D1564924

Dumbarton Oaks

Till the war drum throbbed no longer,
  and the battle flags were furled
In the Parliament of Man, the Federation
  of the World.
There the common sense of most shall hold
  a fretful realm in awe
And the kindly earth shall slumber
Lapt in universal law.
—Tennyson, "Locksley Hall," 1842

Dumbarton Oaks

The Origins of the

United Nations

and the Search for

Postwar Security

by Robert C. Hilderbrand

The University of North Carolina Press

Chapel Hill and London

© 1990 The University of North Carolina Press
All rights reserved
Manufactured in the United States of America

The paper in this book meets the guidelines for permanence and durability of the Committee on Production Guidelines for Book Longevity of the Council on Library Resources.

94 93 92 91 90   5 4 3 2 1

Library of Congress Cataloging-in-Publication Data

Hilderbrand, Robert C., 1947–
    Dumbarton Oaks : the origins of the United Nations and the search for postwar security / by Robert C. Hilderbrand.
        p.   cm.
    Includes bibliographical references.
    ISBN 0-8078-1894-1 (alk. paper)
    1. Dumbarton Oaks Conference (1944)   2. United Nations.
    3. Security, International.   I. Title.
    JX1976.3.H55   1990
    341.23'09—dc20   89-28392
                                                                   CIP

For Jan

Contents

A section of illustrations will
be found following page 107.

Preface

In the two generations since its founding in 1945, the United Nations Organization has come in for harsh criticism. It has disappointed some of its strongest supporters—and to such a degree that even in the United States, the nation that served as its historical midwife, there are now many who doubt whether the birth of a world body was such a good idea in the first place. The reasons for this disenchantment can be found in newspaper headlines almost daily: The U.N. has failed to erect a lasting structure for the maintenance of world peace, or even to prevent the postwar Great Powers, which brought it into existence as a symbol of their continuing cooperation, from drifting into a state of permanent conflict. Whatever may be said of its genuine achievements as a force for order and goodwill in a dangerous and troubled world, the United Nations has not lived up to the larger promises of lasting peace made at the end of the Second World War.

If it is true, as someone has said, that a good way to find out about a people is to study its dreams, then the citizens of all the Great Powers can take just pride in the very idea of a United Nations. As originally developed in each of the Big Four nations, the dream that led to the creation of a new world body was a vision of lasting peace—a dream of ending, once and for all, mankind's curse of war. It was a grand and bold idea, made all the more remarkable by the fact that it called upon the major nations themselves to behave unselfishly at their moment of final victory in the Second World War. Nor did the early plans for putting the dream into effect lack strength or imagination. They envisioned a world where cooperation tempered competition, where power entailed responsibility, where the shared desire for order limited sovereignty. They called for the prevention of war, when necessary, through the enforcement of peace. We know that these dreams and the plans they led to have not been realized. The question we must ask is, Why not?

The answer to this question is not to be found, as the U.N.'s critics seem to suggest, in the way the organization has developed since 1945. We must go back further, to the final plans for the world body itself, plans that made a stronger U.N. impossible by vitiating the strongest features of the Great Powers' original ideas for an organization that would be able to maintain permanent peace. These final plans were drawn up, ironically enough, by the Great Powers themselves during the Dumbarton Oaks Conference of August and September

1944. It was there that the representatives of the United States, Great Britain, and the Soviet Union decided that their own, individual interests were too important to entrust to a world body, that the wartime dream of an international peacekeeping agency might interfere with their own nationalistic dreams of hegemony, and that their differences, highlighted by current events in Eastern Europe, might make their full cooperation impossible and, perhaps, undesirable. It was there that, for those hoping for a strong United Nations Organization, the shadow fell between the word and the deed.

That all of this is not more widely known is due primarily to the fact that so little has been published about the Dumbarton Oaks Conference. No book exists on the meeting itself, and the best of the more general works on the postwar settlement, Thomas Campbell's *Masquerade Peace* and Robert Divine's *Second Chance*, treat the conference ably but in little more than summary form. Thus, one reason for widespread misconceptions about what the United Nations has done is a lack of detailed understanding about what it was really intended to do. A study of the Dumbarton Oaks Conference reveals that the U.N.'s shortcomings did not develop out of a failure of application; they were an intentional part of the plans for the world body as negotiated by the Great Powers in the summer of 1944.

This book is an attempt to explain how this happened—how the wartime dream of world peace led to plans for a postwar organization lacking the authority to achieve it. It is the story of the Dumbarton Oaks Conference. Naturally, I have not undertaken such a project without the assistance of many others, and I am happy for this opportunity to express my gratitude for their generous aid and support. The Office of Research at The University of South Dakota supported my efforts over two summers, one devoted to research and another to writing. Its generosity helped make this study possible. Without research librarians we would all be lost—in the stacks, if not earlier. I have debts to many of them at several facilities: the National Archives, the Library of Congress, the Public Record Office in London, the Franklin D. Roosevelt Library, Alderman Library of the University of Virginia, and Mudd Library at Princeton University. My manuscript has also benefited from the support and advice of my editors and readers at the University of North Carolina Press. This book is dedicated to Jan Hilderbrand, who brought peace and order to my world.

Dumbarton Oaks

Introduction:
Federation of
the World?

For a brief moment in the high summer of 1944 world attention was riveted on the Georgetown estate of Dumbarton Oaks, where delegates from the major Allied powers of the United States, Great Britain, the Soviet Union, and China were discussing plans for a postwar organization to maintain permanent peace. The Dumbarton Oaks Conference, as it was commonly called, took place in the halcyon time after the victorious outcome of the Second World War was already determined (although the fighting went on in both Europe and Asia) and before the development of the new conflict among its own participants that would ultimately result in the cold war. Then the differences between the Great Powers seemed like mere cracks along the East-West fault of the Grand Alliance, although the question of Poland, aggravated during the conference itself by the tragic uprising and massacre of anti-Soviet Poles in Nazi-occupied Warsaw, was giving off the first tremors of the upcoming quake in Allied relations. To most of the world, in that last August and September of the war the possibility that conflict among the Great Powers might produce dangerous leaps on the political Richter scale appeared much less important than the continued cooperation of the Great Powers in drawing up plans for their combined efforts to prevent world wars in the future—precisely the object of the meetings they were holding at Dumbarton Oaks.

No one could have imagined that creating a new world organization would be easy. It had been tried before, of course, at the end of the First World War, with results that were discouraging to even the most optimistic advocates of world order. Not only had the League of Nations failed to live up to its Wilsonian prescriptions for the adjustment and alleviation of international conflict, but it had proved to be almost completely worthless when faced with the round of aggression that produced the Second World War. So fully was the league perceived to have failed, in fact, that its main role in the planning for the Dumbarton Oaks Conference—as, indeed, at the conference itself—was to serve as an example of what the new organization ought not to do. Whatever its actual merits may have been, the creation of the League of Nations represented only the latest stage in the centuries-old dream of bringing order to an almost lawless world—the sort of herculean task that should have made understandable a certain number of missteps and false starts on the part of those who attempted it. What made the league's halting efforts seem so unforgivable at the time was the war that had punctuated that body's ultimate failure with unsurpassed terror; what made the creation of a more effective organization seem so necessary was the development of new weapons that promised to surpass even that terror in the next war. Thus, if the work to be done at Dumbarton Oaks was certain to be difficult, the stakes seemed correspondingly high.

In a sense, however, the errors of the league promised to enhance the new world body's chances for success. At least all of the Great Powers thought that they could learn from the mistakes of the past—an idea that meant several common things to each of them. First, it meant that the powerful nations, especially the United States and the Soviet Union, must this time take part in any world peacekeeping scheme. A chief cause of the league's downfall, it was widely perceived, had been the absence of those states from its councils at critical times. Second, the Great Powers, which would have to play the largest roles in maintaining world peace, must exercise paramount authority in the new organization. Roosevelt's idea of the Four Policemen was just the strongest expression of this popular belief. Third, the new body must have powerful sanctions, including the use of military force, at its disposal to prevent renewed aggression in the future. Before Dumbarton Oaks, proponents of this idea among the Great Powers thought that future peacekeepers should employ strategic bombing—then believed to have proved its value in the Second World War—against the cities of outlaw states. And fourth, the new organization must not disperse its energies by debating every issue to arise on the international scene but should concentrate on matters directly pertaining to the key questions of world peace and security. Had the League of Nations done these things, it was widely believed, there would have been no Second World War; it only followed that if the new body would do them in the future there might not be a third. Thus the Great Powers hoped that their understanding of the mistakes made at Paris in 1919 could prevent similar errors at Dumbarton Oaks in 1944 and might make it possible to create a world organization that would work.

How to make a new world body work was one of the most debated questions of the Second World War. Should it be, as Roosevelt's conception of the Four Policemen seemed to indicate, strictly an extension of the Great Powers' might and authority, to be used as they saw fit to keep the peace? Early in the war, when the horrors of world conflict dominated everyone's thinking about the future, this idea seemed palatable to the public and pundits alike. But such a scheme, appealingly simple as it was, left no role for the lesser nations of the world, whose spokesmen pointed out that life under the total dominance of the Big Four might turn out to be more of a nightmare than a dream of peace. In addition, as the war moved toward its conclusion, the Great Powers began to wonder if they really wanted to create an organization with so much force. Might it not be employed against them? As the postwar period drew nearer, other concerns, especially the protection of their own sovereignty and freedom of action, seemed more important to them than permanent peace. These considerations seemed to suggest the value of creating a revitalized League of Nations that would be less threatening to the Big Four and that would provide the smaller states with at least a sounding board for their ideas. The problem was that the league had been tainted by its own failures; certainly, postwar planners thought, something stronger was required to prevent wars from occurring in the future. The Great Powers, moreover, were even less likely to turn over real authority to a worldwide peacekeeping organization based on the equality of all states—a "Federation of the World"—that could threaten their interests as well as their dominance. The best solution seemed to be a blend of the two ideas. Thus the Great Powers, by the time they came to Dumbarton Oaks, were all working toward the creation of an organization that would be enough like the Four Policemen to keep the peace and enough like the League of Nations to keep the small nations happy. It would, in addition, have to be an organization that they could control, at least where their own vital interests were concerned.

Finding a way to accomplish all of this had engaged the Great Powers in considerable study down to 1944. Especially in the United States, expert committees had drafted and revised a series of plans for a new peacekeeping organization, the last of which was still undergoing important changes by the opening of the conference at Dumbarton Oaks. These revisions reflected both the complexity of the problems the planners faced and the way in which the progress of the war affected their views of the peace. Throughout the process, the experts had to focus on the objective of the organization they were trying to create. The experience of the two world wars suggested that its purpose should be to enforce the peace permanently on the defeated Axis states—something that they were determined the new world body, unlike the old, would be strong enough to do. But the planners knew that other conflicts, often involving less obvious moral choices, would also have to be addressed. Certainly the organization should intervene to prevent wars between small nations from igniting a new world conflagration. But what if a Great Power should be involved? Or if the warring states should include two or more of the Big Four? Could the organization attempt to deal with such conflicts and survive—assuming, of course, that the Great Powers would grant it the authority to intervene in their business in the first place? By August 1944, when the Dumbarton Oaks Conference convened, each of the Big Four was answering these questions in accordance with its own interests. The meetings at Georgetown would reveal just how different those interests had already become.

The rise of conflicting objectives among the Great Powers would place serious limitations on what the delegates could accomplish at Dumbarton Oaks. It would also raise the possibility that the conference might fail—a thought that apparently had rarely occurred to even the most cynical of the planners—and cause the Big Four to depreciate the value they placed on the activities of any postwar organization. Increasingly, the Great Powers would regard their own interests as too important to place in the trust of others, especially another Great Power with which they might disagree, no matter how their behavior might be structured by the charter of an international organization. The result, by the time the conference closed in October, would be plans for a less forceful and authoritative world body than the one envisioned by its original architects, with whose efforts the story of Dumbarton Oaks begins.

1 Preparing for Peace

The preparations in Washington for a new international security organization began even before the United States entered the Second World War. They were a logical outgrowth both of the generation-old Wilsonian prescription for world peace, carefully nurtured by the various League of Nations societies, and of the view of President Franklin D. Roosevelt, already fully developed during the debates over neutrality legislation in the 1930s, that the only way to avoid American involvement in major wars was to prevent new conflicts from developing in the future—or at least to keep them from spreading throughout the world. This was the message of Roosevelt's famous "Quarantine Speech" in Chicago on 5 October 1937. It was also the meaning of his statement, made in a national radio address on 3 September 1939, that "when peace has been broken anywhere, peace of all countries everywhere is in danger." The truth of this seemed to be demonstrated during the next two years as the United States was drawn inexorably into the wars being fought in Europe and Asia. Following the Japanese attack on Pearl Harbor, the appeal of the idea that peace was indivisible—and thus must be protected by an international organization—grew with American power; by the end of the war, leaders in Washington would feel responsible for maintaining the peace more or less everywhere in the world, at least partly because of their desire to avoid the errors of the past and prevent another world conflict.[1]

Early planning for a postwar security organization also had practical utility: it made American involvement in the war seem more palatable to those who doubted its immediate value. For Roosevelt, as for Wilson twenty-five years earlier, the European war presented problems of such enormity that the president doubted his ability to keep the United States outside the conflict despite the unquestioned fact that a majority of the American people wished him to do so. FDR's response, like Wilson's, was in part a public relations campaign to expand the importance of the war for Americans by transforming its ultimate purpose into something larger than the issues of the conflict itself—the establishment of permanent peace through postwar international organization. Thus, in his radio speech of 3 September 1939 addressing "the outbreak of this great war," Roosevelt announced that the influence of the United States would be employed to seek "a final peace which will eliminate, as far as it is possible to do so, the continued use of force between nations." This was—and would continue to be through all stages of planning for the creation of the United Nations Organization—FDR's way of trying to make internationalism respectable in the United States. And here, too, as in the case of the idea that peace was indivisible, the force of Roosevelt's logic grew following the events of 7 December 1941; by the end of the fighting in 1945, millions of Americans shared the view that a permanent peacekeeping organization was necessary to insure that they or their loved ones had not suffered or died in vain.[2]

Roosevelt's efforts produced an almost immediate renewal of public interest in planning for postwar security. On 13 November, a *Washington Post* editorial commented that it was "certainly not too soon to begin thinking about and planning for that new and more orderly world" to be "ushered in when the guns are stilled." A week earlier, a new organization, the Commission to Study the Organization of Peace, had been formed in New York City and elected James T. Shotwell, who had just resigned the presidency of the League of Nations Association, as its first president. This new body would develop and publicize the ideas of the American internationalists, which had been out of favor for a generation in the United States, for a world peacekeeping agency; its initial report, released on Armistice Day, 1940, would set the tone for all efforts in this direction by saying that "the world must evolve from League to federation." Offers of assistance in the administration's postwar planning came from a number of public and private organizations, including the Council on Foreign Relations, whose executive director, Walter H. Mallory, joined Hamilton Fish Armstrong, the influential editor of *Foreign Affairs*, in proposing that the council prepare studies on postwar problems and security and make them available to the State Department. Similar offers of aid came from other groups, including such religious organizations as the Federal Council of Churches of Christ of America, which established its own Commission to Study the Bases of a Just and Durable Peace.[3]

Although these offers were duly acknowledged and accepted, the Roosevelt administration did not make much use of them in its planning for postwar international security. Roosevelt, acting on the advice of Secretary of State Cordell Hull, decided to retain all formal government planning within the Department of State, where on 16 September the secretary appointed Russian-born economic analyst Leo Pasvolsky to be his special assistant for the problems of peace. Pasvolsky, who would become the government's chief planner for postwar organization, had joined the Roosevelt administration as an economic expert after working on the staff of the prestigious Brookings Institution. A model bureaucrat who shunned the limelight, he had entered the State Department in 1936 as Hull's personal assistant, in which capacity he had proved his value as a speech writer and policy drafter. By choosing to work within the State Department, FDR intentionally developed a planning process different from that followed by the Wilson administration during the First World War. The Inquiry, which Wilson had created in September 1917 to study the problems of the postwar world, had been directed by Colonel Edward M. House, Wilson's confidant, and had operated almost entirely outside the State Department by employing experts drawn largely from the nation's colleges and universities. In 1939, the disadvantages of such an independent approach were pointed out by the State Department's Harley Notter in a memorandum to Under Secretary of State Sumner Welles. Notter's arguments were similar to those leveled against the Inquiry in 1917: How could a commission operating outside of the State Department make expert decisions when the information upon which such decisions must be based was lodged only in the department itself? The wisdom of this argument, Notter thought, had been clearly borne out by Wilson's unfortunate experiences at the Paris Peace Conference in 1919.[4]

Roosevelt's decision to work within the State Department represented the first of many times that he would intentionally reverse the practices followed by the Wilson administration during the First World War. Such reversals, in fact, became a rule of thumb for FDR, largely because he could not forget that Wilson had ultimately failed in his efforts to enlist the United States in a world peacekeeping organization. Often, as in the pursuit of better public relations and a stronger liaison with Congress, this policy of reversal would make sense and produce useful results; but in this case it began a long, unhappy process in which the State Department planned—and later negotiated—without possessing the final power necessary to bring its ideas to fruition. The problem was that FDR, like Wilson, was for the most part his own secretary of state and developed plans of his own on important matters often without consulting—or informing—the department. Planning for the postwar world was conducted by an almost powerless Department of State that was too often kept in the dark about the president's real intentions. The seriousness of this problem would begin to grow apparent by the time of the Dumbarton Oaks Conference in 1944.

Pasvolsky and Hull worked, nevertheless, to expand the State Department's role in postwar planning. The secretary of state believed deeply in Wilson's idea of an international organization and saw in the war an opportunity to remold the world along the lines of law and order. He would become the administration's most consistent advocate of a postwar world structured according to Wilsonian principles. For his part, Pasvolsky proposed the creation of a departmental committee on "problems of peace and reconstruction" to survey the "basic principles" that should "underlie a desirable world order" to be evolved following the end of the war. To assist the committee, the special assistant further suggested the establishment of a new division of the department—a departmental version of the World War I Inquiry—to deal with all aspects of the problems posed by the ultimate coming of peace. On 27 December Hull created the proposed committee—the Advisory Committee on Problems of Foreign Relations—but rejected the suggestion for a new departmental division because of the already pressing shortage of qualified professional staff. To strengthen the committee, Hull named Under Secretary of State Welles as its chairman.[5]

The committee's name, arrived at on 8 January 1940 after several days of departmental debate, provided few clues to its purpose. A committee on "problems of foreign relations" might, after all, deal with anything under the authority of the State Department—or even be a working definition for the department itself. Nor did the press release announcing the committee's creation provide the public with much additional information; it said the new group would "gather data on and study" the results of "overseas war measures" and the problems arising therefrom. This obliqueness may have been intentional: Roosevelt, although willing to support planning for a postwar security organization in principle, probably did not want to make it too clear that actual plans were being formulated lest he be called upon to make them public prematurely. Nor did he wish to alarm the large number of Americans who then opposed United States participation in a new world body. Within the department, however, the committee's three-part mission was clearly understood: its fifteen members were, according to Hull, charged with studying means whereby "the war might be limited and possibly ended, the foundations of a peaceful world order laid, and the defense of the Western Hemisphere strengthened."[6]

The administration's public caution continued even after the advisory committee began to function. In announcing on 10 February its preparations for a conference of neutrals to exchange views on postwar cooperation in disarmament and trade, the State Department emphasized that the "conversations involve no plan or plans but are in the nature of preliminary inquiries"—an interpretation very similar to that which the department placed on the Dumbarton Oaks meetings four years later. By then, of course, the planned conference would have taken on a much different character: the leading "neutrals" had all become belligerents, and the responsibility for planning—and for keeping the peace—was no longer to be spread thin among forty-seven nations but was to be concentrated in the hands of the Great Powers. These were changes that could not have been foreseen in 1940, a year dominated by American neutrality and by the general uncertainty caused by the "phony war" in Europe.[7]

It was during this tense hiatus in the war that the State Department produced its first thin draft of a plan for a postwar peacekeeping organization. Reflecting the concerns of the time, the plan called for an organization to be based in Europe, with only possible participation by other states of the world, and contained no specific reference to membership by the United States. The plan's primary objective was disarmament, which would include prohibitions on the manufacture of bombers and other mobile weapons as well as a limitation on the number of soldiers that any nation could recruit. The creation of an international organization came into this proposal by the back door because the planners recognized that to achieve lasting disarmament "some machinery for political decision must exist" and continue to operate in the future. For this machinery to be effective, moreover, the idea of the sovereignty of states needed to be altered—"derogation" of sovereignty in State Department parlance—to permit quick and decisive action by the international body. Thus the committee proposed that the rule of unanimity, placed in the charter of the League of Nations to protect the national sovereignty of its members, be abolished and replaced by some form of majority rule. Still, "practical power" would reside, as always, in the hands of the Great Powers, although it might be divided somewhat by the creation of various—the plan proposed nine—blocs, each with its own representative to the organization and with the presidency rotating among them each year.[8]

The most important power of this proposed political body was to issue commands to another new organization—an international peacekeeping force. Regional and hegemonic in character, this force clearly bore the stamp of Under Secretary Welles, who would continue to advocate regionalism even after he left the State Department in 1943. It was to consist entirely of bombers (along with fighters for their protection), with personnel and commanders recruited from the smaller neutral states, and was to be established at strategic points on neutral or internationalized soil, preferably on islands. The force was authorized to maintain its own factories for the construction of bombers, which were to be outlawed from the possession of individual nations. Members of the advisory committee hoped that such a force would prevent future wars by making aggression impossible or at least impractical; this would, in turn, clear the way for peaceful solutions to international problems through either the political body or a new permanent court of justice. During the next four years, a world police force, with or without bombers, would become the basic prescription for postwar peacekeeping in the plans of all four powers that participated at Dumbarton Oaks.[9]

The abrupt end of the "phony war" in the spring of 1940 forced the advisory committee to put aside such visionary—or at least long-range—considerations. As Hitler's armies overran the European neutrals and forced France to leave the war, the State Department turned to more pressing problems that included the unhappy consequences for the United States of a possible German-Italian victory. These were gloomy days in Washington; certainly no planner could envision a postwar world that would be based on the principles of order and disarmament proposed by the advisory committee if the Nazis were victorious. For the time being, these ideals seemed, like the advisory committee itself, to be a dead issue, replaced in the thoughts of State Department officials by ways to shore up the defenses of the Western Hemisphere against inevitable German pressure and encroachment. This change of emphasis reflected, and not for the last time, the extent to which the problems of war and the problems of peace were invariably interconnected in the minds of the planners, a phenomenon that would ultimately play a major role in shaping the plans themselves.[10]

Following the Battle of Britain, which demonstrated that the war in Europe was not, as some had feared, foreordained to end quickly or in total Axis victory, the State Department intensified its planning for a more orderly postwar world. With previous efforts now splintering off in several directions to deal with problems posed by the war itself, a new, more concentrated round of planning seemed necessary, and in November 1940, Pasvolsky resurrected the idea of creating a new departmental division to deal specifically with postwar questions. Roosevelt added emphasis to this proposal by proclaiming in his annual message to Congress of 6 January 1941 the need for "four freedoms," one of which—"freedom from fear"—called for a reduction of armaments following the war to make any future act of aggression impossible. Hull responded on 3 February by secretly creating the Division of Special Research to conduct "special studies" in foreign relations and to analyze and appraise "developments and conditions" arising out of the European war. The secretary named Pasvolsky chief of the new division and assigned Harley Notter and H. Julian Wadleigh as his principal assistants.[11]

Hull also began to develop publicly his own plans for the structure of the postwar world. In a radio address on 18 May he argued that the time had arrived to lay down at least some of the principles for the establishment of a new world order to follow the end of the war. In the main these principles were economic—Hull's personal brand of Wilsonianism was always found in combination with the open-door doctrine of free trade—and included the end of trade restrictions, economic discrimination, and commercial wars. But the secretary recognized that a new basis for trade could not stand alone; it must be preceded by the establishment of "an international order" in which independent nations could cooperate freely with one another. "We shall not be able to do this," Hull reasoned, "until we have a world free from imminent military danger and clear of malign political intrigue." What was needed, therefore, was a world organization capable of maintaining the peace and of bringing "the menace of conquest" finally to an end. At the same time Under Secretary Welles was reaching a similar conclusion from a different direction. Welles did not share Hull's enthusiasm for free trade, which he considered to be of secondary importance in creating a harmonious world; his particular concern, which was widely shared in the State Department, was with disarmament as the key to peace. Still, "real disarmament," as the under secretary described it in an address at the Norwegian embassy on 22 July, depended—like free trade—on the creation of an "adequate instrumentality" to provide order and to keep the peace. Thus, by the summer of 1941, State Department thinking and publicity on the two most important postwar questions of trade and disarmament had converged on the need to establish an international organization after the war.[12]

But once again planning fell into desuetude. The problem this time was partly structural: the Division of Special Research was neither organized nor sufficiently staffed to make policy decisions; it was best prepared to supply information and support to a policy planning committee that did not then exist. Pasvolsky had proposed the creation (or recreation) of such a committee on 11 April 1941 and Welles had agreed that something like the original advisory group was needed, only without the division into subcommittees preoccupied with war that had splintered the department's previous efforts. What Pasvolsky had in mind was a body that could study the problems of peace in a concentrated and unified way, while resisting the temptation to be distracted by more immediate wartime concerns. In practice, however, the creation of a new committee was itself forestalled by wartime difficulties; the pressure of immediate events intervened at this time, as it did often during the war years, to push postwar planning off everybody's center stage. Thus, after State Department leaders had decided in April to pursue Pasvolsky's suggestion, they failed to do so because their energies were taxed by such current problems as Japanese advances in Asia, Hitler's invasion of the Soviet Union, and the undeclared naval war with Germany on the Atlantic. Under these conditions, planning came to mean little more than concern for the long-range implications of immediate problems.[13]

The obvious importance of genuine postwar planning, however, prevented it from dying on the State Department's vine. On 12 September Pasvolsky again attempted to bring the matter to the forefront, this time in a memorandum addressed directly to Secretary Hull. "In formulating postwar foreign policies," he wrote, three groups of "closely related" problems required consideration: political and territorial settlements, armament arrangements, and trade and financial relations; they could, the planner continued, be considered "fully and adequately only under some unified auspices and well-defined leadership." The vehicle for such consideration did not then exist, however, and Pasvolsky thought that there was "grave danger" that work on postwar policies would be done independently by several agencies of the government or "under other leadership than that of the Department of State." In addition, planning now seemed "hopelessly intermingled" with the consideration of war problems and promised to be carried out "in more or less complete isolation" from the establishment of sound principles for order in the postwar world. The only way to avoid "ultimate confusion" and the loss of valuable time was to safeguard planning from the threat of subordination to current war problems and to organize it "under the formal and active leadership of the Department of State." Although this new advisory committee would place postwar considerations firmly under the aegis of the State Department—which no doubt recommended it strongly to the territorial Hull—it would not consist solely of department personnel but would include representatives of other areas of government and a number of prominent private citizens as well. Pasvolsky thus hoped to mobilize both the entire resources of the administration and the best brains outside of it.[14]

Hull and Welles discussed this proposal with the president in early October and received his oral approval for the creation of a new advisory committee. No action was then taken, however, because the final crisis in relations with Japan occupied most of the State Department's attention for the next two months. Following the Japanese attack on Pearl Harbor, which finally brought the United States into the war and added new emphasis to the need for postwar planning, Hull wrote Roosevelt reminding him of their previous conversation and proposing that a committee be constituted as soon as possible to "work in the inseparably interrelated fields of general security, limitation of armaments, sound international economic relationships, and other phases of international cooperation." The secretary also took this opportunity to cement his own department's position as the administration's clearinghouse for postwar considerations. He not only proposed himself as chairman of the new committee but also reminded the president that it was his (the president's) desire that all recommendations regarding postwar concerns come through the secretary of state and asked that all other departments and agencies be apprised of this fact. Roosevelt "heartily" approved and Hull began to construct his committee as 1941 came to a close.[15]

The new Advisory Committee on Postwar Foreign Policy, which first met on 12 February 1942, commenced wide-ranging consideration in the United States of the questions relating to an international security organization. It had what appeared to be a clear statement of presidential policy to build on: the Atlantic Charter, signed by Roosevelt and British Prime Minister Winston S. Churchill on 11 August 1941, called for "the establishment of a wider and permanent system of general security" to follow the conclusion of the war. This declaration was strengthened when twenty-four other nations, including the Soviet Union and China, subscribed to it on New Year's Day, 1942. The new planning group also benefited from the fact that the United States was now at war and must inevitably be involved in determining the peace. The old "isolationist" argument that the postwar world was none of America's concern seemed, at least for now, forcefully refuted daily by news from the battlefronts.[16]

In fact, the committee's mandate was more ambiguous than it seemed. The records of the negotiations leading to the signing of the Atlantic Charter, which were unavailable to most of the committee's members, suggested that Roosevelt maintained serious doubts about the creation of a true postwar security organization. He removed from Churchill's original draft a reference to an "effective international organization" because he feared the "suspicions and opposition" that such a statement would cause in the United States and because he personally did not favor the creation of something like a new League Assembly until after an international police force had been given an opportunity to function. In Roosevelt's view, the "extreme internationalists" were insufficiently realistic; they needed to take into account the danger of a postwar public reaction like the one that had toppled the plans of Woodrow Wilson. It was only due to the persistence of Churchill, backed by Welles and presidential adviser Harry Hopkins, that Roosevelt permitted the phrase "the establishment of a wider and permanent system of general security" to be included in the Atlantic Charter as a less inflammatory substitute for the words "international organization." Thus, although Welles apparently regarded the two phrases as synonymous, to FDR they were sufficiently different in purpose to suggest that the president might ultimately sacrifice the creation of a true world organization in the name of some higher political realism.[17]

Roosevelt was also then displaying a decided lack of interest in the details of postwar policy questions. As Harley Notter has remembered, the president told Welles that he wanted such questions answered for him now so that he would be able later "to reach in his basket and to find there whatever he needed" to know about such matters as the workings of a proposed security organization; this would free him, in the meantime, to devote himself entirely "to ways and means of winning the war." Certainly putting off distant questions was a sensible approach for an administrator as busy as Roosevelt, but it also reflected FDR's predilection for power politics over representative organizations when dealing with both foreign and domestic questions. Roosevelt may never have believed that a new, Wilsonian international body was the best way to maintain order—his own ideas, as we shall see, always centered on the primacy of the powerful—and was thus unwilling to invest much of his own energy in such a dubious undertaking. If this proved true, any new international organization was destined to be as secondary to "ways and means" in the president's thinking after the war as it was during it.[18]

Moreover, the advisory committee did not itself turn out to be an effective agency of postwar planning. The primary problem was its size, which grew to more than two dozen members following the introduction of representatives from other departments in March and April 1942. So many members made secrecy impossible to ensure, and Welles doubted that confidentiality could be maintained even until policy recommendations were reviewed by the president and secretary of state. In addition, plenary sessions of a large committee did not lend themselves to the goal of slow and incremental planning; instead, they tended to produce finished recommendations that reflected pressing wartime considerations as much as they did a dispassionate analysis of what might turn out to be desirable in the future. Because such decisions could not be based on very complete information, they might, in the secretary of state's opinion, unnecessarily involve "fatal gambles" about the shape of things to come. Consequently, only four meetings of the full committee were held before it was disbanded on 2 May 1942.[19]

Planning, however, continued in the various subcommittees created by the advisory group before its demise. The Subcommittee on Political Problems began its deliberations with the question of whether a general peace settlement should follow immediately after the end of the war or be delayed during a period of transition such as that proposed by Roosevelt in his meeting with

Churchill the previous August. In an attempt to avoid one of the "errors" of World War I, the subcommittee developed a plan proposed by Norman H. Davis for a deliberate peace process that included a "chart" of policy problems to be dealt with in three stages: an armistice, a transition, and the establishment of an international organization. The armistice, which was to last not more than a year after the end of hostilities, would be used to achieve an agreement on an "over-all United Nations authoritative body" to be instituted later. During the longer transition period, the subcommittee expected that the Great Powers would begin to resolve the problems caused by the war as well as use their own means to maintain order throughout the world. Only afterward would a "definitive international organization" be put into effect, although, as the subcommittee recognized, its details may have been agreed upon beforehand. This three-part division of the postwar period, which Davis referred to as a "chronological" approach, became the basic timetable for all early planning but was gradually abandoned later in favor of a more rapid schedule.[20]

In this period some of the cardinal principles of postwar organization were first brought to light. In a meeting on 28 March the Subcommittee on Political Problems decided that the framework for an international organization should be developed during the war itself to "provide machinery ready at hand when needed," to prepare a staff through "acquaintance" with world problems, and to provide a mechanism for reaching decisions during the immediate postwar period. The "United Nations Authority," as the subcommittee thought it might be called, would be composed of representatives from all of the United Nations—those that had signed the declaration on 1 January or might do so in the future. But it would not be majoritarian in character. Primary authority would rest with an executive committee composed of delegates from the "four major powers"—the United States, Great Britain, the Soviet Union, and China—along with representatives from the "regions" of Eastern Europe, Western Europe, the other American republics, the Far East, and possibly the Mohammedan peoples. Although other countries were to be included to "foster a sense of participation" among the smaller united nations, the subcommittee recognized that, "in the last analysis," all the important decisions would have to be made by "the four major powers."[21]

The notion of Big Four superiority, which grew in part out of the concept of the trusteeship of the powerful, was fast on the way to becoming a fixture of all American thinking about the postwar world. Roosevelt had presented the principle—and the connection to trusteeship—in September 1941 when outlining his objectives for the mission of Myron Taylor to the Vatican. He did not wish, he wrote, "to reconstitute a League of Nations which, because of its size, makes for disagreement and inaction. There should be a meeting place of nations for the purpose of full discussion, but for management there seems no reason why the principle of trusteeship in private affairs should not be extended to the international field." The granting of a superior position to the major powers also surfaced in the signing of the Declaration of the United Nations, when the Big Four were placed out of alphabetical order at the head of the list of signatories. FDR commented at the time that he had a feeling that the Soviet Union—not to mention the United States—would not be pleased to be listed below some of the countries that were "realistically making a minor contribution" to the war. Ultimately, these same considerations, extended to the peace, would give rise to the Four Policemen idea that would dominate all of the president's plans for a postwar world structure.[22]

From this early stage in the war, American postwar planning was invariably predicated on the dual concepts of Allied victory and cooperation. Any alternative to the first was unthinkable, especially now that the United States had formally committed itself to the war. As for the second, the attitude of the Soviet Union seemed the chief question mark, which the political subcommittee removed by determining Soviet cooperation to be both essential to world peace and assured by the national interests of the Soviet Union itself. This assessment received credence in the spring of 1942 with the signing of two agreements that promised cooperation in the postwar era: the Anglo-Soviet Treaty of Alliance and Mutual Assistance, dated 26 May; and the Lend-Lease Agreement with the United States, signed by the Soviets on 11 June. Although it was to some extent window dressing, the Anglo-Soviet treaty pledged the two nations "to contribute after the war to the maintenance of peace" and "to collaborate closely" with each other and their allies "at the peace settlement and during the ensuing period of reconstruction." The Lend-Lease Agreement, and particularly Article VII, promised postwar economic cooperation, a principle that Soviet Foreign Minister Vyacheslav Molotov enlarged upon in a report to the Supreme Soviet in Moscow on 18 June. According to Molotov, the agreement implied an understanding between the United States and the Soviet Union about the need for strengthening international relationships to enhance "the stability of peace" in the postwar world."[23]

While these principles were being shaped within the administration a public debate was developing over America's place in the postwar world. The controversy was sparked by Vice President Henry A. Wallace, who began at this time to adumbrate his program for "the American Peace, the peace of the common man." What the lanky Iowan had in mind was a kind of New Deal for the world, including the redistribution of peoples and resources and the spending of at least some of the vast wealth of the United States on world reconstruction. In this way, America could "establish a truly great peace based on justice to all peoples" that would include a program of international social reform. In an address in New York City on 8 June, Wallace presented these ideas wrapped in a mystical, apocalyptic vision of America as "the chosen of the Lord," with the New Deal as the New Islam—or New Jerusalem—divinely inspired to save the world. Such idealism had much to commend it in a war being fought for the lofty goals of restoring freedom and democracy to a troubled world, but it worried other internationalists who feared that Wallace might raise American expectations far beyond the level of the possible. The State Department, which would have preferred to develop its plans in secret, thus found itself, as Harley Notter put it, "in the midst of a great struggle" for control of the public's interest in postwar planning.[24]

One response to Wallace came from Under Secretary of State Welles, who along with the vice president served as Roosevelt's right and left hands in considering postwar matters. Welles spoke as the chief proponent of the more conservative idea of the "American Century" as developed by *Life* magazine publisher Henry R. Luce, which meant, in Luce's words, bringing forth a "vision of America as a world power which is authentically American" and spreading throughout the world the "American way" in economics, technology, and social ideas. Welles responded to Wallace's address in a speech of his own nine days later in Baltimore, where he called for a less visionary approach to the solution of postwar problems. Included in Welles's scenario was a cooling-off period following the war; this would allow for cautious planning in keeping with the political subcommittee's timetable. In addition, Welles contended that the peace arrangements should grow organically out of the seeds sown during the war itself; thus the "five great nations" (the fifth was presumably France) would become the nucleus for a postwar organization, and reconstruction would be conducted under the aegis of Lend-Lease. In this way, the United States would have a large role to play and no rash action or untested agency would undermine the effectiveness of the peace.[25]

The official State Department position was presented a month later by Secretary Hull. Hull's motives were partly the same as Welles's: to warn against the woolly-headed idea that the end of the war would be the "immediate dawn of the millennium." In addition, the secretary wanted it clearly established that serving as the administration's spokesman on postwar international concerns was the prerogative of the State Department and not the vice president. In a worldwide radio address on 23 July written largely by Leo Pasvolsky, Hull argued that the United States must set realistic limits on its expectations for the peace. It was obvious, he said, that "international desperadoes" could only be stopped by force and that it was therefore "plain that some international agency must be created which can—by force, if necessary—keep the peace among nations in the future." Hull assailed the "extreme nationalism" of those who believed that the United States could withdraw from world affairs following the war and warned against any return to "isolationism," such as that being revived by some segments of the anti-Roosevelt press. What was developing, then, was a State Department position that, like the Welles-Luce program, occupied the middle ground between the millenarianism of Wallace and the narrow nationalism of the prewar isolationists.[26]

Another, slightly different, point of view was offered by Republican Governor Harold E. Stassen of Minnesota. Stassen, speaking before the Annual Conference of Governors at Asheville, North Carolina, on 22 June, agreed that the United States must assume leadership in the "winning of the peace." In addition, to insure orderly and peaceful relations in the future, he called for the creation of a "world association" based on the wartime alliance and modeled after the relationship among the states of the American union. Such an arrangement would, he argued, permit the members to retain their respective sovereignties while pursuing concerted international policies. Although sketchy and incomplete, Stassen's anti-isolationist plan represented the most advanced views of the internationalist Republicans. A final position, which found little support in the administration, was that of the unreconstructed Wilsonians, found mostly in the academic community, who continued to believe that a revitalized League of Nations, or something like it, would be capable of solving the problems of the postwar world.[27]

This debate highlighted the need for more detailed planning. On 27 June Welles proposed the creation of a Special Subcommittee on International Organization to prepare draft proposals that might clarify the State Department's vaguely generalized views on postwar organization and preempt whatever plans were being developed by other sources. Although this new group would not survive to shape the administration's final postwar policies, it was important because, with the exception of Welles and James T. Shotwell, all of its regular members—Isaiah Bowman, Benjamin V. Cohen, Green H. Hackworth, Leo Pasvolsky, and Harley Notter—played prominent roles later in the negotiations at Dumbarton Oaks. In some forty-five meetings held during the following year, the subcommittee made intensive studies of several key issues upon which any plans for a future world organization would ultimately have to depend. It began its efforts in July and August with a close examination of each article of the League of Nations covenant for the purpose of answering the basic question of whether the covenant should be revived and amended or replaced with an entirely new organization; it chose the latter primarily because the league retained too many unpleasant associations and might be a political liability in the United States. Another proposal, to base the new organization on the Kellogg-Briand Pact outlawing war, was rejected for similar reasons. At the same time, the subcommittee decided that a transitional, rather than a permanent, organization should be its first objective; this course would permit flexibility and the eventual elimination of whatever structural errors were committed by the new body's planners. These decisions did not come easily, and by September there developed a clash among the committee's leading personalities—what Notter referred to as a "struggle for power"—with "Bowman, Welles, and Pasvolsky at odds" with one another. Although Welles, who was the senior member and best connected with Roosevelt, appeared at the time to have the upper hand in this debate, Pasvolsky, whose views were in closer accord with those of Secretary Hull, would ultimately prevail.[28]

Other fundamental questions proved no less difficult. The subcommittee was most divided on the issue of whether the postwar organization should be regional or universal in its structure and operation. To some extent, the group's ideas on this question had to be influenced by the opinions of the world leaders who would eventually approve or disapprove its efforts; this approach seemed only prudent to several of the subcommittee's more realistic members. Churchill revealed his regionalist views in an address on 21 March 1943, when he called for the establishment of "a Council of Europe and a Council of Asia" to function "under a world institution embodying or representing the United Nations, and some day all nations." Roosevelt was also believed by the subcommittee to favor a regional approach at this time. Nevertheless, some committee members saw only disaster in an organization founded on a regional basis; they argued, as Charles W. Yost put it, that the United Nations must avoid breaking up into regional security "pools" after the war or run the risk of renewed international competition, perhaps among continents led by the Great Powers. Ultimately, the subcommittee put aside these concerns and developed a draft based on regional representation, reflecting their appreciation of the political realities of the time. Another controversial issue dealt with membership in the new organization: should entities not generally accepted as sovereign states, such as dominions or colonies, be admitted, or should membership be permitted only on the basis of independence? The subcommittee decided in December 1942 that only states should be members; it regarded the vitality of the nation-state as continuing to be of primary importance in the postwar world and thought that an organization formed on any other basis was bound to fail.

Similar reasoning also led to the rejection of any plan that might suggest the creation of a world government. The findings of the special subcommittee were by no means definitive—many of its decisions were, in fact, reversed by later groups of planners—but it had begun at least to deal with the hard questions of international organization.[29]

A second, related subcommittee dealt with postwar security. The Subcommittee on Security Problems, which first met on 15 April 1942, considered such issues as the maintenance of security vis-à-vis the Axis states in the transitional period following the war, the control of armaments in that same period before an international organization could be established, and the security provisions to be included in the charter of the new peacekeeping organization itself. Because of its focus on security questions, this subcommittee expanded its membership to include representatives of the military, whose expertise could then be called upon in planning postwar security arrangements. New members at the second meeting on 29 April included Major General George V. Strong of the War Department and Admiral Arthur J. Hepburn of the Navy Department; during 1943 the Joint Chiefs of Staff were represented by Lieutenant General Stanley D. Embick of the army, Major General Muir S. Fairchild of the air corps, and Vice Admiral Russell Willson of the navy. All of these men would later be participants at Dumbarton Oaks, even though the security subcommittee, like its counterpart for international organization, held its final meeting a year before the conference began.

From its first meeting, the Subcommittee on Security Problems viewed postwar security needs from the perspective of expanding American interests. As Notter put it, America's "conceptions of strategy had broadened profoundly, and the requirements of security were being widened correspondingly." This meant that the subcommittee must consider the United States's security objectives not only in light of the American position alone but, Notter continued, "in terms of the world's requirements for peace," with which "our own requirements were merging." Put this way, the United States's goals seemed altruistic, if expansive; America intended to defend the world's security in order to insure its own. But this did not imply that the United States had no interests of its own, or that these interests might not be decisive in shaping its views of the peace. The reciprocal nature of this war-broadened approach to security had been made clear two months earlier, at the first meeting of the parent advisory committee, when committee member Anne O'Hare McCormick of the *New York Times* had asked whether the group's purpose was to examine problems from the American "point of view," to determine "the kind of world we want?" "Exactly," was Welles's reply. Thus, although the United States now viewed its security needs as linked with those of the entire world, it would demand, as the price of a *pax americana*, a determining voice in defining those needs.[30]

The central question for this subcommittee to consider was the kind of international peacekeeping force that ought to be created; upon its answer all other questions of security must to some degree depend. The group began thinking through the issue at its first meeting and debated the practicability of various sorts of international forces in a series of subsequent meetings and memorandums. Two ways of organizing an effective force seemed possible: one was an actual, standing international army, empowered to maintain peace and security anywhere in the world; and the other was an ad hoc force of national units—not a true international police force at all—that could be internationalized and made available in an emergency. Proposals of the latter sort had been made by the French on three occasions, first at Paris in 1919 and then twice more at the World Disarmament Conference of 1932, so that the idea of an ad hoc force was usually referred to as the "French plan" by members of the subcommittee. In addition to an emergency force, the French plan called for the creation of a permanent general staff to plan actions and lead the peacekeeping armies and for the ultimate internationalization of armaments, with all troops and weapons earmarked for international use. The force would also be granted a more immediate worldwide monopoly on "great weapons"—those with strategic significance—such as heavy bombers, which might be used as the first step in disciplining aggressors. Finally, the plan was based on a regional approach, with the peacekeeping contribution of any country determined by its proximity to the conflict. This conception meshed smoothly, of course, with Roosevelt's hegemonic Four Policemen idea, whereby the Great Powers would maintain peace and order in their own sections of the world, and appealed to those who feared that American involvement outside of the Western Hemisphere might otherwise become too extensive.[31]

The subcommittee spent considerable time exploring the advantages and disadvantages inherent in the two types of international force. Members thought that an ad hoc force would have the advantage of being "considerably more acceptable" to governments—including the United States—"in the present state of the world." It entailed no permanent surrender of autonomous military forces and seemed less threatening to traditional conceptions of sovereignty. In addition, subcommittee members believed that it would be "slightly easier" to control than a genuine international police force, which some feared might develop and pursue interests of its own in an otherwise disarmed world. A true international police force also had several advantages. It would be, in the opinion of the subcommittee, considerably more effective than an ad hoc force in pursuing worldwide peacekeeping responsibilities. One reason was the certainty that such an army would always be available for use; with a permanent force there was no danger that member nations might refuse to provide their quotas in a time of emergency. Security could best be ensured, the members agreed, if potential aggressors could be certain that swift retribution would be the result of their actions—what seemed to many to be the main lesson of the League of Nations experience. This led in turn to the second reason for preferring a standing force: intervention could occur more quickly because no consultation or preparation time would be required before action was taken. A third reason was the permanent force's greater prospect of strategic success; a force that trained together regularly and became more nearly homogeneous in performance and outlook was apt to be stronger than an ad hoc army brought together in a crisis. And fourth, a permanent force would make it simpler to promote disarmament. Under the ad hoc plan, it would be necessary for nations to maintain a level of armament sufficient to provide and equip their share of an international peacekeeping force; thus a world organization might find itself in the uncomfortable—and contradictory—position of requesting an increase in the forces of some states while attempting to foster disarmament as a general rule. A permanent force would remove this difficulty and make possible a more consistent policy of disarmament for all nations.[32]

Disarmament presented the security subcommittee with some of its most difficult questions, which were both practical and philosophical in nature. Some members held to the traditional liberal view that disarmament itself provided the ultimate solution to the problems of aggression and war, that it alone would make any sort of an international police force unnecessary by rendering armed conflict impossible. Critics of this idea pointed out that it overlooked the question of enforcement; in their view, any attempt to prevent war—even through disarmament—would have to be enforced by an international organization equipped with a police force and armaments. And where, they asked, would these armaments come from if not from the member nations themselves—at least in the absence of a truly internationalized army? Thus the subcommittee, while perceiving in disarmament a possible final solution to world disorder, decided that its immediate objective should be to establish both minimum and maximum armament levels, at least for the major powers, as soon as possible after the war. Such levels would cover both dimensions of the problem: maximums would promote disarmament—and perhaps lead to further reductions in the future—and minimums would ensure a strong police force for the new world organization.

Another thorny problem was the effect that international peacekeeping efforts, and the establishment of a world police force, would have on current notions of the sovereignty and equality of states. These nineteenth-century concepts seemed in danger of obsolescence in the kind of world envisioned by most members of the subcommittee, a world where certain principles long regarded by some nations as rights would have to be forgone to protect the security of all. Disarmament had to be considered in this context, as did the possibility of developing international bases at strategic points within the boundaries of nations near prospective trouble spots. A similar problem arose from the issue of potential intervention by large states in the affairs of their smaller neighbors, a dangerous situation that might become the usual order of business in a world where security was maintained under the Four Policemen idea. Some subcommittee members thought that a new, more limited concept of sovereignty would have to be developed, and argued that smaller states would have to accept Great Power intervention as the price of guaranteed security under an international organization. This new concept could, more-over, be made more palatable by the terms of the new organization's charter, which might, for example, treat all nations as equal in principle and require Great Power unanimity before any police action could be undertaken, thus protecting the freedom of action of all. Still, all subcommittee members ac-knowledged that it would be no simple task to reconcile the new interests of world order with the more established values of the sovereignty and equality of nations.[33]

The subcommittees all adjourned in the summer of 1943, joining the parent advisory committee in a kind of planning limbo. Ostensibly, the reason for this hiatus was to clear the path for the drafting of a preliminary United Nations charter by a new committee created by Hull in July; adjournment of the subcommittees would enable the technical staff, as the secretary put it, "to carry out the work of intensive preparation" necessary "for a more definitive round of discussion." According to Harley Notter, the timing for this action was determined by the war, which had begun to impinge on the planning process in two important ways. First, the "postwar" period was no longer very far in the future and had, indeed, already arrived in North Africa and parts of Italy, which meant that the time had come for more detailed consideration of the State Department's plans for a prospective international organization. "The great overwhelming fact by which we are confronted this week," the *New Republic* reported on 16 August, "is that we are completely unprepared for a possible victory that may come sooner than anyone has dared to predict." And second, wartime stresses among the Allies, especially those stemming from the Anglo-American failure to initiate a second front during 1943, pointed to the need for

solid planning now, before disagreements might grow and make postwar cooperation much more difficult if not impossible. Hull's belief in the need for swift
action was evident at the Moscow Foreign Ministers' Conference in October
and November, where he displayed his determination to win British and Soviet
agreement to the necessity of establishing an international organization "at the
earliest possible date."[34]

But this explanation is far from the whole story. The summer of 1943 saw
the State Department in a period of turmoil, and the postwar planning process
could not avoid being affected by these profound internal disagreements. At
the heart of the matter was the bitter dispute between Secretary Hull and Under
Secretary Welles, which had smoldered on several levels for many years, and
which now blazed out into the open. The problems between these two most
important State Department officials had been fanned by the bureaucratic
practices of President Roosevelt, whose administrative style depended upon an
absence of secure authority among his subordinates. In this case, FDR had
promoted Welles as his personal representative in the State Department, frequently undercutting Hull in what the secretary regarded as his legitimate area
of authority. This conflict had been exacerbated by policy disagreements between the two, especially in the area of postwar planning, where Hull favored a
universal type of organization and Welles favored a regional system; their
differences of opinion here had resulted in Hull replacing Welles as chairman
of the political subcommittee in January 1943. Still, Welles's views seemed on
the verge of adoption at that time. They were supported by both Roosevelt and
Churchill, and a regional basis for security was included in the first draft of a
proposed United Nations charter, written by the Special Subcommittee on
International Organization and submitted to the president on 19 June. Hull,
however, refused to accept this decision. He successfully lobbied with FDR for
a universal system of security, then took two steps designed to ensure his
victory. First, he adjourned the subcommittees and replaced them with a
drafting committee that could, as he put it, "work out a new draft charter based
on the views . . . that there should be a universal rather than a regional basis for
the world organization." And second, he forced Welles to resign, employing
reports of alleged homosexual activities by the under secretary of state to
remove his chief adversary from the planning process. These actions placed
control of postwar planning securely in Hull's hands and guaranteed that
future State Department proposals for an international organization would be
based on his own idea of a universal peacekeeping system.[35]

Hull thought he had good reasons for taking such strong action; regionalism
might even, as he wrote later, "imperil the future postwar organization" in

several ways. First, an organization based on a regional system would have to deal with continental blocs rather than individual nations, thus weakening its influence. In a world so structured, future conflicts might be between regions instead of nations (or at least between nations supported by regions) and might be of a magnitude beyond the capabilities of the organization to restrain. Second, a regional organization inevitably "set up a special relationship between the one or two great powers and the small states in that region." It was to be expected that the Big Four would dominate their regions as spheres of influence; this was, indeed, a major reason why regionalism appealed to Churchill and Roosevelt (and probably Stalin) in the first place. But Hull feared the abuses made possible by such an approach, especially the development of closed trade areas or discriminatory economic systems that would violate his belief in free trade, and thought that some of the Great Powers, such as England or the Soviet Union, might fail to exercise sufficient self-restraint in their own spheres to prevent a dangerous situation from developing in which closed systems confronted one another throughout the world. And finally, the creation of regional councils might prevent the United States from participating in the new organization, a concern that was never very far from the thoughts of any of the planners. Hull did not think that the American people would favor participation in either a European or a Pacific council, where the United States might have to take on "the undesirable role of mediating between the other dominating powers in those regions" or, worse, European or Asian participation in a council for the Western Hemisphere. This situation, Hull argued and Roosevelt now agreed, would only give comfort to the "isolationists"; nothing but a truly universal system could guarantee enthusiastic American involvement in a postwar organization.[36]

The new drafting committee gave Hull the kind of organization that he desired. Between 4 and 14 August, ten members of the Division of Political Studies, chaired by O. Benjamin Gerig, constructed a "Charter of the United Nations" that envisioned "an organization on the universal pattern" but did not preclude regional developments provided that they were consistent with the purposes of the universal organization. Peacekeeping authority was vested in a council composed of the five Great Powers (the United States, Great Britain, the Soviet Union, China, and France) and three other nations to be elected for annual terms; decisions were to be made by a two-thirds majority vote including three-fourths of the permanent members. The draft charter also spelled out the steps to be followed in the event of a breach of the peace: the council would call upon the offenders to desist; states failing to comply would be regarded as "intending a breach of the peace," and the council would institute measures, including the use of force, for the restoration of peace. Under those circumstances, members would be called upon to make available such armaments, installations, strategic areas, and armed forces as the council deemed necessary, taking into account the geographical position, regional or special obligations, and relative resources of each nation.[37]

The draft charter also provided for disarmament. Members agreed to maintain their armaments at the lowest level "consistent with their internal order" and with the "effective discharge" of their "obligations for maintaining international security." The council was to establish a system of armament regulations, perhaps including both minimums and maximums, with due consideration given to the special responsibilities for security assumed by the Big Five. The limitations and restrictions created by the council would be enforced through a system of inspections carried out by an Armaments Inspection Commission; members would be expected to cooperate with the commission's efforts by opening their military facilities to its scrutiny.[38]

The drafters recognized that their charter resembled that of the League of Nations in that it was based on the principles of universal membership and free association among states. This similarity made their plan vulnerable to attack from those who wished to avoid the mistakes of the past and urged the more potent alternative of creating a superstate through a federal form of organization; but the drafters contended that, given the current condition of the world, only a cooperative type of organization seemed feasible. They argued, moreover, that the proposed organization differed from the league in several important ways. It granted the Great Powers "exceptional and immediate responsibility for security" along with a "permanent preponderance" in the membership and voting procedures of the council; it enabled action to be instituted with less than total unanimity; and it provided for "effective international control" of armaments. Thus the drafters believed that despite its essentially cooperative nature the new United Nations Organization would be an effective force for maintaining world order.[39]

Welles's replacement as under secretary of state was Edward R. Stettinius, Jr., Lend-Lease administrator and former chairman of the board of United States Steel. A young man who radiated strength and vitality—he was forty-two years old in 1943—the new under secretary brought to the State Department a reputation as one of the ablest administrators in wartime Washington, as the man who had prevented the foreign aid program from becoming controversial when, as *New York Times* columnist Arthur Krock put it, "less wise and able management might have made it so." Although Stettinius possessed neither experience in foreign affairs nor a keen intellect—Dean Acheson later wrote that he had "gone far with comparatively modest equipment"—he had demonstrated during his tenure at Lend-Lease exactly the kind of skills Roosevelt and Hull thought the State Department now needed most: a flair for public relations, an ability to get along with Congress, and a talent for organization. Stettinius would put each of these qualities to good use in the next twenty-one months, first as under secretary, then as chief of the American delegation at the Dumbarton Oaks Conference, and finally as Hull's successor as secretary of state.[40]

Relations with Congress on the question of international organization dominated Stettinius's first weeks as under secretary. During the summer of 1943, Roosevelt, mindful of the nightmarish consequences that had befallen Woodrow Wilson and his plan for world cooperation, attempted to line up congressional support for American participation in a postwar peacekeeping organization; this was another of FDR's many efforts to avoid the "mistakes" of the aftermath of World War I. The administration thus backed a resolution, drafted in the State Department and sponsored by Representative J. William Fulbright of Arkansas, "favoring the creation of appropriate international machinery with power adequate to maintain a just and lasting peace" and calling for American participation therein. After cursory debate, the measure passed the House by the overwhelming vote of 360 to 29. Difficulties arose in the Senate, however, where a resolution similar to Fulbright's offered by Senator Tom Connally of Texas had to compete with a more elaborate and detailed proposal made by Senators Joseph H. Ball of Minnesota, Harold H. Burton of Ohio, Carl A. Hatch of New Mexico, and Lister Hill of Alabama. The "B_2H_2" Resolution recommended that the United States sponsor a meeting to create an international organization of "specific and limited authority" to establish machinery for the peaceful settlement of disputes and provide for the immediate suppression of any future attempt at military aggression. This was moving too far too fast for Roosevelt and his supporters, who wanted to build public support for an international organization slowly and feared that such detailed planning might begin a counterproductive debate on the exact terms of the postwar settlement, which might trigger a revival of isolationist sentiment. It also threatened to steal the limelight from Connally, who might well instigate the kind of divisive Senate fight that Roosevelt most wanted to avoid. Resolving this delicate problem fell to Stettinius, the acting secretary while Hull attended the Moscow conference, who succeeded in persuading Connally to accept amendments that slightly strengthened his resolution without making it too detailed. When it was approved by the Senate on 5 November by a vote of eighty-five to five, the Connally Resolution was hailed by internationalists as a great achievement.

"The Senate yesterday undid a twenty-four-year-old mistake," proclaimed the *New York Times* with considerable exaggeration; in fact, the measure was extremely ambiguous, did not spell out the precise nature of American involvement in the peacekeeping organization, and contained the potentially limiting clause that any action taken in this regard must obtain the concurrence of the Senate. Still, the Senate had put itself on record, even if the issue did amount to little more than, as one commentator put it, "voting against sin"; and Stettinius had demonstrated his considerable skill at winning support for the principle of international organization.[41]

The appointment of Stettinius also had an effect on postwar planning through his development of a design for departmental reorganization. The State Department's reputation for efficiency, never high, had reached its nadir in the summer of 1943, when Welles's resignation, surrounded as it was by scandal and controversy, had confirmed the darkest suspicions of the department's critics and added to the popular image of the State Department as a bureaucracy of incompetents and backbiters—or worse. Hull knew that, whatever its merits, such criticism could not help but have a negative impact on the implementation of the department's plans for international cooperation, and he had offered Stettinius the position of under secretary partly to polish the State Department's tarnished image in preparation for the postwar debate. In one of their earliest meetings, the secretary had given Stettinius full authority to begin the reorganization of the department; by late November, the new under secretary had made studies and written a plan described by a skeptical Robert Sherwood as an "impressive chart with myriad boxes in orderly array."[42]

The departmental reorganization, which went into effect on 15 January 1944, attempted to eliminate overlapping jurisdiction, to establish more direct lines of authority, and to clear the way for top officials to pay more attention to the making of policy. It created an Office of Special Political Affairs, directed by James C. Dunn, who was also director of the Office of European Affairs, to handle special matters of an international political nature, including postwar security. This last issue was to be dealt with by a branch of Dunn's office, the Division of International Security and Organization, headed by Harley Notter, which was to have responsibility for international peace and security arrangements—both "general and regional"—including organized international cooperation, relations with international organizations, and liaisons with the War and Navy Departments on questions of postwar security. The new arrangement made two significant changes in the department's way of handling postwar security questions: the planning agencies were now granted regular departmental status, which made their budgets somewhat more secure; and the process of researching and studying postwar questions was for the first time amalgamated with operational responsibilities. In addition, planning now gave way to drafting as the chief function of the Division of International Security and Organization. These changes reflected the continued progress of the war as well as the expanded importance that postwar cooperation had come to play in the State Department's considerations by the beginning of 1944, the year of the conference at Dumbarton Oaks.[43]

2 Preparing for the Conference

Following the Moscow Foreign Ministers' Conference in October and November 1943, where it had been agreed to establish a general peace-keeping organization "at the earliest practicable date," Pasvolsky suggested to Hull that the time had arrived to formulate an official recommendation for the president. Hull agreed and on 9 December assigned the new planning responsibilities to the Informal Political Agenda Group, previously (as the Informal Agenda Group) the department's steering committee for questions of postwar organization. The group's initial members, most of whom would later participate in the Dumbarton Oaks Conference, were Pasvolsky, Bowman, Taylor, Davis, Cohen, Dunn, and Hornbeck; Special Assistant to the Secretary Joseph C. Green was added on 16 March 1944. In addition, Under Secretary Stettinius took part occasionally, and Notter participated throughout as chief of the department's staff of postwar security experts, the Division of International Security and Organization. The group had no formal chairman, but because it met in Pasvolsky's office he usually acted in that capacity. Although it would change its name twice during 1944, the Informal Political Agenda Group would continue to play a leading role in formulating American plans for a postwar security organization, and its assignment to that task in December 1943 marked the beginning of the State Department's serious preparation for the Dumbarton Oaks Conference.[1]

In seventy meetings over the next seven months the group considered all the difficult questions of postwar security and formulated detailed plans for an international organization. Its first task was to develop a new draft charter for the secretary to present to FDR; in so doing, it clarified some issues and raised others that would bedevil deliberations through the Dumbarton Oaks Conference—and after. The easiest questions were those that had been dealt with before, such as whether the new organization should be created as soon as possible (it should), whether it should be permanent rather than transitional (it should), and whether it should be based on the remains of the League of Nations (it should not). Somewhat more difficult to achieve—and a source of more serious problems later—was agreement on Pasvolsky's proposal that the organization should promote cooperation for "the progressive improvement of the general welfare" as well as for the maintenance of peace and security. But this question could at least be resolved (affirmatively) within the group; others could not be, at least not immediately, and were thus left up to the president through the inclusion of bracketed alternatives in the preliminary draft prepared by the group in December.[2]

One such question was the proper size (and therefore constitution) of the council. Previous plans, including the one drawn up by Welles and the Special Subcommittee on International Organization, had provided for both an executive committee of the Big Four and a council that would also include a number of the lesser powers, perhaps distributed on a regional basis. It was this variation of the Four Policemen format that Roosevelt had presented to Stalin at Tehran on 29 November 1943. The projected difference between the two agencies was to be functional, with the executive committee handling all questions of security in accordance with the Four Policemen idea and the council playing a somewhat lesser administrative and deliberative role. Group members disagreed with this structure on two grounds, however, both of which related to what they saw as the need for broadening the responsibility of small nations within the organization. First, they took exception to limiting the maintenance of security to only four powers; and second, they opposed assigning any questions but those of peace and security to a council where the Great Powers would be disproportionately represented and enjoy special voting privileges. As most of the group saw it, the top-heavy earlier plans would have a negative effect on the success of the organization by detracting from the willingness of small nations to join and by making it more difficult to settle disputes between lesser nations peacefully. The answer, according to Pasvolsky, was to eliminate the executive committee of the Four Policemen, lodge authority over security matters in the hands of the larger Security Council, and turn all remaining responsibilities back to a general assembly of all members. This proposal would eventually be adopted as the solution to the problem, but in the meantime disagreement within the group caused Hull to present several alternatives to the president. One was to retain the Four Policemen idea for security matters while eliminating the council; although this option received no real support within the group, it had to be included in light of Roosevelt's well-known views on the matter, which had never really been shared by the Department of State. A second alternative was a council consisting of the four (perhaps more) permanent members and "an equal number less one" of elected members (currently three); and a third was the Big Four and "not less than three nor more than eleven" elected members. Group members clearly favored the principle expressed by the second and third options—more responsibility for the lesser powers—but disagreed on the optimum size for the council and whether or not the Great Powers should always constitute a majority.[3]

A second question requiring alternative proposals was the method of voting in the council. Earlier plans had begun with the principle of unanimity among the Big Four, then modified it to provide for action where at least three of the four permanent members could agree. This approach would make agreement on enforcement easier to obtain and would, in the view of some State Department officials, strengthen the new international organization. But it raised the serious problem of requiring a Great Power to participate in an enforcement action against its wishes, or perhaps—in the worst of all possible cases—against itself. The Informal Political Agenda Group saw no easy way out of this dilemma. As Notter pointed out, the surest way to make the new organization fail would be to require one of the Big Four to take part in peacekeeping activities that it had voted against, particularly if that nation were somehow involved in the dispute. Only the Great Power veto inherent in unanimity could guarantee that this would never occur. This solution would mean that some questions would have to be settled outside the organization, but such a result seemed preferable to the total breakdown of the world structure that might otherwise take place. Pasvolsky agreed with this reasoning but did not want to go so far. He thus offered a compromise proposal whereby a permanent member of the council could abstain from voting on a question of enforcement and be bound by the decision or vote against it and be released from the obligation to take part. Although this would not restore the principle of unanimity—enforcement action could still be carried out with or without the opposing member's participation—it might prevent the organization from dissolving under the pressure of this delicate issue.[4]

Others opposed the Great Power veto on the principle that it gave the organization the authority to suppress aggression only when it was attempted by smaller states. Requiring Big Four unanimity would eliminate the possibility of enforcement action against any of them; it might thus preserve the organization's body at the price of its soul. The problem with this position was that without the Great Powers there could be no effective enforcement action, and it was uncertain whether any of the Big Four would participate in an organization in which it did not have a veto over when and where its forces were employed. This was true even—perhaps particularly—of the United States. As Benjamin Cohen pointed out, American participation might be jeopardized by a loss of public and congressional support for any organization under which the United States could be required to take enforcement action against its interests or wishes. To solve this problem without resort to a Great Power veto, Cohen proposed limiting all council decisions on enforcement to recommendations. Thus no Great Power could ever be required to act against its will, although a recommendation for enforcement action against one of the Big Four was still possible on the votes of the other three. This suggestion, however, was too reminiscent of the League of Nations; without obligatory participation in duly approved sanctions the new world organization promised to work no more effectively than had the old. Cohen's proposal was therefore rejected by the group, which decided that all decisions of the council, unanimous or otherwise, should be binding on all members of the organization.[5]

The most complicated problem of voting was whether or not a Great Power should be permitted to vote when it was a party to a dispute being considered by the council. This issue, which would be a source of almost fatal difficulty at the Dumbarton Oaks Conference, came up twice in group meetings but was not, apparently, very thoroughly discussed. As Benjamin Gerig, who raised the issue, pointed out, voting by a party to a dispute was directly related to the question of Big Four unanimity; even with a veto, a permanent member could not prevent the organization from taking action against itself unless it had the right to vote in cases where it was involved. Thus it was to be expected that one or more of the Great Powers might object on the basis of unanimity to any attempt to limit their right to vote.[6]

In composing its draft plan for the president, the group decided to list alternative voting procedures for four types of important decisions: settlement of disputes, enforcement of council decisions, determination of the existence of aggression, and suppression of aggression. In these areas, the group left it up to Roosevelt to decide whether the decisions of the council should require unanimity or only a three-fourths majority of the permanent members. In addition, if the president selected the three-fourths option, he could choose from three methods for determining the responsibilities of the permanent member that abstained or dissented. The Great Power could be obligated whether abstaining or dissenting, obligated if abstaining but not if dissenting, or obligated under neither circumstance but bound not to obstruct any action taken by the council. On the vital question of whether or not a permanent member should vote when party to a dispute, the group's draft was decidedly negative; the charter stated that in no decision of the council should such a member's vote be counted. Thus the veto could not be used to protect aggression by a Great Power. But, as historian Ruth Russell has noted, this statement appeared in a section of the charter somewhat removed from other considerations of voting, suggesting that the group had not thought through the effect of such a position on the functioning of the council. In any event, much more would be heard of this difficult issue later in the postwar planning process and at Dumbarton Oaks.[7]

A third unresolved question related to general membership in the new organization. This problem broke down into three parts: initial membership, eventual admission to membership, and the expulsion of members that seriously violated the organization's rules. The group agreed that the organization should be "instituted" by the wartime United Nations and their associates, but disagreed on the procedure whereby other nations might be permitted to join in the future. Some thought that the question of suitability for membership should remain in the hands of the initial members, with new states admitted by a vote of two-thirds majority; in this way, the Axis powers and their sympathizers could be made to demonstrate their full rehabilitation before being admitted for future participation. An alternative, which was listed as such in the draft proposal, was that "all duly recognized independent states" should be automatically considered members, with any doubts as to a potential member's status as a sovereign state—but not its politics—being determined by the council. The question of expulsion also remained unresolved. The draft plan contained a bracketed section granting the council the authority to debar from membership, at least temporarily, any member that had "violated the peace of nations." As its opponents pointed out, however, this form of discipline compromised the principle of a world organization for all nations and had the effect of divorcing from the world body precisely those states most in need of its guidance; but, as others argued, the threat of expulsion seemed a necessary sanction for the organization to retain. Each of these questions would be a source of controversy at the Dumbarton Oaks Conference.[8]

Hull transmitted the group's plan to Roosevelt on 29 December 1943. In a covering memorandum he informed the president that this statement of basic ideas was founded on two central assumptions: first, that the four major powers would consider themselves "morally bound" not to make war on each other or on any other state and would cooperate to maintain the peace; and second, that each would keep and equip adequate military forces and would be willing to use them to prevent or suppress aggression. This was a reiteration of a principle on which all State Department planners were agreed: either the Big Four continued to cooperate after the war or there was no hope for the maintenance of peace in the future. The purpose of the group's proposal, then, was to find some basis upon which this continuing cooperation could be achieved.[9]

Roosevelt responded to the draft plan in a meeting with Hull, Pasvolsky, and others of the "consulting group" on 3 February 1944—more than a month after it had been submitted to him. He gave his approval to the "general approach" of the proposal and expanded upon his own ideas for the new international organization. Most important, he accepted the plan for a single council consisting of the Big Four and a number of smaller powers, thus modifying the simple Four Policemen concept to which he had seemed wedded—at least on a metaphorical level—in all previous discussions of postwar security. It would appear that Roosevelt did not now regard this alteration as a major step; he saw the obvious advantages to be gained from the support of less powerful nations and thought that the major powers would dominate the council anyway, which was always the real objective of the Four Policemen idea. To this end, the president preferred the smallest council possible—seven members—but feared that it might prove too difficult to select only three lesser powers to join with the Big Four. On the question of selection, he thought that the General Assembly should elect the smaller states to membership in the council, which meant, as Pasvolsky put it, that "the regional principle goes out." Hull, in particular, must have taken genuine satisfaction from the president's decisions on the council; they meant that FDR was much less inflexible on the key questions of representation and regionalism than the secretary of state had feared.[10]

On voting in the council, Roosevelt favored an approach that Pasvolsky termed "unanimous with abstention." The president was "quite clear" that the interests of the Big Four necessitated their unanimity on "the most crucial matters"; this was in keeping with his often stated view that only cooperation among the Great Powers could guarantee peace in the postwar world. FDR thought that abstention could be used to facilitate Big Four cooperation; with this option, a Great Power could avoid voting in favor of an embarrassing proposal without employing its veto to prevent action favored by the remainder of the council. In any such situation, of course, the abstaining nation would be bound by the council's decision. The record does not indicate that Roosevelt expressed any opinion on the question of a Great Power voting when it was party to a dispute; this matter was not, at any rate, a bracketed provision in the current draft plan. But its omission reflected a potential gap in the president's reasoning. Abstention might, as he argued, preserve the principle of unanimity when the council was dealing with an "embarrassing" question, but only a veto could do so when a Great Power's vital interests were at stake—that is, when it found itself involved in a dispute before the council. These were precisely the "crucial matters" about which Roosevelt was certain that the Great Powers must agree, yet it was here that the draft plan diverged dangerously from the basic rule of unanimity. In part, this contradiction resulted from the difficult nature of the issues involved, but it also reflected the failure of all planners—including Roosevelt—to think through the ramifications of surrendering the principle upon which the new organization was to be based when dealing with the very questions where it was most essential. This failure would cause considerable mischief later.[11]

Another issue that Roosevelt wanted clarified was the nature of the American military commitment to postwar peacekeeping. The president wished to be certain that the United States would not be called upon to furnish armed forces without its consent, something that he knew Congress would never permit in any event. He also wanted it made clear that the United States was not bound to send troops to Europe; this was in keeping with what he had told Sir Anthony Eden in a meeting in Washington in March and Stalin at Tehran in November. Roosevelt thought that American land forces could be sent to trouble spots in the Western Hemisphere, but that only naval and air forces, which were manned by voluntary enlistment, should be employed in other areas of the world. In this way, FDR hoped to retain a part of the organization's regional character and to avoid provoking a renewed public outcry against American involvement in the affairs of Europe that might endanger all participation in postwar security operations.[12]

The president also expressed an intense interest in the physical details of the proposed organization. He continued to prefer a decentralized structure, with the council meeting at a permanent base—the Azores were FDR's first choice, although he thought Hawaii might do—the assembly moving about to various places, and technical agencies situated in several locations, such as the World Court at The Hague. Roosevelt thought that situating the council on an island would make it seem more neutral; rotating the meeting site of the assembly would have a similar effect for that body. In addition, physically separating the organization's agencies would make it seem less like a world government, which the president knew would find little favor among critics of international-ism in the United States. And perhaps most important, a decentralized organi-zation would avoid identification with the League of Nations; thus FDR may have favored a peripatetic assembly primarily because he thought that the only practical alternative was to locate it in Geneva, where it would inspire too many recollections of the league. In a similar vein, Roosevelt asked that the State Department's planners look for some new nomenclature—less reminiscent of the League of Nations—although he thought that the names Executive Council and General Assembly might prove satisfactory.[13]

Roosevelt also renewed another long-standing interest by requesting that the assembly be given authority to investigate the status of colonies and other dependent areas. On several previous occasions the president had indicated that he regarded international trusteeship as the best way to bring colonial peoples to independence in the postwar world; he had stated this view most recently at Cairo and Tehran and in a memorandum to Hull, dated 24 January 1944, in which he argued that Indochina should be liberated from France and come under international guidance following the end of hostilities in Asia. This goal promised to cause difficulties with the British (as well as with the French), who viewed it as an underhanded American attempt to strip them of their colonial possessions, and any suggestion of its inclusion in plans for an international organization was certain to provoke heated controversy. The issue of trusteeship would, in fact, seem so incendiary by the time of the Dumbarton Oaks Conference that it was (although without Roosevelt's knowledge) deferred entirely from consideration there.[14]

The president closed the meeting by agreeing that the State Department should exchange proposals with the British and Russians as soon as possible. Other arrangements had to be made for dealing with the Chinese, however, because Roosevelt feared that any documents made available to Chungking might become publicly known before talks could begin and arouse opposition sentiment in the United States. On 8 February, the department informed the British and Soviet embassies that it was ready to begin a study of the framework and functions of an "international organization for security and peace." It also suggested that each of the three governments should prepare a paper as a basis for discussion; when completed, these papers would be circulated and arrangements made for preliminary talks to begin in Washington as soon as possible. The department projected a short timetable for this process—it thought that it might have its own preliminary outline ready in a week—but in fact the procedure would take much longer, not actually reaching the discussion stage until the conference convened at Dumbarton Oaks six months later.[15]

None of the Big Three was having an easy time shaping plans for a postwar organization. Even the British, who wished to push the timetable for planning ahead as rapidly as possible to guarantee American involvement in the postwar world, found the formulation of concrete proposals extremely difficult; indeed, their problems resembled those of the Americans in several important respects. Down to the spring of 1942, the thinking of the Foreign Office had not progressed much beyond the generalities of the Atlantic Charter; the pressure of the war had left little time or opportunity to give serious consideration to the possible shape of a permanent world peacekeeping organization. Then Sir Alexander Cadogan, the permanent under secretary for foreign affairs who would later serve as chairman of the British delegation to Dumbarton Oaks, requested a study of the reasons for the failure of the League of Nations, with a view toward how the mistakes of that body in the past might be remedied in the future. The result, in outline form, was a draft plan for an organization that its developers hoped would be more effective than the league had been at preventing war and aggression. The Foreign Office began serious consideration of postwar planning in the autumn of 1942, when, as Eden put it, the Allies had "the strategic initiative" and "victory could be foreseen." At that time, a committee of the Foreign Office headed by Gladwyn Jebb, chief of the new Economic and Reconstruction Department, prepared the first more or less formal British plan for a new world organization. In a long memorandum dated 20 October 1942, "The Four-Power Plan," Jebb analyzed the Rooseveltian idea of an organization dominated by the Big Four; in particular, he tried to determine whether control by four powers was practicable and in accordance with British interests in the postwar period. The answer to the first question was uncertain, Jebb wrote, because the vagaries of American policy, the suspicions of the Soviets, and the fear of domination on the part of the smaller powers would all present difficult obstacles. The answer to the second question was decidedly affirmative; there existed, Jebb argued, no satisfactory alternative to cooperation among the Great Powers. Isolation was impossible in a world where Great Britain was unable even to provide for its own defense, and if the Americans could not be induced to cooperate in a continuing alliance, the British would have to line up with the Soviets—or the Germans, if the leaders of the USSR proved recalcitrant.[16]

Eden supported these conclusions, which he presented to the War Cabinet on 8 November. Before the matter could be discussed, however, the situation was complicated by the presentation of another memorandum with a somewhat different emphasis. This paper, prepared by the minister of aircraft production, Sir Stafford Cripps, proposed councils of Europe, Asia, and the Americas to deal with all political, economic, and social questions that might disturb the peace; representatives from these councils, along with two others from the British Commonwealth and the constituent republics of the USSR, would make up a Supreme World Council. Thus the British Foreign Office had its own, less acrimonious, version of the Hull-Welles debate over regionalism, which the War Cabinet failed to resolve on 23 November when it accepted the idea of four-power cooperation in principle and deferred the Cripps proposal for continent-based councils to a later meeting.[17]

A second major problem facing British planners was the unwillingness of the prime minister to take the issue of a postwar organization very seriously. Churchill, who was preoccupied with matters of wartime strategy, responded to the Foreign Office's first attempt to explore the question of peace by arguing that it was a waste of time. "Any conclusions drawn now are sure to have little relation to what will happen," he wrote to Eden. "It is even dangerous to discuss some aspects of the problem, for instance the position of Russia," he concluded. The prime minister also offered his foreign secretary two pieces of advice: He should entrust studies of the postwar era "mainly to those on whose hands time hangs heavy" and should "not overlook Mrs. Glass's Cookery Book recipe for Jugged Hare—'First catch your hare.'" Eden responded the next day, writing Churchill that he was "most disappointed" with his reply. The Foreign Office was not, he wrote, requesting a detailed discussion of the postwar settlement, just the prime minister's general approval of the outline that it was developing. "It is," he argued, "from every point of view bad business to have to live from hand to mouth where we can avoid it, and the only consequence of so doing is that the United States makes a policy and we follow, which I do not regard as a satisfactory role for the British Empire."[18]

Eden's prodding finally caught the prime minister's attention, although not with a result that could have given much comfort to the planners at Whitehall. Churchill make it clear that he did not see much value in the Four-Power Plan, except insofar as it might maintain an American interest in Europe and prevent a return to the isolationism of the interwar years. "I must admit," he wrote in one of his grand geopolitical moods, "that my thoughts rest primarily in Europe—the revival of the glory of Europe, the parent continent of the modern nations and of civilization. It would be a measureless disaster if Russian barbarism overlaid the culture and independence of the ancient States of Europe." To prevent this unhappy outcome, about which he would have so much to say by 1946, the prime minister proposed a Council of Europe consisting of the United States, the United Kingdom, and several confederations of states—Balkan, Scandinavian, Danubian—to administer an international police force and point the way toward the creation of a United States of Europe in the future. It made no sense, from Churchill's perspective, for the British to be, as he put it, "shut up with Russians and Chinese" in a world organization when their vital interests rested primarily in Europe. This was as deeply into the question as the prime minister was willing to go at the time. "It would be easy to dilate upon these themes," he wrote Eden, but "the war has prior claims on your attention and on mine."[19]

As his thoughts matured over the next year or so, Churchill also came to regard regionalism as a matter of common sense. The nations most affected by a breach of the peace were those closest to the dispute, he reasoned; they were the powers that might most reasonably be expected to supply the pressure or sanctions needed to secure a settlement. Faraway countries had less at stake, so that calling upon them for action to quell a disturbance was likely to produce "merely vapid and academic discussions" reminiscent of the pusillanimous behavior of the League of Nations. Thus regional councils would be best suited for handling most peacekeeping duties; a Supreme World Council would maintain final authority and deal with disputes that threatened the peace of the entire world or otherwise outgrew the scope of any one region. Beyond the obvious tactical merits of this argument, however, the real source of Churchill's regionalism was his desire to create a Council of Europe, which he regarded as the key to revitalizing the Continent.[20]

It was also Churchill's primary interest in Europe that accounted for his insistence on the inclusion of France among the postwar Great Powers. Regardless of its wartime inadequacies, France was the only likely candidate on the Continent to serve as a makeweight to the Soviet Union after the end of hostilities; without a renascent France, Churchill thought, the British would either have to balance the power of the Soviets alone or rely upon the always uncertain support of the United States. The prime minister thus pressed at every opportunity for the recreation of a strong France and for its inclusion in a European steering committee "if she recovers her greatness." During 1943 he did so at meetings in Washington in May and at the Tehran Conference in November; thereafter, a strong France became a cornerstone of British postwar policy as viewed from Downing Street. Eden agreed with this assessment. It seemed to the foreign secretary, as he remarked in a telegram to Churchill in March, that the Americans were being "very hard on the French" by denying them an automatic role as a Great Power in the postwar structure then being developed.[21]

Despite their similar views on France, Churchill and Eden disagreed over the principle of regionalism in a way that was reminiscent of the differences between Roosevelt and Hull. In each case the reasons were the same: the president and prime minister emphasized realpolitik (although it understandably meant something different to each) while their foreign ministers sought more of an ideal system for maintaining universal peace; the two were almost certain to be incompatible. Like their counterparts in the United States, British planners worried about interference from their more political chief executive; they feared, as Jebb's assistant Charles K. Webster confided to his diary, that preparations and studies would be completed only to have "precipitate and unconsidered action by the PM . . . take matters entirely out of the hands of the experts." Thus, as historian William McNeill has remarked with some understatement, Churchill's ideas on postwar planning "were not of necessity those of the British Government." In fact, it appears that, at least partly because of disagreement on the most basic questions, neither the cabinet nor the Foreign Office—the "British Government"—had the confidence to develop any very complete plans for a postwar organization down to the middle of 1943.[22]

This diffidence was evident in the Four-Power Plan that Eden made a War Cabinet paper on 8 November 1942. The Foreign Office recognized, he wrote, that it was "premature to chart, in any detail, the course which we intend to follow," so that the plan submitted was nothing more than an attempt to "take a bearing" on the problem of a postwar organization. The reason for Eden's reluctance to go farther was apparent in the plan itself, which adopted a universal perspective and took issue with the prime minister's regional ideas. Any postwar organization, it said, must be more than an Anglo-American alliance to police Europe, no matter how important the Continent was to British interests. Certainly any attempt to write out the Soviet Union was destined to bring trouble, probably in the form of an Eastern European bloc to rival whatever the Anglo-Americans created in the West. Nothing good could come from such a situation because, as the paper put it, "no international organization will be effective if the Great Powers are at loggerheads." Thus, cooperation, not competition, with the Soviet Union should be at the heart of British postwar foreign policy—a view that the anti-Communist Churchill was not likely to accept. The inclusion of China in a four-power agency presented a different sort of problem, but here, too, Eden disagreed with Churchill's view. Although counting China as a Great Power may, he wrote, "seem to us to be a completely unreal conception," granting them a place among the postwar elite was important to the United States, whose cooperation in the plan was essential to its success. Eden was right to be worried about the prime minister's reaction to this paper; Churchill continued to press for a European-centered plan after the inconclusive War Cabinet meeting on 23 November. Thus Jebb and others in the Foreign Office attempted in January 1943 to weave the two ideas together in a memorandum entitled "The United Nations Plan," which contained both a reliance on Big Four cooperation and provisions for a Council of Europe.[23]

"The United Nations Plan," which Eden approved on 16 January 1943, managed to make a gesture toward a regional Council of Europe while emphasizing the paramount role of a universal World Council. Whitehall's basic premise was that the Big Four would have to maintain order for an indeterminate time after the end of the war. They would, the planners thought, act in concert to constitute an international police force and to prevent the rise of social and economic conditions that might lead again to war. Regional groupings might be tolerated or even encouraged within this framework, but it was important to avoid what Eden referred to as a "limited liability" system where a Great Power (especially the United States) would act only in its own sphere. For the new organization to work, planners had to assume that each of the Big Four was "principally interested in maintaining the peace everywhere in the world." Whether that turned out to be true or not, one of the Great Powers' first tasks would be to form themselves into a European Armistice Commission, and it was out of this agency that the Foreign Office now thought a Churchillian Council of Europe might reasonably grow. There might, Eden continued, also be several other regional councils—one for the Americas, others for the British Commonwealth, the states of the USSR, the Far East, and the Middle East. In addition, the affairs of "backward areas" such as Africa, Southeast Asia, or the Western Atlantic might be dealt with by regional councils composed of parent and colonial states. But all would be subject to the authority of the World Council, which the Foreign Office continued to envision as including only the Big Four and eventually France.[24]

When Churchill made it clear that he still preferred the more regionally based Cripps plan, the Foreign Office turned to political arguments to change his mind. Eden and Jebb visited Washington in March and reported that the Roosevelt administration would never accept American participation in a strictly European council. Perhaps to test this thesis, the prime minister came out in favor of postwar regional councils in a radio address on 21 March. The American response was everything that Whitehall's planners might have hoped; the speech was, as a Foreign Office memorandum put it later, "seized upon by Isolationists in the United States," who threatened to keep their country out of a postwar organization altogether if it meant, as Churchill suggested, continued involvement in the internal affairs of Europe. During the following eighteen months of deliberations on the shape of a postwar body, the Foreign Office would repeatedly use the threat of an American return to isolationism as a trump card against Churchill's scheme for a European council.[25]

This is not to say, however, that the prime minister's ideas carried no weight in Foreign Office planning. Whitehall could not ignore Churchill's views any more than their counterparts in the State Department could ignore Roosevelt's; the result was a continuing attempt to find a formula that would be acceptable to both the prime minister and the Americans. One way to do this was to move away from the simple Four Policemen idea toward an expanded council that might include representatives from a number of regional groupings. In this manner, the World Council and regional councils could be blended together, satisfying Churchill's desire for a European council without unduly alarming the more universalist Americans. As Eden put it during a Foreign Office meeting on 12 May, "the more he looked into these matters the more he came to the conclusion that the new international machinery, if it was ever established, would be something like the League of Nations." Thus, although the limited council of the Big Four would have peacekeeping value in the immediate postwar period and "might even endure as a system," a larger council would eventually be necessary.[26]

The Foreign Office attempted to develop such a hybrid plan in the spring of 1943. This new "United Nations Plan," which was the British government's most fully conceived postwar scheme up to that time, featured a council that included the four (or five) Great Powers and other nations chosen on a regional basis—two from Europe, two from the Americas, and one each from the Far East, the Middle East, and the British Commonwealth. This council, meeting at regular intervals in different locations, would link the world together while acting to settle disputes and restrain aggression. Decisions would be made by the unanimous vote of the Great Powers; other council members would have no vote at all, only the opportunity to influence the final outcome of deliberations. The Foreign Office also drew closer to the League of Nations idea by including a World Assembly in its plan. This agency, planners thought, might meet every two years or so to receive and discuss reports from the council and whatever other bodies the new world organization would create. Among these bodies might be regional defense systems, including one for Western Europe that could, the Foreign Office hoped, satisfy the prime minister's desire for regional organization. Planners warned that these groupings must not be dominated by the local Great Power, however, lest they create blocs and "sow the seeds of future war."[27]

The Foreign Office's case against regionalism was reinforced in August when Churchill met Roosevelt at Quebec and the president proposed the creation of a postwar security organization with a worldwide basis. Churchill's grudging acceptance of this proposal marked the beginning of his slow—and sometimes uncertain—retreat from regionalism. His motives for this change of direction were probably twofold and related: worsening relations with the Soviet Union and heightened dependence upon the United States as undeniably the greatest power in the postwar world. By the time of the first Quebec Conference Churchill was losing his wartime faith in Soviet cooperation, without which there was no hope for a successful Council of Europe such as he proposed, especially in light of American rejection of a regional European organization. Under the circumstances, the prime minister had to be certain that the United States would play an active role in postwar European affairs; he could best do this by accepting American leadership on its own terms—that is, as one of the Great Powers in a worldwide peacekeeping organization. Sacrificing a regional plan that was now unworkable anyway must have seemed a small enough price to pay for this assistance. There was, however, a higher price. As William McNeill has pointed out, Churchill was also in effect surrendering his hopes for a truly independent British postwar policy. The United States, rather than a revitalized Western Europe supported by Great Britain, would now have to counterbalance the power and influence of the Soviet Union. No matter, by the end of 1943 the prime minister had apparently abandoned his previous region-alist views and accepted the American idea of a universalist organization.[28]

In the meantime the British were making little additional progress on a comprehensive plan of their own. On 29 July the prime minister suggested the creation of a cabinet committee to consider proposals for the postwar settle-ment. This high-level committee did not, according to Charles Webster, go "very far into the question"; in fact, it met only four times before disbanding under the pressure of more immediate wartime concerns in the aftermath of the first Quebec Conference. A second, more important group, the Committee on Armistice Terms and Civil Administration, chaired by Deputy Prime Minis-ter Clement Attlee, was responsible for preparing papers to be exchanged with other governments, but its efforts failed to produce useful results until 1944 when its name was changed to the Armistice and Post-War Committee of the Foreign Office. A third body, the Post-Hostilities Planning Sub-Committee of the Chiefs of Staff Committee, directed by Gladwyn Jebb, which considered postwar strategic questions, was only somewhat more successful. In general, these committees—along with the Foreign Office—attempted to deal with the same questions then being discussed by the various groups within the Depart-ment of State, although, as Webster has remarked, in accordance with British practice, the organization was less elaborate than in the United States. It might also be pointed out that it was less productive; although British ideas on a postwar organization were beginning to take shape, they were far less devel-oped than those of their American counterparts by the end of 1943.[29]

This was still more true of the Soviets. In the absence of solid evidence, little can be said with confidence about the preliminary ideas of Soviet officials on the question of a postwar security organization; but it does seem certain that no working plans or proposals had been formulated in the Kremlin by the end of 1943. Down to the time of the Moscow Foreign Ministers' Conference at the end of October, in fact, the Soviets were reluctant—although sometimes per-suaded—to discuss postwar planning even in principle, much less to converse in detail about the complex problems of the powers and composition of a new peacekeeping organization. It is not clear why Stalin agreed to cooperate in beginning postwar planning even then. Perhaps he regarded his cooperation as the price of continued American support in the war against Germany, although this interpretation seems excessively Machiavellian and is supported by no hard evidence. More likely, he could not see how agreeing to an organization could do much harm, at least so long as Roosevelt and Churchill continued to operate on the level of such generalities as the Atlantic Charter and the Soviet Union retained privileged status as a Great Power.[30]

That is not to say, however, that Stalin placed no faith in a postwar security organization; the fashionable view of the Soviet dictator as a cynical realist who only humored Roosevelt's fuzzy idealism is surely overdrawn from both angles. As early as December 1941, Stalin had told Eden that after the war he would favor the creation of an international police force, organized under a World Council of some sort and backed by an alliance of the great democratic nations. There is no reason to doubt that he meant it. Still, Stalin's hopes in this uncertain area were clearly linked to his postwar national objectives, and particularly to his paramount concern for the security of the Soviet Union. Thus Stalin, alone among the leaders of the Big Three, emphasized the prevention of future German aggression as the chief goal of the new organization; his greatest worry, as he described it in one of his wartime speeches, was that "Hitlers come and go but the German nation, the German state, remains." At Tehran, he argued that "safeguarding" against Germany should be the most important objective of a postwar organization, even to the extent of taking and maintaining possession of key strategic points within German territory. For Stalin, clearly, the ability to maintain European security against a revanchist Germany would be the primary scale against which any proposed world organization must be measured.[31]

It was for this reason that Stalin—like Churchill—favored an organization based on a Council of Europe. His idea, as he expressed it at Tehran, was for the creation of a European Commission consisting of the United States, Great Britain, the Soviet Union, and possibly one other European state to handle security problems on the Continent. There might also, Stalin thought, be a Far Eastern Commission to deal with problems in that part of the world and a worldwide organization of which the two commissions would be a part. Roosevelt objected to this proposal because, he argued, it would never win the support of the United States Congress or American public opinion; only a truly universal organization would have a chance to do that. As one historian has pointed out, Stalin must have been puzzled by the president's willingness to make a worldwide commitment but not a purely European one; nevertheless, by the end of the conference he had seen the point and informed Roosevelt that he now favored an organization that was worldwide rather than regional. It can only be conjectured exactly why Stalin changed his mind. Most likely, he recognized—as did Churchill—that a Council of Europe that did not include the United States was not worth creating.[32]

Stalin's preoccupation with security also shaped his views on the basic composition of the new organization. He favored a simple structure because he believed that a more complex system would be less effective, especially in an emergency situation—a judgment that he, like the Americans, based on the unhappy experiences of the League of Nations. Stalin was thus cheered at Tehran by Roosevelt's presentation of the hegemonic Four Policemen idea. In the Soviet leader's view, only the Great Powers were capable of maintaining the peace; they must therefore play a dominant role in any security organization if it were to have a chance for success. It does not seem an exaggeration to say that Stalin's heart was never really in the development of plans for the General Assembly or other ancillary agencies of the new organization. More than either Roosevelt or Churchill, he concentrated on the police function of the troika of Great Powers as the one key to a security organization's success.[33]

A corollary to this concentration on security was the importance that Stalin placed on continued cooperation among the Big Three. As Adam Ulam has noted, regardless of how things may have turned out, one cannot accuse the Soviet leader of hypocrisy on this matter. From the beginning, he never wavered from the position that if the major Allies continued to cooperate after the war, peace could be secured; if not, future conflicts were inevitable. Certainly the other leaders grasped this essential proposition, but Roosevelt, in particular, does not seem to have understood quite as clearly as Stalin did that no organizational structure or statement of principles, no matter how finely drawn or precisely worded, could keep the peace in a world where the Great Powers disagreed among themselves. For Stalin, therefore, Great Power unanimity was much more than just a voting principle, although it would have to be treated in this manner at Dumbarton Oaks; it was a sine qua non of any effective peacekeeping organization.[34]

By February 1944, when the United States suggested an exchange of documents, none of the Great Powers had developed any very complete plans for a postwar security organization. Still, it was clear from a circulation of preliminary topics for discussion that the British and American foreign offices were close to agreement, at least in outline form, on the kind of organization they hoped to see created. Less was known about the views of the Soviets. Although the Anglo-American summaries were cabled to them in mid-February, the Russians did not respond with an outline of their own. A month later, in fact, Pasvolsky could only assume that the Soviets were working on a plan for postwar organization; no direct information had been forthcoming from Moscow in this regard. The British knew only that there was a committee in the Kremlin, presided over by Ivan Maisky, to discuss a new world body and prepare preliminary papers. When a Russian response to the summaries finally arrived on 5 April, it was cool and noncommittal in tone and offered little more than commentary on the British and American proposals. It accepted the list of topics—or "questions," as Molotov termed them—as a basis for conversations but pointed out that this did not imply "settlement of all of them in [a] favorable sense" or even their adoption for discussion at a future conference. The Soviet view was that fundamental questions—those dealing with security—should be discussed first; other issues, such as the relationship between the international labor organization and the new security system, had "not been clarified" and should be deferred.[35]

As usual, Soviet motives are difficult to assess. It is possible that their failure to respond sooner resulted primarily from a lack of preparation; they apparently had no plans of their own, even in outline form, to communicate to the British and Americans. In addition, this was a time of perceptibly cooling relations between the Russians and their Western allies. Soviet gains in Eastern Europe, and especially in Poland, caused the State Department and the Foreign Office to question the continued likelihood of postwar cooperation among the Great Powers; perhaps Stalin was contemplating a return to what Hull referred to as "unilateralism" in his postwar foreign policy. Certainly he did not want to foreclose on any of his security—or, as the Anglo-Americans would see it, imperial—options in advance, especially if he feared disagreement with the West over the political and territorial settlement in Eastern Europe. Whatever the reason, there is no doubt that the Soviets had fallen decidedly behind the Americans and British in their preparations for a Great Power conference on the proposed peacekeeping organization.[36]

Drafting by the State Department began in earnest following Roosevelt's approval of the agenda group's preliminary proposals on 3 February 1944. By the end of April planners had completed a "possible Plan for a General International Organization" with the exception of sections on social and economic cooperation, territorial trusteeship, and the method of establishing the new organization. This new proposal resembled the plan of 23 December 1943 in many ways. It called for the creation of a universal organization with four principal organs: a General Assembly, an Executive Council, an International Court of Justice, and a General Secretariat. Real power was lodged only in the council, which was now to consist of eight members—the Big Four and an equal number of other states elected by the General Assembly. Voting on substantive matters was to follow the rule of Great Power unanimity, with other questions settled by a majority vote. No mention was made of the issue of a permanent member voting on a matter in which it was involved; Hull had deleted reference to this difficult question because, as he put it, department planners "differed on this point." He must have feared that the Great Powers would as well. Any member had the right to abstain from voting at its own discretion, but it would still be bound by the council's decision unless it exercised its veto. The plan stated that all members should be prepared to furnish armed forces for the maintenance of peace and security and called upon member states to make agreements on the size of the forces that they could supply. It also provided for the creation of a permanent security and armaments commission to recommend proposals for the regulation of armaments, which would go into effect at a time to be determined by the executive council. With some important modifications, especially pertaining to the council, this plan formed the basis of the draft charter that the State Department eventually presented at Dumbarton Oaks.[37]

The British were also developing basic documents at this time. Since early in the year, when the Foreign Office had faced the "rather frightening" prospect of being invited to a conference at any time, an interdepartmental committee chaired by Minister of State Richard Law had studied alternative provisions for a postwar organization. It reported on 19 April with five memoranda that presented its ideas on the nature of a permanent world organization, the maintenance of peace and security, the military dimension of a postwar security organization, the coordination of political and economic machinery, and the procedures for establishing a new world body. In a covering note Law explained that the committee's plan attempted to retain what was best about the League of Nations while creating a structure that would be both more flexible and more effective in maintaining the peace. The basis for the new organization was to be an acceptance by all nations of certain key principles; the means of putting them into effect were to be determined by the circumstances that arose in the future. Such an organic approach, Law noted, was more likely to appeal to the British, whose institutions had developed in that manner, than to the Russians and Americans, who had a different system of law and always preferred "explicit undertakings, no matter how often they have been broken." This difference might, Law reasoned, require that the British agree to changes in their plan, although the committee thought that their general and nonprescriptive proposals represented the practical limit of international cooperation then possible.[38]

The first of the committee's memoranda—referred to as Memorandum A— called for the creation of a "United Nations" organization with four principal agencies: a World Assembly, a World Council, an International Court of Justice, and a Secretariat. The World Assembly, consisting of representatives from all member nations, should meet at least once a year, but it would not exercise the kind of power that had been lodged in the assembly of the league, especially in the area of security. This deemphasizing of the assembly was based in part on the failures of the League of Nations, which haunted British planners much as it did those in the State Department, and in part on a set of principles of world organization then being developed in the Foreign Office. The British did not want to stress the universality of the new body because they thought it was "in fact, though not in name, to be first and foremost, at any rate in its initial stages, a league of mutual security against the aggressors of the present war." Emphasizing the importance of the assembly might also enhance notions of independence and "sovereign equality" among all states, which could lead to troubles with India and was anyway "not consistent with the objectives of a world order, viz. the interdependence of nations and the transcendence of particular sovereignties."[39]

Preventing breaches of the peace was to be the task of the World Council, which would consist of the Great Powers, "upon whom responsibility of maintaining peace principally depends," and of a limited number of other states, perhaps elected by the assembly. Displaying their usual concern for the feelings of midrange powers, British planners regarded the selection of the temporary council members as a matter for "grave consideration"; in their view, the manner in which council decisions would be made—and thus the success of the peacekeeping apparatus—might depend on the method of selection adopted. Thus some means were necessary to insure adequate representation from the various regions of the world, with the overall object that all members of the council command general confidence. A suggestion that one of the dominions should always be represented on the council was omitted for fear that such a provision would provoke the Soviet Union to insist on perennial membership for one of its constituent republics. Although some members of the Armistice and Postwar Committee thought that a Soviet demand for a second seat could be granted without requiring additional places for China and the United States, the majority expressed concern that American isolationists would never tolerate multiple membership for their Communist ally. It would be better, the Foreign Office decided, to let the entire question die.[40]

Memorandum B, which dealt with questions of maintaining peace and security, placed considerable emphasis on the mistakes made in drafting the covenant of the League of Nations in 1919. It argued that the new organization should not, for example, undertake to guarantee the "territorial integrity" or "political independence" of its members as had been attempted in Article X of the league covenant. Guaranteeing boundaries, according to the British, would only open the new organization, as it had the league, to charges of protecting the status quo and would not permit such alterations in frontiers as might become necessary in the future. The concept of political independence was so difficult to define that it could not be guaranteed by a threat of concerted action, although it was thought important enough to be regarded as one of the essential principles of any new world organization. Omitted altogether from these principles was the use of justice in settling disputes, which planners decided against trying to include "in view of the ambiguous legalistic implications of the term" and because some states might have to tolerate minor injustices in the interest of maintaining the peace. The use of the term "aggression" presented a similar problem. In the British view, the League of Nations had erred in basing sanctions on the punishment of aggressors; this approach required that too much time had to be spent defining aggression as it applied in every case, time that was used by such nations as Japan to confuse the issues involved and prevent the organization from mediating disputes and resolving conflicts. Similarly, experience suggested that a rigid definition of when enforcement or other action was necessary would likely hinder the maintenance of peace and security; thus no attempt should be made to list the various circumstances under which the organization might take it upon itself to act. Instead, the World Council should be empowered to take action "in accordance with the principles and objects of the Organization," with each specific application to be determined by the events of the future.[41]

The military dimension of postwar security was the topic of Memorandum C. This paper argued that, whatever its form, the proposed world organization would fail unless the Big Four continued to cooperate and retained the will to enforce peace in the postwar era. As Cadogan put it, "procedure is rather a secondary matter. Everything depends on the unity of purpose of those Powers who are able to impose their will." The primary objects of Big-Four cooperation should be to disarm Germany and Japan, to keep them disarmed, and to prevent them or any other nation from again destroying the peace of the world. To achieve these goals, the organization would have to rely primarily on the combined military forces of the United Nations, and particularly on the Big Four, cooperating in a way similar to their Grand Alliance during the current world war. The memorandum ruled out the establishment of a true international police force. Although such a plan had "theoretical merits," British planners wrote, it required greater international cooperation than states were as yet prepared to grant, implying as it did the existence of something like a "world State." In addition, a standing police force would give rise to practical questions of size, cooperation, maintenance, location, and command that could not be resolved in the present condition of the world. As the British saw it, a better approach to military organization would be the creation of a Military Staff Committee to advise the council on such questions as the military quotas of the various states and the forces that should be called upon to meet whatever emergency situation might arise in the future. It would also be up to the staff committee to see that the national forces cooperated as smoothly as possible by providing for joint garrisoning of troops and combined exercises during peacetime.[42]

Memorandum D foresaw the need for specialized international agencies to deal with economic and social questions and argued that, so far as possible, these bodies should be coordinated with the efforts of the new world organization. To facilitate cooperation in these areas, the British proposed the creation of an economic and social secretariat to bring before the council questions of this nature potentially affecting world peace. Noticeably absent from the British plan, however, was any mention of a colonial or trusteeship council such as still existed under the aegis of the League of Nations. The Colonial Office was adamant on this issue because it disliked the restrictions imposed by the league's system and because it feared that the United States would push for even more controls as part of its expected effort to undermine the empire in the postwar period.[43]

The final memorandum proposed that the principles of the new organization should be agreed upon by the Big Four "at the earliest possible moment," with the working out of details relegated to a later stage in the planning process. Early agreement—preferably before the war ended—would heighten the world organization's chances for success; it would also bind the United States to participation before postwar isolationism could have an opportunity to set in. The British hoped that a draft declaration could be written at the upcoming Washington conference, then scheduled for sometime in July, followed as quickly as possible by a meeting at which all of the united nations could approve the basic structure of the new organization.[44]

Churchill responded to these memoranda with one more plea for regional councils, now expanded from his focus on Europe to include Asia, the Americas, and perhaps Africa. In a paper dated 8 May 1944, the prime minister stressed the importance of regional organization and called for the creation of a United States of Europe at some time in the future. He had two main goals for the postwar era. One was an alliance, or a "fraternal association," with the United States that would include maintaining the Combined Chiefs of Staff system developed during the war. The prime minister understood that this could best be achieved through the creation of a more general postwar organization, which was his basic reason for going along with this utopian American idea. Churchill's other goal was to find a way to let the "glory of Europe rise again" through the development of a unified Continent that might be modeled after the pattern of the British Empire and dominions, "with all the added intimacy which would come from geographical proximity."[45]

The Foreign Office objected strenuously to this proposal. Planners regarded the idea of a Council of Europe as impracticable because, if it included the United States, it was indistinguishable from the World Council and, if it did not, it was of little value anyway. Whitehall also revived its argument that the United States would revert to isolationism if presented with the prospect of a strictly European council. The important thing was to create a world organization with the Americans safely inside it; then, as Webster put it on 9 May, "we could still work for such regional organizations, and if they could be made to work . . . much of what the Prime Minister desires could be obtained without undue risk." But to follow Churchill's more direct course and endanger the world organization while even the possibility of creating regional bodies remained "so problematical" would be "to give up the substance for the shadow." A month later, Eden expressed similar views. When a Foreign Office draftsman referred to a United Nations of Europe, the foreign secretary replied, "No, *please*. This is quite unreal, at least in the near future. We try for too much, our papers are too long, our aims too complicated and the result is—we get nowhere."[46]

The Foreign Office also feared that the proposal for a United States of Europe—the exact meaning of which the planners thought was unclear—might be regarded by the Soviets as an attempt to set up a bloc against them that might include a revitalized Germany. (This was essentially what, in fact, would happen by 1950.) The prime minister's proposal revealed a basic difference of opinion between his views and those of the Foreign Office on postwar relations with the USSR. Churchill thought that for the foreseeable future, at least, "there will be a vastly powerful Russian state in the East of Europe" and the United Kingdom in the West, with only "a litter of broken states, disarmed, and smarting from their wounds" in between. Under such circumstances, nothing but Western European unity, including a restored Germany, could prevent Soviet encroachment as far west as France. In the Foreign Office view, however, Churchill's prescription for recovery was as dangerous as the malady he was trying to cure. Eden thought that any postwar alliance of Western European states had to be for the "sole purpose of preventing a renewal of

German aggression" and described any attempt to aim it at the Soviet Union as fatal. The British government must, he reasoned, avoid the creation of two spheres of influence in Western and Eastern Europe, with Germany as a kind of no-man's-land in between. Although Eden recognized that this outcome was to some extent inevitable, given the genuine differences between the two Great Powers that sat at opposite ends of the European Continent, he thought that minimizing its effects would be less dangerous and would best serve British postwar interests.[47]

At least partly in response to the prime minister's prodding, the Foreign Office was by this time basing its postwar planning on three primary options. One, which might be called the Eastern strategy, was an alliance with the Soviet Union against Germany. The Western strategy called for an alliance with the United States, including American assistance to keep the peace in Europe. And the Central strategy proposed the creation of a Western European defensive union or alliance—essentially going it alone with the support of neither of the other Great Powers. Ideally, the final result would be some combination of all three approaches, which meant that the main problem for British planners was how to avoid becoming locked into one to the exclusion of the others. It was for this reason that Foreign Office thinking always returned to the idea of a postwar world organization; only under its umbrella could the United Kingdom retain its two main wartime alliances while building a defensive relationship with the states of Western Europe. Churchill did not disagree with this reasoning, of course, as he made clear even in his criticisms of the planners' five memoranda. But from the perspective of the Foreign Office, the prime minister's preoccupation with a Council of Europe to contain the Soviet Union threatened to make one, or maybe two, of the planners' postwar objectives mutually exclusive of the third.[48]

It was thus a worried group of planners who went looking for allies at the Dominions Prime Ministers' Meeting on 11 May. The outcome, as Jebb described it to a member of the embassy staff in Washington, was an immense success for the Foreign Office—so much so that in the face of almost total opposition Churchill agreed to withdraw his idea of regional councils as the building blocks of the new world organization. Eden thought that this settled the matter, but he soon learned that the prime minister had only retreated, not surrendered, on the issue of a Council of Europe. In withdrawing his own paper of 8 May from further consideration, Churchill instructed the Foreign Office to redraft its five memoranda to include at least the possibility of a regional European council, then take them to Washington "as a guide, not as a rule." Cadogan, who as head of the British delegation would have to try to negotiate from such an ambiguous position, remarked that what the prime minister wanted drawn up was too equivocal for instructions, "being a combination of incompatible views."[49]

Churchill's new approach, which Jebb characterized as "completely off the mark," left Whitehall with two options. One was to try to persuade the prime minister to change his mind; the other was to try to win his agreement to only small changes in the original memoranda that would do no real damage to the planners' conception of a world organization. Webster preferred the first option, which seemed more honest, but his colleagues, who did not want to risk a direct confrontation with the stubborn prime minister, thought that the second course seemed wiser tactically. The Foreign Office thus prepared what one planner called a "re-hash" of its memoranda that presented Churchill's idea for regional organization but stated plainly the arguments against it. If this was less than the prime minister had asked for, planners hoped that his lack of interest in postwar organization might permit it to slip through anyway.[50]

Churchill was not so easily fooled, however. He informed Eden that the Foreign Office had apparently misunderstood his instructions. "We were not," the prime minister wrote, "to declare ourselves against regional organizations nor in favor of them, but to leave the arguments in a balanced way on each side." Jebb's retort that this would result in "two alternative and mutually contradictory plans" did not seem to worry the prime minister, who regarded the upcoming talks as nothing more than exploratory in nature. Like it or not, the Foreign Office had no choice but to try to weave Churchill's plan into the fabric of its own, at least tightly enough to win the prime minister's approval.[51]

But then Churchill seemed to lose interest in the issue altogether. A month later, the Foreign Office, which was growing increasingly concerned about American impatience at the slow progress in getting the Washington talks organized, was still waiting for the prime minister's response to their revised memoranda. Jebb predicted "grave difficulties" if the papers were not approved soon and suggested that only the personal intervention of the foreign secretary would prompt Churchill to take immediate action. Eden, who agreed that written approaches to the prime minister "do not seem to work very well at the moment," promised to speak to him at the earliest opportunity. As the situation grew into a crisis, even the usually even-tempered Cadogan complained that Churchill's "backwardness" on the issue was preventing the completion of instructions for the British delegates to the postwar conference. The prime minister's new approach of ignoring the whole matter made Whitehall wonder why it had tried so hard to compromise with him in the first place. Planners had put in a European regional council, Jebb wrote on 8 July, "for the sole purpose of getting the Prime Minister to agree to the paper as a whole." But now that he "seems to be throwing his hand in and disinteresting himself in the future of the world" it would have been better not to have put it in at all. It was by then too late to make any changes, however, so that in their final form Memorandum A was expanded to include provisions for a regional organization for Europe, "if only to prevent a repetition of the circumstances that have caused two world wars to originate in that area," and Memorandum C was revised to point out the advantages of basing military peacekeeping operations on a regional system. As amended, the memoranda became the basis for the British plan of world organization presented in August at Dumbarton Oaks.[52]

While British and American experts were drawing up their proposals, Under Secretary Stettinius journeyed to England. The reason for this trip was partly courtesy—the English wanted an important American official to return the recent visits of Churchill and Eden to the United States—and partly to discuss topics of interest to both the United States and the United Kingdom. One such topic was the proposed postwar security organization. On 15 April, Stettinius and Isaiah Bowman, who as a member of the Informal Political Agenda Group served as the under secretary's chief expert on world organization, discussed the new peacekeeping body with Churchill at Chequers, the prime minister's country home. Churchill, obviously harassed by wartime concerns, seemed unwilling at first even to consider postwar issues; he said, according to Stettinius, that "we had to see the war through first and take up world organization afterward." Later, when Bowman returned the conversation to the question, Churchill sketched what he called a "tripod of world peace." At its apex stood the Great Powers, which would operate through a Supreme Council—the "main show," as Churchill called it—that possessed the force to act in the interest of world security. Beneath the Supreme Council the prime minister drew three legs—regional councils of Europe, Asia, and the Americas, the object of which was to settle regional affairs locally and thus avoid having "every nation poking its finger into every other nation's business the world over." Bowman and Stettinius might have been sorry they asked. They certainly could not have taken much comfort from this outline, which indicated that Churchill's views, at least, remained surprisingly far removed from those of the American planners.[53]

The situation seemed considerably brighter a few days later, however, when the Americans discussed world organization with Eden and other Foreign Office representatives. Eden and Law described an organization that more closely approximated the State Department's universalist plan, complete with an assembly and one world council to maintain security. Eden, in particular, took issue with the prime minister's idea regarding regional councils, calling their inclusion in any postwar planning a mistake. According to Stettinius, the general feeling at this meeting was that the official British and American views were now fairly close and that the two sets of planners would have very little difficulty reaching an agreement in the future. Perhaps for this reason, the British pressed the Americans to speed up plans for conversations on postwar organization, and the two sides agreed to begin the conference in Washington about 20 May and to issue a joint statement to that effect.[54]

This more rapid timetable was ruled out by both Churchill and Hull. The prime minister, still in no hurry to consider postwar concerns, argued that rushing the Washington conference would be bad politically in both England and the United States; it would interrupt the "psychological trend" of the war and start the public thinking prematurely about peace. He proved willing only to agree that the talks should go forward within the "next few months," and then on nothing more than a preliminary basis. From Washington, Hull cabled the under secretary that the proposal for an early conference was impossible for practical reasons—neither the American plans for world organization nor projected discussions with congressional leaders could be completed before the end of May. Hull also opposed the issuance of a joint communiqué based on the London talks because, as Stettinius explained it to Eden, it would be fatal both domestically and with the Soviets if it were made public that the British and Americans had discussed plans for the postwar organization privately. No statement was released.[55]

Although the extent of agreement between the Foreign Office and the State Department turned out to be "surprisingly great," one major issue still threatened to undermine Anglo-American cooperation in postwar planning. This was the question of colonial trusteeship, which Bowman brought up repeatedly in London, prompting Cadogan to refer to it as "a regular King Charles's Head" for the American expert. The Foreign and Colonial Offices both hoped to keep this matter off the postwar agenda altogether; certainly they did not appreciate being pressed on colonial considerations by what they regarded as unsympathetic Americans. But the State Department's planners showed no signs of letting the issue die. As Bowman explained to Jebb in a meeting at the Foreign Office on 12 April, the United States needed the concept of trusteeship to control Japanese islands in the Pacific. Outright annexation of this territory would be seen as a violation of the Atlantic Charter, he said, so the Americans "would be bound to camouflage their actions" through the new United Nations organization. This much the British might have been willing to grant, but they feared that the Americans had worse things in mind. Bowman himself raised the question of Indochina, where the Roosevelt administration wanted the French to grant the United Nations an "interest." Surely, Whitehall reasoned, an attempt to encroach upon the prerogatives of the British Empire could not be far behind. Still, the British recognized that the State Department was under great pressure to obtain results on this matter and suspected that without the inclusion of some sort of trusteeship provision any plan for a postwar organization would have a hard time winning approval among the American public and in congress.[56]

Hull was at this time endeavoring to build public and congressional support for a peacekeeping organization. On 25 April he began a series of consultative meetings with a select senatorial committee that included Democrats Tom Connally of Texas, Walter George of Georgia, Alben Barkley of Kentucky, and Guy Gillette of Iowa; Republicans Arthur Vandenberg of Michigan, Warren Austin of Vermont, and Wallace White of Maine; and Progressive Robert La Follette, Jr., of Wisconsin. This committee, which had been constituted at Hull's request, was another of the Roosevelt administration's attempts to insure that its plans would not be defeated, as Woodrow Wilson's had been at the end of World War I, by senatorial jealousy over its prerogatives in determining foreign policy. Hull promised to share responsibility and commenced the meetings by giving the senators confidential copies of the department's "Possible Plan" draft of 24 April, which became the basis for the new committee's deliberations.[57]

In four meetings over the next month the senators raised a series of questions concerning several major areas of the plan. Some were easily answered, such as those dealing with regional representation as a basis for council membership, the need to consult with South American countries on the effect of the plan on hemispheric security, and the application of congressional authority regarding the use of force. This last issue might have posed serious problems but was finessed by Hull's assurance that any agreement to supply troops for the new world organization would be submitted in advance to the Senate for approval. More difficult were questions about the principle of Great Power unanimity, over which the senators were themselves divided. Most were relieved to discover that the United States would have the power to veto key decisions, but Senators Gillette and Austin objected to the granting of too much power to the less trustworthy members of the Big Four. Hull responded that a veto was essential to the plan's acceptance by both the American people and the governments of the other major powers; without it, there was little chance that there would be any world organization at all.[58]

Most troubling—in part because it came unanticipated—was the objection that the early creation of a world organization might imply its use to maintain a bad peace. Here senators were drawing on the lessons of World War I; they did not want to see the United States committed in advance to protect a peace settlement as unfair as that signed at Versailles in 1919. Such a development might lead to American involvement in a World War III, they thought, just as the inequities of the Versailles treaty had led to the Second World War. Senator Vandenberg, in particular, refused to have his fears assuaged by Hull's argument—similar to Wilson's of a generation before—that only an effective international organization could remedy the arrangements of an unfair peace. The Republican senator was also concerned about the political ramifications of accepting the draft proposal; this was, after all, an election year, and the Republican convention was only a month away. He thus refused to endorse the State Department's plan without the reservation that its ultimate acceptability depended upon the justness of the terms of peace, a position also adopted by Senator La Follette. When Hull found that he could not gain the committee's unqualified approval of his plan, he decided to make the best of it, drafting and releasing a statement in which he described himself as "definitely encouraged" by his "frank and fruitful discussions" with the senators, stating his readiness to begin talks with the British, Russians, and Chinese, and promising that the "door of nonpartisanship" would continue to be "wide open" at the Department of State in dealing with questions of postwar organization.[59]

His domestic flank covered, Hull was now prepared to proceed with Great Power conversations. On 30 May, he met at the State Department with the British and Soviet ambassadors and asked them to request their governments to fix a date—"as early as might be convenient"—for the conference on postwar world organization to begin, adding that the United States would be ready as soon as the others were. The secretary of state then reviewed the "China angle" for the ambassadors and made what he described as a most earnest appeal that they try to persuade their governments to include the Chinese at the conference table.[60]

What Hull termed "the China angle" was in fact an extremely difficult problem—or set of problems. From the beginning of his consideration of a postwar security organization, Roosevelt had included China among the Great Powers. In his simplest scheme the Chinese were to be the fourth policeman, with responsibility for maintaining order in Asia; in maturer plans they became the fourth permanent member of the Security Council. It should not be supposed that FDR had any illusions about China actually functioning as a Great Power at the time of World War II or in the near future. But his vision of the postwar world depended upon the development of an Asian power to replace the defeated Japan as the leading nation of the Far East; the alternatives were revolutionary chaos, a return to colonialism, or Russian hegemony—none of which held any appeal for Roosevelt. In addition, the president thought it reasonable to hope that the China of Chiang Kai-shek (Jiang Jieshi) could someday become a Great Power in the liberal American mold (although this seemed less likely in 1944 than it had earlier) and argued that treating the Chinese as responsible Asian leaders might foster their development in that direction. For these reasons, Roosevelt treated Chiang as a major ally during the war and endeavored to include China as a Great Power in all plans for postwar security as well as in the conferences where such plans would be perfected.[61]

Churchill disagreed with this reasoning, which he thought reflected a "wholly unreal standard of values." He saw no likelihood that China would ever become a Great Power, particularly in light of the civil war that seemed certain to develop there between Chiang's armies and Communist forces led by Mao Tse-tung (Mao Zedong). In the British prime minister's view, Roosevelt's goal was to make China strong enough to police Asia while leaving it weak enough to be dependent upon the United States, a relationship that would be cemented—and made more potentially dangerous to British interests in the Far East—by the basic anticolonialism of each. It was for this reason that Churchill complained of China as a potential supporter of the United States—a "faggot vote"—in its future attempts to dismantle the British Empire, and refused to take China seriously as one of Roosevelt's Four Policemen.[62]

Churchill expressed his continuing doubts about China in his discussions with Stettinius during April 1944. In describing his view of the prospective postwar organization, the prime minister referred repeatedly to the Big Three and China rather than the Big Four because he thought it "nonsense" to list China among the Great Powers. He said that he had little confidence in the Chinese—the "pigtails," as he called them—either to unite after the war or to be of much value as a keeper of postwar peace in the Pacific. Further, he worried that in the future the Chinese might go the way of the Japanese and arm themselves for aggressive purposes. Churchill thought that the Chinese compared unfavorably to the French, who had also caused the Allies "no end of trouble" and must also play a major role in the postwar world but were far better candidates to achieve Great Power status in the next few years. Clearly, Churchill's views were colored by his colonial predilections—by his tendency, as State Department China expert Stanley K. Hornbeck described it, "to look at China and the Chinese" in light of the "British experience in India" and thus to place little faith in China as a sovereign nation at all.[63]

Eden shared many of these views, although perhaps to a less extreme degree. In meetings with Roosevelt in Washington in 1943, the British foreign minister had stated his pessimism regarding China's future stability, especially if something should happen to Chiang Kai-shek. And even if China managed to avoid a revolution, Eden told the president, he "did not much like the idea of the Chinese running up and down the Pacific" after the war. Thus he joined Churchill in doubting whether it was either sensible or prudent to treat China as one of the Great Powers in planning a postwar organization.[64]

Nevertheless, as historian Christopher Thorne has noted, the British did not present any serious obstacles to Roosevelt's plans for a powerful postwar China. Churchill and Eden, prompted by experts at the Foreign Office, perceived the need to humor the naive American fondness for China because they recognized that the real significance of the China question was its potential impact on relations with the United States—the key to all their hopes for the future. Thus, despite his periodic grousing on the subject, the prime minister invariably included China in his outlines for postwar security (at least when Americans were present); and the Foreign Office listed the Chinese among the permanent council members in its preliminary proposal for a world peacekeeping organization—what Churchill described as adding a "pigtail" to the tripod of Great Powers. In addition, the British always supported the inclusion of the Chinese in meetings where postwar plans were to be developed. During preparation for the Tehran Conference, for instance, Churchill agreed to Roosevelt's suggestion that they include Chiang Kai-shek, wiring FDR that he should "by all means" invite the generalissimo, even if Stalin objected. This attitude also prevailed in planning for the conference at Dumbarton Oaks. On 4 June, less than a week after Hull's "earnest appeal" to the ambassadors, the British accepted both the invitation to attend and the inclusion of the Chinese as full members of the conference.[65]

As always, Stalin's views and motives are more difficult to plumb. What is clear is that he agreed with Churchill rather than Roosevelt on the question of China's potential for effectiveness in any postwar organization; he said at Tehran, for example, that he "did not think China would be very powerful at the end of the war." This evaluation prompted the Soviet leader to speak out against the inclusion of the Chinese in a world security council, because to do so would give them the kind of authority over Europe that he thought some of the smaller nations of the continent "would probably resent." Although such reasoning must seem strange coming from the Soviet leader, it was to avoid this sort of situation that Stalin suggested at Tehran the creation of a divided organization, with either European and Far Eastern committees (a proposal similar to Churchill's regional plan) or with separate European and worldwide organizations. Despite his objections, however, Stalin soon yielded to Roosevelt's position and did not further question the creation of a seat for the Chinese among the future peacekeepers, perhaps because he, like the British, recognized that a strong China was a key factor in the American equation for the postwar world.[66]

While giving way on the postwar lineup, the Soviets posed a more serious problem with respect to Roosevelt's more immediate goal of Chinese representation in the planning process. At the Moscow Foreign Ministers' Conference in 1943, Molotov objected to including China in the Four-Power Declaration on General Security; indeed, the Russians had attempted to keep the matter off the agenda altogether because they feared it might lead to some involvement with the Chinese. Stalin relented, and permitted the Chinese ambassador to sign the declaration, only after being subjected to heavy pressure from the Americans. No amount of pressure, however, could cause the Soviet leader to change his mind about Roosevelt's proposal for a meeting with Chiang at Tehran a few weeks later; he cabled FDR that "it goes without saying" that the conference must include only the Big Three and that representatives of other governments—that is, the Chinese—must be "absolutely excluded." Separate arrangements thus had to be made for an Anglo-American meeting with Chiang at Cairo before Churchill and Roosevelt went on to Tehran.[67]

Something similar was also going to be required for the inclusion of China at what was then being referred to as the Washington Conference on Postwar Organization. When on 9 July the Soviets finally responded to Hull's invitation of 30 May, they reminded the secretary of state that some sort of "double negotiations" would be required at the conference. They refused to meet with the Chinese themselves but accepted Hull's proposal that the Americans and British meet separately with the Russian and Chinese delegations. The British Foreign Office found this arrangement cumbersome, preferring instead to keep the Chinese ambassador informed behind the scenes at the meeting site, but ultimately acquiesced in the American idea—designed to protect Chinese dignity—of two conferences. The result would be in essence two meetings at Dumbarton Oaks, the first including the United States, Great Britain, and the Soviet Union, and the second, of far less significance, including the United States, Great Britain, and China.[68]

It is impossible to say for certain why Stalin objected so strenuously to China's inclusion. His stated reason was fear that wartime conferences with the Chinese might jeopardize Soviet neutrality in the Pacific conflict, thus subjecting the beleaguered Red Army to the risk of a two-front war. Considering the damage inflicted on the Soviet Union by the war in Europe, this explanation is certainly plausible and should perhaps be accepted at face value. But Stalin would not have been human (or a good statesman) if he did not have other strategic considerations in mind as well. The Soviet Union was an Asian power as much as a European one, and its position in the Far East after the war had to be in Stalin's thoughts now that the outcome of the struggle in Europe was no longer in doubt. Under the circumstances, he had no reason to desire the establishment of a strong postwar China, particularly one that was likely to be a client of the United States. Nor did he have any need to enhance through personal meetings the stature of Chiang Kai-shek, whose treatment of the Chinese Communists both before and during the war had been far from exemplary. Whatever objectives Stalin hoped to achieve in the Far East after the end of hostilities—and they do not appear to have been very ambitious at this time—their fulfillment could not be made more likely by encouraging the rise of China to world power or by adding luster to the reputation of Chiang Kai-shek.[69]

Russian acceptance of Hull's invitation cleared the way for the completion of plans for the conference, which the secretary of state hoped could begin on 2 August. Hull met with Liu Chieh, the Chinese chargé d'affaires, in Washington on 10 July and informed him of the decision to hold two conferences, a development that the American said he deeply regretted. The secretary could not say for sure whether the meetings would be concurrent or consecutive; further discussions would be necessary, he said, "so as to have everybody satisfied with the arrangements." The State Department's initial approach was to follow the British idea of simultaneous conversations held at the same site, thus giving the Chinese and Soviet phases of the talks equal status—at least officially. Although Hull did not anticipate any objection to this from the Russians, he soon discovered that they were indeed dissatisfied with the way the arrangements were developing. On 13 July Deputy Foreign Minister Andrei Vyshinski requested further assurance from Harriman that the talks would be kept entirely separate; he also wanted a public explanation of the reasons for this decision, probably to dispel rumors in the United States, where his country's image was beginning to tarnish, that the Russians were anti-Chinese. A day later the Soviets stated their preference for consecutive conferences, although they were indifferent as to which should occur first. After further negotiations Hull accepted the Russian plan and announced that the Soviet phase of the talks would precede conversations with the Chinese.[70]

A further complication arose from the American desire to follow the four-power talks with an expanded international conference. In an aide-mémoire to the Soviets dated 12 July, the State Department expressed its expectation that "subsequent discussions with the other United Nations" would be the next stage in planning a postwar organization. For the Soviets this was stepping onto uncertain ground; Vyshinski described it as introducing a new element into the negotiations and said that it raised questions of timing, subjects suitable for discussion, and representation at the meetings that must be resolved in advance. If the Russians had good reasons for wanting to avoid direct contact with the Chinese, they had even better ones for wishing not to take part in meetings with some other governments, especially in Eastern Europe where serious difficulties were certain to arise. Ultimately, however, Harriman succeeded in convincing the Soviets that the answers to Vyshinski's questions could be postponed until later.[71]

A more difficult problem related to the agenda for the conversations themselves. In accepting Hull's invitation to the conference, the Soviets indicated that they preferred to limit the "first phase of the negotiations" to "questions of primary importance," which they described as security, the scope and nature of the new organization, and procedures for establishing it. This list eliminated two major areas of British and American concern: the pacific settlement of disputes and the coordination of economic and political machinery within the new organization. Such an approach was consistent with Stalin's desire to concentrate the efforts of the postwar organization on the maintenance of security; it also probably reflected the fact that the Soviets were lagging behind the Americans in developing detailed plans for a more extensive kind of organization. In response, the State Department reiterated its view that the primary purpose of the organization would be the peaceable adjustment of disputes, procedures for which must therefore be an integral part of any effective plan for a peacekeeping body. It also stressed the importance of postwar international economic relations and the need for specialized social and economic agencies to prevent conflicts from arising. The Americans stated that they intended to express their views on these matters—and on trusteeship as well—at the forthcoming conference and hoped that the Soviets would "feel disposed" to enter into preliminary discussions with them. This dispute was only resolved during the conference at Dumbarton Oaks itself.[72]

On 17 July Hull announced publicly that the talks would begin soon, probably early in August. All sides had tentatively agreed to a starting date of 2 August, but procedural problems soon forced a series of postponements. In its aide-mémoire of 20 July the Soviet government proposed to start "approximately on August 10," a revised opening date that was accepted by both the British and Americans. A week later the British pointed out that their negotiators could not arrive in Washington by then unless they traveled by airplane, a risk that they wished to avoid; similar doubts had also arisen about the ability of the Russians to reach the United States on time. Thus the starting date was pushed back to 14 August. Early in the month, however, Vyshinski asked Harriman for a few more days "to study the American proposals in order to instruct their delegation on the questions raised." The American ambassador thought that the Soviets had expected more general conversations and were taken by surprise by the detailed and comprehensive nature of the State Department's tentative proposals. The opening of the talks was now set for 21 August.[73]

During these final preparations Hull and Roosevelt made a further attempt to secure public support for a postwar organization. What made this effort necessary was renewed criticism of the president's plan for Great Power dominance in "policing" the world after the end of hostilities. On 31 May, for example, Eelco van Kleffens, the minister for foreign affairs of the Netherlands government-in-exile, issued a statement warning that no international organization could be effective that did not enjoy the full cooperation of the smaller states. In van Kleffens's opinion, it was a mistake to exclude the minor powers from the peacekeeping council; the necessity that modern wars be conducted by only the few—from which the idea of Great Power dominance naturally grew—did not, he argued, carry over into the maintenance of peace, where the support of all nations was required. He thus advocated a system of rotation to permit the smaller states to take turns on the council side by side with the Big Four, which could still have permanent representation if they so desired. Although van Kleffens's proposal was not very different from the State Department's current plans for a security council, his statement contained implicit criticism of all of the American planners' efforts, with potentially damaging effects in the United States.[74]

Hull responded on 1 June with a public statement of his own that emphasized the important role of the smaller states in any future world organization. As the secretary put it, the peacekeeping body would be a "mutual affair" reflecting the "common interest" of all nations, both large and small, in maintaining security. It would be "all-inclusive" in nature, with all peace-loving states, "irrespective of size and strength," joining as partners in a system of general security designed to prevent future wars. Such sentiments were a far cry from the original Four Policemen idea, and clearly understated the primary role Hull envisioned for the Great Powers, but they reflected the direction in which American plans for a postwar organization were then maturing.[75]

Roosevelt followed these remarks with the release of a more detailed statement on 15 June. Although written by Pasvolsky, the message was attributed to the president to insure publicity and to quell rumors that FDR did not personally support the efforts of the secretary of state. To this end, it revealed that the president had been conferring on questions of international organization with State Department officials for a period of eighteen months, a practice that the message claimed had enabled him to give personal attention to the progress of the department's postwar work. In addition, the release pointed out that all plans and suggestions from organizations and individuals had been carefully considered, and stressed that the administration's consultations had been entirely nonpartisan in nature. More substantively, the presidential statement set forth the basic outline for world organization, emphasizing that the maintenance of peace and security must be the task of all nations, large and small. There would be, accordingly, a "fully representative body," or assembly, to deal with questions of world relations and to facilitate international cooperation through the creation of such agencies as may prove necessary. There would also be a council, including the four major nations and others elected annually by the assembly, to promote the peaceful settlement of disputes and to prevent breaches of the peace. And finally, there would be an international court of justice to deal with justiciable disputes.[76]

The president also took pains to reassure those who feared that the plans might be going too far. "We are not thinking," he said, "of a superstate with its own police forces and other paraphernalia of coercive power"; the world (like the United States) was not ready for that. Instead, the American planners were seeking effective ways to arrange for all nations to maintain forces adequate to prevent war and to make impossible deliberate preparation for war. Such forces would be available to the organization for "joint action" whenever it might become necessary. This was by far the most complete official statement at that time of the Roosevelt administration's plans for a postwar organization; nothing more detailed would be released until after the meetings at Dumbarton Oaks were completed.[77]

Roosevelt's statement did not prove altogether persuasive. It was, of course, intentionally vague, a fact that such anti-Roosevelt newspapers as the *Chicago Tribune* pointed to as evidence of a presidential attempt to leave the door open for American domination of the world. Some internationalists, on the other hand, took FDR at his word and criticized his failure to speak forcefully in support of an international police force or the automatic application of sanctions to halt aggression. Roosevelt had, according to the liberal *Nation*, failed to learn the lesson of "the tragic 1930's." *Time* magazine probably spoke for the great majority in the middle when it said that "most Americans found the

program unexceptionable—what there was of it." The British were also unim-
pressed with FDR's remarks. Jebb wrote that Roosevelt had been far too
cautious and complained that "if the world organization is to have virtually *no*
powers there is really not much point in setting it up." Still, the president's
statement probably accomplished the objectives that Roosevelt and Hull had
set for it. It affirmed presidential interest in an international organization,
alerted the public to the broad outlines of the administration's postwar policy,
and—for good or ill—focused the attention of most Americans on the deliberations about to begin at the Georgetown mansion known as Dumbarton Oaks.[78]

3 *The Conference Begins*

Quod severis metes. The inscription on the mansion built in 1801 at Dumbarton Oaks was fitting, for the delegates who gathered there in the late summer of 1944 would indeed reap as they sowed. But whether their harvest would be bitter or sweet would not be known for many weeks, the outcome to be determined by the success or failure of the conversations held at the stately Georgetown mansion made available by Harvard University. For the time being, Dumbarton Oaks, the former estate of Robert Woods Bliss, onetime minister to Sweden and ambassador to Argentina, ceased to be a scholarly center for Byzantine studies and became the center of world attention, as representatives of the United States, Great Britain, and the Soviet Union (and later, China) gathered to discuss the shape of the organization that they hoped would bring lasting peace to the postwar world.[1]

Why Dumbarton Oaks? In June, while the British and Americans were awaiting the Soviet reply to Hull's invitation, Eden had requested that "in view of the heat" the State Department should try to find a cool place for the proposed meetings. No government building could meet Eden's requirement —air conditioning was at a premium in the Washington of 1944—and non-public space was almost unavailable in the bustling wartime capital. In addition, the British and Americans agreed that for ease of communication the conference should be held as near to Washington as possible, a consideration that ruled out moving the meeting to a location like Bar Harbor, Maine, or Bretton Woods, New Hampshire, where a United Nations monetary and financial conference convened in July. The Foreign Office also wanted to meet in a place where its representatives could consult with the embassies of the dominions. Alger Hiss, a State Department employee who had recently joined the postwar planning group, suggested Dumbarton Oaks, whose nearby location above the Rock Creek Parkway, shaded grounds (complete with lily ponds and formal gardens), and generous size made it seem an ideal place to hold the conversations.[2]

For all of the attention they were about to receive, the delegates who gathered in the pink brick buildings at Dumbarton Oaks were unaccustomed to the limelight; this conference was not to be a meeting of the Big Three leaders, or even of foreign ministers, such as had been held in the past. Hull had planned initially to serve as titular chairman of the American delegation—he would open the proceedings before turning the negotiations over to Stettinius—but agreed to withdraw when Eden objected on the grounds that the foreign secretary would then be required to attend as the head of the British group. Instead, Eden preferred that the talks be conducted at the high technical level—what the British called the "official" level—with a foreign ministers' meeting to follow based on the preliminary agreements reached by the experts. To head the British delegation, Eden selected his permanent under secretary for foreign affairs, Sir Alexander Cadogan, whose experience as chief of the League of Nations section at the Foreign Office since 1923 made him a logical choice for the job. The Soviet group was headed by a figure of even lower rank, Andrei Gromyko, their young ambassador to the United States, who was currently in Moscow for consultations. Pasvolsky, commenting on the Soviet group for State Department intelligence, described Gromyko as "not strong or experienced enough" for the job. As Roosevelt alone seems to have understood, such low-level delegations would make it difficult for the conference to live up to its advance publicity, because in the absence of top officials it was unlikely that final decisions could be made. Still, the Americans acquiesced in the wishes of their allies and appointed Stettinius as chief negotiator for the United States.[3]

Cadogan and Stettinius would find it easy to work in tandem. They had discussed postwar problems at length during the American under secretary's visit to London in April and had discovered no fundamental difference in their basic points of view. In addition, the two delegation chiefs took an immediate liking to one another, with Stettinius describing Cadogan in his diary as "calm, intelligent [and] . . . very quick on the trigger" and Cadogan responding—in his own diary—that Stettinius "looks like a dignified and more monumental Charlie Chaplin." Gromyko was more of a mystery. At age thirty-five he seemed an unlikely choice to head the Russian delegation. Although he had been in Washington since 1939, his views on world organization were almost totally unknown to the Americans; certainly his reticent personality—he later earned the sobriquet "old stony face"—did nothing to make his opinions more fathomable. It was thus not surprising that on personal as well as political grounds the Soviet ambassador often felt himself the odd man out at Dumbarton Oaks, or that Cadogan and Stettinius frequently operated as a team in trying to work out their joint disagreements with the Russians.[4]

Stettinius renewed his acquaintance with Cadogan following the arrival of the British delegation in New York on 12 August. Although this early arrival was unintentional—the British had decided not to change their travel plans when they learned while boarding the Queen Mary that the conference had been postponed for a week—it provided a welcome opportunity for Anglo-American consultations before the meeting with the Soviets. While preparing for the conference Hull had stressed the importance of close cooperation with the British; "we can't keep in line with the Russians," he told Stettinius, "unless we all work together." As it turned out, working together presented few difficulties. After just one conversation with Cadogan, Stettinius reported to the secretary of state that the British had only one or two problems with the American proposals. The most important difference, according to the under secretary, was over trusteeship and colonial policy, which the Americans agreed to "breeze through" and postpone for future consideration. A relieved Cadogan reported to London that he was "glad to say that the vexed question of territorial trusteeship seems to have been put into cold storage, at any rate for the time being." Additional talks, which included Hull and Acheson among others, brought the two delegations even closer together. By the eve of the conference they were consulting on the finer points of strategy, with Cadogan agreeing to talk to Gromyko about using the American plan as what Stettinius called a "neutral paper" to serve as the basis for discussion at Dumbarton Oaks.[5]

The Russians arrived on 20 August, just one day before the conference opened. They had left Moscow twelve days earlier and, after being delayed by fog in Siberia, first landed in American territory at Fairbanks, Alaska. As their DC-3 bearing the Red Star of the Soviet Union taxied down the runway at Washington's National Airport, Stettinius noted that it was apparently a Lend-Lease airplane—not a surprising observation for the former administrator of that agency to make. Gromyko was welcomed with the appropriate pomp and courtesy in a reception ceremony that was, according to Cadogan, exactly the same as the one afforded the British on their arrival a week earlier. Still, there were differences. The Soviets were met by both the Americans and the British, which may have made Gromyko feel a bit ganged up on. (There would be ample evidence of this the next day.) And the Russians would not have time, of course, for advance consultations with their hosts.[6]

The conference began with an opening ceremony at 10:30 the next morning. Secretary of State Hull presided, calling the meeting to order with a gavel made from a plank of the U.S.S. *Constitution*. For the occasion, the tapestried Renaissance music room at Dumbarton Oaks had been transformed, its usual overstuffed furniture replaced by a long U-shaped table at which the three delegations were seated; in addition, a portrait of Paderewski, the Polish composer and patriot, had been removed to avoid giving offense to the Soviets, whose armies were then fighting in Poland. The press corps was there in force as were the still and motion picture cameramen; the delegates found it hot work performing in front of what Cadogan referred to as the "blazing searchlights." It must have been a relief later, when the diplomats adjourned to the cooler garden for more photographs. The highlights of the first meeting were brief speeches by Hull, Gromyko, and Cadogan about what they hoped to achieve at Dumbarton Oaks. As befitted the situation, these remarks were general and filled with platitudes, as all three men stressed the significance of their upcoming labors and the need to act quickly. In addition, they agreed that the new organization must be granted sufficient authority to maintain the peace and that it must respect the rights of all nations, big and small. There were perceptible differences, however, in what the speakers chose to emphasize. As Stettinius noted in his diary, "Mr. Hull especially stressed the necessity of justice to all nations while Ambassador Gromyko placed especial emphasis on the greater responsibility of the Great Powers in maintaining peace and security. Sir Alexander's remarks followed a middle course between the views just mentioned."[7]

The delegates commenced work that afternoon with a meeting of the Joint Steering Committee. This small group—it consisted only of Stettinius, Dunn, and Pasvolsky for the Americans; Cadogan and his deputy, Gladwyn Jebb, for the British; and Gromyko and his deputy, Arkady Sobolev, for the Soviets; with Hiss serving as secretary—was intended originally to decide only matters of conference procedure. As the deliberations progressed, however, it became the organ where substantive decisions were made, largely because the Russians preferred the security of working in a small body. The first issue to be settled was the official language for the conversations, with the delegates agreeing that both English and Russian would be regarded as of equal importance, although everyone expected (as turned out to be the case) that English would be used more frequently. In fact, although he sometimes elected not to use it, Gromyko's English was quite good, a fact that caused Stettinius to conjecture that the Soviets' real concern over the matter of an official language was only for the record.[8]

As head of the host delegation, Stettinius was named permanent chairman for the conversations; Cadogan and Gromyko would have it no other way. This decision was confirmed the next morning in the first plenary session of the conference. The steering committee also discussed relations with the press, which would become an embarrassing issue over the next few days. The members agreed that all news statements must receive the approval of the three chairmen, and that the initial press release, to be issued at noon the following day, would state that the delegates were proceeding to the discussion of general principles of international organization, with the Soviet group presenting its ideas first. On the question of record keeping, the British and Soviets agreed to the American suggestion that brief informal minutes were preferable to a full stenographic transcript. Verbatim records would be made only of proposals, votes, and amendments; arguments and explanations would be summarized and attributed to delegations rather than to individuals.[9]

The most difficult question discussed at this first meeting concerned which of the three proposals should be used as the basis for the conversations. Following the opening ceremony that morning, Cadogan had kept his promise to Stettinius and asked Gromyko to consider basing discussions on the American plan. The Soviet ambassador refused, perhaps because he thought that the British and Americans were combining against him; his language, at any rate, was forceful enough to convince Cadogan that it would be better not to push the matter further. When the issue was raised in the steering committee, Stettinius, who had decided in a meeting with Dunn and Pasvolsky not to be adamant on this question, agreed to begin discussion on the Soviet plan, which the British delegate Charles K. Webster referred to as "a bad decision." In fact, the Soviet proposal held the floor for only one morning; the decision to take it up first convinced Stettinius of the need to discuss the British and American plans in sequence, a procedure that Cadogan regarded as a waste of time but acquiesced in to please the Americans. As Stettinius probably expected, the result of this approach was that the American proposal, which was by far the most complete and detailed of the three, became—albeit unofficially—the basic frame of reference for building a plan of world organization. As in the case of selecting an official language for the conference, Gromyko's objection to beginning with the American plan was apparently more formal than substantive.[10]

The opening day concluded with a dinner for the three delegations at the Carlton Hotel—an example of what Webster described as the "abundant and imaginative hospitality of our American hosts." Selected congressmen and reporters were also in attendance. The mood was festive, with Gromyko and Cadogan exchanging toasts with Stettinius. Although the American under secretary had sworn more than once that there would be no speeches, Cadogan decided to prepare a few words anyway, especially when he noticed near the end of the meal that Gromyko was drafting a speech on the back of his menu. When called upon, the Englishman noted that in making arrangements for the conference the Americans had struck a nice balance between friendly cooperation and military display, a combination that he thought might be reproduced in the plans drawn up in the discussions that followed.[11]

Original plans for the conversations had called for frequent plenary sessions;

it was in such meetings that the Americans envisioned much of the conference's real work being accomplished. The first plenary meeting was held on the morning of 22 August—and the second that afternoon to hear the British and American presentations—but these turned out to be the only plenary sessions convened until the one that marked the closing of the first (or Russian) phase of the conference. In practice, as has been noted, the Joint Steering Committee became the center stage at Dumbarton Oaks, with the delegation chiefs reserving the most difficult negotiating and decision-making for themselves, much as the Big Three had done at Tehran and would do again the following January at Yalta.[12]

The Joint Steering Committee met between the first day's two plenary sessions "to determine further questions of procedure," such as the formulation of subcommittees to deal with the various aspects of creating a world organization. The use of subcommittees had been anticipated by the State Department as early as 11 July, when the American planning group had been divided into three working sections, each responsible for a different topic that would have to be addressed at Dumbarton Oaks. The first, headed by Pasvolsky, dealt with the structure and establishment of the new organization; the second, under State Department Legal Adviser Green H. Hackworth, studied arrangements for the pacific settlement of disputes, including provisions for a world court; and the third, chaired by Dunn and including military representatives, was responsible for postwar security arrangements. The steering committee at Dumbarton Oaks adopted this pattern and established three subcommittees organized along the lines of the American sections—the Subcommittee on General Questions of International Organization, the Legal Subcommittee, and the Subcommittee on Security Questions. These bodies, of which the legal group was the smallest and the security subcommittee the largest, made specific recommendations for consideration by the Joint Steering Committee.[13]

The steering committee also created a fourth group—the Drafting Subcommittee. The delegation heads expected that this body, which consisted primarily of legal experts, would be utilized at the later stages of the conference, after decisions had been made and needed to be put into proper form for transmittal to their governments. In practice, however, drafting could not be so easily divided from the formulation of proposals, which required on a day-to-day basis the kind of precise phrasing that the Drafting Subcommittee had originally been envisioned to provide. The Joint Steering Committee thus decided on 25 August to institute small formulation groups for the two larger subcommittees; these would be responsible for drafting specific proposals as the subcommittees arrived at them—a process that had already begun informally during the first week of meetings. The creation of the two formulation bodies, which met together from the first and were later merged into the Joint Formulation Group, caused members of the steering committee to question the necessity of the Drafting Subcommittee; certainly much of its editorial function had been taken over by the new agencies. The result was that the drafting group, although not abolished, held only one meeting near the conclusion of the first phase of the talks and did not play an important role in shaping the conference's recommendations.[14]

Because of the emphasis placed on the wording of proposals, the Joint Formulation Group—or Formulation Group, as it came to be called later in the conversations—played a key role at Dumbarton Oaks. It was second in importance only to the steering committee, next to which it gave, according to Notter, "the most detailed and analytical consideration" to all provisions advanced for the proposed international organization. Throughout the conference the Formulation Group worked closely with the Joint Steering Committee; its task, as Stettinius described it, was to "draw together" the work accomplished by the substantive subcommittees and to put their conclusions into a suitable form for approval by the delegation chiefs. Controversial issues were almost always deliberated by the two bodies together. When the Formulation Group could not resolve its differences on a difficult point, it asked the steering committee for a decision; alternatively, problems that the Joint Steering Committee could not solve were often referred to the Formulation Group for the drafting of an acceptable compromise formula. The group thus represented the highest technical level of the conversations, and its work became, in Notter's words, "inherently indistinguishable" from that of the steering committee—except, of course, that only the latter body had the power to make decisions.[15]

Later in the conference two additional subcommittees were created to deal with problems as they arose. The first was the Special Informal Military Group—its initial name, which was changed because it seemed excessively formal, was the Special Military Subcommittee—which grew out of the deliberations of the security subcommittee on 23 August. Chaired by Admiral Willson of the American delegation, this group of military advisers was created to deal with the technical aspects of the Russian proposal for an international air force, about which more will be said later, and subsequently extended its discussions to include all questions of a military nature relating to the implementation of an international organization. Each of the three groups included a full contingent of uniformed members, although the British had originally envisioned them attending only as observers. The second additional body was the Subcommittee on Nomenclature, established on 23 August by the Subcommittee on General Questions of International Organization. Its task was to recommend the names and titles for the new organization, its various organs, and its officials—a chore that proved considerably more difficult and controversial than anybody expected.[16]

Conference procedures were also established during these first days of conversations. Although the British and Soviet Groups were assigned private space in the outbuildings at Dumbarton Oaks, they found such offices unacceptable for security reasons and used their embassies for most of their meetings, arriving at the estate each day just in time for the first meetings of the morning—normally 10:30 A.M. Only the American group carried out the lion's share of its daily activities at Dumbarton Oaks itself. The Americans met at 9:30 each morning in the grand formal dining room described by Stettinius as "the most used room" in the mansion; it was at these meetings that unresolved issues were discussed, drafting duties were assigned, and decisions were made. All three groups kept in close touch with their governments, a time-consuming practice made more necessary than usual by the relatively low rank of the chief negotiators. The Americans found this contact easiest, of course, with Stettinius—sometimes joined by other members of the delegation—talking with Hull daily and with Roosevelt on occasion. The under secretary also kept the president informed about the conference through daily memoranda. In the case of the Soviets, the need for continuing instructions would prove a particular problem. Gromyko was authorized to accept only the terms contained in the Russian proposal; any deviation therefrom would require consultations with Moscow, a practice—not unusual for Soviet diplomats—that contributed to the conference lasting longer than anyone expected.[17]

On 22 August, as on a typical day, the delegations remained at Dumbarton Oaks over the noon hour for a buffet luncheon arranged by the State Department and catered by a Washington restaurant. Tables were set outside on the terrace overlooking the estate's exquisite gardens in good weather and in the orangery in bad. Tea was served in similar fashion each afternoon. The three delegation chairmen often sat together at these times and discussed their differences in an informal manner; the result, as Stettinius noted in his diary, was that some of the most difficult issues were settled during luncheon and tea breaks.[18]

Security for the conference was extremely tight. The grounds at Dumbarton Oaks were (and still are) protected by a heavy iron fence, around which military policemen stood guard throughout the conversations. Additional military police, along with secret servicemen from each country, protected the delegates themselves, both in Washington and on weekend trips to Virginia and New York. From the State Department's perspective, such measures seemed clearly necessary—this was, after all, still wartime and there existed the danger of assassination as well as espionage—but they left many Americans, who were worried about America's role in a postwar organization and anxious to learn what was going on behind the curtain of security, fearing that their government had something to hide in its conduct of the negotiations.[19]

Secrecy at Dumbarton Oaks would cost the Roosevelt administration dearly in its relations with the press. Despite the widespread belief that, as journalist Edgar Ansel Mowrer put it, "Woodrow Wilson came to Dumbarton Oaks" in August 1944, the conference was never intended to be open diplomacy—not even in the limited Wilsonian definition of the term. Michael McDermott, the American delegation's press officer, explained to reporters that secrecy was made necessary by the preliminary and exploratory nature of the talks, which represented only the early phase of continuing negotiations for a postwar organization. At this stage, too much publicity could be an error that would make the delegates' work more difficult and success perhaps impossible to achieve. The conference, therefore, was in no sense to be a "dress performance" for the press to record; but if an agreement were reached, McDermott concluded, the reporters could be certain that full publicity would be forthcoming about its terms.[20]

Newsmen were dissatisfied with these arguments. It was to placate them—and also to catch the public's interest in a peacekeeping organization—that the State Department had agreed to turn the opening ceremonies into what McDermott called a dress performance, staged primarily for the benefit of the press. Even this had its limits, however. The American group had turned down journalists' requests for radio broadcast of the opening speeches by Hull, Cadogan, and Gromyko and agreed to newsreel photographers only as a compromise. The result was an elaborate ceremony photographed "ad infinitum," as Webster put it, but without any likelihood that reporters would mistake it for the substantive kind of public information that their editors craved. By the second day of the conference, in fact, newspaper reporters were already beginning to complain of what they regarded as excessive secrecy at Dumbarton Oaks.[21]

The worst was yet to come. On 23 August, James Reston of the New York Times published the substance of the three secret proposals, a coup that set the other reporters "absolutely on the warpath." Citing "an unimpeachable source," Reston described the American, British, and Soviet plans with remarkable accuracy and detail, scooping the rest of the press corps on the biggest story of the summer. Understandably, the other correspondents were, to use Cadogan's word, "furious"; they interpreted Reston's exclusive information as the result of privileged treatment by friendly State Department officials. As the reporters saw it, this unfair advantage for one of their number was exactly the kind of thing that could be expected to happen as the result of too much secrecy; the only remedy was for the conferees to be equally open with all of the correspondents. Reston's story—one of a series on Dumbarton Oaks for which he would ultimately win a Pulitzer prize—was threatening to blow the lid off the press policy established for the conference.[22]

The reporters asked for a meeting with the chairmen of the three delegations at Dumbarton Oaks to state their case for more publicity. Stettinius, after consulting with Cadogan and Gromyko, agreed to hold such a conference, apparently in hopes of appeasing the angry correspondents. This was not to be the result, however. In the meeting on the morning of 24 August, the journalists' sixteen representatives—the Committee of the State Department Correspondents Association, as they called themselves—complained that press releases containing the times of sessions and the appointment of committees were not "news"; what they needed was more "substantial information" instead of "reports of meaningless mechanics" and dry procedures. They thus asked that the delegation heads reconsider their policy of secrecy, which they described as both dangerous because it created a "news vacuum" on an important subject and impracticable now in light of Reston's articles.[23]

The chairmen responded with what Cadogan described as a "most discouraging reply." They reiterated the informal and exploratory nature of the talks and stressed that agreements made at Dumbarton Oaks could not be released immediately because they were tentative and subject to approval by the participating governments. Stettinius, Cadogan, and Gromyko promised to release statements when to do so would not "interfere with smooth and rapid progress toward agreed recommendations," and they agreed, at the reporters' urging, to consider holding additional—perhaps twice-weekly—meetings with the press. In addition, also at the correspondents' request, Cadogan and Gromyko promised to consider the release of synopses of their governments' proposals in a form similar to Roosevelt's statement of the American plan on 15 June. Not surprisingly, in light of the fact that the conference was already under way, such synopses were never prepared or made public. The meeting did little to correct the fundamental problem between the conferees and the press; this result could only have been accomplished, as Stettinius noted in his diary, through a "complete reversal" of the conference's restrictive publicity policy.[24]

As Stettinius predicted, this meeting did not satisfy the reporters, who continued to chafe at being denied the kind of information that Reston was now publishing daily. In an attempt to improve relations with the journalists, Stettinius agreed—against his instincts—to conduct a joint press conference with the other delegation chairmen. Stettinius, Cadogan, and Gromyko met the almost two hundred correspondents in the music room on the morning of 29 August; their purpose, as described by Cadogan, was "to tell them that we weren't going to tell them anything." Following the issuance of a very general statement outlining the type of organization being discussed at Dumbarton Oaks, the reporters were permitted to ask questions. Stettinius, who served as spokesman for the chairmen, found them impossible to answer because they dealt with matters still under consideration; the result, again according to Cadogan, was that the correspondents soon "got tired of it" and gave up. Still hoping to appease them, Stettinius gave the reporters a statement offering additional explanations of the need for secrecy. To his previous arguments, the under secretary of state now added that the governments involved might suffer embarrassment if information were released prematurely and that nothing could be final anyway until after the upcoming meeting with the Chinese. In addition, he cited secrecy in the American constitutional convention—an argument prepared by Breckinridge Long, who had written a book on the subject—as an example of a productive use of this procedure in the past.[25]

The press conference did not silence Stettinius's critics, who now pilloried the under secretary for his failure to give them any information of value. The *Detroit Free Press*, for instance, discounted the importance of Stettinius's responses, "all of which," it said, "could have been written on a postal card a year ago." Only the well-positioned *New York Times* seemed satisfied with the under secretary's explanations, a fact that no doubt added to the fury of other members of the press corps. All of this led Stettinius to the conclusion that his initial reaction had been correct, that it was a mistake for the delegation heads to conduct joint press conferences about their efforts at Dumbarton Oaks; and he resolved to hold no more of them in the future.[26]

Continued criticism, however, convinced Stettinius that something needed to be done to improve the conference's unsatisfactory press relations, and he agreed to meet reporters on his own on 4 September. Without Cadogan and Gromyko present, the American delegation chief felt less restricted—he genuinely sympathized with the journalists' desire for real news—and came away from the meeting fearing that he had perhaps revealed too much of substance about the status of the negotiations. He thus asked aides to inspect the session's transcript to find "the things they got me in the corner on." Despite the under secretary's willingness to be more informative, this effort at personal press relations also proved a failure. He seemed patronizing to reporters, who especially disliked his attempts to gain their confidence by calling them by their first names. He was also halting in his framing of answers and seemed to lack confidence in some of his replies. This was Stettinius at his worst. A shy and somewhat nervous man in public, he was never comfortable in the spotlight—an ironic shortcoming for one so skilled at masterminding public relations behind the scenes. (He had, it will be recalled, been recommended as under secretary of state on the strength of his ability in this dimension.) Not surprisingly, Stettinius decided not to repeat this "gruesome experience," delegating McDermott to meet with small groups of influential reporters on a daily basis. This arrangement could not possibly correct the conference's poor press relations, which remained an unresolved problem for Stettinius both during and after the meetings at Dumbarton Oaks.[27]

To a considerable degree this problem had been caused by the Roosevelt administration's ambivalent approach to the conference's publicity. On the one hand, the State Department had highlighted the conference to build up the public's interest in a postwar organization; but in so doing, it created among the press and public a desire for information that none of the governments involved really wanted to satisfy. As Assistant Secretary of State Acheson told Stettinius: "We failed fundamentally in having a secret conference too highly played up." The situation was also made worse by holding the conversations in the nation's capital, where news-hungry reporters were ubiquitous. Under the circumstances, it seems unlikely that anything Stettinius might have done could have materially improved the conference's poor relations with the press.[28]

Considering what it could cost them, it is not surprising that State Department officials tried hard to locate the source of Reston's information. As early as 6 July, Stettinius had grown concerned that the *New York Times* reporter seemed to have all the details of plans for the upcoming conference on world organization. After a check revealed that no one at the State Department was talking, Stettinius concluded that Reston's information must be coming from one of the other governments involved in the planning. He thus asked his friend Michael Wright, counselor of the British embassy in Washington, to see if he could locate the leak, but nothing came of Wright's investigations. Following Reston's publication of the substance of the American, British, and Russian proposals on 23 August, the State Department stepped up its efforts to find his informant. Stettinius still suspected the British delegation, several members of which—including, privately, Cadogan himself—had expressed the hope that a more liberal press policy might be adopted for the conference. In addition, the

British, who were intent on committing the United States to a postwar security organization, seemed to have the most to gain from promoting the idea among the American public. The suspicion became so intense that Lord Halifax refused to have any contact with Reston at all. But a study conducted by the State Department's Division of Internal Organization and Security, based on a detailed analysis of the *New York Times* articles, suggested that it was the Chinese, and not the British, who were responsible for the leaks. The study revealed that Reston knew least about those matters, especially the Soviet proposals, on which the Chinese had not been fully briefed. Stettinius apparently remained unconvinced by this argument, which Reston later admitted was accurate, but even if he had believed it, he could hardly have refused to keep the Chinese—who already felt mistreated by the Soviet Union's unwillingness to meet with them—abreast of what was occurring at Dumbarton Oaks.[29]

Reston's articles gave the British and Russians reason for complaint against their hosts. Even Cadogan, who thought the State Department's press policies unnecessarily restrictive, expressed some annoyance at the leaks. But the real difficulty was with the Soviets, who had in the past suggested that the American government could not be trusted with secrets because of its inability to keep them from its own public. Probably the Russians were astounded at Dumbarton Oaks by the aggressiveness of American reporters and by the unpredictable workings of a free press; certainly Reston's articles confirmed their belief in the superiority of their own system of closely controlled reporting. Adding to the problem was the now familiar Soviet paranoia. As Soviet interpreter Valentin M. Berezhkov wrote in his memoir of the conference, Soviet delegates at Dumbarton Oaks and their superiors in the Kremlin both viewed leaks and articles criticizing the conference as stemming from those who wished to sabotage cooperation between the Soviet Union and the West. At best, then, Reston's revelations were a diplomatic embarrassment; at worst they threatened to make friendly negotiations with the Soviets—already troubled by strains within the Grand Alliance—considerably more difficult.[30]

Conducting the conference in secrecy also provoked another incident that embarrassed the administration. On 20 August, Gerald L. K. Smith, a demagogic evangelist who in 1944 was the presidential nominee of the miniscule and isolationist America First Party, telegraphed Hull with the demand that he invite a "nationalist" to take part in the meetings at Dumbarton Oaks. Smith suggested two names: Senator Robert R. Reynolds, Democrat of North Carolina, and Colonel Robert R. McCormick, publisher of the isolationist *Chicago Tribune*; and he warned the secretary of state that if one of these men were not included to represent "true nationalism," he would present himself at the conference as spokesman for the "millions of inarticulate nationalists who are determined that there shall be no super state and no world police force after this war."[31]

Smith, whose politics had moved considerably to the right since his days as an organizer for Louisiana senator Huey P. Long's "Share Our Wealth" movement, proved true to his word. When the conference opened with no "nationalist" representative, he traveled to Washington to present his ideas to the secretary of state in person. Hull refused to see him and assigned the case to Assistant Secretary Long, who told Mrs. Smith "snippily" over the telephone that as an American citizen her husband was welcome to present his views on any subject to the State Department in writing. Although in Long's opinion this concluded the matter, Smith was not satisfied and continued to bombard Long's secretary with importunate phone calls. Rebuffed repeatedly, the Smiths threatened to take their case to the American people. "All right then," Mrs. Smith finally told Long's secretary, "there will be another election."[32]

Although he was not much of an electoral threat, Smith did subject the Dumbarton Oaks Conference to a dose of negative publicity—something that it already had in more than sufficient quantity during these first days of meetings. On the morning of 25 August, Smith caused a sensation by showing up in front of the gates to the mansion and demanding that the military policemen admit him to take part in the conference. Stettinius was called out of a meeting of the Joint Steering Committee and delegated Long to meet with the isolationist "representative," but by then Smith had made his point and departed. This scene at Dumbarton Oaks provided sensational publicity for Smith's criticisms of the conference, which he had written in a letter to Hull and distributed among the press corps and in Congress on 23 August, and which—in an untimely coincidence—reinforced the problems caused by the State Department's restrictive press policy.[33]

According to Smith, the Dumbarton Oaks Conference was being conducted in a way "foreign to our American tradition"; he regarded the exclusion of the press and Congress as distinctly "un-American." This procedure was, moreover, part of a consistent policy of secrecy practiced by the Roosevelt administration, which Smith viewed as nearly dictatorial in its conduct of foreign affairs. Smith also criticized the Republican John Foster Dulles, who had consulted Hull on postwar issues, for giving the talks a nonpartisan appearance; this was an illusion, Smith argued, because Dulles was a "known internationalist." The heart of Smith's letter consisted of seven accusations against the State Department. He accused the department of making secret covenants in secret meetings; of attempting to make treaties without the consent of the Senate; of having already made a secret deal with the Soviet Union over Poland; of violating the Constitution; of setting up a conference on American soil and filling it with foreigners, then surrounding the place with soldiers to keep out the American people; of making facts available to agents of Great Britain and the Soviet Union that were being kept secret from Americans; and of taking the United States into a League of Nations—or something like it—while the war was still going on. Smith concluded that when the truth was finally brought out the American people would realize that "someone should be impeached."[34]

The foreign delegates at Dumbarton Oaks were not charmed by the comic aspects of the Smith imbroglio. Isaiah Berlin, who served during the war as head of the Special Survey Section of the British embassy in Washington, pointed to the episode in his weekly intelligence summary for London as an example of the way in which "even irresponsible circles do not seem wholly beyond the . . . ken" of the Department of State. He was astounded to note that Hull had turned Smith—whom he described as a "notorious Fascist dema- gogue"—over to Assistant Secretary Long and that Long was supposed to keep in touch with "this disreputable figure." Berlin could only surmise that the Americans' willingness to handle Smith gingerly was a reflection of their nervousness about public support for the conference and postwar interna- tionalism. Given this British reaction, one can only wonder what the Rus- sians must have thought about Smith—who was openly and extravagantly anti- Soviet—and his apparently evenhanded treatment by the American State Department.[35]

Other groups also complained about being excluded from the conference. As head of the American delegation, Stettinius received mail critical of the fact that no women were involved in the discussions at Dumbarton Oaks, with several writers pointing out that if men had special aptitudes for war women were more familiar with the ways of making peace. The State Department was careful not to make this same omission at the U.N. organizing conference in San Francisco the following spring; Durward V. Sandifer of the International Security and Organization Division drew up a list of a dozen women qualified to be delegates, and Virginia Gildersleeve, dean of Barnard College, was se- lected to be among the representatives of the United States at that meeting. Other critics reversed Gerald L. K. Smith's position and argued that the Ameri- can group at Dumbarton Oaks was too narrowly conservative. Dorothy Detzer, of the Women's International League for Peace and Freedom, for example, expressed displeasure to Alger Hiss because her organization had not been invited to take part; in Detzer's view, the State Department's consultants for

Dumbarton Oaks all represented conservative internationalism, what she called the "right wing of the peace organization movement" in America. Although disturbing, these complaints did not produce the kind of bad publicity engendered by the American group's problems with the reporters and Smith.[36]

As the conference progressed—and disagreements mounted—Stettinius attempted to find ways to relieve the tensions developing among the three delegations. These diversions included trips to New York City and rural Virginia, during which the Americans attempted to give their guests two quite different views of American life while they relaxed and rested from their labors at Dumbarton Oaks. At four in the afternoon on Friday, 25 August—following the conclusion of the first week's meetings—the delegates were flown by a U.S. Army plane from Washington to New York's La Guardia Airport, where they were picked up by military vehicles and whisked, their escort's sirens blaring, to rooms at the Waldorf Astoria. After dinner, Stettinius treated the party to a midnight floor show at Billie Rose's Diamond Horseshoe, a popular New York nightclub. The Russians (excluding Gromyko, who had not made the trip) were mesmerized. Here was capitalism at its most decadent, and they assumed, because of the familiarity with which Stettinius greeted the waiters, that attending such late-night entertainments was typical behavior for senior American officials.[37]

All of this was done in secrecy—"naturally," according to *Time* magazine, because "no Russian wanted Joseph Stalin to hear too many lush details of bouncing about in night clubs"—and Stettinius even denied in his press conference on 29 August that the delegates had attended a floor show in New York at all. But security broke down, not surprisingly considering the blaring sirens, and the foreigners found themselves hounded by inquisitive reporters when they emerged from their rooms on Saturday morning. The day was spent sight-seeing and included visits to the Empire State Building, the New York Stock Exchange, several museums, and Rockefeller Center. That evening, the party went to Radio City Music Hall, where the chief attractions were a floor show and Katharine Hepburn performing in *The Dragon Seed*. They also attended a cocktail party hosted by Nelson A. Rockefeller, who was then coordinator of Inter-American Affairs in the Roosevelt administration. Afterward, Stettinius and Rockefeller took the delegates backstage to meet the Rockettes, to whom the under secretary asked Cadogan to explain the significance of the meetings at Dumbarton Oaks. There is, unfortunately, no record of the Englishman's response. The foreign visitors also received a glimpse of the future, as the Americans showed them a working model of a television set. After another night at the Waldorf, the party flew back to Washington on 27 August.[38]

Two weeks later, on Sunday, 10 September, the four delegations—including, this time, the Chinese—toured the historic sites of Virginia. One group, led by Stettinius and including the British and Chinese, departed Washington in sixteen government limousines with motorcycle escort; Cadogan, Ambassador Halifax, H. H. Kung, Wellington Koo, and Ambassador Wei rode with the under secretary. After a morning spent touring the Civil War battlefield at Bull Run and the Skyline Drive along the Blue Ridge mountains, the party stopped at Big Meadows for a picnic lunch complete with iced cocktails. Next was a visit to the campus of the University of Virginia at Charlottesville, designed by Thomas Jefferson, then on to the great estates of the Virginia dynasty of presidents—Jefferson's Monticello, Madison's Montpelier, and Monroe's Ash Lawn, where mint juleps were served. All the while Stettinius held forth, in what Cadogan described as "his showman manner," on the beauties of the scenery, "as if he not only owned it but had painted it." At 6:30 P.M. the cavalcade arrived at Stettinius's home, Horseshoe, where the party ate a buffet supper and was entertained by a negro quartet singing spirituals.[39]

A second group, composed of members of the Soviet group but excluding Gromyko, who once again elected to stay in Washington, received a separate tour of Virginia on 10 September, an arrangement made necessary by the Russians' unwillingness to participate in any activities with the Chinese. This party stopped at Mount Vernon and the Luray Caverns and was escorted by Dunn and Bohlen, whose descriptions of the scenery placed—for whatever reason—special emphasis on the battle sites of the Revolution and the Civil War.[40]

It seems unlikely that these junkets had much effect on the negotiations at Dumbarton Oaks. Stettinius had conceived of the tours, according to contemporary news accounts, after Roosevelt related to him Al Smith's dictum that a settlement to any labor dispute could be reached if you could only get the negotiators for the unions and management to relax together. Other members of the American group were doubtful; the dour Pasvolsky, for one, thought that it was all just "too frivolous." Wasteful or not, the trips did not appear to bring the delegations any closer together, especially considering that the Russians, with whom difficulties of the labor-management sort (the president did not say which group was which) had by then begun to emerge, were escorted separately on 10 September. Cadogan's reaction to the Virginia tour indicated its failure to draw even the British and American groups any closer together. The head of the British delegation wrote that he found the evening at Horseshoe to be an "astonishing scene": "admirable food . . . which one collected and took to an armchair or sofa. Flashlight photographers followed one—also the negro 'spirituals.' And meanwhile the motor-bike police strolled about the house smoking cigarettes." It was "all very pleasant but unintelligible." Later, describing the experience to his wife, Cadogan concluded that the Americans were "extraordinary people," who were "in some respects rather like ourselves but (as you can see) so utterly different." Whatever their value, sightseeing trips could not accomplish the primary objective of the conference; that could only be done in the daily meetings at Dumbarton Oaks. It is on these that we, like the delegates, must now focus our attention.[41]

4 Plans and Principles

The negotiations at Dumbarton Oaks began, as the State Department's Harley Notter has written, "energetically and with common desire for success." The preliminary proposals drawn up by the three powers had revealed a broad base of common ground, and the delegation chiefs continued to emphasize these areas of agreement in their initial presentations to the plenary sessions held on the second day of the conference. What differences existed then appeared to be mostly matters of emphasis or misunderstanding—just the sorts of things that the conference of experts at Dumbarton Oaks was designed to resolve. Thus optimism was the dominant mood as the delegates turned on 23 August to the task of determining the structure of a new world organization that they hoped might produce a workable system for the maintenance of world peace.[1]

The first topic raised was the most general: the overall aims and objectives of the new international organization. At Gromyko's insistence, the Soviet Union's plan served as the basis for discussion in the opening meeting of the organization subcommittee, inaugurating a formal procedure that would be followed throughout the early rounds of talks and would be abandoned only when the Joint Formulation Group began to produce drafts of the conference's own recommendations, which were usually closer to the American plan. The Soviets thought that the organization should have three principal purposes: the maintenance of general peace and security through collective measures for the prevention or suppression of aggression, the settlement by peaceful means of international disputes that might lead to breaches of the peace, and the adoption of other measures to strengthen world peace and to develop friendly relations among nations. These general goals were not controversial and were, indeed, similar to those presented in the British and American plans. But they failed to go far enough, the other groups thought, by omitting any reference to the basic principles and objects of the organization, including the importance of the rule of law; this was, as radio commentator Upton Close put it, like "building a motor to operate without considering what fuel you will use." The British and Americans thus requested that the Drafting Subcommittee explore ways to expand the Russian statement into the philosophical realm. In addition, Cadogan expressed doubts about the Soviets' use of the term "aggression" because of the myriad difficulties that it had posed for the League of Nations, with the result that the supplementary phrase "or other breaches of the peace" was eventually added to "the suppression of acts of aggression" in the final Dumbarton Oaks proposals.[2]

The seemingly innocuous question of the organization's basic aims contained the seeds of one major disagreement. The Soviet Union's proposal did not include the fostering of social and economic cooperation among the purposes of the new body; it said only that it might be desirable to establish a separate organization or organizations, "not connected with the inter-national security organization," to carry out this objective. This Russian approach did not satisfy the British and Americans, who by the time of the Dumbarton Oaks Conference viewed arrangements for social and economic cooperation as integral parts of any world organization, and who listed them among the primary purposes of the new body. Thus, when tentative agreement was reached on the Soviet statement of aims, Stettinius raised the issue of including a social and economic agency and suggested that this "important question" be referred to the Joint Steering Committee for further consideration. The British and Russians agreed. This decision established what would become two of the conference's fundamental procedures. The first was that difficult questions, which might provoke lengthy and even heated debates, were handled by the small and informal Joint Steering Committee, where the heads of the three delegations could hammer out a final agreement. The Soviets, in particular, seemed to prefer this approach. The second was that difficult issues would be deferred until later in the conference. Gromyko had proposed this strategy on 21 August because he thought it would be useful to create as wide an area of agreement as possible before turning to more troublesome points. Cadogan and Stettinius agreed, perhaps hoping in this way to produce a positive atmosphere in which all disagreements could ultimately be resolved. The result, in the early days of the conference, was to put the delegations in a mood that was almost euphoric with success—although, as Cadogan noted, this was achieved "at the expense of leaving a lot of the more difficult questions for further consideration." Ultimately, this procedure would contribute to the conference's difficulties—and to the delegates' sense of failure—as the agenda was slowly reduced to questions that seemed all but impossible to resolve.[3]

Faced with Soviet intransigence on the issue of an authoritative social and economic council, the Americans wavered in their dedication to creating such an agency within the United Nations Organization. As early as 21 August Stettinius had told Gromyko that he regarded the subject as "very debatable," even though, he said, the United States and United Kingdom had "definite views" about it. Now the president and his chief of staff, Admiral William D. Leahy, proposed a compromise that threatened to take the teeth out of the American plan. In a meeting at the White House with leaders of the United States delegation on 24 August, Roosevelt expressed the view that although the General Assembly should have adequate functions with respect to social and economic problems, the actual provisions for this authority could be written into the proposal in general terms. There was no reason to risk disagreement by being too specific on this issue at Dumbarton Oaks. To Stettinius, this approach seemed to indicate the president's desire not to press immediately for a social and economic council, an interpretation that was confirmed later in the day by Admiral Leahy. In a discussion with Stettinius at a White House reception for the President of Iceland, Leahy stated his own opposition to American insistence on establishing a specific welfare agency. Instead, Leahy, who claimed to have discussed this matter intermittently with FDR for several months, thought that the Dumbarton Oaks proposals should give the assembly the authority to create subsidiary organs later—which could, of course, include a social and economic council.[4]

The issue was the first to be discussed at the next morning's meeting of the Joint Steering Committee, held in Stettinius's office in the downstairs library at Dumbarton Oaks. Cadogan began by stressing the British view that important economic and social questions should "somehow" be dealt with by the new organization. He argued that the Soviet planners' distinction between security and other matters, on which they based their desire to keep economic and social questions in a separate organization, was an artificial one. What it overlooked, he continued, was the fact that differences on social and economic issues might lead in the future, as they often had in the past, to conflicts that threatened the world's peace and security. The prevention of war required that something be done about its roots, which the British thought were generally found in just the kinds of questions that the Soviets were proposing to remove from the direct authority of the new organization. The least that was required, according to Cadogan, was a close liaison, such as that which their combined inclusion in an international organization might effect, between the agencies dealing with welfare and those handling security questions.[5]

The Russians responded earnestly and exhaustively by urging the desirability of a separate economic and social organization. Gromyko pointed out that the League of Nations, which had failed so spectacularly in its efforts as a peace-keeping body, had actually considered more questions relating to general welfare than it ever had to international security. According to Soviet estimates,

77 percent of the matters dealt with by the league had not been directly related to the maintenance of peace; thus, too much of that body's time had been spent considering what Gromyko referred to as "secondary matters," a fact that he thought explained its inability to accomplish its main goals of peace and security. It was an awareness of this problem, the Russian chairman argued, that had produced a worldwide "general aspiration" for an organization that could concentrate solely on the preservation of peace. In the view of the Soviet Union, therefore, "the primary and indeed the only task" of the international organization should be the maintenance of peace and security. Other, less important, matters should be dealt with somewhere else.[6]

Stettinius agreed that security should be the main task of the proposed organization and the only task of the council. He thought that the views of the three delegations were not very far apart; the only real question was where to deal with the relatively less important matters of welfare and economics. The American position differed from that of the Soviet Union just in its opinion that there should be one overall organization—"one tent," as Stettinius phrased it— to cover international relations generally, including both threats to the peace and the causes of those threats. The exact nature of the social and economic organization was not important, he said, and the American group had no desire to press its own definite and detailed plan in this connection. Thus, according to the American chairman, the reference to an Economic and Social Council consisting of twenty-four members contained in the United States proposal was merely a suggestion—not an absolute requirement. As a compromise, Stettinius proposed Leahy's idea that the conference agree to a formula that would permit the assembly to create subsidiary commissions or other bodies that it regarded as necessary to the preservation of peace and security. Although the American group still had, according to the under secretary, an open mind on the subject, it agreed with the British view that some way should at least be left open for the international organization to act in this secondary but important field.[7]

Pasvolsky also attempted to explain the American position. He said that planners within the State Department, like those in the Soviet Union, had recognized that one of the league's chief difficulties was that the council had been given too much responsibility in areas that inevitably diverted its attention from the key questions of peace and security. Not only did this arrangement work poorly for keeping the peace, they thought, but it also failed in its goal of promoting social and economic well-being because the council members' expertise lay in the area of political rather than welfare questions. These problems had been revealed in the report of a special committee of the league chaired by the Australian representative, Stanley Bruce. The Bruce Report, submitted in August 1939, had recommended the creation of a Central Committee for Economic and Social Questions that could free the council from its responsibilities in welfare areas. Although mooted, at least as far as the league was concerned, by the onset of the war in Europe, this recommendation became the basis for the American proposal of a social and economic council in the new organization. Thus, according to Pasvolsky, it was the same league experience—and failures—of which the Russians complained that had prompted the Americans to include a welfare agency in their plans.[8]

But why not, as the Soviets argued, separate these matters from the proposed United Nations altogether? Pasvolsky said that the Americans thought it desirable to bring as many economic and technical questions as possible within the scope of the new organization, which should be able to promote peace simultaneously on several fronts. The goal here was coordination, not control; the various agencies, the American argued, could remain autonomous under the aegis of the new world body. The Economic and Social Council would normally operate independently. But if a serious conflict arose in regard to a social or economic matter, especially if it threatened the peace, the question could easily be transferred and taken up by the Security Council. The Americans, like the British, thought that the organization should deal as much with eliminating the causes of war—with what Stettinius called "the maintenance of conditions conducive to peace"—as with actual threats to security.[9]

No decision was reached on this question on 25 August. The discussion revealed a serious difference in the perceptions of the Soviets and the Anglo-Americans about the proposed world organization—a difference of perception that Stalin had described in another context as that between the Westerners' "algebra" and his own "practical arithmetic." "I do not wish to decry algebra," he had said, "but I prefer practical arithmetic." Still, Stettinius emerged from the meeting of the Joint Steering Committee confident and encouraged by the attention that Gromyko and Arkady Sobolev, the deputy chairman of the Soviet delegation, had paid to the British and American arguments, a view shared by Gladwyn Jebb. Gromyko agreed to report fully to Moscow and the topic was deferred to a later meeting.[10]

Although the issue of a social and economic council remained deadlocked in the first meetings of the Joint Formulation Group on 28 and 29 August, there still seemed reason to hope for a successful conclusion. The Soviets continued to participate "constructively," as Stettinius put it, in discussions about including social and economic cooperation in a draft statement of the new organization's objectives, even though they refused to make any concessions until they received instructions from Moscow. Gromyko also showed signs of softening his own views on the matter. After the press conference on the morning of 29 August, he talked privately with Stettinius in the garden near the swimming pool. Gromyko said that he was impressed by American arguments for the creation of a social and economic council and would be happy to discuss the question in more detail whenever Stettinius wished. The Russian chairman's attitude left Stettinius with the impression that it would not be too difficult to reach a satisfactory solution on this issue.[11]

The under secretary's assessment proved essentially correct. Although retaining a reservation on the subject, the Soviets took part in drafting a section on social and economic cooperation in the Formulation Group meeting of 6 September; then, in keeping with what would become standard procedure for the conference, the disputed section was placed in brackets pending final approval or rejection by Moscow. The group agreed to use virtually the entire text of the American proposal, except that the size of the Economic and Social Council was reduced from twenty-four to eighteen members and a new concept was added empowering the agency to assist the Security Council upon request. Gromyko also continued to be encouraging, informing Stettinius at lunch on 7 September that he believed the issue should be resolved during the Dumbarton Oaks Conference. This proved to be the case; in fact, on the next day the Soviets withdrew their objection to the operation of the new organization in the social and economic sphere so that all that remained was, as Stettinius termed it, "perfecting the draft."[12]

Perfecting the draft turned out to be a bit more difficult than Stettinius expected. In a meeting of the Joint Formulation Group on 9 September, Gromyko proposed two changes in the draft plan: the inclusion of technical problems and the substitution of the phrase "other humanitarian problems" for "educational and cultural problems" among the social and economic concerns to be dealt with by the new world organization. The Americans objected strenuously to these alterations. Several members of the group, including Rear Admiral Harold Train and Major General George V. Strong, feared that the inclusion of the word "technical" might obligate the United States to share secret technical and research information with other countries of the world, including, of course, the Soviet Union. They thought that the effects of such disclosures could be disastrous, not only on commerce and industry, but on military secrecy as well. Benjamin Gerig, who was a former official of the League of Nations, pointed out that similar concerns had prompted the Bruce Committee to use "economic and social" instead of "technical" to describe its proposals for a nonpolitical agency of the league. Pasvolsky agreed that the term "technical" should be avoided, although he doubted that the Soviets expected the provision to require the sharing of secret military information. Pasvolsky also favored retaining the phrase "educational and cultural problems" because "other humanitarian problems" was too vague.[13]

Although Stettinius expressed concern that rejecting Gromyko's proposals might cause the Soviets to reconsider the whole question of social and economic cooperation, he agreed to bring the matter up in the Joint Steering Committee. He did so on 12 September with no success. Later in the day, however, while the chairmen were sharing afternoon tea, Gromyko offered a compromise: the Soviets would withdraw their demands for technical cooperation if the Americans would drop their insistence on the inclusion of specific references to educational and cultural matters. Stettinius and Cadogan, sensing that this was the best they could do, agreed to the trade.[14]

On 9 September, just as the question of social and economic cooperation was about to be resolved, the Americans added a new complication to the discussion of general principles. They wanted the inclusion of the Wilsonian issue of human rights, which had been omitted from the State Department's original plan despite pleas by internationalists for some sort of worldwide bill of rights to embody Roosevelt's Four Freedoms. The new American proposal, which was written by the president's personal representative within the American group, Benjamin Cohen, stopped well short of accomplishing the internationalists' objective, probably as a result of concern about congressional reaction to the idea of a prospective world body investigating the racial and immigration policies of the United States. Backing into the subject, it said that the international organization should refrain from intervention in the internal affairs of any state because it was the acknowledged responsibility of each state "to respect the human rights and fundamental freedoms" of its own people and to govern "in accordance with the principles of humanity and justice." The idea here, as Pasvolsky explained it to the American group, was to reduce the likelihood of the world organization interfering in the internal affairs of its members by placing the responsibility for respecting human rights on the member states themselves, while noting for the record that such respect was an important international principle.[15]

Stettinius found little support for this proposal in the Joint Steering Committee. Cadogan thought that the statement was too vague in the absence of any universal agreement about what constituted human rights and was concerned that the provision might give the world body the right to criticize the internal organization of its members—criticism that he feared might be leveled against British rule in India and elsewhere. Cadogan may also have viewed the proposal as an American attempt to raise the forbidden colonial question indirectly. The British chiefs of staff, usually passive concerning political questions, cabled that it found the proposal "objectionable *in toto*" and requested that Cadogan try to persuade the United States to withdraw it "in its present unhappy form." Gromyko argued that in his personal opinion any reference to human rights and basic freedoms was not germane to the main tasks of an international security organization and should not be included in the Dumbarton Oaks proposals. Both agreed, however, to consult their governments.[16]

When the matter came up again ten days later the British continued to object to its inclusion in the draft plan. The Soviets, however, were less obdurate, indicating that they would accept the proposal on human rights provided that it could be coupled with a provision stating that fascist or fascist-type states were excluded from membership in the new organization. This reflected the Soviet view that the new organization should be directed against Germany and Japan and was apparently an attempt by Gromyko to define what was meant by human rights violations. As such, it proved unacceptable to the Americans, who feared its effect on certain Latin American nations—such as Argentina—which might under this provision be denied membership in the world body. In addition, both the British and the Americans thought that the term "fascist" was far too ambiguous to be included in the draft charter. Cadogan pointed out that the British used it only when referring to Mussolini's Italy, and Pasvolsky remarked that in the United States "fascist" was not applied to Japan. Gromyko responded that the task of determining which states were covered by the terms could be left up to the Security Council.[17]

The American group reacted to all these developments on 20 September by voting, as Gromyko had suggested, to exclude both technical cooperation and a specific reference to cultural and educational affairs from the plan; at the same time, it also issued a statement urging that a reference to human rights be included somewhere in the Dumbarton Oaks proposals. At a meeting of the Joint Steering Committee late in the day, Stettinius persuaded Gromyko and Cadogan to postpone a decision on the matter until Cohen, assisted now by Isaiah Bowman, could draft a new proposal. The Americans suggested three places where a brief reference to human rights could be inserted: in the chapter on the assembly; among the purposes of the world organization; or in the chapter on social and economic cooperation. The Russians preferred the last, and with their assent the phrase to "promote respect for human rights and fundamental freedoms" was added to the section on the responsibilities of the Economic and Social Council. The British also granted their approval because, as Gladwyn Jebb told Alger Hiss, it would be farcical to give the public impression that the delegates could not agree on the need to safeguard human rights. This left the draft plan without a statement explicitly restricting the power of the organization to interfere in the internal affairs of member states, a defect that was remedied by a British proposal forbidding the Security Council from involving itself in domestic questions unless they presented a direct threat to world peace. American acceptance of this provision, which had been a part of Cohen's original proposal on human rights, assured British approval of the compromise statement. The Russians also agreed, despite Gromyko's initial reaction that the council should be free to consider any question it wanted to. Overall, the outcome was gratifying to the American group, which had successfully finessed a difficult political problem by satisfying both the internationalists, who favored a statement on human rights, and congressional critics, who feared interference in the domestic affairs of the United States. In addition, FDR expressed pleasant surprise that the Soviets had yielded on this matter, which he referred to as an "extremely vital" provision for the success and acceptance of the world organization.[18]

Less successful was an American attempt to include a statement of sexual equality in the new body's charter. Isaiah Bowman raised this issue during an American group meeting on 13 September with the statement that he regarded it as a refinement of the clause on human rights then under consideration by the conference. Cohen agreed but thought that the question should be broadened to include the equality of the races, along the lines of a provision in the Chinese proposal for Dumbarton Oaks. The group voted to approve a statement that "no person shall be precluded from holding any position in the organization because of race, nationality, creed, or sex." Although he seemed to have little hope for it, Stettinius agreed to bring this provision before the other delegation chairmen; if they disapproved, he said, the proposal would at least be in the minutes and could be raised again at the upcoming general conference to found the new organization. That afternoon in the meeting of the Joint Steering Committee, the under secretary found that Cadogan and Gromyko thought the point unnecessary and were "rather negative" on it. Even though Stettinius asked that the British and Soviets think about the proposal and respond later, the Americans let the matter die quietly following approval of a general clause supporting human rights in the draft charter.[19]

There was much less difficulty in determining the basic shape of the new world body. The organization subcommittee agreed without much debate on 23 August to the creation of four principal organs: an assembly of all member nations, a smaller council to handle questions of security, an international court, and a secretariat presided over by the chief executive officer of the organization. This structure was similar to that of the League of Nations and had been included, despite all previous objections, in the preliminary proposals of each of the three nations. In addition, the subcommittee agreed that the international organization should be empowered to establish such subordinate agencies as might become necessary.

The question of membership proved considerably more controversial. At its initial meeting on 23 August, the organization subcommittee discussed the Soviet proposal on this issue: only the United Nations—those which had signed the declaration of 1 January 1942—were to be "founder-members" of the organization, with the eventual admission of other "peace-loving" states to be determined by the assembly on the recommendation of the council. This differed from the British and American plans in several ways. The Americans, in particular, thought that limiting charter membership to the United Nations was just too restrictive; they favored the immediate inclusion of the pro-Allied associated powers and "such other nations as the United Nations may determine" to make the organization more truly universal in scope. The British, who had not developed a firm position on initial membership, seemed inclined to favor the American view, especially after they considered that some of the dominions might be omitted in the Soviet plan. Some Americans also objected to the Russians' use of the adjective "peace-loving," which they regarded as a mere affectation; they decided not to argue against its use, however, because of its recognized value in winning popular support for the new organization, which was always an American goal.[20]

The definition of procedures for eventual admission was even more problematical. State Department planners had originally favored a combined council-assembly formula much like the one proposed by the Russians; they hoped in that way to retain a veto over membership in the council without angering smaller nations that desired a voice in the matter in the assembly. By the time the American proposals for Dumbarton Oaks were drafted, however, a majority of the planning group had decided that the traditional principle that all states involved should have an equal vote on decisions concerning membership was too important to ignore. Besides, the assembly, where the Americans now wanted to lodge all authority for determining membership, would contain enough clients of the United States to prevent the admission of unacceptable nations, at least in the foreseeable future. British thinking on the subject had followed a similar path, although by the time the conference opened they still favored some sort of participation by the council in the admission of new members. When the topic came up in the organization subcommittee, Stettinius and Cadogan—now fully won over to the American view—proposed that the admission of new states be left entirely to the assembly, and Gromyko skeptically agreed to take the matter under consideration.[21]

From the Soviet perspective, these two membership questions were linked by a concern over being perpetually outnumbered—and outvoted—in the new world organization. The United States and United Kingdom could always count on a wealth of friendly nations, including in the case of the British the dominions, to support their positions in the United Nations. Not so for the Soviets, whose fear of being isolated was drawn from their experiences following World War I and in the League of Nations, and by their ideological view of the inevitable enmity of encircling capitalist nations. Nothing could entirely eliminate this fear, of course, but it could be alleviated somewhat by limiting the initial size of the organization and by blackballing questionable nations— such as Egypt, Iceland, and the six "associated powers" of Latin America (Chile, Ecuador, Paraguay, Peru, Uruguay, and Venezuela)—that would otherwise add to the already comfortable majorities enjoyed by the United States and Great Britain. Thus it seemed important to the Soviets to retain their veto on questions of membership by always involving the council in the deliberative process. Even more appealing was the possibility of including friends of Moscow, such as the sixteen constituent republics of the Soviet Union, among the initial members of the new world organization. This tactic would never change the balance of power in the peacekeeping body, which would inevitably contain a large majority of non-Communist states, but it would lessen the Soviets' sense of isolation and guarantee some support for their views, especially if the votes of the constituent republics could be combined with those of a few satellite states to be created in Eastern Europe. Still, the constituent-republics proposal can have seemed like little more than a pipe dream to the hardened realists in the Kremlin, who probably saw it as a bargaining chip to trade for something more feasible.[22]

Pipe dream or not, Gromyko raised the issue in the Joint Steering Committee on 28 August. Following a lengthy debate on the questions of voting and membership in the Security Council, about which more will be said later, the meeting turned to the problem of initial membership in the organization. Stettinius wanted it made clear that the American proposal included, in addition to the United Nations, those "few additional countries" that had broken relations with Germany and were "cooperating" in the war effort, whereupon the delegates agreed that a tentative list of such states should be drawn up by the Joint Formulation Group for further consideration. It was at this point that Gromyko dropped what Stettinius called "the bombshell" by blandly remarking that all of the sixteen Soviet republics should be included among the initial members of the organization. The Russian's statement left Stettinius and Cadogan "breathless," according to Cordell Hull, but they swallowed their shock and responded in a similarly unexcited tone. The Briton said that he had no comment to make on the matter at this stage, but that he thought his government would want to discuss the international status of the Soviet republics with the Kremlin—a remark that was, as Stettinius observed, an attempt to divorce the question from the Dumbarton Oaks talks. The Americans said only that they would have to think about Gromyko's proposal and moved on to another topic.[23]

The fact that the Soviet chairman raised this issue at the end of a discussion concerning the delicate problems of voting and membership in the council has led historian Gabriel Kolko to interpret it as an extemporaneous response to the Russian's fear of isolation in a capitalist organization. But surely this can not have been the case, because Gromyko would never have raised such an important issue, with its potential for imperiling the conference, without prior instructions from Moscow. In fact, the Soviets had been laying the groundwork for this proposal for some time. On 1 February 1944, the Supreme Soviet had amended the constitution of the Soviet Union to say that each of the constituent republics had the right to conduct its own foreign relations, which provided something of a legal basis for later claims that they were independent states. Even earlier, in December 1943, the Kremlin had requested that the British grant representation on the War Crimes Commission to several of the republics, contending that they were no less sovereign than the British dominions and that their suffering during the war gave them a moral right to be represented. The British had rejected this proposal, but were still considering, on the eve of the Dumbarton Oaks Conference, the possibility of sending diplomatic representatives to each of the sixteen republics. It thus seems likely that Gromyko had instructions, at least, to bring up the matter of the republics if the British and Americans attempted to expand the size of the organization, and that this order explains his decision to raise the issue when he did on 28 August.[24]

Nor could the Americans have been as surprised by Gromyko's action as they professed to be. Hull, for example, wrote that "no such question had ever entered the minds" of those involved in postwar planning in the United States. But this was far from the truth. The British had informed the Americans of the Soviet request for multiple membership on the War Crimes Commission, and the State Department had immediately begun to consider the implications of this for the proposed postwar organization. And in February 1944, while Hull was on vacation, Roosevelt and Stettinius had discussed in detail the possibility of a Russian demand for membership in the world body for each of the sixteen republics named in the recent amendment to the Soviet constitution. It was, in fact, the fear of such a demand that had originally caused the State Department's planners to favor participation by the council in determining new members—thus insuring the United States a perpetual veto over granting membership to the Soviet republics. When the American group reversed itself on this procedure, it did so not out of an assurance that the Soviets would decline to press the matter but because the planners thought that the pro-Western assembly could be counted on to keep the republics out.[25]

The Americans and British were genuinely shocked, however, that the Soviets decided to raise such an inflammatory issue at Dumbarton Oaks. When informed of this development, Roosevelt responded, "My God," and instructed the under secretary to explain to Gromyko "privately and personally and immediately" that the United States could never accept the proposal, that it "might ruin the chance of getting an international organization accepted in this country." FDR thought that it would make as much sense to include the entire forty-eight United States among the members of the new body and warned that the Russian provision might cause the British to increase their voting power by creating new dominions out of their colonies and islands. He asked Stettinius to point out these dangers to Gromyko. The American chairman said he would do so but that he thought resolving the issue might require direct communications between the president and Stalin.[26]

After their pained surprise wore off, the Americans' first concern was to maintain secrecy—to guarantee that the Soviet proposal was never made public. They feared that, armed with such information, domestic critics of world organization and continued cooperation with the Soviet Union could eradicate any possibility of the public's acceptance of the Dumbarton Oaks proposals. Adding to their concern was the conference's increasingly unsatisfactory relationship with the press, especially the damage done by the leaks to James Reston of the New York Times, and the fact that the three group leaders had a press conference scheduled for the next morning. Stettinius thus went to extraordinary lengths to keep the Soviet request secret. He ordered that no member of the American delegation except for those present at the Joint Steering Committee meeting (himself, Pasvolsky, and Dunn) be informed of the proposal; the remainder of the group learned of it only on 16 October—a week after the close of the conversations. He also attempted to have all references to the question expunged from the minutes of the committee, but failed when Gromyko refused on the principle that "what was said was said." For the remainder of the conference, Stettinius always referred to the topic as the "X-matter" in his notes and memoranda, arranged that official papers containing references to it be distributed only to the delegation chairmen, and kept all American copies of such papers locked in his office safe.[27]

The British were less troubled by the principle involved in Gromyko's request than by the effect they feared it might have on opinion in the United States. Foreign Office planners understood that the Soviets might feel isolated in the kind of world organization then being proposed and thought that the additional seats would not in themselves present a problem in an assembly where the USSR would still control less than one third of the votes. The real difficulty was the likely reaction of the United States. If the Soviet proposal did not drive the Americans away from the idea of a world organization altogether, it might lead them to demand more seats in the assembly for themselves—surely the isolationists would never sit still for being outvoted by the Soviets sixteen to one. This outcome could give rise to the principle of proportional representation for all states, which the Foreign Office regarded as a farce and a danger to acceptance of the world body by smaller nations. Regardless of its views on the subject, the Foreign Office recognized that the inclusion of the dominions in the new organization left its delegates in a weak position to say too much about the Soviet request for similar treatment at Dumbarton Oaks, with the result that it advised Cadogan to stay out of the debate on the issue as much as possible and let the Americans handle Gromyko.[28]

The Americans wasted no time making their objections known to Gromyko. Stettinius raised the issue on the morning of 29 August, while he and the Russian chairman were walking in the garden at Dumbarton Oaks. The under secretary said that Roosevelt and Hull regarded the Soviet request as out of order and warned that pressing the point at that time might jeopardize the success of the entire conference. He made what he described as an "earnest appeal" to Gromyko for the withdrawal of the topic, adding that it might more properly be presented to the international organization itself following its creation. Hull reiterated these sentiments in a private meeting with Gromyko two days later. He said that in his view the Soviet proposal might "blow off the roof" of the proposed world body. The secretary of state thought, moreover, that plural membership was unnecessary for the Great Powers, which due to their leadership and military preponderance would have no difficulty in getting their ideas heard, no matter how many votes they had. The United States certainly did not want more than one vote, he said, but still felt that its influence would be sufficient to assert itself in the new organization—a view that could not have struck the Soviet chairman by surprise or given him much comfort. Gromyko's response was "cooperative." He indicated that he had raised the X-matter merely to inform the British and Americans that the Soviet government had it in mind and agreed not to mention it again at Dumbarton Oaks.[29]

Despite Gromyko's assurances, however, Roosevelt decided to take Stettinius's advice and send a telegram on the subject directly to Stalin. What the president wanted was the Soviet leader's assurance that the topic would be avoided not only at Dumbarton Oaks but at all meetings until the international organization was firmly established. He said that in his opinion the question was so volatile that to raise it before the world body was functioning "would very definitely imperil the whole project," certainly in the United States and probably in other important countries as well. Like Stettinius, FDR held out the possibility of discussing the matter later, at which time the assembly would, he said, have full authority to deal with it. Stalin's response said that he attached exceptional importance to the issue. He reminded Roosevelt of the constitutional reforms that had broadened the authority of the republics in conducting foreign relations and pointed out that some of the constituent parts of the Soviet Union, such as the Ukraine and Byelorussia, surpassed both in population and political influence "certain countries" that "all of us agree" should be among the initiators of the international organization. He hoped therefore to have an opportunity to explain to Roosevelt the "political importance" of the question to his government.[30]

This response, which Stettinius described as discouraging, reflected Stalin's concern that plans for the new organization were moving too far away from Roosevelt's idea of the Four Policemen and were placing excessive emphasis on the role of the smaller powers. British and American planners had indeed been traveling in this direction, in part because of complaints from lesser governments that their interests and sovereignty were not safeguarded in earlier plans for the world body. But the Soviets continued to view the matter in light of the experience of the League of Nations, where as they saw it "pseudo-democratic" ideas about the principle of the equality of states had permitted small nations to play a role "altogether disproportionate" to their actual importance in world affairs. The result, according to the Russian analysis, had been the inability of the league to act, especially in crisis situations. Stalin also instinctively opposed the idea of smaller nations judging and criticizing Soviet behavior; only Great Powers could understand each other's needs and responsibilities well enough to do that. Still, the Soviets found themselves constantly giving ground on this issue at Dumbarton Oaks, and Stalin had to recognize that guaranteeing some protection for the interests of the minor countries would be a feature of the conference's ultimate proposals. It thus seemed reasonable to demand similar protection for the Soviet republics, which he thought deserved to be ranked as highly in international affairs as did many of those states destined for initial membership in the United Nations. Doing so afforded Stalin the opportunity both to protest the expanded role of the secondary powers and to assuage strong nationalist sentiments in the Soviet republics—what the Russian leader meant by the "political importance" of the question.[31]

Gromyko raised the issue once more at Dumbarton Oaks. On 27 September, the next to the last day of the Soviet phase of the conference, the Russian chairman remarked in the Joint Steering Committee that his government's agreement on any date for a general conference to establish the United Nations depended, in part, on British and American acceptance of the Soviet proposal that the sixteen republics be among the initial members of the organization. Gromyko chose not to elaborate on the point, and neither Stettinius nor Cadogan commented about it. When Stettinius reported this development to Roosevelt, the president said that he was disturbed by the news, then shocked the under secretary by saying that he had reviewed the matter, about which State Department security had been so tight, with the Brazilian ambassador to the United States. FDR had learned, he said, that Brazil consisted of twenty-one states and planned to use this fact in debating the matter with Stalin. The question of the Soviet republics proved, of course, to be unresolvable at Dumbarton Oaks and became one of the key issues settled by the Big Three at Yalta in February 1945.[32]

At the meeting on 29 August where he had agreed not to press membership for the republics, Gromyko had also accepted the Anglo-American idea that the United Nations and their associates should constitute the new world organization. This was not quite the concession that it seemed, however, because the Soviet chairman defined "associated nations" as limited to those which had signed the United Nations Declaration after 1 January 1942, not those which, as in the broader British and American definitions, had failed to sign but were cooperating in the war effort. Thus in the Soviet view no state that had failed to declare war on the Axis would be included among the initial membership. The difference between these two interpretations surfaced on 31 August, when Pasvolsky presented his list of United and Associated Nations to the Joint Steering Committee. Gromyko, who obviously disagreed with some of the nations included, responded that he regarded this information as strictly supplementary, that he opposed any attempt at that time to draw up an actual list of initial members, and that the recommendations of the present conference should not go beyond the stating of a formula for determining membership. Following this course would make it possible for the conferees to avoid the difficult problem of compiling a list—and would also keep alive the Soviet claims to inclusion of the sixteen republics. Then, at a subsequent meeting, the Soviet chairman argued that the formula should include only the United Nations—signatories to the declaration of 1 January 1942—and not what Pasvolsky referred to as "Associated Nations" in his list. The Americans objected that this was not consistent with the participation, already agreed to by the Soviet Union, of these nations in the United Nations Relief and Rehabilitation Administration,, the Food and Agriculture Organization, and the International Monetary Fund, but Gromyko would concede only that the other nations might be admitted to membership "immediately after" the United Nations.[33]

By the end of the first week in September it was evident that the conference was deadlocked on this question. On 13 September Stettinius proposed an alternative formula suggested by the British and approved by the American group that morning: the initial members would be the United Nations "and such other states as those nations may invite," provided that the four powers could agree at Dumbarton Oaks on which states they should be. Discussion of this formula in the Joint Steering Committee was inconclusive, however, leading Stettinius to speculate that the Russians did not fully understand what the Americans had in mind. It seems more likely, however, that Gromyko understood only too well; this new approach required a definite list to be drawn up at Dumbarton Oaks and implied the inclusion of at least some states that the Soviets were attempting to keep out. It would also exclude the sixteen republics. The American proposal did nothing new except remove the inference that the objectionable nations had earned the right to membership by virtue of participation in the war, which was not the issue for Stalin and Gromyko. The Russians therefore rejected it, as did Cadogan, who now agreed with Gromyko that the conference should confine itself to drafting a general principle on the subject. The Soviets then added to the confusion with the demand that any attempt to define membership specifically must exclude "fascist" states. Ultimately, the conferees at Dumbarton Oaks found it impossible to agree on the question of initial membership and postponed the issue by determining only that membership "should be open to all peace-loving states." This problem, too, was resolved at Yalta, where it was decided that the associated nations (along with Turkey) would be invited to join if they declared war on Germany by 1 March 1945.[34]

Closely related to membership was the question of provisions for the suspension, expulsion, and withdrawal of member states. The Soviet proposal, on which the initial discussion of this issue was based, gave the assembly the authority to expel offending members on the recommendation of the council. No provision of this sort appeared in the American or British plans, although both groups had considered the question and arrived at Dumbarton Oaks with mixed opinions on the matter. For the Americans, suspension, expulsion, and withdrawal posed too many unresolved difficulties about the nature of membership in the organization. To be effective, they reasoned, the world body would have to gain compliance with certain of its principles—such as the peaceful settlement of disputes—from all nations, whether members or not. And certainly member states should not be permitted to escape their obligations by withdrawing or be freed from them through expulsion. The obvious solution to this problem, and one that appealed to many of the American planners, was to make membership automatic and irrevocable. But this raised as many questions as it answered: Would an unwilling state be likely to accept unwanted responsibilities merely because it was declared to be a member? Did anyone want Germany and Japan in the organization initially? How could the State Department answer congressional critics who would howl if membership were made explicitly irrevocable? By the eve of the conference it seemed safest to most of the American group to omit any reference to the entire matter and hope for the best. Hull made this decision on 19 August, and Roosevelt confirmed it, after the conference was under way, on 24 August.[35]

The British view lay somewhere between those of the Soviets and the Americans. Although their draft plan called for the consideration of "conditions under which a State shall cease to be a member of the Organization," they joined the Americans on 23 August in objecting to the specific Soviet provision on expulsion. Their reason, as Cadogan put it, was that "expelled states had a habit of drifting into a kind of limbo in which, unconstrained by rules, they might do a certain amount of mischief." Cadogan also expressed his desire to omit any direct reference to withdrawal from the Dumbarton Oaks recommendations. Two days later, the British chairman offered a compromise: the organization could suspend rather than revoke the membership of states against which the council took action. Gromyko did not think this went far enough. He insisted that the power of expulsion was necessary to "discipline" members, but neither Stettinius nor Cadogan could see how this would work in practice. The Americans thus reiterated their view that the document should include no provisions for expulsion or withdrawal; it should simply be assumed that all members would remain within the organization no matter what happened. Despite Russian objections, the British proposal for suspension was accepted by the Joint Steering Committee pending further consideration. By the time of the committee's next meeting Gromyko had drafted a counterproposal of his own: the British idea on suspension should be included, but as a supplement to, not a substitute for, the Russian provision permitting expulsion. This solution did not appeal to either the British or the Americans, whose view on the matter was supported by President Roosevelt late in the day.[36]

This topic then became the object of diplomatic horse-trading. On 7 September, Gromyko announced that the Soviet Union agreed to the elimination of their proposal for the expulsion of offending nations and hinted that his motive was to begin a round of concessions by all three powers. Cadogan responded, perhaps in an effort to minimize the importance of the Russian concession, by saying that he had been prepared to resolve the issue the other way by agreeing to the inclusion of a provision on expulsion. Stettinius, too, had been authorized to yield on this question, especially if he "could get something in return." Apparently no one had very strong convictions on this matter. Less than twenty-four hours later, when the three chairmen met to discuss unresolved subjects, Stettinius and Cadogan reversed the earlier compromise and accepted an expulsion provision in exchange for Gromyko's approval of the Economic and Social Council as part of the new organization.[37]

This agreement meant that the Dumbarton Oaks proposals would contain provisions for both the suspension and the expulsion of members. In drafting this section of the document, the British and Americans attempted to emphasize the difference between the two concepts to guarantee that the latter would not be exercised lightly. Cadogan, in particular, thought that the lesser penalty of suspension had the important advantage of making it easier to reinstate an offending member, which could be done simply through a vote of the council; once a state was expelled, however, it could only be readmitted through the regular admission process. Thus suspension was to be applied routinely to any member "against which preventive or enforcement action" was taken by the Security Council, whereas expulsion was to be reserved for a nation that "persistently violated the principles" of the world organization.[38]

Any statement on withdrawal was omitted entirely from the Dumbarton Oaks agreement. The British and Russians agreed with the American view that such a provision would serve no useful purpose and might prove dangerous in light of the experiences of the League of Nations. The Americans and British differed, however, on how explicitly this position should be stated. The Americans preferred to leave the matter open and vague; they hoped in this way to finesse congressional criticism about infringement on United States national sovereignty while maintaining the principle that member states should not look upon withdrawal as a way of expressing their displeasure with future actions of the international organization. The British, on the other hand, saw no reason not to confront the issue directly. They contended in their official commentary on the proposals that the omission meant that "states would have no right of withdrawing voluntarily" because "the intention is that membership of the Organization shall be permanent."[39]

All three delegations shared the view that some procedure for future revision of the charter was necessary "if the Organization was to be able to adapt itself to the rapidly changing world of today." They also agreed that to be effective amendments must be binding on all members, whether they approved of them or not. One solution to the problem this posed was to require that all changes be made with unanimous consent, an approach that each of the powers thought would make the amendment process practically impossible to carry out. Thus, some voting formula was needed to make changing the charter difficult enough to satisfy those who might be in opposition without ruling out revision altogether. The American plan, presented to the organization subcommittee on 24 August, called for amendments to be proposed by a majority of the assembly and to be ratified by two-thirds of the member states, including all permanent members of the council. The logic behind this procedure was similar to that for changing the United States Constitution: amendments should be relatively easy to propose but harder to ratify. Neither of the other groups was entirely satisfied with this formula, although they agreed that the Great Power veto was justified by the responsibilities of the Great Powers for maintaining the peace, which they could hardly be expected to fulfill under conditions not agreed to by themselves. The British, in particular, thought that it might be difficult to impose an amendment on the one-third that refused to ratify it, and both they and the Russians decided to draft their own voting proposals.[40]

The British plan reversed the American system of voting. Because they thought that in the experience of the league it had been more difficult to obtain final ratification than initial approval—often for reasons of inertia rather than policy—their proposal required the assembly to adopt amendments by a two-thirds vote and permitted ratification by a simple majority of member states including, of course, all of the permanent members of the council. The Soviets, who had apparently decided to place all of their faith in their own veto, proposed simple majorities for both the vote in the assembly and ratification. The Americans responded with a compromise plan: procedural amendments would need only a majority vote whereas substantive changes would require something more. At this point the discussion of amendments completely broke down, and on 20 September the chapter providing for them was removed from the draft charter altogether. It appeared that this might prove to be another question that the conferees at Dumbarton Oaks would have to leave unresolved for possible settlement by the Big Three. But the issue only seemed more difficult than it was, perhaps because it had become linked with the vitally important problem of voting in the council. On 27 September the Soviets announced their willingness to accept a draft from the Joint Formulation Group—already approved by the Americans—that embodied the British formula, and a chapter on amendments became part of the Dumbarton Oaks proposals.[41]

It would also appear from subsequent references that the Joint Formulation Group discussed, in addition to amendments, the possibility of a general reconsideration of the organization's charter after ten years. This idea, which is not mentioned in the official records of the conference, was apparently rejected for two reasons: it would diminish the prestige of the organization by implying that the charter was not intended to be permanent, and it was unnecessary because of the general principle that any organization has the inherent right to review its constitution whenever it chooses to do so.[42]

The less substantive issues of nomenclature and location proved to be much more difficult than anyone expected. The Americans came to Dumbarton Oaks determined to carry the wartime term "United Nations" over into the postwar organization. They thought that employing the name of the victorious alliance, already commonly in use to refer to postwar cooperation, was only logical and would serve to enhance the prestige of the peacekeeping body. Stettinius expected no difficulty in persuading the British and Soviets to accept this view—the British used the term themselves in their preliminary proposals—and this prediction seemed to be coming true during the early, informal discussions of the organization's name. The ad hoc Subcommittee on Nomenclature, which was chaired by Henry P. Fletcher of the American group, reported in favor of the name "The United Nations" despite some concern that neutrals might object because of the term's specific wartime connotation. The Soviet representatives, Sergei A. Golunsky and Sergei B. Krylov, preferred the name "International Security Organization" but were outvoted by the British and Americans. Gromyko also objected in the organization subcommittee to the use of "United Nations"; he argued that the term had a special connotation relating to the war against the Axis that would be undesirable for the future world organization. The Soviet chairman also thought that it might be advantageous to have the word "security" in the body's name—hence the Russian proposal of "International Security Organization"—but conceded that this might not be necessary if the term was added to one of the organization's major agencies, such as the council. The organization subcommittee accepted the nomenclature group's report on 4 September, although the Soviets still maintained a reservation on the title "United Nations."[43]

Gromyko renewed his objection when the issue was raised in the Joint Steering Committee five days later. He now suggested the name "World Union," which was far too suggestive of a superstate to suit American tastes. It was for this reason that the name "Commonwealth of Nations," which some of the State Department's planners had originally preferred, had been ruled out by Hull and Roosevelt in the spring of 1944. Cadogan then surprised the American group by announcing that he did not believe the British government to be too "keen" on the term "United Nations," and that it had at one time considered an alternate title containing the word "union." When the Americans refused to yield, however, Gromyko grudgingly accepted the name "United Nations" on

12 September. The Foreign Office still disliked the term but decided not to object because it was "reluctant to take the initiative in producing another wrangle in the conference."[44]

The remainder of the new body's nomenclature presented fewer difficulties. The Americans took issue with the Fletcher committee's recommendation of the name "World Assembly" for the organization's plenary body because that body would not, in fact, be an assembly of the world but only of member states. They proposed "General Assembly" instead, a title that the other groups subsequently accepted. As suggested above, "security" was added to the name of the council to satisfy Soviet desires for the inclusion of that term; this change presented no problem because everyone agreed that the name accurately reflected that organ's primary function anyway. For the organization's chief executive officer the Americans preferred the title "Director-General" but acceded to the Soviets' choice of "Secretary-General," which had been the title for that officer under the League of Nations. There was general agreement that the name "International Court of Justice" should also be continued.[45]

Location was the subject of only informal discussions at Dumbarton Oaks. FDR expressed the most interest in it, quizzing Stettinius repeatedly about the progress being made on the topic at the conference and lobbying for his own choices. The president's strongest opinion was that Geneva should not be the site of the new organization's headquarters because he did not want to see the United Nations associated with the failures of the league. Roosevelt thought that only the secretariat required a fixed seat of operations and suggested the Empire State Building or the newly constructed Pentagon as the home for that body. The assembly, in his view, could be peripatetic, holding meetings at different locations in the manner of the Pan-American conferences, except jumping "from hemisphere to hemisphere." The president wanted the council to have two or three locations. His choices were the islands of Flores in the Azores and Niihau in the Hawaiian group, which he described as the most "heavenly spot he knew of on earth." He also spoke favorably of the Black Hills of South Dakota, saying that they were located four hundred miles from civilization in every direction, contained two good hotels, and were filled with well-stocked trout streams.[46]

Stettinius had doubts about FDR's proposal. He thought that it would be a mistake to separate the secretariat from the council, that to locate the support staff on the mainland and the council on an island "just would not be practical." He also feared—as did other members of the American group—that situating the secretariat in the United States (and especially in the Pentagon) would not prove acceptable to the British or the Russians. The under secretary preferred Geneva as the site of both because the climate was good, the facilities excellent, and it was readily accessible to the major nations of Europe. The only drawback was the "bad name of the League," which Stettinius thought could be overcome by the success of the new world organization. For Roosevelt, however, who was more sensitive to public opinion in the United States, this one disadvantage was decisive. He would not go beyond locating the world court, which he thought had a better "history" than the league, in Geneva, although he admitted that perhaps the secretariat could also be situated there.[47]

The Russian view seemed closer to Stettinius's than to Roosevelt's. Sobolev thought that the seat of the new organization should be in Europe but not in one of the larger countries, thus narrowing the choice to only a few places. Pasvolsky responded that Prague might satisfy the Soviet criteria, as would Geneva. Sobolev acknowledged the latter by saying that the Russians were considering a proposal for internationalizing a portion of the city around the present League of Nations buildings. Sobolev's initiative may have been less than sincere. The Kremlin was still nursing a grievance against the Swiss for their treatment of the Soviet Union in the interwar period, and Jebb, who himself favored the creation of "a sort of District of Columbia" in Europe, thought that the Russians would never accept Geneva as the site of the new organization. Still, the Fletcher committee agreed with the Soviet idea, reporting that outside of the United States the best site for the permanent headquarters would be the small strip of Swiss territory containing the league structures and the adjacent French territory of the Pays de Gex. No decision was reached on the question of location at Dumbarton Oaks.[48]

As the delegates at Dumbarton Oaks soon learned, the creation of a new international organization was a thicket of difficulties. If this was true of the discussion of such general—and apparently innocuous—issues as nomenclature and location, it was even more true of attempts to define the world body's principles and to set standards for the admission and expulsion of members. But such issues, complex as they may seem, were simple compared to the thorny problems raised by attempts to establish the form and function of the assembly, world court, and council—the agencies that would perform the peacekeeping tasks of the new organization. As everyone knew, the answers to questions about these organs would materially affect the fortunes of the powers, great and small, and would determine how—and if—the United Nations would work.

Stettinius addresses a plenary session during the Chinese phase of the conference. Courtesy Edward R. Stettinius, Jr., Papers (#2723), Manuscripts Division, Special Collections Department, University of Virginia Library.

Military police guarding the main gate at Dumbarton Oaks during the conference. Courtesy Edward R. Stettinius, Jr., Papers (#2723), Manuscripts Division, Special Collections Department, University of Virginia Library.

The three delegation heads confer. *Left to right*, Cadogan, Stettinius, and Gromyko. Courtesy Edward R. Stettinius, Jr., Papers (#2723), Manuscripts Division, Special Collections Department, University of Virginia Library.

An informal meeting in the library at Dumbarton Oaks. Cadogan, Stettinius, and Gromyko are seated second, third, and fourth from left. Courtesy Edward R. Stettinius, Jr., Papers (#2723), Manuscripts Division, Special Collections Department, University of Virginia Library.

Delegates to the conference picnic at Big Meadows while sightseeing in Virginia. Cadogan is third, Koo sixth, and Stettinius eighth from left. Courtesy Edward R. Stettinius, Jr., Papers (#2723), Manuscripts Division, Special Collections Department, University of Virginia Library.

The opening session of the Dumbarton Oaks Conference. Seated at the head table are, *left to right*, Cadogan, Lord Halifax, Hull, Gromyko, and Stettinius. Courtesy Edward R. Stettinius, Jr., Papers (#2723), Manuscripts Division, Special Collections Department, University of Virginia Library.

Dumbarton Oaks. Courtesy Edward R. Stettinius, Jr., Papers (#2723), Manuscripts Division, Special Collections Department, University of Virginia Library.

An informal meeting of delegation heads following the opening of the Chinese phase of the conference. *Left to right*, Koo, Stettinius, and Cadogan. Courtesy Edward R. Stettinius, Jr., Papers (#2723), Manuscripts Division, Special Collections Department, University of Virginia Library.

5 *The Assembly and the Court*

As the discussion at Dumbarton Oaks of principles for the organization revealed, the three victorious powers remained far apart in their perceptions of what was required for the creation of a just international order for the postwar world. The Americans, British, and Russians had a difficult time agreeing whether or not the United Nations charter should include references to such things as human rights and aggression—let alone defining what those concepts meant or should mean in the future. Such differences, which would be even more pronounced among the representatives of all of the United Nations, had often been the source of disagreements—and wars—in the past; thus one of the primary goals of the Dumbarton Oaks Conference was to construct an apparatus whereby terms could be defined, issues discussed, conflicts resolved, and justice achieved. In extreme cases, these objectives would be the task of the Security Council's peacekeeping forces, but ordinarily, before conflicts reached the point of threatening war, they would be achieved by two of the world organization's other main agencies—the General Assembly and the International Court of Justice.

All three nations included a general assembly of all members in their preconference proposals, then agreed to its creation in the first meeting of the organization subcommittee. The most fundamental question to be resolved about the assembly at Dumbarton Oaks was how far its authority should extend into the area of peacekeeping—a field that originally had been reserved for the council. Under FDR's initial conception of the Four Policemen, in fact, there had been no need for a general assembly at all; security was to be the sole purpose of the new organization and security was the task of the power-wielding council of Great Powers. Such an organization could not be expected to win the support of the smaller nations, however, because it left them with no role to play in either peacekeeping or policy-making. Nor would it satisfy Wilsonian internationalists in the United States. Thus planners in all three nations evolved a general assembly, patterned after that of the League of Nations, to give vent to the opinions of all nations, placate the lesser powers by recognizing the "sovereign equality" of all members, and make the organization more truly a world body.[1]

In the field of peacekeeping, which everyone recognized as the most important task of the new organization, the function of the assembly would be clearly secondary to that of the council. As Gromyko put it on 23 August, the assembly would "discuss" and the council would "decide and act" on all questions of security, peace, and arms limitation. The Americans, in agreeing with this view, thought that the role of the assembly should be paramount only in handling social, economic, and humanitarian concerns—in areas, that is, which might lead ultimately to breaches of the peace but not in dealing with violations of security themselves. And the British, who had originally thought it "unwise to stress the antithesis between the assembly as a forum for discussion and the council as a center of action," now viewed such a dichotomy as essential, at least where peacekeeping activity was concerned. There was also general agreement that the assembly should attempt to define universal standards of behavior, including, in the American proposal, the development and revision of rules of international law. In addition, all three draft plans contained provisions that involved the assembly in the actual peacekeeping process, at least up to the point where a conflict had led or was about to lead to war. Even the Soviets, who generally favored limiting the authority of the assembly, thought that it should be free to consider all questions concerning international security once they were raised by the council. Such questions should be left for the council, however, to decide how to proceed if peacekeeping action was required. The British and Americans wanted to go ever farther and permit the assembly to make recommendations of its own for the peaceful settlement of questions affecting the general welfare. Gromyko disagreed with this view on 24 August, for reasons similar to those that caused his initial rejection of an economic and social council to deal with welfare matters. He also reversed his government's initial position and argued that the assembly should defer discussion of all questions of peace and security until after the council had examined them. But, in general, as Stettinius noted a few days later, there was "striking unanimity" among the three delegations on the status and role of the General Assembly.[2]

This unanimity resulted by the end of August in agreement on the basic functions and powers of the new assembly. It would have the right to consider questions relating to the maintenance of peace and security, but not to take up any such matter on its own initiative when it was already being dealt with by the council. The General Assembly could also make recommendations about questions of peace and security, except when the matter was already in the hands of the council. The intent here, as Gromyko made clear, was to differentiate between the powers of the two organs in a manner that would insure the dominance of the council in peacekeeping and avoid the kind of interference by the assembly that had hampered the activities of the League of Nations. Thus, if the structure of the assembly was patterned closely after that of the league, its more limited peacekeeping functions and powers decidedly were not.[3]

Directly related to peacekeeping was the question of the assembly's responsibility for the regulation of armaments—a topic that only the Soviets had included among that body's responsibilities in their tentative proposals. When the Russian representatives raised this issue in the security subcommittee on 5 September, the British and Americans objected that they saw no reason for singling out arms reduction among the many subjects that the assembly might profitably discuss. They thought that the topic could safely be considered covered by the assembly's basic right to make recommendations on important questions relating to security. The Soviets persisted, however, and Stettinius and Cadogan relented during the general give-and-take on disputed points that occurred three days later. The Russians also wanted a specific reference to disarmament, not just to arms regulation; but the British, who feared the consequences of too few arms at least as much as they did too many, balked at the use of this term anywhere in the Dumbarton Oaks agreements. This time Stettinius, who regarded disarmament as a laudable if impractical ideal, took Gromyko's side, and the outnumbered Cadogan was forced to permit both disarmament and the regulation of armaments to be named as principles of international cooperation for the General Assembly to consider.[4]

The assembly was also given the authority to approve the annual budgets of each of the organization's bodies and agencies. In principle everyone agreed that the power of the purse should rest with the General Assembly; all member states would, after all, share the organization's expenses and should have a voice in determining the uses to which its revenue would be put. The Americans, however, worried that the assembly might use this power to influence the decisions of the council by voting or withholding funds in response to its activities, and considered granting the council at least concurrent control over its own budget. It was difficult to see how such sharing of authority would work in practice, though. As a substitute, the American plan called for weighted voting on budgets in the assembly, with each state having voting power in proportion to its contribution to the organization's expenses. This seemed equitable because it related participation in the budgetary process to the amount of financial burden that each nation assumed. It would also give the council, whose members would probably always account for more than half of the total contributions to the organization, an indirect control over its own budget—and, incidentally, over the budgets of all the other agencies as well. But this violated the important principle that each state should always have an equal vote in the assembly—and probably also seemed to the British and Russians to be a bit self-serving on the part of the rich Americans. It was therefore not included in the Dumbarton Oaks proposals, which simply empowered the assembly to approve the budgets of the new organization. At the revenue end of the budgetary process, the assembly received the authority to apportion the world body's expenses unequally among it members, thus insuring that the wealthy nations, which would be outnumbered in the plenary sessions, would always be called upon to pay the lion's share.[5]

Another responsibility of the General Assembly was the election of nonpermanent members of the Security Council. Here, too, the three delegations considered violating the principle of voting equality—this time for reasons that were more political than practical. The British, prompted by a desire to win the support of middle-sized powers for the world organization, proposed that the election of nonpermanent council members should be carried out with "due regard being paid to the military contribution of members of the organization toward the maintenance of international peace and security." Gromyko expressed doubts about the wisdom of such a policy when it came up in the Joint Steering Committee on 9 September. He thought that the contribution of members should, of course, be taken into account in the periodic election of members to the council but wondered whether any statement of this principle might not appear to be a form of Great Power pressure on the assembly. Cadogan defended the British proposal by pointing out that certain nations— which, he observed in passing, were too important to fit easily under the rubric of "smaller powers"—would make such valuable contributions to the success of the organization that they deserved preference in election to the council as opposed to states that would realistically make no contribution to the organization at all. The British had two groups of nations in mind—the middle-sized states of Europe, on which they were counting for support in policing the Continent, and the larger commonwealth nations, whose interests they felt bound to protect. Such motives did not recommend the British plan to the Soviets, of course. As a compromise, Cadogan suggested that the British provision might be broadened by deleting the word "military" and adding, at the end of the clause, the words "and towards the other purposes of the organization."[6]

The Americans sided with the Soviets. Although State Department planners had previously considered a formula similar to that proposed by the British, they had rejected it before the opening of the Dumbarton Oaks Conference as a violation of voting equality. On 9 September, Dunn agreed with Gromyko that it would be inappropriate to include the British provision in the draft charter; he thought that the question should be taken up, if at all, during the general United Nations conference when smaller powers would be in attendance and could speak for themselves. The American was concerned that the British proposal would establish three separate categories of states—"the great powers, those who made special contributions, and the remainder"—and feared that other nations, especially in Latin America, would see this invidious arrangement as a serious step away from the principle of the sovereign equality of states. It was one thing, he reasoned, to ask smaller nations to accept a special status for the Great Powers, which had presumably earned some right to it during the present war, but quite another to expect them to tolerate a privileged place for their only slightly larger and more powerful neighbors. Dunn therefore did not think that the British view would meet with general acceptance. Jebb disagreed; in his opinion, the proposal would help win the approval of the states whose support the conference (or at least his government) most wished to insure—the so-called middle-sized powers. It was thus a political asset, not, as the American thought, a liability.[7]

Pasvolsky also criticized the British plan. He pointed out that the provision would have the effect of making it impossible for some states ever to serve on the council. The sharp-tongued Jebb replied that this might be a good thing. Cadogan, however, was more conciliatory; he said that in his view the proposal would not necessarily have that result—it would simply mean that the assembly could reject the inevitable pleas for an automatic rotation of council terms among all member states. If this meant that larger states would serve more often, Cadogan thought this acceptable because their representation was needed in determining security questions; the new organization should avoid, he said, "lumping . . . powerful 'medium states' like Canada along with the likes of Salvador and Iraq." Pasvolsky responded that this result would probably occur in practice anyway. Under the league, he observed, some states had never been elected to the council whereas others had served several terms. The initial debate on this matter proved inconclusive. Gromyko finally said that his group would have to study the issues thoroughly—which meant he wanted to ask for instructions from Moscow, where the full importance of the British plan could be considered. Stettinius also reserved his opinion until he could discuss the question with Hull.[8]

The British agreed tentatively on 19 September to omit this provision, which, following American insistence, was eliminated altogether from the draft plan one day later. The Dumbarton Oaks proposals said simply that the General Assembly "should elect" the nonpermanent members of the Security

Council. They also gave the plenary body the authority to elect members of the Economic and Social Council and the International Court of Justice, about which there was no controversy during the conference.[9]

The question of voting, which in the case of the council would almost wreck the conference, proved less difficult where the assembly was concerned. As mentioned above, the principle of one-state-one-vote would turn out to be inviolable, primarily because it seemed basic to the idea of the sovereign equality of all members. Before the Dumbarton Oaks talks began, however, the American planners had toyed with and rejected a voting scheme that was more in line with that of the council—the Great Powers would all have to concur in the making of any major decision. The goal here was to neutralize the inevitable numerical superiority of the smaller nations in the assembly, which might be utilized, in the absence of the Great Power veto, to take action that might go against the interests of the United States. The major objection to this plan, in addition to its obvious violation of the principle of voting equality in the plenary body, was that it was unnecessary. Because its recommendations on security were nonbinding, the assembly lacked sufficient authority to endanger the vital interests of any of the Great Powers; thus losing an assembly vote was a risk that the United States could safely take in the interest of creating a true world organization. The result was that the Americans, like the British and Soviets, called for voting equality in the assembly in their tentative proposals for the new United Nations.[10]

Among American planners the defeat of the veto idea gave rise to the proposal that a two-thirds majority should be required to decide important questions in the assembly. This provision would grant the Great Powers a sort of indirect veto because as the organization's leaders they should be able to wield enough influence, perhaps individually and certainly as a group, to prevent themselves from becoming part of a one-third minority. In addition, a two-thirds majority would help insure the kind of compliance and support for the new organization that might be lacking if a controversial question could be resolved by a bare 51 percent. With these considerations in mind, two related voting questions had to be answered at Dumbarton Oaks: whether the normal voting procedure should be by a simple or two-thirds majority and how to determine what the exceptions would be. The Americans wanted a simple majority to be the norm; they argued that this procedure would be more in keeping with the root principle of sovereign equality. The Russians and British disagreed, arguing that it would be easier to enumerate the procedural questions that could be carried by a simple majority than it would be to list the "important decisions" requiring a two-thirds vote. The problem, as the British and Soviet delegations saw it, was that because future questions were unforeseeable it was impossible to know what kinds of issues might produce important decisions in years to come. If a simple majority served as the normal voting requirement, they thought, such unprecedented questions were likely to be settled by 51 percent of the members when the intent of the planners was to require a two-thirds vote. Despite these objections, however, the American view prevailed when the Soviets changed their minds. Gromyko did not say why, but his reasons probably had something to do with the usual Soviet desire to keep the charter as simple as possible. The Joint Formulation Group also added a stipulation that all majorities should be determined by the number of members present and voting in the assembly.[11]

This decision made enumerating the assembly's "important decisions" seem extremely important. There was no real disagreement on what kinds of questions the delegates had in mind: the lists compiled by the three groups all included recommendations regarding the maintenance of peace and security, election of nonpermanent members to the Security Council, election of members of the Economic and Social Council, admission of new members to the organization, and suspension and expulsion of members. Budgetary decisions were added following the defeat of the special American scheme for handling them. The trickiest question was how to add new items to the list of important decisions in the future. The British, in particular, wanted to make this procedure as easy as possible, and the Soviets and Americans accepted Malkin's proposal that new questions could be added by the approval of a simple majority. This provision did not altogether solve the problem, however, because 51 percent of the members could still defeat attempts to make an issue an important decision and then approve it as a procedural question.[12]

Although it was readily agreed that each member should have one vote in the General Assembly, there was some debate about the size and composition of each nation's delegation. American planners thought that the assembly might better mirror world opinion if it included representatives of the national legislatures of the member states, thus extending the parliamentary process into the international sphere. They therefore considered including a suggestion that each nation's delegation should reflect its "various national interests." Two things seemed wrong with such a provision, however: it might be seen as interference in the internal affairs of the organization's members, and it would probably result in a plethora of special-interest groups demanding representation on the American delegation to the assembly. To avoid these problems the Americans decided merely to limit the total number of each nation's delegation to six. The British and Russians agreed with the principle of leaving the determination of representatives entirely up to the states but disagreed on the optimum number of delegates. The question could not be resolved at Dumbarton Oaks, where on 14 September the three groups decided to say only that each member "should have a number of representatives to be specified in the Charter," thus deferring the matter to the general United Nations conference in San Francisco, where the number was set at five.[13]

The hopes of all three delegations for a world based on law depended on a revived and more effective world court. The central idea here was the nineteenth-century notion of an ordered world, where nations agreed to submit their differences to an impartial tribunal for resolution in accordance with the principles of international law. Theoretically, at least, such a court could function in the international arena, preventing disputes from deepening and resulting in conflict and war, much as its domestic counterparts did in their national settings. In practice, however, the present court had been beset by serious difficulties of sovereignty and jurisdiction that limited its effectiveness, until by 1944 the Second World War had rendered it as moribund as its parent, the League of Nations. Thus one of the goals of the Dumbarton Oaks Conference was to find a way to reestablish the court on a footing that was firm enough to permit it to dispense justice and contribute to the preservation of peace in the postwar world.

Each of the Big Three's tentative proposals contained provisions for a world court, but only the Americans had gone so far as to produce a draft statute. At one time the State Department had thought of the world court as, to use Bowman's phrase, the "pillar" of international institutions, but had moderated that view as it focused its attention on the question of security. The final American plan suggested few revisions in the court; like the league's tribunal, it would consist of fifteen judges nominated by national groups, would sit at The Hague, and would be competent to decide all issues of law and fact that nations might bring before it. Two major changes were included: the court was to be granted jurisdiction over certain kinds of cases by the charter of the international organization itself, thus making the tribunal more clearly an instrument of the new world body; and amendment of the court's statute was made possible by vote of a two-thirds majority of the United Nations including all the permanent members of the council.[14]

Only one question concerning the court remained unanswered by American planners at the time of the Dumbarton Oaks Conference. This was the matter of ad hoc judges, which the league's court had allowed to sit for nations that were party to a dispute but were not already represented on the tribunal. The continuation of this practice was supported by both equity and expedience because it permitted an ad hoc jurist to defend his country's position while explaining its legal principles to the remainder of the court. On the other side of the issue was efficiency—the court had fifteen regular members and the addition of up to two more made it seem excessively large—and the Americans' dislike for the idea of advocacy on the part of judges who were supposed to be impartial. The last point raised a related difficulty: if ad hoc judges were eliminated, would it not be only fair to disqualify any judge from hearing a case in which his own country was involved? Would the Senate accept this in the case of an American judge? After debating these questions exhaustively in the days before the conference, the American group finally decided that ad hoc judges were a matter of policy that would have to be settled by Roosevelt and Hull. Although Hull was personally opposed to the principle of ad hoc representatives, he thought that political considerations should prevent the United States from protesting against them too vehemently. For one thing, the vast majority of smaller nations, which would not otherwise be represented on the court, supported the practice of appointing special judges; and for another, the United States would be open to the criticism that it could afford to oppose ad hoc judges because it could always count on having at least one of its citizens sitting on the world court anyway. FDR agreed with this reasoning and decided on 24 August that the Americans should speak against ad hoc judges for the record but give way when it became politically necessary to do so.[15]

At Dumbarton Oaks the question of the world court was referred to a special Legal Subcommittee chaired by the State Department's legal adviser, Green Hackworth. The subcommittee met first on 24 August and decided to base its discussions on the American draft statute, which was the only plan it had available. Sir William Malkin, the British legal expert, raised two general questions that he thought needed to be cleared up before going into the problem of the court in more detail: first, whether the present court should be continued or a new court established; and second, what the exact relationship of the world court should be to the new international organization. The first issue was the more technically complex. Retention of the Permanent Court would insure continuity in both jurisprudence and organization, whereas creation of a new tribunal would leave the status and operation of a number of treaties that assigned jurisdiction to the league's court in a kind of legal limbo. On the other side of the matter was a serious difficulty over membership: several parties to the statute of the present court were not members of the United Nations, and a number of United Nations, including the United States, had never adhered to the original statute. If the Permanent Court were continued, neutral states—which were not yet being admitted to the general international organization—would retain membership in the court, and the United States would somehow have to be added to the court's membership.[16]

The Americans found the arguments for continuing the present court to be persuasive. Their draft proposal said that the Permanent Court, "as adapted to the purposes of the general international organization," should be the chief judicial organ of the new world body. The British agreed, apparently for reasons that were as much sentimental as practical. The Soviets, however, favored a new tribunal; they strongly opposed the continuing membership of certain neutral states in the world court—as they did in the new international organization—and feared that continuing the Permanent Court would grant such nations an unimpeachable status. In addition, the Russians thought that whatever problems were raised by creating a new court would turn out to be only theoretical in nature and could, in any event, be resolved by the new tribunal itself. This disagreement, like all disputes over the world court, was not settled at Dumbarton Oaks but carried over to the general United Nations conference at San Francisco, where the delegates decided to create a new court.[17]

There was also disagreement on Malkin's second question concerning the relationship of the court to the new international body. The Americans, it will be recalled, had taken special pains in their draft statute to strengthen the organic relationship between the court and the world organization; they envisioned the two agencies tied together at least as closely as the League of Nations and the Permanent Court had been. The British, however, took the opposite view. Malkin pointed out that his country's legal experts now thought there should be no integral relationship between the two organizations, that the court would function more effectively on its own. This view, he argued, was supported by the experience of the league court—usually a telling argument with the Americans and Russians as well as with the British. In addition, the British position had been supported by the report of the Inter-Allied Committee on Statute Revision, a delegation of representatives from eleven European and commonwealth nations that met in 1943 to suggest changes in the Permanent Court. That body's main reason for favoring separation, ironically enough, was to prevent a recurrence of previous American objections to the world court's connection with the League of Nations. Still, the Briton was far from inflexible on this matter and said that he thought his government would ultimately go along with the American proposal. The Russians had not studied the question and made no comment. A close relationship between the two agencies, along the lines of that proposed by the United States, was eventually established at San Francisco.[18]

Two related questions were discussed at the subcommittee's second meeting on 31 August. The first came up when Hackworth mentioned that the American group favored retaining as much of the existing court statute as possible. This remark was probably a response to Malkin's reference to the report of the Inter-Allied Committee, which unlike the American plan suggested some radical departures from the league court's structure and procedures. The most important of these dealt with the creation of regional chambers—on either a permanent or ad hoc basis—and was an attempt to satisfy earlier American complaints that a unitary court situated in Europe "might not altogether satisfy the needs of the world," by which they meant particularly those of the Western Hemisphere. At the time when the Inter-Allied Committee was meeting, planners in the United States—then in their regionalist phase—had similarly proposed that the court might be divided into separate chambers for Europe, the Middle East and Africa, the Far East, and the Americas; but by the summer of 1944 the Americans had decided in favor of a universal court in a universal organization. There was no real disagreement on this issue. Both Malkin and Soviet group member Sergei Golunsky expressed their approval of the American view.[19]

The second question dealt with membership in the world court. The American draft statute provided for automatic membership for all states that belonged to the United Nations Organization; others could be admitted by the assembly acting on the recommendation of the council. Stanley Hornbeck of the American group thought that this procedure seemed invidious and suggested that the court should have the authority to determine its own membership. The British and Russians—as well as the remainder of the United States group—agreed with the American plan, however, because it would provide another link between the court and the world organization and make it possible to keep out undesirable nations. Ipso facto membership for all states in the world organization and the American formula for admitting new member nations were thus both included in the brief chapter on the world court in the Dumbarton Oaks proposal.[20]

The delegates had more difficulty determining the specific relationship between the court and the all-important Security Council. Ideally, there would be a division of labor between the two agencies, with the court handling legal questions and rendering judicial decrees and the council dealing with political matters and enforcing its own security decisions. But how extensively should each be involved in the activities of the other? Should the court, for example, answer legal queries for the council? Or, alternatively, should the council be empowered, or perhaps required, to enforce the court's decisions? The real influence—and power—of the court in the new organization depended on the answers to these questions.

The first question did not prove too much of a problem. The Joint Formulation Group decided on 1 September that the council should be permitted to refer issues to the court for legal advice, which it would then utilize as it saw fit in arriving at its own decisions. This procedure had been followed by the league and had, in the opinion of all three national groups, facilitated the league council's peacekeeping activities. Also on 1 September the Joint Formulation Group agreed that justiciable disputes should "normally" be referred by the council to the court. The difficulty here was defining "justiciable"; all of the Great Powers had reservations about what kinds of disagreements fell into that category and were certain to oppose the removal of some important issues from the political bailiwick of the Security Council—where they enjoyed a veto—to the much less certain venue of the world court. Thus the council's own ultimate interpretation of what it regarded as a justiciable dispute suitable for court action was the real key to determining the court's power in this direction, and no attempt was made to settle this issue at Dumbarton Oaks.[21]

The second question seemed even more dangerous. By making the council the executor of the court's decisions, as had been attempted under the covenant of the League of Nations, the conferees threatened to replace the political hegemony of the Great Powers with the legal authority of a panel of more or less independent jurists. If made mandatory, such a provision would render the veto meaningless following a court decision—a development that both the United States and the Soviet Union would never be willing to accept. The Foreign Office was also opposed to such a scheme, although Churchill's views were less certain and included what Jebb described as some "fantastic ideas" about the world court dealing with political disputes. In addition, mandatory enforcement of court decisions would give the new organization too much of a supranational aspect, which all three nations wished to avoid for political reasons. Thus, although nothing was included on the question in the Dumbarton Oaks proposals, the three powers would go to San Francisco united in their opposition to a provision of this sort. There the Big Three paid some deference to the views of smaller nations and agreed to a compromise whereby the council could decide, at its own discretion, to enforce a court decision. This outcome preserved the dominance of the council and therefore of the Great Powers, yet lent some authority to the decisions of the court.[22]

The most difficult—and most important—of the general issues was whether the court should have compulsory jurisdiction in handling certain kinds of questions. Without compulsory jurisdiction, the court would be potentially as ineffectual as its League of Nations counterpart, which had been handcuffed by a provision that left jurisdiction at the option of the nations involved in a dispute. Smaller nations, in particular, regarded compulsory court settlement as their best defense against domination by the Great Powers, which naturally stood to win any contest of strength but were theoretically equal before the world court. Yet for all its usefulness compulsory jurisdiction seemed politically impossible, particularly in the United States where the Senate would be certain to object to it at the end of this war as it had at the end of the last. Nor could the Soviets be expected to see much merit in the idea. The statute of the Permanent Court had sought a way around this dilemma by permitting pairs of nations to declare in advance their shared willingness to grant the tribunal authority over certain classes of legal disputes, and American planners—many of whom favored compulsory jurisdiction but thought it unrealistic—included a similar provision in their own draft plan. The question could not be resolved at Dumbarton Oaks. Only the British, who usually expressed the greatest concern for the sensibilities of smaller powers, thought that compulsory jurisdiction might become a fixture of the new world court. The Americans stood by their compromise voluntary proposal—which, of course, released the United States from any threat of compulsion—and the Russians, "motivated by the necessity of defending the interests of the socialist states," as international law professor and Dumbarton Oaks delegate Sergei B. Krylov put it, rejected any sort of compulsory jurisdiction entered voluntarily or otherwise.[23]

The Legal Subcommittee met for the last time on 6 September. By then it was evident that the troubled Dumbarton Oaks Conference would not be able to produce both a set of proposals for a general world organization and a new statute for the world court; indeed, with serious differences developing between the Soviets and the Anglo-Americans, there already existed some doubt as to whether it could do even the first. Subcommittee members thus decided to disband and concentrate their energies elsewhere. This meant that the conference's proposals would contain only five basic statements dealing with the world court: that there should exist a world court as the principal judicial organ of the international organization; that its statute should be part of the charter of the organization; that it should have either a new statute based on that of the Permanent Court or should continue the league court's statute with modifications; that all members of the peacekeeping organization should be automatic members of the court; and that new members should be admitted by the assembly on the advice of the council. The subcommittee suggested that a special meeting of all the United Nations be held two weeks before the start of the general conference on world organization to make recommendations on the other, more controversial questions, and to write a draft statute.[24]

The conversations at Dumbarton Oaks would not produce a world based on universal law. Probably no member of any of the three delegations seriously thought that it would, although some must have hoped to come closer than the conference ultimately did. There were those, at least, who wanted to include what Charles K. Webster has called "aspirations which the authors know cannot be immediately realized, to make, as it were, an appeal to posterity." But such an appeal was unrealistic, not just because the world was far from ready for a utopian international order but also because the governments that were represented at Dumbarton Oaks had no desire to see the creation of anything too visionary. As the politically astute Jebb had written earlier in the summer, "when we get together, it will become clear that something very simple and preliminary is what we shall be able jointly to recommend." Put simply, a world of universal law and sovereign equality posed too many dangers for the Great Powers that would have to create it; they preferred to retain enough of the old, political way of doing things to preserve their own dominance. This was the same combination of forces that had plagued Woodrow Wilson at Versailles, and it seemed likely, in fact, that the new organization would be even more the creature of its leading founders than its predecessor had been—the Great Powers' own national interests and desire for security made anything else impossible. The result was to guarantee the primacy of the Security Council, the true heart of the matter, which as everyone expected became the subject of the longest debate and the most divisive controversy at Dumbarton Oaks.[25]

6 The Security Council

All postwar planners agreed that the League of Nations had failed to prevent World War II because of an inherent weakness—its lack of enforcement power. The league's covenant had given its council only the authority to recommend armed action against an aggressor nation; it contained no provision that bound member states to make whatever military commitment might be necessary to preserve the peace. In practice, this had made the league's council so pusillanimous that it never even proposed military sanctions, much less attempted to enforce them. Thus all planners saw the need for putting teeth into the peacekeeping provisions of the new organization, a realization that was primarily responsible for the great appeal of the Four Policemen idea in the years prior to 1944. By the time of the meeting at Dumbarton Oaks, each of the Big Three had developed proposals for a world body that blended the universality of the league with the certain military power of the Four Policemen. These plans lodged the authority necessary to maintain peace and security in the all-important Security Council, which became, not surprisingly, the center of most discussion—and dissension—at the Dumbarton Oaks Conference.[1]

The first major topic of debate on this subject was membership in the new Security Council. As an outgrowth of Roosevelt's Four Policemen concept, the council would naturally have a core composed of the United States, Great Britain, the Soviet Union, and China—the Great Powers participating in the conference at Dumbarton Oaks that everyone agreed should have a permanent place in the executive body. Beyond this, however, differences abounded. At the head of the list was the question of a permanent seat for France, a nation that the British, in particular, wished to see returned to Great Power status despite its ignominious defeat at the hands of Nazi Germany in the spring of 1940. Before the conference began, the Soviet Union had objected consistently to the inclusion of France among the permanent members on grounds that the French—like the Chinese—had contributed too little to the war effort to prove themselves worthy of so lofty a position in the postwar structure. France would be, in Stalin's view, a "charming but weak" country after the war. This objection was not renewed at Dumbarton Oaks, however, where the Soviets quickly acquiesced to the British proposal that a permanent seat be reserved for the French.[2]

The problem with France was determining when it would take its place on the Security Council. The United States, in particular, wanted to reserve judgment on this question until the nature of the government of postwar France could become known. Hull had decided in preconference meetings to put off the French until they could elect a government that was recognized by the other four Great Powers. In the meantime—Cadogan thought that this process would require at least eighteen months—France was to be granted a provisional council seat without the special privileges of a permanent member. FDR, however, advised the American delegation not to be "too explicit" on the question of creating a permanent seat for France for fear that "difficulty might arise over the word 'recognize'" at a time when the United States was uncertain what to make of Charles de Gaulle's French Committee of National Liberation. Concern over recognition was also probably why the Americans rejected the request of Vice Admiral Raymond Fénard, chief of the French naval mission to the United States, that his nation be represented at the conference and why they were so concerned when the United Press published the canard that France had been invited to attend. Under the circumstances, Roosevelt would agree only to accept "some provision" that would grant France a permanent council seat "when she has a permanent government." As Bowman had warned the British in April, the question of France was one on which the president could not "be influenced by the usual methods of argument." When the matter came up in the Joint Steering Committee on 28 August the Americans agreed to reserve a seat for the French until they had a generally recognized and responsible government. Cadogan, responding to what he saw as invidiousness in the American tone, said that he was not sure it would be wise to have the council decide when France had achieved a responsible government; perhaps, he argued, the Big Three might want to determine this question for themselves at Dumbarton Oaks. Either way, he pointed out, he was certain that his government's intention was to bring the French into the council as quickly as possible. This caused Stettinius to fear that Cadogan might ask to admit France immediately—a proposal that Roosevelt had rejected out of hand. In the absence of agreement on this issue, the Dumbarton Oaks proposals simply stated that France would be granted a permanent seat "in due course."[3]

The United States also hoped to make room on the Security Council for Brazil, the only Latin American nation with troops actually fighting in the Second World War. In meetings of the American group before the Dumbarton Oaks Conference opened, Hull decided to request a permanent seat for Brazil based on its size, resources, and active participation in the war against Germany, all of which made it seem possible that the Brazilians could one day achieve Great Power status. This decision reflected Hull's awareness of Latin American dissatisfaction with its inconsequential role in the proposed world organization—although, as the State Department's Latin American specialists pointed out, promoting Brazil to a council post would only be likely to antagonize its neighbors ever further. Still, no other nation in the region could possibly qualify for the spot, and Washington was in the position of being damned if it did and damned if it didn't find a place for Brazil. Hull may also have feared that Brazil itself would refuse to join the new organization if it did not receive a permanent council seat; it had, after all, resigned from the League of Nations in 1926 after being denied just such a position.[4]

Roosevelt agreed with Hull's analysis. He met with Stettinius on 24 August and helped the under secretary map out plans for winning a permanent seat for Brazil. Because he expected objections from the Russians and British, the president advised the American group to approach the matter obliquely—that is, that they should only raise the question of an additional permanent seat in general terms before making informal reference to Brazil in the ensuing discussion. FDR also thought that it would be unwise to press the matter too hard. He would not insist on the inclusion of the Brazilians at this time, but he clearly hoped to provide a place for them eventually on the council.[5]

Roosevelt was right to expect objections from the other two participants. When the topic of council membership came up in the Joint Steering Committee on 28 August, Stettinius cautiously voiced the American position on Brazil. The United States, he said, might want to consider adding a sixth permanent seat for one of the Latin American countries—just as it had previously come to accept the British idea of a fifth seat for France. Gromyko, sensing trouble, asked whether the United States had a particular Latin American nation in mind and, if so, which one. When Pasvolsky replied Brazil, Sobolev inquired as to when the Americans thought it should be added. This was going too far too fast for Stettinius, who remarked that the United States was not making an actual proposal for the inclusion of Brazil and could not, therefore, suggest any particular time for the creation of a sixth seat on the council. Gromyko refused to be put off, however, and wondered whether the Americans contemplated making a reference to a council seat for Brazil in the Dumbarton Oaks proposals. Stettinius responded that it would not be necessary to go that far, that it would be sufficient to state that a place should be reserved for France and another for one of the Latin American countries. If the under secretary thought that he had maneuvered the Russian ambassador into a corner, however, he was soon disappointed. Gromyko closed the discussion by saying that his group wanted the others to understand that it definitely opposed any expansion of the number of permanent council seats beyond the four Great Powers and France. The British, too, were cool to the idea of creating a sixth place on the council, which they thought would "stir up a hornets' nest." Still, they let the Soviets do most of the objecting—perhaps because they sensed (as they were supposed to) that the Americans might link together the similar issues of council seats for France and Brazil.[6]

Despite this setback, Roosevelt still hoped to bring Brazil into the Security Council. When Stettinius reported that both the British and Soviets had reacted negatively to the idea of a sixth seat, the president suggested a different approach. Specific mention of a permanent seat for Brazil could be omitted from the Dumbarton Oaks proposals, he said, if the other Great Powers would agree to a general provision for expanding the size of the council later. Thus Roosevelt hoped to leave the door open for a Big Three conference where he thought he might be able to persuade Churchill and Stalin to admit Brazil to the charmed circle before the new organization could be launched.[7]

Most of the American delegation did not share Roosevelt's optimism, however. They responded to British and Soviet objections by proposing to drop all suggestion of a council seat for Brazil. In the group's regular morning meeting on 31 August, Pasvolsky pointed out that a sixth permanent seat would mean adding another elected member to the council if the group wished to avoid violating the principle of more elected than permanent seats. The result would be a council of thirteen—an "unlucky" number that Roosevelt would never accept. Pasvolsky's statement prompted Bowman, who said he was speaking for several members of the American delegation, to list a number of reasons why a permanent seat for Brazil would be as intrinsically undesirable as it was procedurally awkward. For one thing, he said, Brazil's presence on the council was primarily justified by the idea of regional representation for Latin America, which might reopen the question of regionalism in general and encourage the other Great Powers to make counterdemands for the inclusion of lesser states—Czechoslovakia, for example—from other areas of the world. For another thing, Brazil not only fell far short of any definition of a Great Power, but its future unity, form of government, and military potential remained uncertain as well. And third, the inclusion of Portuguese-speaking Brazil would fail to placate other Latin American nations, which would probably ask that permanent representation also be granted to the much larger Spanish-speaking population. At worst, the situation could result in demands for a seat for Argentina, whose pro-Nazi sympathies had led to strained relations with the

United States. Perhaps, Bowman argued, it would be better to reach an understanding that a Latin American state would always occupy one of the elected
seats on the council.[8]

John Moors Cabot, the American group's Latin American adviser, echoed
Bowman's sentiments. He had discussed the matter with Norman Armour,
acting director of American Republic Affairs at the State Department, he said,
and learned that Armour too was strongly opposed to a permanent seat for
Brazil. After Stettinius promised to pass these views along to Roosevelt and
Hull, Breckinridge Long proposed that the United States continue to sponsor
Brazil for the council—but only for the purpose of bargaining with the British
to withdraw their sponsorship of France. Long still favored a council composed
of the Rooseveltian Four Policemen and thought it would be enough for France
to be permitted to stand for election to successive terms. This approach seemed
inadvisable to others, however, because as Pasvolsky reported, Gromyko believed that the size of the council was set with five permanent and six elected
members, and there was no point in reopening that issue now. As the meeting
closed, the group was virtually unified in opposition to continued support of a
permanent seat for Brazil.[9]

To convince the president, Dunn and Pasvolsky gave Stettinius a memorandum setting forth their reasons for withdrawing the American sponsorship of
Brazil. In light of the Soviet objection, they wrote, the American group had
reconsidered the matter and was now unanimously opposed to granting Brazil
a permanent seat. Their arguments included those presented at the group
meeting, as well as the probability that the United States would be held
accountable for Brazil's performance as a permanent member of the council
and the likelihood that including a nation of Brazil's dubious military capabilities would undermine the chief justification for assigning permanent membership (and special privileges) to nations with primary peacekeeping responsibilities. In short, they thought that a place for Brazil on the council would
prove more of a liability than an asset for both the United States and the new
world organization.[10]

Roosevelt was less than convinced by these arguments. The American
group's criticisms of Brazil might, after all, be just as easily applied to China
and France, neither of which was a Great Power in 1944 or was certain to
become one in the future. A study by the Joint Chiefs of Staff indicated that
China could not become a Great Power in the foreseeable future and ranked
France below Great Britain in future war-making potential, except in a land war
on the European continent. The Joint Chiefs did not bother to analyze Brazil.
Similarly, all the other arguments against expanding the number of permanent

seats on the council to six might also have been made against expanding it to four or five. It was all a question of where one chose to draw the line, and Roosevelt thought he had good reasons for wanting to draw it later rather than sooner. One such reason was probably to facilitate the expansion of American influence in the world. As historian Gabriel Kolko has observed, the addition of Brazil would put another American client on the Security Council; certainly this was one reason why the British and Soviets opposed it so strongly. Conversely, the possibility of a seat for Brazil could be held as an American bargaining chip to prevent the other powers from sponsoring additions of their own, as the British had done in the case of France. A second reason was that Roosevelt, unlike most of the American group at Dumbarton Oaks, continued to believe in a kind of watered-down regionalism as the best approach to peacekeeping. This was the logic behind the president's sponsorship of China, and it seemed equally valid for Brazil and perhaps for other leading states in the various regions of the world. And third, Roosevelt may have thought that a larger number of permanent council members would enhance international support for the new world organization, a consideration that he ranked above any hairsplitting concern over which nations were and were not worthy of Great Power status.[11]

With some effort, Stettinius finally persuaded Roosevelt to agree that the American group should withdraw its request of a permanent seat for Brazil. But this did not mean that the president had given up on the idea of expanding the council. He remarked to the under secretary that Brazil was still "a card up his sleeve," and that he would also consider proposing a permanent seat for a Moslem state in the future. Stettinius informed Gromyko and Cadogan of Roosevelt's decision on 3 September, indicating that it had been made in deference to their objections. Following FDR's lead, the American group leader also attempted to use the Brazilian seat as a bargaining chip. He commented, in what he described as "a somewhat jocular aside," that he hoped the voluntary American withdrawal from this position would serve as an example for the others to follow. This remark fell on deaf ears, however, as Stettinius soon learned. To the American's next suggestion—that the Dumbarton Oaks proposals contain a general provision authorizing additional permanent seats—Cadogan replied that he regretted being the first to depart from Stettinius's example but that he hoped no such provision would be necessary. If expansion proved desirable later, he said, the number of seats could be changed through the process of amendment. Gromyko seconded Cadogan's position, and no mention of a sixth seat appeared anywhere in the proposals.[12]

Closely related to the question of permanent membership was the number of elected seats on the council. As the British pointed out in their preconference proposals, any decision on the membership of the council had to be governed by the two contradictory principles of size and efficiency. Thus, although the smaller the council the better for reasons of efficiency, it was necessary to elect enough nonpermanent members to guarantee support for the organization among the second and third rank of nations, including the dominions. The problem expressed by the British was also apparent in the changing views of President Roosevelt, who had begun by emphasizing the first principle—hence the Four Policemen—but ended by adopting the second and favoring a council that was larger than anyone else thought feasible. American planners had discussed the question with the president in a long meeting at the White House on 15 June. Roosevelt thought that there should be enough smaller powers on the council for their role to be described as "ample," but Stettinius objected, proposing the word "suitable" as more in line with the State Department's intentions. At that time, before the final preparations were made for Dumbarton Oaks, the United States had favored seven elected representatives to join the four Great Powers on the council, but American planners subsequently had lowered this number to six when the acceptance of France raised the number of permanent members to five. The British and Soviets agreed with this reasoning, only to have it all called back into question by the American position regarding Brazil. In the Joint Steering Committee on 28 August, the Americans proposed a council of six permanent and six elected members or, if an odd number seemed preferable, six and five. Pasvolsky favored six and seven in order to maintain a majority of nonpermanent seats, but there was general agreement that a council of thirteen was too large (and too subject to superstition) to be efficient. This difficulty was resolved, of course, when the United States dropped its sponsorship of Brazil six days later.[13]

Another factor favoring six nonpermanent council members was the length of their term of service. Each of the three powers came to Dumbarton Oaks with a different idea on this question: the British wanted three-year terms to give the council continuity and the elected members a chance to gain experience, the Soviets favored two years, and the Americans only one. By 28 August, however, the groups had agreed to a compromise that included two-year terms with rotating retirement. It was this last provision, which was included to insure continuity and experience, that supported setting the number of elected positions at six because, as Pasvolsky pointed out in the Joint Steering Committee, an even number would make it possible to elect half each year. Cadogan agreed with this reasoning, and the number of nonpermanent members was set at six, each elected for a term of two years, with half retiring annually. To create staggered terms, three of the initial six electees were to be chosen for two years and the remaining three for one.[14]

How often the council should meet also proved to be a difficult question. The American group thought that the council should remain more or less in continuous session; this would ensure the kind of immediate response to disputes that Roosevelt had envisioned in the original Four Policemen idea. Continuous sessions seemed essential for the organization's success to some of the Americans; indeed, Pasvolsky defended the idea so tenaciously that Webster thought he must have invented it. Although the British did not oppose this procedure in principle, they feared that the need for permanent representatives would result in officials of second-rate capacity and authority dealing with the kind of important issues that ought to be reserved for discussion by responsible cabinet ministers. The Soviets, who apparently had not considered this question before coming to Dumbarton Oaks, proposed a compromise: in addition to regular sessions, there might be periodic meetings of the council at which member states could be represented by "a responsible member of the government or other plenipotentiary representative." The Americans saw two problems with this suggestion. They feared that the national leaders attending these special sessions would overshadow the regular delegates, thus diminishing the authority of the council when it sat in regular meetings; at worst, this could result in a situation in which all important questions required the presence of outside officials and ordinary council members were reduced to the status of caretakers. In addition, the Americans were concerned that any application of the term "plenipotentiary" to the council would cause difficulties with Congress. The result, after considerable debate and redrafting, was a compromise that included a council organized to function continuously, occasional meetings at which council members could be represented by cabinet officers, and the replacement of the term "plenipotentiary" with the words "some other special representative."[15]

The role to be played by the Security Council was also the subject of intense debate at Dumbarton Oaks. All three powers were in basic accord on the council's important place as a peacekeeper when nations resorted to war—although, as we shall see, they had different ideas on how that vital task might best be accomplished. But they also understood that for the new world organization to be successful the responsibilities of the council could not be limited to peacekeeping after the outbreak of hostilities. Because they viewed peace and security as indivisible in the modern world, they thought that some way had to be found to prevent disagreements from escalating and resulting in war. Thus, provisions empowering the council to engage in the peaceful settlement of political and diplomatic disputes were included in each nation's preconference proposal, and they became a major topic of discussion at Dumbarton Oaks.

The main issue was how much authority the council should have for settling peaceful disputes. The Soviets, expressing concern that such disputes had frequently led to war in the past, thought that the council should be empowered to take "all necessary measures" to settle disputes and conflicts before they reached the stage of violence and threatened the peace and security of the world. The British, however, disagreed with any use of compulsion where peaceful disagreements were concerned. They feared that the organization's members would be unwilling to bind themselves in advance to accept the council's decisions under threat of enforcement or to enforce such decisions against other nations who might refuse to be bound, thus undermining from the beginning the authority of the new world body. In dealing with peaceful disputes, the British argued, the council should be limited to making recommendations and advancing them through persuasion. Otherwise the council would become a judicial body employing the kind of power best reserved for domestic courts. The American position was less clear-cut. In April, the State Department had favored a provision permitting the council to "take necessary measures to insure compliance with the terms of any settlement determined under the authority of the international organization"; but by July, when the United States' tentative proposals for Dumbarton Oaks were completed, the Americans wanted the council to have authority only to "encourage and facilitate" the execution of any peaceful settlement it might propose.[16]

The American group continued to be divided on this issue during its preconference meetings in mid-August. Those who favored granting the council the authority to impose pacific settlements argued that the organization would be seriously weakened by a failure to do so. Such a decision, they contended, would leave the world body unable to act in any positive way until a crisis reached the flash point where the peace was actually broken and world security threatened. Those who supported the British view, however, argued that the organization should not be the first to break the peace—even if it did so in the name of security. As long as a dispute had not yet resulted in violence, they reasoned, there remained a chance that it might be settled peacefully through persuasion and not require the use of force at all. Like the British, this group wanted to emphasize the council's police function—to keep the peace—over its judicial function—to make a settlement—and feared that consolidating the two would turn the organization into something too close to an international superstate. As a compromise position, it was also suggested that the council might be granted authority for compulsory settlement only in serious cases of the sort that clearly threatened world peace.[17]

In a meeting of the American group on 17 August, Pasvolsky proposed another reason for favoring the British view: it might offer a solution to the difficult problem of whether or not a Great Power should be permitted to vote when the council was deliberating a dispute in which it was involved. This question, which would almost wreck the Dumbarton Oaks Conference when relations with the Soviets grew strained, had the American delegation split at this time. As a compromise, Pasvolsky thought that if settlements of peaceful disputes were made nonbinding, the Great Powers might willingly surrender their right to vote on such cases while retaining their veto (perhaps in a modified form) where enforcement action was concerned. Whether Hull accepted this logic or not—and the evidence that he did is not conclusive—he decided two days later to support the British position of limiting the council's power for settling pacific disputes to one of persuasion.[18]

Roosevelt agreed with this decision—despite the fact that it represented a considerable dilution of his original Four Policemen idea. In a meeting with Stettinius and other key members of the American group on 24 August, the president approved a statement denying the council the right to "impose" the terms of a settlement concerning a peaceful dispute; instead, he would limit the council's role to promoting a peaceful settlement, making recommendations to the parties involved, and issuing authoritative judgments only at the request of the disputing parties themselves. Thus the conference opened with the United States shifting from the Soviet to the British view on the best method for settling peaceful disputes.[19]

Cadogan explained the British position in a plenary session held at Dumbarton Oaks on 22 August. The British chairman stressed the need for establishing a flexible organization—one that could promote peaceful change without imposing terms of settlement over every international dispute that might arise. The experience of the League of Nations had pointed out how difficult this combination could be to achieve. Under the league, Cadogan said, members had promised not to settle their disputes by force but had not promised always to settle their disputes; the result was to put the organization in the posture of habitually defending the status quo. The British viewed this as the result of placing too much emphasis on the machinery of peacekeeping and not enough on the spirit of international cooperation. They thought that for the organization to succeed all disputes must be settled—even if settlement meant only the recognition of a legitimate grievance for which no satisfactory remedy could be found. On balance, it seemed to them a good thing that the requirement to settle disputes should favor change; they thought that the status quo would be sufficiently safeguarded, as it had been under the League of Nations, by the very existence of a universal system of security.[20]

The settlement of disputes promised to be even more difficult when Great Powers were involved. The British could do no better here than to hope that the big nations' "habit of cooperative leadership" during the world war and the restraints imposed by their promises to one another might prove sufficient for them to arrive at a peaceful settlement; certainly the machinery of the organization would not be strong enough to force them to do so. In addition, the Great Powers must, Cadogan thought, take the lead in promoting the principle of peaceful change, which as the league experience demonstrated could not be mandated by a clause in a charter or covenant but only obtained through continual discussion and compromise. Thus, only if the great nations showed a willingness to be guided by principle and to work through established procedures could the cooperation of the smaller states be guaranteed. Ultimately, the success of the new world body would depend on whether enough states of all sizes came to regard the continuation of the organization as more important than the protection of all of their own interests so that they were prepared to run risks and make sacrifices to support and preserve it.[21]

The British and Americans presented a united front when the issue was discussed in the organization subcommittee. They agreed that although the council should be empowered to consider means for the settlement of peaceful disputes, it should not have the authority to impose a settlement unless an actual breach of peace was involved. Surprisingly, the Soviets did not object and even "seemed to agree," according to Stettinius. Two factors might explain this apparent reversal of the USSR's preconference position. First, the Soviets were probably not as certain about this issue as their earlier proposal had made them seem. What they wanted was a strong council—one that could act forcefully to prevent wars as well as to end them. This might be achieved through a clear statement of the security body's right to intervene in all disputes, even those of a peaceful nature, but only at the risk of involving the council in so many minor disagreements that its energy and power would inevitably be dissipated. Thus the Soviets' desire to enhance the power of the council by streamlining its authority, which made granting the power to intervene even in peaceful disputes appear advisable, might also have made such a course seem impractical.[22]

Second, the Soviets had to reassess their position on peaceful disputes in light of the disagreement over voting in the council. This deepening controversy called into question their right to veto peacekeeping action for disputes in which they were involved—a right that they had never doubted before coming to Dumbarton Oaks. Under such circumstances, it is not surprising that the Russians lost some of their certainty that a strong council was automatically a good thing; they now had to worry that the power thus created might be used against them, especially considering the growing dispute over postwar control of Eastern Europe. By 24 August, when the Soviets yielded on the question of peaceful enforcement in the organization subcommittee, the larger voting issue had by no means been settled, but it seems reasonable that the Russians may have viewed weakening the council as a prudent safeguard following the Anglo-American challenge to their absolute veto.[23]

Whatever his motives, Gromyko's acceptance of the British position eliminated a potentially serious source of controversy among the Big Three. By 1 September the Joint Formulation Group had drafted a section on peaceful disputes and sent it to the Joint Steering Committee for approval. There the matter found relatively smooth sailing—despite the inevitable debate over changes in wording and emphasis. The committee's most important addition was designed to enhance the status of the Security Council; it placed at the beginning of the section a paragraph empowering the council "to investigate any dispute," or any situation that might lead to a dispute, that was likely to endanger international peace and security. This statement established the right of the executive body to be a sort of world watchdog and emphasized its preeminent position within the new international structure. As such, it was a reflection of the original Four Policemen concept and of the Soviet view of the new peacekeeping apparatus.[24]

Other changes were made at the urging of the Americans—although not as a result of the usual decision-making process within the American group. They were proposed by Governor Thomas E. Dewey of New York, Roosevelt's Republican opponent in the upcoming election campaign of 1944. Before the Dumbarton Oaks Conference began in August, Hull had contacted the Republican nominee in hopes of generating bipartisan—or, as the secretary of state preferred to put it, nonpartisan—support for the proposed peacekeeping organization. Dewey, who wanted to make it clear that despite his criticism of the "coercive power" contained in the new organization he had no connection with the isolationist wing of his party, accepted Hull's offer of a briefing and designated John Foster Dulles, the international lawyer who served as his adviser on foreign affairs, to meet with the secretary. Their conversations began in Hull's office on 23 August, just as the delegates were beginning their own deliberations a few miles away in Georgetown, and continued over the following two days. The present and future secretaries of state (Dulles would become the first

Republican secretary in twenty years when he joined the Eisenhower administration in 1953), so different in manner and philosophy, sparred warily over
virtually every aspect of American foreign policy. They also had very different
political goals for the meetings: Hull wanted Republican support for Democratic policies, whereas the Republican Dulles hoped to win a share of the
credit for developing a new world organization while retaining his freedom to
criticize it. Their joint statement of 25 August reflected these differences but
managed, despite a stiff and formal tone that resembled—fittingly enough—
diplomatic communiqués issued by rival governments, to convey their basic
agreement on the need for a postwar peacekeeping organization.[25]

Although basically satisfied with this result, Dewey had a few problems with
the details of the State Department's plan for the United Nations. On 8 September, while the Joint Steering Committee was completing its deliberations on the
peaceful settlement of disputes, he sent Hull a memorandum suggesting several changes in the proposed charter. Three of these dealt directly with the
matter at hand. First, the Republican presidential nominee proposed that all
states, not just members of the organization, should have the right to bring
questions before the Security Council. This would broaden the council's moral
authority and avoid the impression that the new organization intended to use
its power in support of its members and against states that did not belong—
that the United Nations would be simply an alliance of the strong to police the
weak, a criticism that Dewey had previously made of the idea of the Four
Policemen. Second, Dewey recommended that the council be empowered to
investigate matters that might lead in the future to friction between states. And
third, he suggested that the paragraph on subjects suited for the council's
attention should specifically include a reference to treaties, which he hoped to
see enhanced in the postwar era as the building blocks of international law and
behavior.[26]

Hull regarded these changes as unnecessary—especially the specific reference to treaties, which he thought the draft charter already "took ample care
of" by granting the council the power to consider any situation likely to
endanger international security. Still, because he wanted Dewey's support and
saw no reason to risk losing it by rejecting what he regarded as insignificant if
meddlesome requests, the secretary sent the Republican candidate's suggestions to Stettinius with the recommendation that they be included in the
Dumbarton Oaks proposals. By this time the section on peaceful disputes was
already formulated, but the American group agreed to add the first two items if
the British and Russians did not object. They did not, and Dewey's suggestions
were simply incorporated into the proposals by the Joint Steering Committee.

The third proposal proved to be more of a problem, however. The American group shared Hull's view that a reference to treaties would require the listing of all such matters open to the council's consideration or risk a later interpretation excluding anything not specifically enumerated. When private talks indicated that the British shared this reservation, the Americans decided not to bring Dewey's third suggestion before the conference.[27]

The British also requested a couple of last-minute changes. One concerned justiciable disputes—those hinging on a point of law instead of national interest or policy—which the British group thought should be differentiated from those subject to consideration by the council and referred directly to the new international court instead. The Soviets and Americans approved this idea, along with a provision that the council be empowered to ask the court for advice on legal questions that arise during its deliberations over generally nonjusticiable disagreements. The second British proposal turned out to be more controversial. It involved excluding all domestic questions from the council's procedures for settling peaceful disputes, an idea that the British proposed on 14 September in response to the conference's approval of an American-sponsored statement affirming the world organization's support for human rights. In the British view, which was motivated by concern for the sanctity of the empire, any reference to human rights opened the door for the council to meddle in strictly domestic matters—matters that they thought should be left under the jurisdiction of the states themselves. To prevent such interference, Cadogan suggested that the conferees add a paragraph to the section on pacific disputes eliminating from the council's consideration all "situations or disputes" that arose out of "matters which by international law are solely within the jurisdiction of the state concerned." The Americans, whose original proposal on human rights had included just such a disclaimer, quickly agreed. Not so the Soviets, however. Gromyko thought that the council should not be limited in this way—that it should be free to consider any question it regarded as presenting a threat to the peace. He also probably saw no reason to protect British imperial interests. The Russian objection caused the provision to be removed from the Joint Steering Committee's working draft on 20 September, although Gromyko promised to wire Moscow for further instructions on the matter. When these instructions arrived a week later, after the usual delay, they reflected the Kremlin's desire to compromise on nonessential questions and perhaps to avoid future troubles of their own. Gromyko thus expressed approval of the British proviso, which was added once again to the Dumbarton Oaks proposals.[28]

In the end, the conference established a procedure for settling peaceful disputes that was very similar to the initial British position. It began with the idea that the parties to a dispute should obligate themselves to seek a solution of their own through negotiations, mediation, or arbitration—or any other peaceful means that they might choose. At this stage of a disagreement the role of the Security Council would be only to call upon the nations involved to seek a peaceful settlement, not to make any suggestions of its own. This was in keeping with the British view that the structure of peace should not be imposed by the council but should evolve from the negotiations of states with conflicting interests. Such a procedure could not, of course, always be expected to work. Sometimes nations would fail to resolve their differences, leading to the possibility of armed conflicts. Then, according to the conferees, the disputing parties should obligate themselves to refer the matter to the Security Council for consideration. This decision raised the practical question of who ought to decide whether a dispute was in fact likely to endanger the peace and should therefore be taken up by the council; the answer, provided by the Soviets, was the council itself.[29]

If the council decided to take action, what could it do? From early in the conference it had been agreed that the British view—no force—would prevail in the handling of peaceful disputes. This left two possibilities: the council could suggest a method for resolving a conflict that had been referred to it, or it could propose the actual terms for what it regarded as a reasonable settlement. Once again the British argued for the weaker option of suggesting only a method. Cadogan's concern, as usual, was for the sensibilities of the weaker powers, especially in Europe, without whose support he feared the new organization would fail. If the council could impose—or even suggest—the terms of a settlement, he said, smaller states would fear that the Great Powers intended to use it to force settlements upon their weaker neighbors—as they had done at Munich in 1938. Cadogan's reference to Munich, which already stood as a symbol of the failure of strong nations to live up to their responsibilities to the weak, proved decisive, and the three groups decided to grant the council only the authority to "recommend appropriate procedures or methods of adjustment." In dealing with peaceful disputes, at least, the new Security Council would not be the kind of powerful body that some postwar planners had hoped for.[30]

It would be different where an actual breach of the peace was concerned, however. Here all three nations agreed that the council must have real power—that it should be authorized to take "any measures necessary," including the use of force, to restore international peace and security. This was the potent role of the Security Council as Roosevelt had envisioned it in his original Four Policemen plan; its continued appeal down to 1944 was apparent in its inclusion in each of the preconference proposals drawn up by the participants at Dumbarton Oaks. The Soviets were most attached to the idea of creating the strongest possible council. As they saw it, the new United Nations would stand or fall on its ability to generate unified action to halt future aggression; failure in this regard had been responsible for the downfall of the League of Nations. The British and Americans essentially agreed, and there would be no serious discussion at Dumbarton Oaks about diminishing in any way the power of the council to act forcefully once the peace had been broken.[31]

An immediate problem arose, however, over the Russians' use of the term "aggression" to define the reason for action by the council. The Soviets thought that the "suppression of aggression" should be the main object of the security body; they could not, in fact, imagine how peacekeeping would work except through the chastisement of aggressor nations. It made no sense, in their view, to punish both sides for breaking the peace; surely effective sanctions should be employed only against the aggressor, not against its intended victims as well. And certainly, Gromyko thought, any state had a right to defend itself before the council could act on its behalf. This approach was in keeping with the Russian view of the future United Nations as an organization that would maintain peace primarily through the use of its power—especially as embodied in an international air force capable of bombing the cities of nations that did not obey its rules. It also reflected their perception of the Security Council as a continuation of the Grand Alliance, punishing aggressors in the postwar world as it had Nazi Germany during World War II. Thus Gromyko made the suppression of aggression in the manner of the Rooseveltian Four Policemen the main task of the council in his initial presentation of the Soviet Union's views on 22 August.[32]

Cadogan was quick to disagree. He argued that "aggression" was too difficult to define and thereby be of any use in determining action by the Security Council. All past attempts at such definition had failed, he contended, including those developed by the League of Nations. In fact, in the British view, reliance on the concept of aggression in Article X of the covenant had accounted for many of the league's most significant failures. Too much time had been wasted arguing whether a conflict represented aggression by one nation or another, they thought, even when it was obvious which side had initiated the hostilities; the result, on several key occasions, was that the league had failed to act quickly enough to prevent the bloodshed from spreading or the aggressor from gaining an advantage. Cadogan thought that this problem could only be avoided by omitting any mention of the offending term from the

United Nations charter and replacing it with something broader and more useful, such as "breach of the peace."[33]

The Americans sided with Cadogan. They thought that the phrase "act of aggression" was too value laden to be applied easily by the Security Council; besides, they considered its meaning to be included within the scope of Cadogan's more general—and less loaded—phrase, "breach of the peace," which they preferred to use. The Soviets refused to relent on this point, however. As was so often the case, their motives were not made clear. Perhaps they thought that a reference to preventing aggression would add legitimacy to the new world organization; smaller nations, in particular, might be more willing to accept the authority of a coercive organization that protected them from the threat of aggression than they would of one that only policed "breaches of the peace." Or perhaps the Soviets hoped to use the inevitable confusion about determining aggression for their own purposes, to protect themselves against the threat of action by the Security Council in their own Eastern European sphere of influence. In any event, they argued that the term "aggression" had gained such wide currency in recent years that the power of the council to deal with it should be stated specifically in the charter. Although they still disagreed, the British and Americans gave in to a compromise on this issue, and the final document authorized the council to take action against either a "breach of the peace" or an "act of aggression."[34]

This raised the question of attempting to define aggression, at least in so far as action by the council was concerned. The British were particularly insistent in opposing this idea. As they saw it, any definition would be likely to limit the breadth of the council's powers, especially in light of the rapid changes in the technological nature of warfare in the twentieth century. Who could say what new forms of aggression might be invented in the future? It would be wiser, they argued, to grant the council full discretion to decide whether or not any particular action ought to be designated as aggression and should fall under its authority for action. The Soviets and Americans readily agreed, and no attempt to define aggression was included in the Dumbarton Oaks proposals.[35]

The conference turned next to implementation—to what the council should be empowered to do once it had decided that action was necessary. All three nations agreed that force should be the last resort, to be employed only after other less dangerous measures for restoring order had been tried and had failed. They disagreed, however, over whether the Dumbarton Oaks proposals should include a list of the council's nonmilitary sanctions. The battle lines were familiar: the Soviets wanted to be as specific as possible, the British favored only a general statement, and the Americans were somewhere in between. In their preconference proposal, the Russians had produced a list of methods for combating aggression that began with an appeal or warning by the council. If ignored, this plea could be followed by "measures of economic pressure"; severance of diplomatic relations; termination of commercial, financial, and economic contact; interruption of postal-telegraphic, rail, or air connections; naval and land blockades; and naval and air force demonstrations. As usual in matters of this sort, the British view was diametrically opposed to the Russian view; their reasons had been stated best by Sir John Simon a decade before when he told the House of Commons that it was not "an Anglo-Saxon habit to make defined engagements out of undefined circumstances." The American plan contained a list that was much briefer and more general than the Russians', requiring members of the organization to take part in "concerted diplomatic" and "collective economic, commercial, and financial measures" against a state found guilty of breaking the peace.[36]

When the topic came up in the Joint Steering Committee on 4 September—Labor Day—the debate was almost predictable. Gromyko pushed for his country's idea of enumerating the actions that the council might be authorized and expected to take; otherwise, he argued, there was too much danger that the new organization would follow the league's example and do too little or nothing at all. Cadogan viewed the problem from the reverse angle and contended that listing the council's powers might have a limiting effect and weaken the enforcement action of the new United Nations. Pasvolsky supported the English position. There was, in his opinion, no reason to enumerate nonmilitary sanctions, which he thought could be covered adequately by the inclusion of a phrase such as "other measures not involving the use of armed force" in the final proposal. Gromyko refused to bend, however, and the committee instructed the Joint Formulation Group to draw up a list of possible measures of nonmilitary enforcement—just in case it should turn out to be needed. Three days later the Americans returned to their original position, agreeing to the idea of a list but insisting that it be general rather than specific. In the end, the Dumbarton Oaks proposals included most of the items enumerated in the Russian plan; only the phrase "measures of economic pressure" was deleted because it seemed, ironically enough, too imprecise to the British and Americans.[37]

Even as they approved the list of peaceful sanctions, however, representatives of the Big Three recognized that such actions would never, by themselves, be enough to prevent future wars. Only the threat—and, almost certainly, the use—of force could deter a nation that was bent on finding a military solution to its problems with other states; surely that, if anything, was the lesson of the failure of the League of Nations. A realization of this fact had prompted all three nations to make provision for the council's use of force in their preconference summaries, and from the beginning of the meetings at Dumbarton Oaks the participants were certain that military sanctions would be included among the powers of the Security Council. If the principle was simple, however, the details were bewilderingly complex. How should a United Nations force be constituted? How should it be led? What kinds of military power should it employ? And how much authority should it have to use the resources or the territory of less powerful states? All of these questions would raise difficult issues that would have to be dealt with at Dumbarton Oaks.

The composition of an international force was widely recognized as one of the keys to the success of a postwar peacekeeping organization. Because the new United Nations would need to employ military power both swiftly and effectively, planners in the governments of each of the Great Powers began their deliberations by favoring the creation of a true international police force. The Soviets thought that the failure to provide such a force was a major reason for the downfall of the League of Nations—a view shared by many analysts in Great Britain and the United States as well. State Department planners regarded a standing force as superior to one organized on an ad hoc basis for several reasons: its troops would always be available, they could be employed speedily, and they might form a homogeneous force that would fight with more esprit than would national contingents brought together at the last minute. In addition, the formation of a true international police force might make it possible for nations—perhaps even the Great Powers—to disarm and remain secure. Among British leaders, Eden seems to have envisioned a permanent international force growing naturally out of the Grand Alliance at the end of the war; policing the world of the future would, in his view, be a logical consequence of the victory over Germany and Japan.[38]

As the conference neared, however, all three nations drew away from this somewhat visionary position. American planners had foreseen the reasons for this as far back as 1942; by 1944 their arguments seemed decisive to each of the governments involved. For one thing, an ad hoc force made up of national contingents would be slightly easier to control than a true international army, minimizing the danger that the police force might itself become a threat to world security. Similarly, the absence of an ongoing force with its own command apparatus would help to alleviate the fears of those concerned that the United Nations was designed to be a superstate. Most important, an ad hoc force would be more acceptable to governments in what State Department planners called "the present state of the world." This referred to the fact that nations were not prepared to surrender their identities any more than they were their sovereignty; even the Great Powers, which would surely dominate any international army, wanted to keep their own forces under their own control except in an emergency situation. The Soviet Union's new position was revealed in July 1944 in an article in *Zvezda*, attributed to "N. Malinin" but probably written by Assistant Foreign Minister Maxim Litvinov, that referred to an international police force as "impractical."[39]

The same word was then being used by the State Department—and for the same reasons. Some were explained by Alger Hiss in a radio broadcast after the close of the Dumbarton Oaks Conference. Hiss argued that "under modern conditions" an effective military force required a "national basis in terms of munitions, equipment, training, discipline, tactics, and everything else." The Dumbarton Oaks participant also pointed to the problem of determining how to distribute an ongoing force. If widely distributed, the police force would have difficulty maintaining its effectiveness and its morale, and would also suffer from a lack of coordinated training. If, on the other hand, such a force were concentrated in one place, it would not be promptly available where it might be needed—which was, after all, the primary argument in favor of a unified force in the first place. Troublesome as they were, such difficulties might have been overcome had the Big Three been determined to do so; distribution, for example, was not a problem for an ad hoc force only because the national contingents were by definition dispersed and unavailable for rapid deployment. What could not be overcome, however, was the problem of national sovereignty, which was reasserting itself everywhere as the war moved toward its conclusion. The Great Powers might be willing to contribute their military forces to police the postwar world, but they wanted to keep control of them in their own hands both before and after their use.[40]

The British spelled out the problem in their preconference proposals. It was "being maintained," they wrote, "in some quarters" that the best way to preserve world peace was through a completely international police force. Although they conceded that this idea had technical merits, British planners thought that it postulated more of an advance in international cooperation than nations were yet prepared to make—especially because it implied the existence of something like a world state. Such practical questions as size, command, composition, maintenance, and location would result in controversies that would render the force impotent; not even (they might have said especially) the Great Powers could be counted on to permit their forces to operate in ways that were not of their own immediate choosing. Thus, the British concluded, no matter how valuable it might turn out to be in the future, "the time has not yet come" for the creation of such an international force under the aegis of the United Nations.[41]

There did seem to be one way out of this dilemma—the creation of an international air force to punish aggressor states. Such a force might meet all of the postwar planners' criteria for effective action: it could respond quickly, bring awesome force to bear against a guilty nation, and would not require the Great Powers to commit all of their military forces to the new world organization. Its earliest proponent in the United States was Vice President Wallace, who by late 1942 had come to see a United Nations air corps as the palladium of world peace. "When this war comes to an end," he remarked then, "the United Nations will have such an overwhelming superiority in air power that we shall be able to enforce any mandate." A little later, he told a graduating class of Army Air Force cadets—a clear case of preaching to the choir—that an international air force, "consisting of adequate numbers of planes and strategically located bases," was all that would be needed to maintain peace and security in the postwar world. The method for doing so, as Wallace described it in March 1943, was to "bomb the aggressor nations mercilessly" until they laid down their arms.[42]

State Department planners also saw merit in the idea of such a force, at least partly in recognition of what they termed "the revolutionary rise of air power in modern warfare." In addition, they regarded a true international air corps as more acceptable than other types of unified forces for several reasons. First, it would not interfere with the national status of the more traditional services, which might be strong enough bureaucratically in the immediate postwar era to resist internationalization. The air force presented less of a political obstacle, however; it was just too new to have developed either a tradition or a very powerful constituency of its own and could be more easily sacrificed to the needs of an international organization. Second, reliance on air power alone would not require "sending our boys overseas," eliminating one of the main domestic difficulties involved in creating a United Nations force. Planners hoped that even Congress, which was then expected to raise all sorts of objections to the use of American soldiers and sailors to police the world, might accept without too much criticism a proposal limited to an international air force. Third, because under the international air force scheme other types of national forces would still continue to exist, states would be able to provide for their own security in case the new organization should fail. This would answer the criticisms of extreme nationalists as well as of those who regarded the peacekeeping force as impractical and unlikely to succeed. And fourth, an international police force based on air units would require fewer personnel, making it less costly to maintain than one employing the more traditional services.[43]

The development of these arguments did not mean that the State Department was firmly wedded to the idea of an international air force, however. Some planners doubted from the beginning the effectiveness of a peacekeeping agency relying entirely on an air corps; "air power alone," they contended, "has not yet proved decisive in modern combat." To some, this meant that more traditional forces would still be needed both to punish aggressors and to occupy territory that might be in dispute between warring nations. In addition, the experience of World War II had shown that conventional forces were needed to protect air bases that might otherwise be overrun by an aggressor and rendered ineffective. Thus, although planners included an international air corps in their 1943 outline for the United Nations, they remained only lukewarm to the idea and left the matter open for future consideration following an analysis of the details by a panel of army and navy experts on aviation.[44]

The army and navy were also uncertain how to respond to the various ways of constituting an international force. In September 1943, the Joint Chiefs of Staff rejected as premature the assumption of General George C. Marshall that the United States would furnish a major share of an international police force after the end of the war. This did not mean that military leaders were opposed to the idea, however; they recognized that participation in such a force might legitimize American power, enhance postwar service budgets, and guarantee a leading role for the United States in world affairs. Still, the Joint Chiefs' martially heightened sense of nationalism made them even more sensitive than the State Department to the danger that a police force might pose a threat to American sovereignty and freedom of action. From their perspective, too strong a world organization was every bit as dangerous as none at all. They had, as Livy said of Rome, reached the point where they could bear neither their vices nor their cure. An international air force offered the possibility of a compromise between the two; it might deliver the advantages of expanding the United States commitment to world security without threatening America's independence—or the autonomy of the more traditional services. In addition, an international air corps might serve as a means to obtain overseas bases for America's own postwar air units, bases that seemed essential to their mission of extending the nation's defense perimeter but that might otherwise prove unavailable. Still, the generals and admirals could not ascertain exactly how a true international force would affect their particular services, and any plan—especially one relying on air power—had to be considered in light of the struggle, already developing by 1944, over each branch's share of the postwar military budget. Mostly, military leaders adopted a wait-and-see attitude.[45]

The Soviets were much more certain of the need for an international air corps. In their view, the postwar organization's raison d'être was the provision of a quick and ready force to combat aggression—what Stalin referred to in a conversation with Poland's Stanislaw Mikolajczyk on 9 August as the "sword" that was about to be forged at Dumbarton Oaks. By then, however, the United Nations' sword had already been dulled by agreement among the Big Three on the impracticality of a true international police force, a development that worried the military-minded Russians much more than it did the British or Americans. As a substitute, the Kremlin clung to the idea of a U.N. air corps that could provide the organization's enforcement efforts with the kind of speed and certainty of deployment that an ad hoc police contingent seemed to lack. Thus Litvinov's July *Zvezda* article, while conceding that a police force was now out of the question, argued that an international air corps could feasibly be attached to the postwar organization. This view was repeated, with some embellishment, in the Soviet Union's preconference proposals a month later.[46]

Not surprisingly, the British took the opposite position. As they saw it, all of the arguments against an international police force—which they presented most clearly in their advance proposals—could just as easily be applied to an integrated international air corps. English planners did not, in fact, take the idea of a U.N. air contingent very seriously before coming to Dumbarton Oaks or really consider it apart from the more general concept of a postwar police force—due perhaps, in part, to the lack of interest in postwar peacekeeping expressed by the one person who was temperamentally most likely to be drawn to the air corps idea, Prime Minister Winston Churchill. This did not mean that the British were opposed to the use of air power by the United Nations; they expected the new organization to employ airplanes on the same ad hoc basis that it used land and naval forces. But it did mean that they went to Dumbarton Oaks opposed to the Soviet Union's idea of a unique role for air power, a position that they refused to change despite Churchill's later flirtation with the Russian scheme.[47]

The idea of an international air corps dominated the debate about military questions at Dumbarton Oaks. Gromyko brought up the Soviet proposal at the first meeting of the security subcommittee on 23 August, describing a United Nations air force as essential because it would provide the "advantage of speed at a time of crisis." Cadogan immediately expressed the British objections to such a plan, and Stettinius displayed his own lack of enthusiasm for an international air force while stating that the American experts were still studying the idea. Gromyko attempted to respond positively. The details of the plan had yet to be worked out, he said, and the Soviets remained flexible on the air corps' size, staffing, and composition. The Russian chairman even backed away from the idea of a true international force; perhaps, he said, an ad hoc corps could be created on the basis of national quotas. Clearly, there was some room here for negotiation, but not in the security subcommittee. The group seemed too unwieldy—its seventeen members made it the largest of any of the conference's committees—for the sort of detailed work required on the air force plan, which seemed to call anyway for the special expertise of uniformed planners. Thus, before adjourning an initial meeting that, as Cadogan put it, "didn't go badly," the three chairmen agreed to the creation of a new group, called the Special Military Subcommittee (later changed to the Special Informal Military Group), to study the technical aspects of the international air force idea.[48]

The American representatives on this committee were the same officers who had been involved in postwar planning since mid-1943. Although they had discussed postwar military issues endlessly over the past year, they had not arrived at any firm position on the creation of an international air corps by the time the Dumbarton Oaks Conference convened. This wavering caused Stettinius to develop doubts about their personal competence and to describe the generals—Stanley D. Embick, George V. Strong, and Muir S. Fairchild—as being "on the second or third string side." Secretary of War Stimson apparently shared this view; he asked for a dinner meeting with Stettinius and Assistant Secretary of War John J. McCloy on 29 July because he "lacked confidence" in his delegates to the upcoming conference. Stimson also had his doubts about Stettinius. After their dinner on 31 July, he expressed misgivings about what he saw as the under secretary of state's ignorance concerning the League of Nations and international affairs in general. The Navy Department fared somewhat better in its choice of representatives; at least no one expressed an absence of faith in either Admiral Russell Willson—who would chair the Special Military Subcommittee at Dumbarton Oaks—or Admiral Arthur Hepburn.[49]

As the opening of the conference neared, only General Fairchild—the army air force's representative on the planning group—clearly favored the creation of an international air corps. His reasons were basically parochial: he thought that his branch of the service stood to gain in prestige and appropriations if singled out for action against aggressors by the new peacekeeping organization. In addition, the United Nations promised to provide army fliers with the kind of forward overseas bases that they would need to play a worldwide role in postwar affairs; otherwise American air power might be limited to targets in the Western Hemisphere or to aircraft carriers—which would, of course, only benefit the rival navy air wing. And finally, operating under U.N. auspices would make the use of air power more widely acceptable in the postwar period. As Fairchild understood, the widespread use of terror bombing by both sides during the Second World War threatened to produce a backlash against air warfare that could decimate his branch's budget appropriations after the conflict ended. Bombing aggressor states would seem less reprehensible if carried out under the clear moral authority of the United Nations, however, a fact that might prevent a public outcry against the continued use of air power from developing in the future.[50]

Meanwhile, the representatives of the other services were beginning to worry about how postwar reliance on an international air corps might affect their future fortunes as well. Their concern did not, however, cause them to oppose the creation of such a force, but only to question the exclusive emphasis that the new world organization might place on it for peacekeeping. As Admiral Willson put it in the first meeting of the security subcommittee on 23 August, "informed" military and naval experts now "challenged the effectiveness of air power as a single . . . weapon for assault purposes," which meant that the new world body would need the kind of land and naval contingents that the other services could provide as well. Thus, although the army and navy planners continued to include an air corps as part of their proposal for a postwar force, they thought that it should be organized on the same basis as other peacekeeping units and utilized only in conjunction with traditional land and naval forces.[51]

The first meeting of the military subcommittee on 24 August revealed that the Russians were alone in supporting a true international air corps as the world organization's first line of defense against aggression. General Nikolai Slavin, who was serving during the war as liaison officer between the Red Army's general staff and the American and British military missions in Moscow, was charged with presenting the Soviet case. He argued that for the new organization to be effective it must have a ready force available for immediate use against aggressors; this was, the Russian general thought, the paramount lesson to be learned from the experience of the League of Nations and the outbreak of the Second World War. An air force would work best for this purpose, he said, because it would be available instantaneously and because its mobility would make it possible to strike offending nations before they could reap any benefits from their aggression. Speed and mobility could afford protection, the Russian went on, even for smaller, more remote countries—Slavin cited the example of Czechoslovakia, which must have made the British wince—that might otherwise be overrun before outside assistance could arrive. In addition, an international air corps would provide the United Nations with a force it could use immediately, without first obtaining its members' consent, thus eliminating any concern that the new organization might prove to be as much of a paper tiger in practice as its predecessor had been. And finally, Slavin pointed out the deterrent value of an air force as an instrument of terror, the "very existence" of which would make potential aggressors "think twice" before attacking their neighbors.[52]

The British and Americans had an answer for each of Slavin's points. Admiral Willson did not think that the need for speed required an integrated air corps because quota forces—with a given number of planes and pilots always available from participating members—could react to aggression just as quickly. The British went a bit further. Admiral Sir Percy Noble, the ranking member of the United Kingdom's military mission in Washington, argued that for technical reasons an ad hoc force would be even speedier than a true international air corps. The most important of these reasons was the necessity for training; according to Noble, trained national units could be combined for rapid deployment and reach their targets faster than a polyglot multinational force. In addition, an international air group would, like its ground force counterpart, present too many difficult problems of "shipping, supply, and reinforcement," and would have to be extremely large to be available for action all over the globe. Each of these problems could be handled more easily, the British thought, by an ad hoc force employing national contingents.[53]

The Anglo-Americans also argued that speed was not the sole criterion of a successful peacekeeping force. Effectiveness was equally important, they thought, and they doubted the effectiveness of the Soviet plan. Here, too, training was a key element. Noble noted that quota forces would be better trained—and therefore more accurate over their targets—than a force that attempted to integrate disparate national units on a permanent basis. Equipment was also a factor. The British doubted that separate U.N. air groups would have access to each contributing nation's latest equipment; there might be too much temptation on the part of all countries to reserve their best planes (and pilots) for their own forces. And, once again, the Americans pointed out that an air corps could not maintain the peace alone but must be supported in modern warfare by land and naval forces. Slavin seemed overwhelmed by all this criticism, which he apparently had not expected. The meeting had also grown painfully long because Slavin and his naval counterpart, Admiral Konstantin Rodinov of the Soviet Naval Ministry, spoke little English and required almost constant translation. Exhausted, the Russians asked that all three nations take a week to study the question in more detail.[54]

The Americans made use of the time to develop an in-depth assessment of the kind of an ad hoc air force that they and the British were moving toward. Two things continued to trouble them. One was the fact that under any ad hoc plan an aggressor state would have its own national air contingent at its disposal. This would not only diminish the force available to the peacekeeping organization but would make the aggressor potentially invulnerable—a particular problem if the offending nation happened to be a Great Power. To avoid this difficulty, some advocates of a true international air corps had linked their proposal to the eventual outlawing of all military airplanes except for those in the U.N. force. But the uniformed planners viewed such a plan as naive, if not dangerous, and preferred the risk of facing an aggressor's air power to that of any disarmament scheme. Second was the problem, raised in the military subcommittee by General Slavin, that some states might decide not to release their national contingents in a crisis—thus duplicating the failure of the League of Nations. As the American group saw it, this danger could not be avoided; proponents of peacekeeping could only hope that the Great Powers had learned the lesson of the league experience and would be willing in the future to pay the price required to halt aggression. Much would depend, they thought, on the vitality of the organization they were shaping at Dumbarton Oaks.[55]

The Americans also uncovered some new reasons for opposing a true international force. Such a force might encourage an arms race, they feared, because potentially aggressive nations would attempt to build air power of their own to surpass that of the peacekeeping body. This meant that for an international corps to be effective it would have to be coupled with a limitation on the national aircraft of all states—including perhaps civil airplanes, which might otherwise be armed and used for military purposes. An ad hoc force, on the other hand, whose size could be expanded as necessary, would not offer a potential aggressor an inducement to surpass a fixed number of planes and might prevent a worldwide buildup of air power from developing. It would also lessen the threat of any imposed limitation on national air power. A second problem was loyalty. American planners, perhaps influenced by Hollywood's romanticized depiction of war in the air, thought that airmen tended to be loyal primarily to other airmen, raising the possibility of what they termed a "supranational *esprit de corps*" that might threaten world security as much as any aggressor. On balance, this study left the American officers more firmly committed to a national quota plan as they prepared for the second meeting of the military subcommittee on 30 August.[56]

Admiral Willson opened the meeting with a presentation of the American formula for a peacekeeping force—what he described as an attempt to meet the Soviet Union's position without creating a rigid military organization. His plan called for an agreement that would oblige member nations to maintain a ready quota of air, sea, and land forces, which would go into action against an aggressor immediately upon receipt of an order from the council. Once engaged, these forces would come directly under the command of the security body and would remain so until the offending state had been defeated and peace restored. This formula received hearty approval from the British, who saw in Willson's plan essentially an embodiment of their own ideas for a flexible military force, which they called "earmarking." It won no praise from the Soviets, however. Slavin wondered whether the American plan would necessarily exclude an international air corps maintained directly under the council's control—such a force now seemed an irreducible minimum to Russian military planners. The Americans replied that a separate air force was unnecessary, that their plan was really more comprehensive than the Soviet proposal because land and sea forces, as well as air power, would be available when needed by the council. They also argued that the ad hoc nature of their formula made it more practical than a standing international air force. As before, the meeting of military experts ended with the Soviets asking for more time to study the issue.[57]

Just as the American military planners were presenting this plan, however, the State Department was developing what Cadogan described as "cold feet" over the power of the president to commit the American quota of armed forces to action. This potentially explosive issue, which Hull and Stettinius thought had already been settled, surfaced again during the secretary of state's meeting with senatorial leaders on 25 August. At that time two senators, including the powerful Arthur H. Vandenberg, took the position that congressional approval must be obtained before the American force was used, at least in some instances. As Hull saw it, this idea threatened the very concept of a peacekeeping organization: it might dangerously extend the council's time for reacting to aggression, make automatic response impossible, and scare off the British and Russians about the intentions of the United States to keep its end of a postwar peacekeeping bargain. The secretary thus replied that leaving any decision concerning the use of force up to the executive was the "only practicable way" to make the security organization work, but that he presumed the president would consult Congress before taking action in important instances.[58]

Vandenberg responded in writing four days later. "When our Delegate casts his affirmative vote" for military sanctions, he argued, "it is a clear commitment on the part of the United States to promptly engage in the joint military action." This was "tantamount to a declaration of war"—a power that the senator pointed out was lodged by the Constitution in the Congress, not the executive.

Vandenberg did not intend to be rigid in his definitions, however; he acknowledged that there were situations short of war where "our long-time practice"
recognized the legitimate right of the commander-in-chief to employ military
force without a congressional declaration. He was not sure, though, how best
to generalize this distinction in practice. Perhaps it could be done on a regional
basis, with the United States accepting North and South America (under the
aegis of the Monroe Doctrine) as an area of special responsibility and authorizing the president and his delegate in the Security Council to take military
action there under U.N. auspices. But what if action should be required
elsewhere? Or if a regional intervention grew too extensive and threatened a
world war? Then the senator could not see how it would be possible to escape
the need for congressional consent. Despite its damaging implications, Vandenberg's letter was a sincere attempt at an accommodation with the secretary
of state and represented an important way station on the Michigan senator's
journey from confirmed isolationism to postwar acquiescence in a world role
for the United States.[59]

Hull was suspicious, however, and overreacted—perhaps because the Republican senator's plan limiting United States responsibility to the Americas
was too reminiscent of Welles's scheme for a regionally based organization.
Then, too, the secretary could not see what direction Vandenberg was heading
in or know that he would eventually abandon his isolationism rather then
revert to it. Hull thus responded vigorously, ordering State Department legal
adviser Green Hackworth to prepare a study of the executive's right to conduct
military operations without a declaration of war. This would not be the department's first such memorandum. In April, it had sought advice on the subject
from University of Virginia law dean Frederick G. Ribble, who argued that
disputes among members of an international organization were ordinarily
regarded as something like civil conflicts, not as war "in a legal sense"; hence
the United States could participate in U.N. peacekeeping action with no
congressional authorization beyond an initial agreement to join the postwar
body.[60]

Hackworth's memorandum relied upon Ribble's logic. Once the Senate had
approved the treaty creating the United Nations, it said, the president would
have the right to contribute armed forces for peacekeeping without further
recourse of Congress. Hackworth also attempted to demonstrate that presiden-
tially ordered military action was nothing novel by appending a list of seventy-
six previous instances where forces had been employed by the commander-
in-chief without congressional approval. Hull circulated this memorandum
among members of the Senate Foreign Relations Committee and used its

arguments as the basis for discussion in another round of meetings with leading senators. There was some danger here. Telling senators that if they were in for a penny they were in for a pound might discourage them from entering the postwar bidding at all, but Hull thought that he had no real choice in the matter. The effectiveness of any postwar organization hinged on the Senate's acceptance of Hackworth's point. To take off some of the edge, the secretary also emphasized that the Dumbarton Oaks Conference was attempting to create an organization for peace, not for war, that would employ the "peace powers" of Congress—stated in the Constitution as the power "to define and punish . . . offenses against the Law of Nations"—instead of its powers for war. These arguments apparently won over Vandenberg, who ceased his objections on the issue.[61]

This new round of senatorial criticism caused considerable worry at Dumbarton Oaks. Stettinius expressed his growing concern by telling Cadogan on 1 September that because of arguments like Vandenberg's the United States might have to put in a reservation providing for the employment of "constitutional processes before the American quota of forces could be used." Cadogan thought this "pretty serious"; there was no telling how Gromyko might react to it. He asked Stettinius if it might not be possible to hold off on the issue for now on the hope that it might prove unnecessary later. Still, the English chairman concluded that it was for the Americans "to say what they can and what they cannot do"; the important thing was to get them inside the new world organization in the first place. He therefore expressed his sympathies with Stettinius over his domestic difficulties and raised no objections to the under secretary's warning about a possible American reservation.[62]

Cadogan soon had domestic difficulties of his own to be concerned about. Churchill, it seemed, had finally taken an interest in the Dumbarton Oaks talks and was worrying the Foreign Office with his views. In particular, the prime minister could not understand why the British delegation was resisting the Soviet proposal for an international air force, which he thought had merits that were both technical and political. In late August, after the conference had already begun, Churchill swung his considerable support behind the Russian position, which, he wrote, "raises very large questions of principle and cannot be decided on purely military grounds." He had, he said, favored such a force following the last war; it seemed, if anything, even more necessary now. On 4 September, the Foreign Office telegraphed a warning to Cadogan that the British position on this issue might be about to change. "Please go slow on this matter," Eden wrote; the prime minister was "disturbed" by the Foreign Office's position and the entire question was being studied in London "urgently."

"Meanwhile," he concluded, "it is important that no further criticism should be made of the Russian proposal." Cadogan replied that he intended to inform Stettinius; he did not want to surprise the Americans—with whom the British were cooperating on a number of issues—by making a complete shift to the Russian viewpoint. "We and the Americans have fought this thing together," he wrote in his diary, "and we can't suddenly desert them on the field of battle."[63]

Despite his concern over its impact on Anglo-American understanding, Cadogan was himself wavering in his opposition to an international air corps. He had spent the afternoon of 4 September in a "tiresome" meeting with representatives of the dominions in which Canadian Ambassador Lester Pearson had argued—in terms reminiscent of Stettinius's recent reservation—that Canada must be consulted before its quota of forces could be deployed by the Security Council. "Bless my soul," Cadogan responded, "if we put in such provisions, the world will say 'Where are the teeth you promised to put into the Covenant. We are back where we were before.'" A standing international air force could solve this problem by eliminating the national quotas and thus the need for consultation. Cadogan still thought the Russian idea "technically unsound" but could see how its practical difficulties might be outweighed by its political advantages, especially if member nations chose to make potentially devastating reservations about the use of their other military contingents.[64]

The next day, after lunching with Stettinius at the Soviet embassy, Cadogan pulled the American chairman aside to tell him his news. Stettinius did not seem unduly disturbed by it, according to Cadogan. "I do not know with what degree of real conviction [the] Americans have been opposing this proposal," he cabled Whitehall, "and Mr. Stettinius professes not to know himself." In fact, however, the American chairman found the information "rather alarming" and reported his concern to the secretary of state immediately following his press conference later that afternoon. Hull, too, was worried. He was having trouble enough with the Senate over the much looser American plan for national quotas and could only guess how Vandenberg—or worse, genuine isolationists—would respond to a standing international air force. Ironically enough, one of the important merits that Cadogan now saw in the Russian scheme was its potential effect on the political climate in the United States. He had talked on the evening of 4 September with Senator Harold Burton, a strong supporter of a postwar organization, who had expressed a desire to see the United Nations equipped with the kind of a ready force that an air corps could supply. But Cadogan was viewing only one side of the senatorial equation. Hull was more concerned with the reaction of the U.N.'s potential opponents, on the assumption that Burton and other internationalists in the Senate would support the world organization whether it turned out to be as strong as they hoped or not.[65]

Cadogan also had the unpleasant task of informing Great Britain's military delegates—whom he called "our men o' war"—about the prime minister's latest whim. They maintained their technical objections, with which Cadogan also still agreed, but were willing to admit that the idea might have political advantages. In London, the chiefs of staff were also making a slow retreat before the forces of the prime minister, which were growing daily now that he had made his opinion known. On 1 September, the British military leaders reported to Churchill that they saw "some difficulties" in his proposal, which called for an international air force to be quartered with its national counterparts but wearing different uniforms and insignia. The military's foremost objection was "the security aspect," which meant, the chiefs of staff explained, that new equipment would be exposed to fliers of all nations and that it would be impossible to keep the international force's plans a secret from all governments. But these concerns were not enough for the military leaders to stand up to the prime minister. They thus cabled their joint staff mission at Dumbarton Oaks that in view of Churchill's attitude "it was desirable to meet the Russian request for specific reference to an International Air Corps." In so doing, however, the chiefs cautioned that their delegates should avoid accepting anything too specific that might "tie our hands" in the future.[66]

The American military planners reacted even more negatively. They were upset to learn that the British might change their minds on an international air force and encouraged Stettinius to continue his efforts on behalf of the national quotas plan. They thought that the chairman might have to ask Roosevelt for help with Churchill and that he should at least persuade Cadogan to keep Great Britain's possible defection a secret for the time being. Although they had taken a long time to make up their minds on the subject, the uniformed Americans now seemed certain that an international air force would be a disaster for the success of the new United Nations.[67]

This view was shared by FDR. The president had never been a supporter of the international air corps idea; he thought it impractical and politically dangerous in the United States. As he had written Clark Eichelberger in January, there were just too many problems with a force of this type, although he admitted that one might be developed later "especially if everyone spoke basic English." When Stettinius raised the matter in a meeting at the White House on 6 September, he was not sure that the president completely understood it. Finally FDR said, "You mean an international air force that will have American planes with international insignia on the planes and uniforms with a United

Nations insignia? I cannot agree to this." Neither would the Russians. As Gromyko informed Stettinius on 29 August, the Soviet proposal did not mean "a new uniform with a special insignia on the plane under command of some officer of the Council" but only joint operations conducted by an Allied command. Anything more was too much of a threat to national pride. Still, Stettinius—anxious for the president's support—warned Roosevelt that Churchill seemed to be pushing the British delegation to vote in favor of such a visionary force and said that it might prove necessary for Roosevelt to raise the issue with the prime minister during their meeting at Quebec the following week. The president agreed to do so.[68]

From the American standpoint the air force problem was reaching crisis proportions. Stettinius feared that the Russians and British might succeed in having the idea written into the Dumbarton Oaks proposals before Roosevelt could have a chance to change Churchill's mind. He now recognized that the decision to hold the conference in Washington—which had made many things easier for the American delegation—also had it disadvantages: he could not, under present circumstances, very well stall for time by employing the excuse of waiting for instructions from home as Cadogan and Gromyko had done. He thus proposed to his superiors that if the air force question could not be resolved properly until after the Quebec meeting, which was scheduled to begin on 11 September, it might be best to recess the Russian phase of the conversations and hold discussions with the Chinese in the interim. Roosevelt and Hull agreed, but the secretary of state doubted if the Russians would.[69]

Stettinius also raised the possibility of a recess with Cadogan, who was once again firmly opposed to the air corps idea. The British leader was at the time "quite disturbed" over a cable he had just received from London that left Churchill's new position intact. He feared that because the prime minister was already on his way to Quebec and would not arrive until the following Monday he might not hear anything on the international air force question for as long as a week. In the meantime, he would have to support the Russian position. Stettinius asked if he would consider adjourning the Soviet talks and meeting with the Chinese, reminding Cadogan of his often-stated desire to conclude the conversations and return to London as soon as possible. The British chairman "did not respond very enthusiastically" to the idea. He would go along with it, he said, if the American wanted, but he did not think that Eden would like it very much.[70]

Things looked brighter the next morning. Before the 10 A.M. meeting of the Joint Steering Committee, Cadogan showed Stettinius a new telegram from the Foreign Office that practically defused the issue. The message authorized the

British chairman to propose a "*very* slight concession" on the Russian proposal that included an examination of the international air force idea sometime after the new world organization had been created. This was much less than Stettinius had feared, and he readily agreed to Cadogan's suggestion that the British delegation present it at the upcoming session. Stettinius also showed his delight with this new development by attempting to appear flexible at the meeting; he suggested that part of an American air quota might be brigaded with forces of other states—and succeeded so well that Cadogan thought "he might go even further" than the Foreign Office proposed. Clearly, the threatened break in the Anglo-American united front, which seemed more important with each day's news from Poland, had now been closed.[71]

All of this had been kept secret from the Soviets, of course, who were about to change their own views on the subject. On 8 September, during his meeting with Roosevelt and Stettinius in the president's bedroom, Gromyko made the dispute over an international air force seem only a matter of semantics. In a way that Stettinius described as "perfectly open minded," the Russian chairman said that it was just a question of saying the right thing in the right language. He was sure, he told Roosevelt, that all three powers were talking about the same thing, and if the United States objected to the term "international air force," or to the proposal as he had originally phrased it, his government would be willing to drop the entire issue. A relieved Stettinius replied that he was confident the section on security forces could be written in a way that would satisfy everybody's objectives—without, that is, a standing international air corps.[72]

Gromyko proved true to his word. In fact, it seems likely that the dispute over the air corps issue had never been as serious as Stettinius feared, that the obduracy of General Slavin and the Soviet uniformed planners had exaggerated the Kremlin's more lukewarm commitment to a standing force. The Russian chairman had, after all, expressed a willingness to compromise his plan away as early as the 23 August meeting of the security subcommittee, only to have his nation's position appear to stiffen in the more detailed sessions of the Special Military Subcommittee. What this probably suggests is that in their zeal to negotiate successfully the Russian military delegates forgot—if indeed they ever knew—that the international air force idea was one to which their political counterparts were less than firmly wedded. Moscow also may have seen, in the Polish controversy and the veto dispute, reason to divorce itself from the air corps scheme. At any rate, Gromyko withdrew the Soviet proposal in a meeting of the Joint Steering Committee on 12 September. His explanation sounded nervous and defensive. The purpose of the USSR in proposing an air corps, he said, had been merely to insure the effectiveness of the new organization. The

Soviet Union had no greater interest in this matter than did Great Britain or the United States and if the other two nations thought that a standing force was unnecessary he was willing to go ahead without one.[73]

This left the conference with two plans concerning air power: an American proposal that required member states to hold air force contingents in readiness and make them available to the Security Council as needed; and a British alternative that provided for a future study of the feasibility of creating a combined force with a "supreme" commander. Stettinius, strengthened by the Soviet retreat, argued forcefully for the American plan; there was no longer any need, he reasoned, for the kind of compromise that the Foreign Office had suggested. Cadogan resisted this conclusion—he knew that Churchill still saw merit in the idea of a standing force—but gave in on 20 September and permitted the American national quotas idea to become part of the Dumbarton Oaks proposals.[74]

The conference also adopted the American plan for land and sea forces. This was the formula presented by Admiral Willson to the Special Military Subcommittee on 30 August: each member should, in accordance with a special agreement, supply "armed forces, facilities, and assistance" to the Security Council "on its call." These agreements, which were to be negotiated as quickly as possible, would govern the numbers and types of forces, as well as the kind of facilities and other assistance, that each state promised to provide. Loose as such a system was designed to be, Stettinius still worried that it might arouse Republican and congressional criticism. He thus arranged for the inclusion of a statement in the final proposals that made each agreement subject to ratification by the signatories "in accordance with their constitutional processes"—a provision that he also hoped would bind the Senate to an acceptance of subsequent decisions by the Security Council.[75]

Once formulated, the U.N. force would have to be organized and led. The British had spent the most time thinking about this question before coming to Dumbarton Oaks, and their plan for a Military Staff Committee would ultimately form the basis of the conference's proposal. What the British had in mind was essentially an extension of the Combined Chiefs of Staff system that they and the Americans had developed for fighting the war in Europe. It would include the supreme military authorities (or their representatives) of each of the Great Powers, which the British thought deserved permanent membership on the Military Staff Committee—as they did on the Security Council—because of their primary responsibility for keeping the peace. Other major states, such as elected members of the council, would be represented in some way—perhaps in proportion to their contributions to peacekeeping—as would those states having a special interest in whatever conflict was under discussion. The Military Staff Committee's duties would include both planning—to prevent renewed aggression by Germany, Japan, "or any other" state—and command of the forces supplied by member nations. It would also advise the council on general military questions, such as the regulation of armaments.[76]

Cadogan presented this plan to the Joint Steering Committee on 25 August, explaining that British military leaders regarded it to be "of very great importance." The Americans agreed—it was of great importance. But they had not, despite considerable study, decided upon any detailed arrangements for what their proposal called a Security and Armaments Commission. On the question of membership in the commission, for instance, State Department planners had considered an international staff drawn from the permanent secretariat of the new organization, then rejected the idea for the reason that only national military establishments contained a ready reservoir of suitable military experts. They also discussed the possibility of a widely representative body elected by the General Assembly. In the end, the best the Americans could come up with was a commission composed of a high-ranking officer from each member of the Security Council, a plan that they were too uncertain about even to include in their preconference proposals. The Soviet plan was even less detailed. Thus both Stettinius and Gromyko asked for time to study the British General Staff proposal.[77]

Determining membership on the Military Staff Committee turned out to be something of a problem. The Russians thought that it should include representatives from all members of the Security Council, not just the Big Five as proposed by Great Britain. The Americans, despite their earlier attachment to what became the Soviet formula, supported the British point of view, which was finally adopted by the conference. Much more difficult was the question of command during a future enforcement action. Here none of the delegations had a proposal beyond the general idea that it should be exercised in some way by the Military Staff Committee. The problems inherent in any international military plan, including divided loyalties, tangled lines of communication, and easily wounded national pride, had been made only too clear by the Anglo-American war experience; they were certain to be even worse when a multinational and multilingual peacekeeping force was involved. The Americans had considered three possible ways of handling this delicate matter: continuing staff talks among member states, with an ad hoc command determined at the time of need; consultation between the military committee and national general staffs, with military decisions left to the latter; or the creation of a standing general staff, with individual commanders selected from within its ranks. The last seemed the most satisfactory to the State Department—as it apparently did to the British and Soviets as well. Still, there was no agreement on the details, which were potentially very troublesome, so that the Dumbarton Oaks proposals simply left them to be "worked out subsequently."[78]

Providing the new organization with an armed force had proven to be a difficult task. In particular, the Soviet proposal for an international air corps—which seemed to the Americans to be going much too far—had once again called into question the whole issue of United States participation in postwar peacekeeping activities. For a while, at least, the problem had appeared serious enough to cause Stettinius to consider adjourning the conference and working with the Chinese. This episode raised the worrisome specter of failure—the possibility that the Dumbarton Oaks Conference might not be able to construct the outline of a new organization acceptable to all three powers. It would not be for the last time. In the weeks that followed a number of even more troublesome issues, including the use of the Great Power veto, would threaten to divide the conference irreparably before any final agreement could be reached.

7 A World of Troubles

From almost the beginning of the conference, debate over the Security Council revealed serious differences among the Big Three—differences that reflected above all the importance each placed on questions of security in a dangerous world. Although united initially by their desire to create an effective postwar organization, the three nations would find it increasingly difficult to agree on the details of a council designed to wield the kind of power that this required. Mistakes here could be critical—could even lead to the creation of an organization that was detrimental to the Great Powers' own security interests, which were, in the waning months of the war, beginning to replace general security as the primary concern. Thus, as discussions of the council continued, the delegates found themselves emphasizing their differences—which were becoming only too apparent in Eastern Europe—and considering the idea that an effective peacekeeping organization based on their cooperation might not be possible to create after all. This growing sense of pessimism would prove especially pronounced where the knotty question of voting in the council was concerned, but it could also be seen in the debates over such other issues as disarmament, the creation of regional security organizations, and the requisition of bases for peacekeeping purposes.

To one degree or another, disarmament figured into just about everybody's plans for the postwar world. Certainly all agreed that the Axis states had to be disarmed and removed as threats to future peace, although, as the Americans pointed out, the extent to which this goal should be pursued would have to be determined at a peace conference and not at Dumbarton Oaks. Still, there was agreement on the principle that the defeated states were to be deprived of the weapons of war—and that the enforcement of this decision was to be one of the tasks of the new world organization. As they did so often, the Big Three were reacting here to the experience of the League of Nations, which had failed to prevent the rearmament of Germany in the 1930s, and were determined that the same thing not happen again in the aftermath of the current conflict. Thus, creating an organization that would be strong enough to keep the Axis powers weak was to be the lowest common denominator concerning disarmament in the postwar period.[1]

Beyond this point, however, the Big Three found disarmament a difficult subject. Each even had a different idea about what part of the new organization should be responsible for it: the Americans thought the Security Council, the Soviets the General Assembly, and the British the Military Staff Committee. This problem would be solved at Dumbarton Oaks by deciding to distribute the task of disarmament among the powers of all three agencies, with the Security Council receiving the formal authority for the key task of developing a weapons-reduction plan to be submitted to all member nations and the others concerned with planning and monitoring. More difficult was the question of how extensive such a plan should be. The British put the least faith in the idea of limiting weapons, refusing, in fact, even to use the word "disarmament" in their preconference proposal, where they employed—over the objections of the chiefs of staff, who thought even this was going too far—the less trouble-some phrase "regulation of armaments." The problem here was partly one of definition: disarmament implied the elimination of all "offensive" weapons— those beyond the minimum needed for national defense—and thus continued a distinction that many believed to have been outmoded by the technological advances of the Second World War. In the postwar world, they argued, "offen-sive" and "defensive" weapons would often look the same, especially where air power was concerned. In addition, any reasonable definition of defense would now have to involve more than the ability to protect one's own borders against the immediate threat of aggression; it would, at least for the Great Powers and their supporters, also include defending weaker states from the first advances of future Hitlers and Tojos. This was, after all, what the new world organization was designed to empower the Big Four to do, and the British planners did not want to see an excessive regard for disarmament—as opposed to the more limited regulation of armaments—impair their ability to do it.[2]

Considering their reputation for realpolitik, the Soviets placed a surprisingly strong emphasis on disarmament. Their motives were murky as always, but there is no reason to doubt their sincerity, especially in light of their desire to place authority for the matter in the hands of the General Assembly, where they would not be able to exercise a veto. Apparently the Russians believed—as had the designers of the League of Nations—that for peacekeeping to be effective, it must be joined with a general reduction in the level of armaments to reduce the risk of arms races and preventive wars. The Soviets would, at any rate, prove to be the most vigorous supporters of disarmament in the meetings at Dumbarton Oaks.[3]

The Americans shared the Soviet belief in disarmament, at least before the formal conversations began. They had spent most of their preconference efforts considering not whether but how disarmament was to be achieved—and had decided that any success in this area would have to depend on the efforts and authority of the new international organization. Certainly, "in view of past experience," they knew that simply asking outright for the cooperation of all states would not work. Other ideas had also been considered in Washington, including having the Big Four disarm to set an example that other states might follow, announcing a worldwide policy of disarmament and pressuring all nations to accept, and adding other potentially troublesome states to the list of Axis powers to be forcibly disarmed at the end of the war. But in the end American planners saw no real alternative to employing the auspices of the new United Nations, which they hoped might serve as a neutral agency for securing a workable regulatory agreement among its members. As the Americans saw it, use of the U.N. might take some of the sting out of disarmament for lesser nations by alleviating both the specter of direct dominance by the Great Powers and the fear that regulation might be used as a tool of imperialism— concerns that had led at the same time to watering down the Four Policemen idea. In addition, they thought, the international organization could perform a number of tasks that might induce states to accept an agreement for disarmament. It could create a more secure world in which nations would not have to fear attack and would need fewer arms, bring worldwide moral and diplomatic pressure on recalcitrants, and if necessary use force by interpreting a refusal to disarm as a potential threat to peace. Thus the Americans thought that a strong United Nations might provide the kind of practical leverage that had always been lacking in previous unsuccessful disarmament schemes.[4]

When disarmament came up in the Formulation Group on Security, the plan presented was an odd fusion of the American formula and British terminology. Under its terms, the new international organization would be authorized to initiate negotiations for a general agreement—but only for the regulation of armaments, not disarmament. In this way, the British and American positions, so different before Dumbarton Oaks, were combined to present the Russians with a united front, an alliance that Charles Webster attested to when he wrote in his diary that he might have said more on the subject of arms "if it had not been our role at this time to let the Americans do the running." The changed American position also reflected the influence of the military planners, who had always feared that disarmament might go too far. The Soviets agreed to the basic American plan but continued their objection to the use of the weaker British term, producing a deadlock that forced the question to be discussed at a higher level of the conference.[5]

Oddly, in light of the apparent Anglo-American entente, the polarities of the conference were reversed on another aspect of the disarmament issue. This was the American reference to making provision for the regulation of "armed forces" as well as armaments, to which both the British and the Russians objected in the 5 September meeting of the Formulation Group. The Europeans thought that the size of a nation's army should be left to its own discretion; only offensive weapons that represented a threat to world peace required regulation by the international organization. The Americans yielded on this point, again reflecting a movement away from their earlier faith in disarmament, and only armaments were referred to in the Dumbarton Oaks proposals. (Another aspect of the American plan calling for the regulation of the manufacture and international sale of arms was never even discussed.) The Soviets also raised another difficulty. They wanted to mention the regulation of armaments, if not disarmament, specifically among the topics that the General Assembly could discuss and make recommendations on, but as we have seen, neither the British nor the Americans could think of any reason for singling out this one subject from among the many that the assembly might treat.[6]

The general debate on disarmament was continued in the Joint Steering Committee, where Gromyko presented the Soviet case for a stronger proposal. As the Russian chairman saw it, the "regulation" of armaments sounded too neutral to do much good; any plan for the new organization should specify disarmament or at least the reduction of arms to indicate clearly the direction that the planners intended to go. Pasvolsky disagreed, arguing that too few weapons could prove just as undesirable as too many; surely this was one of the lessons of the years following the First World War, he thought, when the victors had too readily agreed to disarm and paved the way for the aggression that led to another conflict. Charged with the blanket responsibility for regulation, Pasvolsky reasoned, the United Nations could set minimums as well as maximums, thus preventing the error of leaping to either extreme in the production of armaments. Cadogan was quick to support this argument—he too had been letting the Americans do the running on this subject but now had something of his own to add. The British chairman warned that the idea of reduction must not be carried too far; any regulation of armaments should be directly related to the commitments made by member states to provide forces for maintaining the peace. This, he reminded Gromyko, was why they were creating a world organization in the first place, and it would make no sense to weaken the states upon whose strength its success would have to depend. In addition, Cadogan insisted that any agreement on the regulation of armaments must be sufficiently generous to permit each nation to meet its requirements for "local defense and internal security." Nor should the idea of local defense be taken too literally. When asked to be more specific about what the term meant for Great Britain, Cadogan gave the example of defense of the northwest frontier of India.[7]

Three days later, when the matter came up again, Pasvolsky and Cadogan still wanted to omit any reference to reduction or disarmament. Gromyko, however, was ready to compromise. The Russians would accept "regulation" instead of "reduction," he said, but they still thought it would be desirable to put the word "disarmament" somewhere in the conference's final proposals, even if only as a "slogan" for the future. Stettinius, although not much given to sloganeering, signaled his agreement, and Pasvolsky assented grudgingly. The British continued to object even to the principle, however; as late as 14 September they were still insisting that the word "disarmament" be placed in brackets wherever it occurred in the draft proposals to indicate that they had not yet agreed to its use. When they did finally give in, it was only to permit use of the word in the section describing topics open for discussion by the General Assembly, not in the more formal—and potentially more effective—plans for developing an agreement on arms in the Security Council. Cadogan was more interested in devising a clear statement of principles underlying the "regulation of armaments," a topic that he thought was important enough to be placed in a separate chapter of the Dumbarton Oaks proposals. Such a chapter was drafted by the Formulation Group, which included the British stipulation that consideration be given to the special needs of the Great Powers for meeting their peacekeeping responsibilities, for providing local defense, and for maintaining internal order. But the Russians were less than enthusiastic about this new chapter and argued that if it was adopted at all, it should include at least some reference to disarmament. Because a renewed debate on this issue threatened to unravel the loose fabric of the Soviet-American compromise, the idea of a separate chapter was dropped, and the principles of a system for regulating armaments were left for future determination. Too much disagreement existed among the Big Three for anything of substance concerning the important question of disarmament to be accomplished at Dumbarton Oaks.[8]

The conferees also disagreed on the role to be played by regional organizations within the new world body. Before arriving at Dumbarton Oaks, the Americans had found regionalism to be a particularly difficult problem; it had been, as we have seen, the basis for the postwar planning dispute between Cordell Hull and Sumner Welles, which had ended, at the time of Welles's resignation, in a clear victory for the secretary of state and his more universalist ideas. For a while, at least, regional organizations had been so discredited as to be eliminated from the American plans altogether, leaving full responsibility for peacekeeping in the hands of the worldwide Security Council. Several factors caused the planners to reconsider this decision later, however, including the British proposal for a Council of Europe, potential difficulties with Congress over sending American troops outside of the Western Hemisphere, and concern over European involvement in what the United States regarded as its primary defense region in the Americas. Albeit grudgingly, even Hull was admitting some sort of a role for regional organizations by the time the American proposals were drafted in the summer of 1944.[9]

The American group at Dumbarton Oaks discussed regionalism at some length in a series of meetings before the conference opened. The reason for these discussions was the ambiguous nature of the United States proposals, which allowed for the existence of regional organizations "not inconsistent with" the purposes of the world organization, permitted them to function on matters of security and peace "appropriate for regional adjustment," and provided for their employment by the world body for peaceful settlement purposes "where feasible." Maintaining such a qualified position seemed unwise in light of what seemed to be clear-cut British support for European regionalism in their preconference memoranda, so the Americans decided to review the matter in order to develop a more detailed understanding of their own point of view. One thing was certain: the central organization had to be the master, not the servant, of any regional bodies. Dunn and Bowman outlined the reasons for this in a meeting on 16 August: Dunn because the emphasis must be on the universal nature of the new world organization to avoid a breakup into spheres of influence, and Bowman because it was difficult to define a region and because in order to achieve a workable world settlement, the council had to be above any region. These widely shared convictions prevented the Americans from changing their minds altogether on regionalism, with the result that the preconference discussions at Dumbarton Oaks basically ratified the long-standing position of the United States in favor of a primarily universalist organization.[10]

Pasvolsky produced an official interpretation of regionalism in the American plan in a memorandum circulated the next day. The "Role of Local and Regional Agencies in the Maintenance of Security and Peace" established the clear authority of the Executive Council, which would be empowered to sit in judgment on the legitimacy of any regional association by determining whether or not it was consistent with the purposes of the world organization. Local and regional agencies might be authorized—or even encouraged—to promote peaceful settlement of disputes in their own areas, but would be permitted to conduct enforcement action "only with the prior specific or general authorization of the executive council" and while keeping the council "fully informed of the action contemplated or taken." The council, moreover, could assume jurisdiction or take action of its own to resolve a regional dispute, and any member of the world body would have the right to bring a dispute before the council—

even if it was already being dealt with by a regional association. Thus, although recognizing that regional bodies might have their uses, the Americans wanted it clearly understood that they were to be of secondary importance and influence, especially where enforcement action was concerned.[11]

The British government's version of the Hull-Welles dispute over regionalism had ended in more of a stalemate. Churchill, who viewed a regional association for Europe as of paramount importance, was outvoted in May 1944 by the Foreign Office, which favored a more powerful World Council, and by the dominion prime ministers, who feared that regionalism would foster isolationist tendencies in the United States. The result was a compromise in the British preconference proposals, with a regional Council of Europe receiving special mention within the framework of a global security system. Although the prime minister appeared to have yielded, and even to have lost interest in the subject, the ultimate outcome would depend on where the British government placed its final emphasis; the "old boy" could still, as Charles Webster noted, "play the devil" with the Foreign Office's more universalist designs. No one could be certain that the mercurial Churchill would not later turn intransigent on the question of regional organization and go back on his compromise with the Foreign Office.[12]

The proposed membership of the Council of Europe posed a special problem for American planners. Churchill's plan emphasized the active participation of the United States, which in conjunction with Great Britain and the Soviet Union might be able to promote peaceful tendencies in Europe, heal the Continent's wounds, and prevent Germany from again becoming dominant— all of which the British leader thought would be required to prevent Europe from "becoming the centre of a third world tragedy." This was just the sort of thing that the State Department feared the Senate would never accept; the Treaty of Versailles had floundered on the issue of too much involvement on the Continent, and whatever attraction regionalism held for American planners had partly resulted from the idea that limiting the primary responsibility of the United States to the Western Hemisphere might enhance the new organization's chances in the Senate. The British plan for emphasizing the European region thus threatened to transform regionalism from a political asset into a domestic liability, which only reinforced the State Department's natural preference for a universally based organization. Under the circumstances, the unstable compromise between Churchill and Eden over regional organizations did not reassure the Americans, who went to Dumbarton Oaks wary of any British attempt to use regionalism to draw them into a strictly European council.[13]

When the question of regional organizations came up in the Joint Steering

Committee on 25 August, the British suggested a postponement until after the general shape and character of the world organization could be determined. Thus regional organizations were not discussed at Dumbarton Oaks until 7 September, when Cadogan presented the British view that they should be empowered to undertake enforcement actions voted by the Security Council. In keeping with this idea, the British chairman also proposed the creation of regional subcommittees of the military advisory body, which could plan, organize, and conduct peacekeeping activities of a less than global nature. This was going too far for the Americans, who thought that such a plan placed too much emphasis on the dangerous concept of regionalism. The United States did not, according to Pasvolsky, mean to rule out the use of local organizations for peacekeeping altogether, but thought that they might work best in arranging for the peaceful settlement of disputes. In addition, Pasvolsky said, special groups of nations formed to handle disputes need not be strictly regional; they might also include other states with an interest in the issues or locality involved. Either way, the most important thing for the Americans was that the overriding authority of the globally based council be preserved and emphasized.[14]

Gromyko stayed out of the debate over regionalism because his delegation had not yet had time to study the matter. The Soviets were, however, apparently coming to appreciate how regional organizations could be useful for creating a sphere of influence—a view that the pseudonymous "N. Malinin" would later set forth in an article in *War and the Working Class*. According to the author, who again was probably Assistant Foreign Minister Litvinov, regional arrangements were required to create "security zones" that could provide the kind of safety from attack no longer afforded by national borders and defenses. This need had arisen with the long-range weaponry of modern warfare, which had made it possible for England, for example, to suffer extensive damage from air and artillery attacks during the present war without being invaded. Thus, no one could object if England formed an agreement with Belgium or Holland to prevent such attacks from originating there in the future. "Likewise," the article went on, "no one should object if the Soviet Union, for the same purposes, wished to establish friendly relations with its immediate neighbors." Such an arrangement would serve the security interests of both great and small powers—especially the latter, according to Litvinov, because they have always been damaged and sometimes devastated by attacks within their territory aimed at their Great Power neighbors. Thus, according to this reasoning, a Soviet agreement with Poland would be as much in the interests of the Poles as of the Soviets themselves. Litvinov also outlined two conditions that had to be observed in the making of regional agreements. The independence of smaller states must not be infringed upon, and defensive frontiers should be defined and delimited only by the leading states of any continent. He did not say what would happen when, as seemed likely, these two conditions proved to be contradictory, when the principles of justice and power conflicted. Considering the growing Anglo-American suspicions about the nature of Soviet interests in Poland and elsewhere, it was just as well that the Russians did not present this interpretation of regionalism at Dumbarton Oaks. Never mind that the Americans had a similar view of their own role in the Western Hemisphere; they would have been put into a panic by any plan requiring them to accept a U.N.-sanctioned sphere of influence for the Soviet Union by ratifying their position as the dominant regional power in Eastern Europe.[15]

Even without having to face a direct Soviet threat, however, the Americans wanted to place clear limits on the ability of regional organizations to employ force. They thought, for example, that no enforcement measures should be undertaken without the authorization of the Security Council, where the United States could use its status as a permanent member to prevent ill-advised action by any of the regional groups. This restriction would make it difficult for the other Great Powers to use regional organizations as instruments of dominance. And it would also give the United States an effective veto over the peacekeeping activities of a Pan-American organization—something that it seemed too impolitic, in the days of the Good Neighbor policy, to exercise directly. Although the other groups accepted this idea in principle, Cadogan feared that it might raise difficulties over the enforcement of the German surrender terms, which were to be handled in the immediate postwar period by the victors acting as a kind of regional group for Europe. More important was the related question of arrangements for global security in the interim period between the end of the war and the establishment of the new world organization, during which the Great Powers "and other states in position to do so" would be required to provide whatever peacekeeping activities might be called for, especially in relation to Germany and Japan. The State Department's planners, acting on the advice of military experts, had included such a transitional plan in their preconference proposals; they thought it would, in addition to providing interim security, serve as a litmus test of continued cooperation between the United States and its European allies. Now these transitional arrangements were being threatened by Cadogan's interpretation of the Americans' own plan to employ the Security Council to limit the power of regional groupings.[16]

To meet this problem the United States proposed an exception to its own general rule. It would permit regional groups to take action without prior approval by the council when they were dealing with the former Axis states. This idea worried the Soviets, however, who thought it might allow all regional groupings to have a say in dealing with the defeated enemies. They understood that such authority was to rest directly with a special control commission of the Allied powers until it could be handed over to the Security Council; the alternative, as they saw it, was power far too widely dispersed to be effective. The Americans, mystified by this interpretation of what they perceived as an innocuous provision, suggested the simpler alternative of adding a special section on transitional arrangements that would include a statement that nothing in the document should "preclude action taken or authorized in relation to enemy states as a result of the present war" by the governments "having responsibility for such action." This wording satisfied the Soviets, who agreed to its inclusion in the Dumbarton Oaks proposals.[17]

But now the Americans began to have doubts about including interim arrangements in the draft charter at all. Perhaps this change of mind was caused by the Soviet Union's all too apparent willingness to take its share of the responsibility for enforcing the terms of surrender in Europe, the details of which had yet to be determined. More likely, considering the timing, it stemmed from domestic concerns arising out of Hull's recent conferences with senatorial leaders, when Senator Vandenberg had raised the question of requiring prior congressional approval for any use of United States forces in international enforcement action. The secretary of state had finessed this issue by interpreting the Senate's consent to join the new organization as a blanket authorization for any use of troops approved by the Security Council; he now feared that a section on interim arrangements, which would involve a commitment of American power before the United Nations could be established, might revive Vandenberg's interest in the matter. Endangering senatorial approval seemed just too great a risk to run for the relatively minor purpose of clarifying the role of regional associations in the immediate postwar period.[18]

Stettinius raised the problem in the American group's meeting on 13 September—one day after Hull's meeting with the leading senators. The secretary, he said, preferred that interim arrangements be omitted from the Dumbarton Oaks proposals and left for a separate set of negotiations to be conducted later. General Strong objected to this suggestion, citing the military's interest in creating a European high commission to handle security arrangements in the immediate aftermath of the war. This objective, he reminded the group, was why a section on transitional arrangements had been included in the American proposals in the first place, and nothing had changed to make advance preparations any less necessary. Predictably, however, the State Department's representatives sided with their secretary. Pasvolsky thought that there was too little time to negotiate detailed interim arrangements at the present conference anyway, and pointed out that the Russians would resist any attempt to do so, especially with respect to Japan. The meeting ended with the Americans deciding to recommend the deletion of interim arrangements from the Dumbarton Oaks proposals.[19]

This American about-face found little support among the other delegates in the Joint Steering Committee. Cadogan, apparently amused by the situation, said he could see merit in both the old and the new American positions. Because the question was transitory in nature, he reasoned, it could certainly be treated in a separate protocol, as he had himself proposed to the Foreign Office in July, but he had no objection to including it in the Dumbarton Oaks document either. Gladwyn Jebb proposed a compromise solution: a chapter on interim arrangements could be included in the conference's proposals with a provision that its transitory nature should preclude its being made a part of the final U.N. charter. Gromyko proved the most negative, arguing that a set of proposals relating to peace and security would be incomplete without a provision for dealing with them in the interim period. He agreed with Jebb, however, that a section on the issue might not actually have to appear in the organization's final charter.[20]

There was also disagreement over how the transitional provisions should be phrased. The Soviets wanted language at least as strong as that in the original American plan and suggested even that the Big Four should "assume full responsibility" for the maintenance of peace and security in the interim period—a kind of temporary Four Policemen. This was exactly the sort of thing that Hull wished to avoid, however, to prevent senatorial difficulties. Thus Stettinius explained to Gromyko that the American chief executive could not under his nation's established constitutional procedures assume such wide-ranging responsibility before Congress approved a special agreement for providing armed forces to the new international organization. (Indeed, Halifax had previously hoped that an interim arrangement might force the United States to do just that, thus cementing American participation in the new world organization.) If the Dumbarton Oaks proposals were to contain a section on interim arrangements, Stettinius said, it could not restrict the freedom of the United States to act or not as it saw fit. The delegates finally agreed to adopt the language of the Moscow Declaration, which said only that the Great Powers should "consult with one another" on the possibilities for "joint action" to maintain peace and security in the immediate postwar period.[21]

This decision, combined with the previously agreed to exception regarding the use of force in the interim period, answered Cadogan's objections and returned the conference's attention to the basic issue of regionalism. The outcome was a compromise between the British and American positions that Gromyko finally accepted on 19 September. Although based on Pasvolsky's "Role of Local and Regional Agencies," this section differed in several ways from the American planner's views. It was less explicit than the American plan about subordinating regional organizations to the authority of the Security Council. It also stated the delegates' approval of regional bodies in more negative terms, saying only that "nothing in the Charter should preclude the existence of regional arrangements or agencies." And it omitted the part of the American proposal that permitted any state to bring an issue before the Security Council, even if it was already being dealt with by a regional association. (This idea, stated in more general terms, was later included in another chapter of the Dumbarton Oaks proposals.) Given their own ambivalence over regionalism, the Americans could not have resisted these changes very strenuously. If they did not want to encourage excessive reliance on regional agencies, neither did they want to invite the council to interfere in Pan-American handling of questions pertaining solely to the Western Hemisphere. Perhaps the Americans could not have it both ways, but this section, which mildly discouraged regional bodies while enhancing their autonomy, was about as close as they could come.[22]

The Americans also wanted to have it both ways on the potentially more divisive issues of postwar bases and territorial trusteeships. Their goal here, as the British had perceived it at the time of the Stettinius mission to London in April, was to use the authority of the new United Nations to permit them to take over strategic islands and bases in the Pacific while continuing to pose as the champion of the world's dependent peoples resisting colonial rule. This dual objective was to be accomplished through a system of territorial trusteeships, much like the mandates granted by the League of Nations, that would sanction United States control of key island bases under the friendly auspices of the new world organization. To this purpose, the American preconference proposal called for the creation of a trusteeship council directed by the General Assembly to supervise the administration of designated trust territories, including both former league mandates and other possessions that might be detached from the defeated enemy states, for the ostensible purposes of promoting their economic advancement, developing their political skills toward eventual independence, guaranteeing their good treatment, and furthering international peace and security.[23]

The British saw plenty to be worried about in this proposal. They viewed the trusteeship council as the entering wedge of an American attempt to use the postwar organization to deprive them of their own colonial possessions, something that they intended to resist as strenuously as possible. Issuing vague statements about self-government in such documents as the Atlantic Charter was one thing, they reasoned, but the American trusteeship plan, which might permit the new United Nations to inspect a colony without the mother country's consent or to take petitions directly from dependent peoples, was quite another. It would lead to no end of meddling in what London regarded as its private business and promised, at least eventually, to encourage independence movements throughout the colonized world. These fears made the Americans' self-serving motives for proposing trusteeships seem all the more annoying. Not that the British disapproved of the United States taking over strategic bases within the Japanese mandates; on the contrary, they made it very clear that they did not. But they objected to the way in which the Americans proposed to escape the political consequences of their acts, to avoid being tainted by imperialism while taking new possessions throughout the Pacific region. It would be much better, from the British standpoint, to force the Americans to own up to what they were doing; then, at least, they might feel constrained to cease their excessive moralizing about the treatment of other nations' colonies.[24]

Realists in the Foreign Office understood that this outcome was unlikely, however; the Americans would never be willing to reveal the true nature of their goals in the Pacific, even if they were honest with themselves. The best that might be hoped for was to limit the notion of trusteeship in a way that would give the United States what it wanted territorially while preventing the United Nations from interfering in the colonial affairs of others. What was required was some form of international trusteeship system limited to "ex-enemy dependent territories," which the Foreign Office hoped would satisfy the desire of the Americans "to find a cloak for their intentions in the Pacific" without threatening British control of the empire. Planners at Whitehall spent the summer working on such a compromise formula, although without much expectation that they would succeed in appeasing their counterparts in Washington.[25]

In fact, they had difficulties much closer to home. The Colonial Office opposed making any reference to mandates and territorial trusteeship at the Dumbarton Oaks talks—so much so that it had declined to send anyone to Washington in order to avoid provoking comment on the issue. What the Colonial Office really wanted was an end to the league's mandate system, which it had found excessively restrictive; any new system, no matter how circumscribed, was almost certain to be worse. To put it gently, the Colonial Office did not trust the Americans, and it saw no reason to placate them on an issue it saw as vital to British interests. This view, always dominant in the office, became even stronger after Sir Hilton Poynton became head of the Defense and General Department following the reorganization of May 1944. Historian Wm. Roger Louis has written that there began then "a perceptible hardening of the line not only towards the Americans but also towards the Foreign Office" that would make it hard to reach any sort of a compromise, either in London or at Dumbarton Oaks.[26]

In July, with the United States threatening to press the trusteeship issue vigorously at the upcoming conference, the Foreign and Colonial Offices attempted to reach agreement on a unified British position. Because the troublesome question of creating a trusteeship council was now included on the American agenda, Poynton decided that he should travel to Dumbarton Oaks himself to present his government's case. He still opposed giving away anything of substance to the Americans, although he was willing to consider the Foreign Office's idea of a trusteeship system limited to former German and Japanese mandates as the least the United States would accept. But now the Foreign Office thought that this would not be enough. The Americans seemed certain to insist on some sort of a trusteeship and colonial bureau to oversee the administration of at least the former mandates and probably other colonies as well. Cadogan thought that such an agency might not turn out to be so meddlesome in practice as the Colonial Office feared in theory. If the goal of the United States, he wrote, was primarily "to give an air of respectability to their annexation of the Japanese islands, I don't think we need be very frightened. I should doubt whether the Americans would submit themselves to very tight control." Others in the Foreign Office regarded agreement to something in this area as necessary to insure American involvement in the new world organization. Jebb predicted that the United States delegation at Dumbarton Oaks might take the view that a colonial bureau was necessary to win the approval of the Senate. If so, he reasoned, the British group should acquiesce because "it would be enormously in our interest to strike the bargain."[27]

The Colonial Office disagreed. It did not think that the topic of colonial administration should be discussed in Washington at all, much less that the British delegation should be prepared to yield ground on it. The conflict that developed over this issue between the Foreign and Colonial Offices was a natural one, based on the primary interests of each. For the Colonial Office, nothing could be more important than the protection of British freedom of action in dealing with the empire, but the Foreign Office, concerned with somewhat larger issues, had to be willing to sacrifice at least some colonial autonomy to achieve its paramount goal of American participation in the postwar world organization. The Foreign Office prevailed, at least in the instructions that the government issued to its delegates. The British group was authorized to approve a trusteeship system and, "as a last resort," to agree to the creation of an international colonial bureau to collect annual reports. "But," Jebb wrote, "I very much doubt whether this will be found satisfactory to the Americans." If not, he continued, the Foreign Office should keep in mind how important a commitment by the United States to a postwar body would be to British security and be prepared to "go a long way towards adopting American theories in regard to 'territorial trusteeship.'"[28]

British objections had some effect on State Department planners, who reduced the authority of the trusteeship council in their final preconference proposal. Especially to those concerned with bases, winning Great Power support for the trusteeship plan seemed most important; surely some other way could be found to persuade the British to move their colonies toward independence later. As Isaiah Bowman told Webster on 4 August, the Americans now recognized that their original plan had been far too "academic," by which he meant naive. It had been written, Bowman said, by young men, one of whom had openly described himself as an "idealist" in the State Department and had been warned "never to use that word again." Still, even the revised trusteeship plan seemed too strong to Webster, who described it as the only "snag" in the American preconference proposal, and to Cadogan, who said that the issue was "going to be nasty" at Dumbarton Oaks.[29]

Webster and Cadogan need not have been so worried, however, because objections from a more important source would cause the trusteeship plan to be removed altogether from the American agenda for Dumbarton Oaks. That source was the United States military, which had been operating under the assumption that the mandated islands conquered from Japan would remain firmly and permanently in American hands as bases for their postwar operations. Secretary of the Navy Frank Knox, for example, told the House Committee on Foreign Affairs on 9 March 1944 that the Japanese mandates "have become Japanese territory and as we capture them they are ours." Because any plan for trusteeship threatened unfettered American control over the islands, which military leaders now regarded as vital to the nation's security and theirs by right of conquest, it promised to become a major point of dispute in postwar planning between the Departments of State and War—the equivalent, in American terms, of the British conflict between the Foreign and Colonial Offices.[30]

The War Department's view was set forth in a report by Admiral Richard E.

Byrd, the famed polar explorer, who had been commissioned by President
Roosevelt to investigate the postwar needs of the United States for bases in the
Pacific. Byrd's study, completed in May 1944, emphasized the requirement for
a strong American military posture in the postwar period. It argued that the
United States should maintain a powerful army and navy (as opposed to any
reliance upon disarmament or the peacekeeping forces of an international
organization), assume almost sole responsibility for keeping the peace in the
Pacific, and, to this end, hold on to island bases seized there from the Japanese.
As Joseph Grew, the State Department's director of Far Eastern Affairs, pointed
out, this report was completely out of step with the ideas of both the president
and the department for a trusteeship agency within the new world body.
Perhaps, Grew proposed, some way could be found to satisfy everyone's objectives—to harmonize the need for national defense with a system of international cooperation.[31]

State Department planners were willing, at least, to try. They suggested that
their trusteeship plan be considered only in the most general terms at Dumbarton Oaks, leaving any discussion of its eventual application to specific territories until after the new world organization was created. Then the United States
could quietly exempt, "in the interests of peace and security," whatever island
bases the War Department considered vital to the defense of the Pacific. In
addition, planners advanced a change in the proposal itself, shifting responsibility for reports and inspections on military matters within the trust territories
away from the trusteeship committee and to the Security Council, where the
United States would have a veto over any questions affecting its Pacific bases.
Hull, who regarded a new trusteeship plan as essential to the success of any
international organization, hoped that these concessions would placate the
military leaders.[32]

They did not, however. When the State Department submitted its tentative
plans to the Pentagon in late June, the result was a storm of criticism. The new
secretary of the navy, James V. Forrestal, called Stettinius on 7 July to ask if the
trusteeship draft was a serious document and if the president was already
committed to it. About the Japanese mandates, Forrestal said, "that's one place
we should not have any doubt about who runs those islands." At Hull's urging,
Roosevelt now stated his support for the State Department's view, writing to the
Joint Chiefs of Staff on 10 July that he was "working on the idea that the United
Nations will ask the United States to act as Trustee for the Japanese mandated
islands." But even this did not satisfy the military, who thought that FDR was
failing to understand the important security interests at stake for the United
States. Where the nation's defense was concerned, they argued, trusteeship
authority was just not good enough; only outright ownership could provide the

kind of total control that the Joint Chiefs of Staff thought the situation required. They thus continued to object to any plan for a trusteeship council
within the new world organization. Under these circumstances, State Department planners decided not to risk making a proposal that they might have
to repudiate later and deleted the section on trusteeship from their final
preconference recommendations, although not from the plan's table of con-
tents, before sending them to the British and the Soviets on 18 July.[33]

The debate over trusteeship continued in meetings of the American group
leading up to the conference at Dumbarton Oaks. This time the military
representatives—Generals Strong and Fairchild, Admirals Willson and Train—
took a different approach, emphasizing the impact of trusteeship on Soviet-
American relations. As the generals and admirals saw it, discussion of trusteeship at Dumbarton Oaks was dangerous because it might encourage the Russians to make territorial demands of their own in the Far East that, if rejected,
could reduce their promised support for the war in Asia. From a military
standpoint, the uniformed delegates argued, nothing was so important as to
risk Soviet participation in the fighting against Japan; thus any reference to the
postwar territorial settlement must scrupulously be avoided.[34]

This argument, which military leaders would also employ in other policy
debates during 1944 and 1945, was repeated in a memorandum from the
Army Chief of Staff, General George C. Marshall, to Hull on 3 August. Should
Russia stay out of the fighting in Asia, the Army leader argued, because of the
Americans' "untimely" pressing of the "territorial settlement" issue, the United
States "must be prepared to accept responsibility for a longer war." In emphasizing the importance of the USSR, Marshall—who would himself serve as
secretary of state under Truman—also advised the State Department to consider that the Soviets, like the Americans, would be "dominant in their respective areas" of the postwar world; presumably, this entitled each to special
territorial concessions after the war. Although viewing the problem from an
opposite standpoint, Hull too saw the connection between trusteeship and
United States relations with the Soviets. "It was not hard to see," the secretary of
state wrote later, "that Russia would not oppose outright acquisition of these
islands, but it was also not hard to see that Russia would use this acquisition as
an example and precedent for similar acquisitions by herself." Thus, Hull
thought, American adherence to trusteeship rather than outright ownership in
the Pacific was important to keep the Russians in line in Eastern Europe and
elsewhere.[35]

As was usually the case in debates of this type, immediate wartime considerations carried the day. By mid-August the American group had decided not to
discuss the question of trusteeships at Dumbarton Oaks—although the mili-

tary representatives, acknowledging that previous United States expressions of interest in the subject might prove embarrassing for the American negotiators, thought that the Joint Chiefs of Staff would be willing to reconsider if the British or Russians insisted on discussing the matter. They need not have worried about the British, however, who were delighted to learn that the entire trusteeship problem would be deferred for later, although Halifax warned Eden that the Foreign Office would still have "the sentimentalists and American politics to reckon with" in the future. London may have regarded the United States military as an unlikely ally for defending its colonial policy, but on the issue of trusteeships, at least, the two had a genuine community of interest arising from the War Department's determination to guarantee its ability to insure American security by retaining strategic bases in the postwar period.[36]

The Russians reacted less favorably. They had already demonstrated that they were not shy about discussing postwar territorial questions, especially now that their victorious armies were spreading out over Eastern Europe, and apparently saw no reason why trusteeship should not be dealt with at Dumbarton Oaks. The issue, moreover, seemed a promising one for them. Not only might the principle of trusteeship legitimize territorial gains made by the Soviet Union—Stalin certainly was not above taking territory with the blessings of the West—but it held out abundant opportunities for pointing a finger at the negative aspects of British colonialism as well. And if the problem of imperialism should provoke disagreements between his Western allies—something that Stalin doubted was very likely—so much the better for the Soviet cause. Thus Gromyko wasted no time before introducing the issue at Dumbarton Oaks, interrupting the presentation of the American proposals on 22 August to inquire about the missing section on trusteeship. Stettinius, apparently embarrassed, could only reply that the United States was still considering the matter and would not be able to bring forth a plan on the subject during the current talks. Gromyko raised the question again three days later, this time in a meeting of the Joint Steering Committee, where Pasvolsky repeated the noncommittal answer given by Stettinius.[37]

Trusteeship also came up in a luncheon conversation between Pasvolsky and Arkady Sobolev toward the end of the conference. Sobolev, the deputy chairman of the Soviet delegation, handled the issue with much more tact than Gromyko had displayed. He began by remarking that it was a "pity" that the trusteeship question had not been discussed in the course of the meetings at Dumbarton Oaks. The Americans could be assured, he continued, that the Soviet government was interested in the problem, even though it had little to contribute to a discussion of the question because it lacked both colonies and—here he must have had to suppress a smile—"experience in colonial administration." He also said that the plan presented by the United States at the Moscow conference in March 1943, which had emphasized independence as the goal of a system of trusteeship, had been "very favorably received" by his government; too bad that it had been rejected by the British. Pasvolsky refused to rise to this bait, however, and remarked—not quite truthfully—that one of the plan's key features had in fact been first suggested by London.[38]

Sobolev also tried to learn something about the State Department's future plans regarding trusteeship. After commenting that there was no doubt that any new international organization would be "an incomplete structure" without some machinery for trusteeship purposes, he asked about the Americans' projected timetable for handling the issue. Should the whole question be held in abeyance until the "big conference" could meet? Or might some preliminary steps be taken in advance? Pasvolsky, always cautious in dealing with the Russians, replied that the United States had not as yet considered the matter, but that either approach seemed feasible to him. Sobolev thought that the Soviets would prefer to have an exchange of views before the next conference and would be especially happy to receive American documents on a trusteeship plan because, he reiterated, they had "done very little" in this area themselves and were waiting to follow the lead of the more experienced United States.[39]

With the trusteeship question off the agenda, the Soviets sought another method of securing United Nations sanction for the establishment of military bases outside their borders. On 31 August, during a meeting of the security subcommittee, the Russian representative proposed a general agreement whereby smaller member states would be obligated to provide facilities, including bases, for use by the peacekeeping organization. In addition, the Russian suggested, the Security Council should be empowered to make whatever supplementary agreements along these lines it regarded as necessary to handle an emergency situation. There was nothing very new in this idea. Roosevelt and Churchill had agreed at Tehran to the creation of "strong points" near Germany and Japan for enforcing peace terms on those countries. Both the British and American plans also contained similar provisions, which the military of each nation regarded as essential to the success of future peacekeeping operations, and members of the Formulation Group hardly debated the provision before adding it to their draft proposals one day later.[40]

The situation began to change on 4 September, when Gromyko elaborated on the Soviet idea in the Joint Steering Committee. What the Russians wanted, he said, was a provision that would require states with meager armed forces—

and therefore little of a tangible nature to contribute to U.N. peacekeeping efforts—to provide the Security Council with bases. Pasvolsky responded that he thought this was already included in the draft proposals; anything more would be, as the British Joint Staff Mission put it, "unnecessary and undesirable." But Gromyko insisted on the need for more explicit language. The next day the Soviets raised the question again in the Formulation Group, arguing that "member states not having sufficient armed forces for carrying out enforcement action" should "make available territory for bases for this purpose." The American and British delegations repeated Pasvolsky's argument and objected to the invidious phrasing of the new proposal, which they thought sounded discriminatory against smaller nations.[41]

This new development alarmed the American delegation. The Soviets, they felt certain, were up to something here; most of the group thought that they intended to use this provision to acquire bases for themselves in neighboring countries, such as Finland or Korea, with U.N. authority. This was, of course, the same purpose for which the Americans had devised the idea of trusteeship in the Pacific—and was also the goal of the State Department's current negotiations with such nations as Brazil—but it seemed somehow illegitimate when pursued in this manner by the Soviet Union. As Stettinius put it in his "flash items for the President" on 6 September, the "abrupt" Soviet insistence on receiving bases and sites from small powers was "a most disturbing element." It would have to be resisted as firmly as possible.[42]

Why this change of mind? Why did the Americans, after approving—even proposing—the furnishing of bases by member states, suddenly object to this new provision? Part of the explanation may have been the more explicit Soviet reference to small states, although the British preconference document had used similar terms—and a similar rationale—without attracting the State Department's attention. More important, however, was the manner in which the conversations were progressing at Dumbarton Oaks. The mood, as the American group perceived it, had changed from cooperation to intransigence on the part of the Soviets. There had developed, Stettinius wrote to Roosevelt, a "sudden Soviet insistence on maximum use of exact phraseology of several sections of the Soviet plan," of which the bases proposal was only one manifestation. This had first occurred, according to the head of the American delegation, during a 1 September meeting of the Joint Steering Committee; it had since grown into a general tendency. Stettinius was not sure what this hardening of the Soviet position signified, but it aroused his suspicions as well as his competitive instincts. If the Russians wanted this new proposal so badly, he reasoned, there must be something wrong with it.[43]

Worse still, this shift in tone paralleled what the State Department viewed as a change in the general behavior of the Soviet Union. Stalin's refusal to cooperate over Poland—by this time the Warsaw uprising had completed its first unhappy month without assistance from the Red Army—was calling into question all American hopes that the Soviets might decide to turn away from a course of ruthless domination in Eastern Europe. As W. Averell Harriman, the United States ambassador in Moscow, put it on 10 September, "the job of getting the Soviet Government to play a decent role in international affairs is . . . going to be more difficult than we had hoped." This did not mean that the State Department was about to give up on the question of postwar cooperation—Harriman, for example, described himself as "disappointed but not discouraged" by the turn of events—but, under the circumstances, it was hardly surprising that the Americans' perception of this trend should have reinforced their concern over the Soviet group's demand for bases from their smaller neighbors.[44]

Stettinius found the Soviet proposal so troubling that he convened a special subcommittee of the American group to study the problem. This subcommittee, which consisted of Admiral Willson, Generals Embick and Fairchild, Stanley Hornbeck, and Charles Bohlen, reported on 5 September with what amounted to an indictment of the idea. The taking of bases, it said, "might be interpreted as a threat to the sovereignty of small nations" and might even prevent them from ratifying the charter and joining the postwar organization. The subcommittee also regarded the provision as unfair. "The proposal," it argued, "could obligate a weak state to accept on its territory the permanent stationing of the armed forces of another state," with political consequences that might be disastrous for the success of the new United Nations both at home and abroad.[45]

The American group as a whole then discussed the issue in its regular morning meeting at Dumbarton Oaks. Stettinius explained that the problem with the Soviet proposal was that it "seemed to include the transfer of sovereignty" and would never, as such, be accepted by the smaller states. The American leader also objected that the provision would be "in the form of an obligation." Someone wondered why the Soviets should have brought up this question now. Admiral Willson replied that it was because most of the bases the Soviets had in mind would already be in existence by the end of the war; putting in this provision now before they could be dismantled would, presumably, save them the trouble of constructing new ones later. Several members of the group thought that an alternative formula might be devised whereby bases could be leased instead of turned over outright, but no way of saying so was found that seemed satisfactory to anything like a majority of the Americans.[46]

At this point, the military representatives began to waver. What was developing seemed to be precisely the kind of territorial squabble that they had feared might jeopardize Soviet participation in the war against Japan. Nor was the State Department's forceful position exactly in keeping with the United States military's hopes for worldwide bases of its own in the postwar era—a worrisome consideration for those uniformed delegates whose internationalism was always designed to serve nationalist purposes. Admiral Willson thus expressed doubt whether "total disapproval" was the "correct attitude" for the United States to take; perhaps, he hoped, some way could be found to defer this troublesome issue until a later meeting. Hornbeck, who for his own reasons apparently shared this hope, proposed a compromise that he thought might buy time: the council could be given the authority to ask a smaller nation for a site and begin construction of a base, with terms to be worked out later. Although the uniformed delegates saw merit in this idea, a majority of the group still opposed any compromise and favored continued outright rejection of the Soviet plan. Thus, with no acceptable alternative plan in sight, the American position was growing firm in opposition to the compulsory granting of bases.[47]

It became hard as a rock later in the day, when Stettinius raised the question in a meeting at the White House with Roosevelt and Hull. At first the head of the American delegation had difficulty gaining either of his superiors' "settled interest" in the bases issue; Roosevelt, in particular, seemed too involved in plans for his upcoming trip to Quebec for a meeting with Churchill. But when Stettinius explained what was involved—the demand of territory or bases by the Security Council—both Roosevelt and Hull voiced "violent objections." They thought that it would be a "great mistake" at that time to try to compel smaller nations to furnish bases for use by the new international organization. It would be much better, they thought, to grant the council authority to request, but not to demand, such facilities.[48]

The Americans and British presented a united position on the Soviet request for bases, which Cadogan was now describing as "rather sinister," in the Formulation Group meeting on 7 September. They raised three main objections to the Soviet proposal. First, it would violate the principle of the sovereign equality of all states by assuming that weaker nations, including, of course, some of the British dominions, must accept a provision that stronger powers undoubtedly would not. Second, it would place "special obligations" on the weaker states. And third, it would obligate some nations to accept the permanent stationing of the armed forces of a foreign state on their territory. The

Soviets quickly retreated in the face of these arguments, permitting Stettinius to report to Hull on 8 September that the question seemed to have "somewhat diminished in importance" for the Soviet group. This assessment proved accurate. Four days later, Gromyko withdrew the Soviet proposal regarding bases, and within a week the last remaining reference to it had been eliminated from the draft agreements. The Soviets had not conceded as much as it seemed, however. Gromyko's withdrawal did not affect the original, more general, provision on bases, which remained in the Dumbarton Oaks document without British or American objection. (They had, of course, not only approved but proposed this general statement.) Thus, if the Soviet Union wished to use the world organization to sanction the establishment of bases inside its neighbors' territory, it could still find a way to do so under the terms of the proposed charter.[49]

The small nations' lack of military and economic resources also posed another problem for the conference. This time the issue was raised by the United States, which thought that the better-off members of the new world organization should "join in mutual efforts to afford relief and aid to states assuming undue burdens" as a result of enforcement measures instituted by the Security Council. In making this proposal, the State Department was reacting to yet another lesson of the League of Nations period, when it seemed that members had been excessively wary about voting sanctions because of the hardships that they might pose for themselves. The Americans, who assumed that the Great Powers would accept the burdens of maintaining peace in the postwar period, feared that the more difficult circumstances of lesser nations might prevent them from participating wholeheartedly in future actions of the Security Council.[50]

The Soviets objected to this proposal when it came up in the Joint Steering Committee on 4 September. They argued that the inclusion of such a provision would only be misleading because no specific measures of assistance or compensation could as a practical matter be devised. More important, the Soviets viewed this idea in the same light as they did the American proposal for a social and economic council within the new world organization. Such provisions, they said, might cause the United Nations to degenerate from an organization concentrating on international security—its true purpose in their view—to one dealing primarily with international relief. Nothing should be included in the charter, the Soviets contended, that might detract from the effectiveness of the new body as a peacekeeping force.[51]

The British and Americans disagreed with this view, however, emphasizing what they regarded as the practical importance of a provision of this kind.

They argued that many states, and especially those with meager resources, would find it difficult to accept even the commitment involved in United Nations membership unless provisions for assistance and compensation were included in the charter. This might prevent some nations from joining the peacekeeping organization initially and later limit the cooperation of the body's weaker members, especially in cases where they might be economically dependent upon the states against whom measures were being taken. Thus, the British and Americans argued, the provision was not a matter of relief in the sense that the Soviets seemed to be using the term but an important means of guaranteeing the effectiveness of sanctions voted by the council.[52]

The result of this dispute was a compromise that left the principle of compensation intact while answering the main Soviet objection. The Dumbarton Oaks proposals said that any state, whether a member of the world organization or not, that experienced special economic difficulties as a result of carrying out measures voted by the Security Council, would have the right to "consult" with the council about a solution to its financial problems. Although relief would not be automatic, it remained at least a possibility, a consideration that the State Department hoped might reassure weaker nations nervous about taking on the responsibilities of membership in the new U.N.[53]

As these debates revealed, any question pertaining to the Security Council was bound to present difficulties. Certainly none of the Big Three wanted to create an agreement that might add to its postwar problems or limit its postwar opportunities—dangers that really only entered the picture where the actions of the all-powerful council were concerned. Still, the delegates at Dumbarton Oaks managed for the most part to find compromise solutions to their disagreements over the executive body; to do otherwise would have been to admit that a genuine security organization of the sort they all envisioned was impossible. This irenic spirit went only so far, however. Voting in the Security Council, upon which all peacekeeping activity had to depend, would prove to be a particular problem. And on one issue—the Great Power veto—the representatives of the Big Three would find that the stakes were too high to compromise; the result would be a dispute that drove the conference to the point of impasse.

8 *Impasse*

For most of the conference at Dumbarton Oaks, the delegates refused to consider the possibility that they might fail. They drew confidence from their careful preparations, including the exchange of remarkably similar preliminary proposals, as well as from the assurances expressed at Tehran and later by the Big Three leaders that they shared the planners' view of the importance of a postwar peacekeeping organization. All that remained by August 1944 was to work out the details—no small task, they thought, but one that certainly could be accomplished. Failure, moreover, seemed unthinkable; it would allow the world to continue in its present state of anarchy, leave open the door to a World War III, and possibly result in conflict among the Great Powers themselves. Ultimately, of course, these considerations added to the participants' concern when the unthinkable appeared about to happen, when the issue of the Great Power veto in the Security Council threatened to end the conference without agreement on plans for a workable postwar body.

The issue of voting in the council was both controversial and complicated. It contained two parts—the size of the majority needed to win a vote and the use of the veto by permanent members—neither of which would prove easy to get a firm grasp on, much less to resolve. Perhaps the best mark of the difficulties involved in answering these questions was the inability of the Great Powers to know their own minds. All three nations would vacillate on the majority problem, in part because each was willing to trade its position here for an advantage in settling the more important question of the veto. The veto issue turned out to be even less tidy, with only the Russians maintaining a clear and consistent position on it through the summer and fall of 1944. The British and American views were extremely muddled—so much so that it is often difficult to ascertain from the conference record exactly what they were—and at times seemed a mystery even to their own delegations. The Westerners also reversed themselves on this question at Dumbarton Oaks and immediately after, with the Americans turning away from and the British eventually turning toward the fixed Soviet position. Yet, despite this confusion, the issue of the veto would seem so vital to all three nations that they would prove willing to break up the conference—and jeopardize all their hopes for creating a postwar organization—rather than accept what they regarded as an unsatisfactory formula for its use.[1]

The most vexing issue was what to do when a permanent member of the Security Council was involved in a dispute. Should a Great Power then be permitted to use its veto—and if so, at what stage of the controversy? Or should it be denied its usual right to prevent the council from acting and be bound by the decision like any other nation would be? Either option was certain to violate one important principle or another; there seemed no way to maintain both Great Power unity, on which the idea of the veto was based, and some reasonable conception of equity with smaller nations. Nor did compromise appear likely in light of the emphasis that each of the Big Three placed on the matter. In time, these problems would cause the delegates at Dumbarton Oaks to question all of their premises about postwar organization and to consider starting over with an entirely different design.[2]

The American group outlined both sides of the veto argument in its preconference meetings. Those who favored an unlimited veto emphasized the need for unity among the Great Powers, without whose resources the world organization could not hope to succeed. In this view, their involvement in the peacekeeping body was more important than any consideration of fairness; hence the rights of smaller nations must not be safeguarded in the new world body by sacrificing the all-important support of the Big Four (or Five). Besides, they saw no possibility of disciplining the behavior of the Great Powers even if they were stripped of the veto when involved in a dispute. A judgment against one of the Big Four, they argued, would probably drive it out of the world organization; the result would be the next world war that the United Nations was designed to prevent. The situation would be even worse if the Great Power turned out to be the United States or the Soviet Union, because all postwar military estimates indicated that no judgment could be effectively enforced against either of them. Thus, this faction of the American group concluded, questions involving the major powers would have to be dealt with by conventional diplomacy or by some other means outside the framework of the new organization.[3]

Those who wanted to limit the veto had an answer for each of these points. Most important, in their view, was the numbing effect of an absolute veto on the peacekeeping powers of the world organization, which would be prevented from bringing about a settlement in any dispute involving a major power. It would thus be as impotent as the League of Nations had been when it found itself unable to discipline Germany or Japan in the years before the Second World War. In addition, they argued, the new security system would lose its effectiveness if only smaller states were subject to its control; among other things, this would leave it open to the charge of being an alliance of the Great

Powers to maintain the status quo. And finally, if attempting to settle a dispute involving a major power would lead to war anyway, the advocates of a limited veto thought it would be preferable to fight it under the aegis of the international organization. Then, at least, it would be clear which side was supported by right and morality.[4]

This response did not convince the veto's supporters, however. They replied by arguing that limiting the veto would put the power of decision in the hands of the majority of smaller nations on the Security Council—nations that did not have the resources required for enforcement. Such a result would reverse the important principle that the Great Powers, who would be called upon to provide the troops and munitions necessary to keep the peace, should have an absolute say about when and where those resources would be used. One consequence of this reversal, they contended, might be to make the new charter unacceptable to the United States Senate, raising the frightening possibilities of a return to isolationism and a refusal to join the postwar organization at all. Along similar lines, they also argued that the Senate might require an absolute veto to prevent the new body from interfering in American domestic questions, particularly those involving race. And finally, those who favored an unlimited veto raised the practical difficulty of determining what states were, in fact, involved in a dispute. Where should the line be drawn between direct and indirect involvement—always a particular problem where Great Powers were concerned?[5]

The other side saw the importance of small powers in a different light. They argued that peacekeeping would work only if the lesser nations joined and cooperated with the new world organization, and feared that an unrestricted veto might prevent the small powers from ratifying the proposed charter. Only by limiting the freedom of the Great Powers, they thought, could the planners be certain that the United Nations would enjoy the kind of universal support that seemed essential to the international body's success—and to its acceptance in the United States. Opponents of an absolute veto also turned another of its supporters' arguments against them. Because enforcement action could never be taken effectively against the United States anyway, they argued, that nation could easily afford to give up the possibility of being a judge in its own case; thus Senators need have no reason for concern about surrendering the veto. Similarly, they contended that the Senate's interest in reserving domestic questions could be satisfied some other way, such as by the inclusion of a blanket statement about the matter somewhere else in the charter. They also thought that a solution could be found to the practical difficulty of determining exactly which nations were parties to a dispute, perhaps by the vote of a two-thirds majority in the council. An absolute veto, they concluded, was not only unnecessary but might prove detrimental to the fortunes of the new organization as well.[6]

All of this occurred two weeks before the conference opened at Dumbarton Oaks, and the American group still had not arrived at a firm position on the veto. Through the spring and summer of 1944 the majority of State Department planners had favored retaining the absolute veto, even in cases where a Great Power was involved in a dispute. This view reflected in part the position of Secretary of State Hull, who feared the domestic political consequences of attempting to limit the veto power of the United States. As an expression of this concern the secretary had prepared for his meeting with senatorial leaders in April by asking Leo Pasvolsky for a memorandum outlining how the veto would serve to safeguard the nation's interests. The resulting paper stressed that a concurring vote by the United States would be required for any important action by the Security Council, including the assumption of jurisdiction over a dispute, the adoption of terms of a settlement, the determination of threats to or breaches of the peace, the decision to use force, and the inauguration of negotiations for a general reduction in armaments. Any limitation on the veto would eliminate at least one, and possibly most, of these safeguards—something that Hull felt certain the Senate would never accept.[7]

Pasvolsky must have been a less than willing participant in the drafting of this memorandum. Certainly his heart was never in the idea of the absolute veto, which he thought discriminated unfairly in favor of the Great Powers and might lead to abuses by the Soviet Union. In preconference meetings during July and August, he stood out as the veto's primary critic, arguing that some formula had to be devised to deal with a situation where a permanent council member was involved in a dispute. The difficulty lay in finding a satisfactory formula. After considerable discussion, the American planners failed to reach a decision by 18 July, when the United States draft proposal was sent out saying only that "provisions" would "need to be worked out" with respect to this question. During August, Pasvolsky focused his efforts on the possibility of using abstention by the Great Powers as a means to solve the veto problem, but he was never able to find a consensus—or, for that matter, even a majority—in the American delegation to support his limited-veto position.[8]

Pasvolsky raised the idea of abstention at a group meeting at Dumbarton Oaks on 7 August. It represented, he thought, an ideal compromise because it would eliminate the problem of a permanent member voting on its own case while leaving the principle of the veto intact. James Dunn disagreed, however, arguing that no plan for a world body would prove acceptable to the Senate that permitted military action to be taken without the concurrence of the United States. Pasvolsky's supporters responded with a further compromise—retain the veto for enforcement measures but require abstention for all other cases. This might, they contended, appease senators and others worried about protecting American freedom of action where enforcement was concerned. But it did not satisfy the proponents of the unlimited veto, who had a different view of how abstention might work. These planners thought that in practice the Great Powers could be counted on not to vote when involved in a dispute, either voluntarily or in response to the pressures of international public opinion. They thus contended that the issue Pasvolsky was raising might turn out to be no problem at all, that the principle of the unlimited veto could be retained without fear of an awkward situation developing in the future.[9]

Most of the American group hoped, at least, that this analysis would prove correct. The frustrating search for a compromise voting formula was bearing no fruit, and on 10 August, following a long discussion of the veto issue, the delegates voted eleven to four to abandon their efforts and recommend that the Great Power veto be retained without qualifications. This seemed to settle the matter, especially in light of Secretary Hull's previous support of the unlimited veto. It appeared that the United States would go to the Dumbarton Oaks Conference firmly in favor of the principle of Great Power unanimity.[10]

Pasvolsky refused to give up, however. After losing the vote on 10 August, he proposed that the American group send a memorandum to Roosevelt and Hull asking for guidance and outlining arguments for and against permitting permanent members to vote on their own cases. In addition, he suggested that the delegates continue to think about possible compromise solutions—just in case the president or secretary of state should insist that a special formula was necessary or the British and Russians should disagree with the American view. Pasvolsky was not just stalling for time. Although he did not reveal it at the time, he apparently knew that Hull was wavering on the veto issue and did not want the secretary to get the idea that the American group was unified in supporting its unlimited use. He also probably suspected that the question would turn out to be a major source of controversy at Dumbarton Oaks.[11]

Critics of the unlimited veto thus continued to suggest possible voting formulas in meetings of the American group. One new approach came from the representatives of the Joint Chiefs of Staff, Generals Embick and Fairchild, who would later be among the strongest supporters of Great Power unanimity. Embick and Fairchild offered two refinements of the plan for abstention, proposing that it be invoked only when two-thirds of the council, including the other four permanent members, voted to do so and that it not go into effect until after the new organization had been in operation for several (perhaps three) years. This would protect the interests of the Great Powers in the critical immediate postwar period and give them a chance to develop trust in one another. It might also prove more acceptable politically in the United States. Pasvolsky himself offered yet another proposal, which he drew from the British draft outline. The idea here was to limit the council to the making of recommendations where the peaceful settlement of disputes was concerned; then, because no coercion was involved, it might be feasible to deny all parties to a dispute the right to vote on suggested terms of settlement without threatening the privileged position of the Great Powers. In cases involving enforcement action, Pasvolsky now favored the formula suggested by Embick and Fairchild.[12]

All of this further confused the issue. From now on, the American delegates would have to determine whether they were discussing the veto's application to peaceful disputes, enforcement actions, or both. Some apparently never would get it straight. The importance of this distinction grew on 17 August, when Pasvolsky notified the group that Hull had rejected its decision to retain the unqualified Great Power veto. The planners would thus have to resume their efforts to construct a suitable compromise formula almost on the eve of the conference's opening. Pasvolsky's two-part plan—or three-part counting both the immediate and long-term elements of the Embick-Fairchild proposal— served as the basis for discussion. Its chief critic was Benjamin Cohen, the president's personal representative in the American delegation, who thought that limiting the council to offering suggestions about settling potentially dangerous disputes would make it impossible for the new world body to bring about peaceful change. The new U.N., he argued, should try to prevent wars from developing, not just resolve them after the fighting had begun. Cohen also had two suggestions of his own. One was to develop different voting procedures for recommendations and enforcement actions, with a permanent member permitted to vote on its own case only when the council was deciding to act. The second was to require an affirming vote of the General Assembly before the council could issue mandatory settlement terms. Perhaps a bit overwhelmed by so many options, and by no means certain of their own minds, the delegates decided to submit all of the proposed procedures to Hull and let him make the final selection.[13]

Hull took up the issue in a meeting with Pasvolsky, Dunn, and Hackworth in the secretary's office on 19 August. He indicated that he had read the group's minute on possible solutions to the veto question, which stated that Pasvolsky's rather complicated plan had more support than any other within the American delegation, and was now satisfied that this was the best approach to follow. In principle, at least, Hull had changed his mind since April—he now thought that a permanent member should not be permitted to vote on its own case when it came up before the Security Council. Why this change? Pasvolsky's perseverance was no doubt part of the reason; all of his arguments about the ethical complications raised by an unlimited veto had finally taken effect. In addition, two recent events had indicated increasing foreign and domestic support for qualifying the Great Power veto: the British delegation had arrived in Washington with a clear position opposing the absolute veto; and Republicans, including presidential nominee Thomas Dewey, had, as Cadogan put it, "set the cat among the pigeons" by beginning to criticize the idea of what they termed a postwar dictatorship by the Big Four. Hull, who may have wanted to reverse his position on this important question for some time, probably thought that the propitious moment had come to announce the change.[14]

This did not exactly clear up the issue, however. The American position remained ambiguous enough to be misunderstood by both participants and historians. Ruth B. Russell, who began her study of the origins of the United Nations charter in close collaboration with Leo Pasvolsky, has argued that Hull approved only the first part of Pasvolsky's proposal and left the veto in place when enforcement decisions were being made by the council. It seemed impossible, she wrote, that Hull could have meant to surrender the right of the United States to exercise the veto on enforcement questions; thus the new American position could only have covered votes taken through the council's deliberations concerning peaceful settlement. As a later historian has pointed out, however, there is nothing to support this view in the written record. The minutes of Hull's meeting with leading American planners on 19 August said only that "the votes of great powers involved in cases before the council should not be counted in the council's decisions with respect to such cases," making no mention of the distinction suggested by Russell. Hull's memoirs presented his decision in an even more straightforward manner. And Stettinius's diary shows no indication that Roosevelt's approval of Hull's recommendation a few days later included any difference in the Security Council's treatment of settlement and enforcement decisions. The direct documentary evidence all points to Hull having made a firm decision on 19 August against Great Powers ever voting on their own cases.[15]

Still, there is something in Russell's interpretation. As late as 24 August, the American delegation, already in meetings with the British and Russians at Dumbarton Oaks, was unable to state for the record its position on the veto issue. Certainly, as Hull remembered in his memoirs, there was still "some difference of opinion" within the group about whether abstention "should apply only to the pacific settlement of disputes in which one or more of the major nations were involved, or should apply also to enforcement action." There were also those who continued to object to the placing of any limitation on the veto at all, and who would later argue that the American planners had never meant to reject the principle of Great Power unanimity. This confusion may have reflected only poor communication within the American delegation; Dunn, Hackworth, and Pasvolsky apparently failed to communicate Hull's new position clearly enough to the remainder of the group. But there is also some reason to doubt the air of certainty that seems to permeate the documentary evidence. Hull's recollections of events, published in the cold war environment of 1948, were often edited to sharpen the contrast between his ideas and those of the Soviets, who favored a totally unqualified use of the veto. In addition, all of the Dumbarton Oaks summary records refer to the veto question only in general terms, obscuring any distinctions that may have arisen in the debate between peaceful settlement and enforcement action—and therefore any ambiguity that may have remained in the American position. Adding to this problem was the participants' pervasive use of the term "dispute," which some delegates may have been using in its specific sense of peaceful settlement while others employed it as a synonym for international conflict in general.[16]

It seems likely that Hull was responsible for much of the confusion. What he approved on 19 August was primarily a change in principle, not policy, that rejected the idea of the absolute veto without deciding the manner of or the occasion for its limitation. He continued this general approach when he had Stettinius present the question to Roosevelt, perhaps because he did not want to bother the president, who was then trying to resolve a difficult disagreement within the War Production Board, with the complicated details of the problem. Later, when the lines of the controversy formed at Dumbarton Oaks and the secretary's position hardened, he neglected to get word of the change to all of the American delegation, some of whom still believed that Hull favored only a moderate limitation on the Great Power veto—and only if it could be worked out in practice. No matter how great the confusion, however, Russell was wrong on the essential matter: at some point early in the Dumbarton Oaks Conference the official United States policy changed and became the elimination of the veto when a permanent member was involved in any sort of a dispute before the council. Only such a strong position can possibly explain the kind of controversy that Stettinius and Hull were willing to provoke to try to put it into effect.[17]

The British and Soviets, on the other hand, had their minds made up before they came to Dumbarton Oaks. Cadogan presented the British view to the Americans on 14 August: a Great Power should never be permitted to vote and exercise its veto when it was involved in a dispute before the council. This British prohibition included all questions—even those involving enforcement —although the War Cabinet recognized that a case of this kind concerning a Great Power would mean that the new organization had failed, and as historian Sir Llewellyn Thompson has put it, "there is little use in asking what would happen" then. When some of the pro-veto Americans raised similar objections of their own, Cadogan replied that an absolute veto would be strongly opposed by commonwealth nations, such as Canada, which would never understand why the United Kingdom could prevent action against itself whereas they could not. The British chairman also predicted similar opposition from other small powers, especially in Latin America. These arguments seemed so decisive to members of the British group that when they met to discuss the veto issue on 17 August only Jebb favored going over to the American position, which at that time still included an unlimited veto. The Soviet view was just as fixed as that of the British—but on the opposite side of the question. Their preconference proposal made no provision for any deviation from the principle of Great Power unanimity, and their delegation at Dumbarton Oaks would never waver in its support of an unqualified veto.[18]

The three delegations stated their opening positions on this issue when the organization subcommittee met for the second time on 24 August. Cadogan said that the British strongly favored denying the vote to any nation that was a party to a dispute, on the grounds that the veto power of a permanent member might prove difficult, and perhaps impossible, for smaller countries to accept. Gromyko stressed the need for unanimity among the Great Powers, arguing that nothing else was so essential to the success of the new world body. And Stettinius, as he put it, "called attention" to the American group's "interest" in the question of a qualified veto, which he said was still being considered within the United States delegation. British delegate Charles K. Webster later claimed that this meeting was responsible for the impasse that subsequently developed over the veto issue. In this view, the United States was at fault for not taking a clear position on the matter, which encouraged the Soviets to press their point when a united Anglo-American front might have carried the day without much dispute. Considering the importance that the Russians placed on the Great Power veto, however, it seems unlikely that they would have yielded sooner what they would not yield later. The veto controversy could not have been prevented so easily, if at all.[19]

The question of how many votes were needed to make a majority in the council also came up at this meeting. Cadogan expressed the British view that substantive decisions should be determined by two-thirds of the council's membership, a position that the Foreign Office had taken in its preconference proposals. The issue here, he explained, was not added security against a bad decision but fair treatment of smaller nations sitting on the Security Council. If important decisions could be made by a simple majority—including, of course, all of the Great Powers—the concurrence of only one other member would be required, thus enhancing the already dominant position of those with permanent tenure. A two-thirds majority, on the other hand, would have to include the votes of several of the smaller states, giving them a larger voice in the council's decisions, and perhaps making them more willing to participate in the activities of the new organization. As was often the case at Dumbarton Oaks, the British position on this issue reflected their concern for protecting the status of middle-sized nations—a group that included some key members of the commonwealth.[20]

The Russians took the opposite view. Gromyko said that the Soviets preferred determination by a simple majority, which would practically guarantee that any decision made by the permanent members would be ratified by the council as a whole. This position was in keeping with the principle, often voiced by the Soviet Union, that the security body should be run by the Great Powers who would provide most of the military forces needed to carry out its wishes. A simple majority would also make it easier for the council to act, another key Soviet principle. As for the Americans, Stettinius was again required to present a position in a state of flux. In their preliminary proposal, State Department planners had agreed with the Russians and favored a simple majority for all decisions, only to reverse this view in meetings following the arrival of the British delegation in Washington on 14 August. This sudden change produced more confusion within the American group as once again some delegates failed to get the word. Thus Admiral Hepburn reported happily after a meeting with Cadogan and Malkin on 25 August that the British were not entirely certain about a two-thirds majority and might change their minds—while at the same time Roosevelt was endorsing the American change to their position. Even Stettinius could not say for certain what his delegation's preference was on 24 August, with the result that he merely joined Gromyko in agreeing to study the British proposal.[21]

Over the next few days, the Americans developed firm positions on both voting questions. In each case, they moved from the Russian to the British view—a coincidence that could not have escaped the notice of either of the other delegations. Cadogan, at least, observed that the new American position "was in the nature of a shock to the Soviet Delegation." Stettinius announced the first of these changes during a meeting of the Joint Steering Committee on 25 August, declaring that now the United States "could agree" with the British proposal that important questions should be decided in the council by a two-thirds majority. Gromyko did not put up a fight. He "indicated no dissent," according to Stettinius, and said that he would inform his government of the new American position. This response seemed promising to Stettinius but less so to Cadogan, who wondered whether the inexperienced Soviet ambassador really would present the Anglo-American view fairly to the Kremlin—or whether anyone there would pay any attention to him if he did. Meanwhile the more important issue of the veto was deferred over the weekend. When it came up in the Joint Steering Committee on Monday, 28 August, it provoked the first of many long debates on the merits of this all-important question.[22]

Stettinius wasted no time in presenting the American group's new position. As soon as the issue was raised that morning, he said that the United States had come to the conclusion that a "guilty" party should not be permitted to vote on its own case, no matter who that party might be. Cadogan pointed out that this meant that the British and American groups were now in agreement. Gromyko, who Cadogan thought was surprised by the American reversal, said that this blanket prohibition was unacceptable to the Soviets. At least, the Russian leader argued, some "special procedure" needed to be worked out to cover the difficulties that would inevitably arise if a Great Power became involved in a dispute. He did not know what this procedure should be, he said, because his group had not considered the question before Dumbarton Oaks inasmuch as the Americans seemed to be working on a suitable formula. He did not know why they had given up. Cadogan, catching a suggestion of treachery in the Soviet leader's statement, asked if the Russians themselves might be able to devise an acceptable procedure before the conference concluded, to which Gromyko responded that they would surely try.[23]

Pasvolsky jumped to the American group's defense. He said that the planners had given "prolonged consideration" to the veto question before coming to the conclusion that they could not devise a satisfactory procedure for dealing with a dispute in which a Great Power was involved. It was only at this point, he said, that the American delegation had decided to support the British idea of denying any nation the right to vote on its own case—and then only because there seemed to be no other workable alternative. Pasvolsky and other members of the American group emphasized that they would be happy to consider any formula that the Soviet delegation might propose, even though they themselves had been unable to find one. Gromyko responded by again promising to inform the other groups if his experts managed to develop anything on the subject during the course of the conversations.[24]

Cadogan, apparently bothered by the technical way in which the Russians and Americans were approaching the problem, commented on the principle behind the British position on this "most important subject." He said that in his opinion the conference must make it clear that a Great Power involved in a dispute cannot vote; otherwise, they will have put themselves on a very different footing from the rest of the world. Without some sort of limiting provision, he went on, the permanent members would even be able to prevent the council from considering their disputes. This would never be tolerated by smaller nations, Cadogan argued, and the result would be the "greatest difficulty" in winning general acceptance of the new organization throughout the world. As the British chairman saw it, the danger here could not be overestimated; this was the "biggest problem" that the delegates would face at Dumbarton Oaks, and if they failed to find some way out of it, significant difficulties could be foreseen for the future.[25]

Gromyko replied that he disagreed with Cadogan's principle of equality before the council, that in his opinion the Great Powers deserved to have a special position there in keeping with their extra responsibilities for keeping the peace. This did not have to mean an absolute veto, of course, but it did mean that any special formula developed to deal with the problem had to preserve at least some of the privileges that came with power. The task of the conference, then, was to find a procedure that would satisfy both the British and the Russian principles. This, Pasvolsky pointed out, was just what the American group had failed to do, leaving it with no option but to choose between the opposing views. Why had it selected the British position? It did so because the State Department felt so confident that the United States would never decide to use force against its neighbors that it was willing to recommend that it be "put on the same plane" as all other nations regarding the settlement of disputes. The Americans recognized the risks involved in this, Pasvolsky continued, but thought them outweighed by the benefits that would come from creating an organization in which all countries involved in disagreements were treated equally.[26]

As Pasvolsky himself seemed to recognize, this greatly overstated the American case. To the extent that it was accurate, it reflected the idealism of the times; but it failed to take into account the American group's serious doubts about senatorial approval of any plan placing major limitations on the Great Power veto. It also omitted any mention of a likely reservation concerning the sanctity of the Monroe Doctrine, which would be designed to remove any disputes involving the United States and its neighbors from the direct authority of the council. Almost as an afterthought, Pasvolsky did decide to add a couple of qualifications to his high-sounding statement. First, he said that some formula needed to be worked out to prevent the Security Council from considering questions ordinarily regarded by international law as falling under domestic jurisdiction. And second, clarification was needed as to whether the council could call upon a nation involved in a dispute to furnish forces for settling it—forces that could, at least theoretically, be employed against that nation itself. Pasvolsky said that he was certain, however, that both of these difficulties could be worked out.[27]

The Russians wanted to talk about another principle—unanimity. Did not, Sobolev asked, the British and American position violate the basic idea that all decisions must be made jointly by the Great Powers—which had been, after all, the reason for devising the veto in the first place? Gromyko seconded this view, arguing that the Anglo-American stance represented a retreat from the principle of unanimity among the Great Powers set forth by Churchill, Roosevelt, and Stalin at Tehran. Pasvolsky and Cadogan disagreed. They thought that limiting the veto would strengthen the idea of unanimity "in its essential aspects" by bringing it into line with the even more important principles of justice and equity, without which the council's decisions would not be respected by the rest of the world.[28]

The determined tone taken by both sides in the Joint Steering Committee debate spelled real trouble for the negotiators at Dumbarton Oaks, who were for the first time encountering a key issue that they realized might not be resolvable. Sensing this possibility, Gromyko sought out Stettinius for a private talk in the garden on the following day. After they were seated by the swimming pool, the Soviet ambassador said that he and his colleagues in Moscow had been pleased with the State Department's original positions on the veto and majority questions but that he was now "very discouraged" to learn that the Americans had changed their minds. He was afraid, he said, that both of these matters would cause serious difficulty with his superiors in the Soviet Union, and hoped that the United States would be willing to reconsider its views. Stettinius replied that he thought this result was possible where the size of the majority was concerned because that question was still the subject of study by members of the American group. But he could not be so reassuring about the veto. That issue, he pointed out, had been thoroughly explored by American planners and reviewed carefully by both Secretary Hull and President Roosevelt. "Only last night," he told Gromyko, the president had asked him to "explain" to the Russian leader that "it would cause great difficulty in present-ing the plan to the American public" if a party to a dispute could vote on its own case.[29]

Gromyko's response reflected a growing sense of resignation. He said that it was clear that this question had developed into "a point of actual disagree-ment," that each side now seemed able to see the issue only from its own perspective. Perhaps, he thought, the best solution would be for the delegates to find "some general language" to cover the disputed point; thus a definite decision would not be required at Dumbarton Oaks and the issue could be dealt with at a later time. Stettinius rejected this idea, emphasizing that delay would be very disappointing to supporters of an international organization in the United States. He hoped, he said, that it would still prove possible to find a solution "that we could all support" at the present conference.[30]

Stettinius soon discovered, however, that this hope was not even a reality within his own delegation. When the American group met later in the day, it revived its old quarrels over the veto question, belying the certainty that Stettinius had expressed to Gromyko about the United States position. The uniformed members expressed particular concern about relations between the United States and the Soviet Union, with General Embick worrying about the firmness of the Russian position and General Fairchild repeating his previous support for a compromise formula that would require a permanent member to abstain if requested to do so by a vote of two-thirds of the council. A more troublesome issue was raised by Henry Fletcher, the Republican party's repre-sentative within the American group. Fletcher argued that the Senate would never accept the current American position on voting—an opinion that was exactly the opposite of the one then being expressed by Roosevelt and Hull. Breckinridge Long supported Fletcher's view, adding that the Senate might reluctantly approve a qualified veto on settlement questions but not on the use of force. The meeting adjourned without having achieved a consensus, al-though the official American position remained as uncompromising as ever.[31]

The veto question surfaced again at Dumbarton Oaks on 4 September, after a week in which the three delegations had busied themselves with other issues. During a meeting of the Joint Steering Committee on that morning, Stettinius "took occasion" to emphasize the importance that the United States attached to denying all parties to a dispute the right to vote in the council. If this matter could not be resolved, he said, "the success of the whole project for an international organization might be endangered." Cadogan, pleased that "the Americans seem to be increasingly aware of the importance of the point," nodded his agreement with this assessment. So did Gromyko, who added "rather unyieldingly" that he had no other proposal to offer than the one he had already made about finding a special procedure to govern the situation. This attitude worried both the British and American group leaders. Cadogan thought that the situation was now "quite hopeless" because the Soviet Union was unwilling to compromise and doubted whether Gromyko even had the latitude to do so. Stettinius, who was always more optimistic, noted only that the Russian chairman seemed increasingly recalcitrant.[32]

Stettinius and Cadogan met after lunch to plan strategy for dealing with the Soviets. Cadogan said that London had authorized him to yield on three or four points, including the making of council decisions by a simple majority vote, and asked the American chairman if the following day might not be a propitious time to act on them. Stettinius agreed and said that he might have some concessions of his own to make by then. That would put them in a position, as Cadogan put it, to ask Gromyko: "Where are yours?" "Probably won't have any effect," the British chairman went on, "but it's the only thing to do." After Cadogan left, Stettinius continued his discussion of tactics, this time with Pasvolsky and Dunn. The three Americans agreed that it was to their advantage to stretch out the conversations as long as might be necessary to reach a complete agreement. The Russians, they thought, were unprepared to see the conference adjourn without a final resolution because, much more so than the Americans, their postwar status as a Great Power would depend upon the creation of an international organization to ratify it. Thus, holding out might bring them around to the American view. Stettinius blamed Cadogan for encouraging the Soviets' obduracy through his frequent remarks about ending the conference quickly so he could return to England before the war in Europe ended without his being "in at the kill." The Russians, Stettinius thought, must be made to see that they had nothing to gain through delay.[33]

Gromyko, too, thought that the time had come to bargain away some concessions—and with the same end in mind. On 5 September, he invited the top members of the British and American delegations to what Cadogan described as "a quite pleasant lunch" at the Soviet embassy. Between courses, the Russian chairman told Stettinius that he thought the time had come to make some final decisions but that to do so each of the delegations would have to concede on a few points. "I am ready to start to concede," he whispered, "but I want you to know we attach big importance to the voting procedure both on the matter of majority and the matter of dispute." Stettinius replied that the question about a party to a dispute voting was what disturbed the United States most. "I will be ready tomorrow to start getting down to cases," Gromyko concluded.[34]

This conversation spurred Stettinius to look for concessions to trade. The most obvious choice was the other part of the voting issue, about which most of the American group did not have a decided opinion anyway. When the American chairman asked Hull for his view on the question later in the afternoon, the secretary replied that if it meant reaching an agreement, the United States "could easily return" to decision by simple majority of the council. Hull also offered what he thought would happen if the Soviets became immovable and refused to compromise on the veto. It would mean a much longer conference than anyone anticipated, he said, so much so that the delegates might eventually have to explore the possibility of leaving the question open for consideration at a later date. As he had when speaking with Gromyko, Stettinius rejected this idea. He argued that most of the American group thought that this would show weakness and a lack of unanimity among the Big Three and might be seized upon by the smaller nations as an excuse for not attending the full United Nations conference.[35]

Hull and Stettinius raised the whole issue with the president on the following day. Stettinius said that the American group regarded the majority question as something on which it might be wise to yield, "particularly for trading purposes." With a Security Council consisting of eleven members, he explained, the difference between a simple majority and two-thirds meant only one vote—actually, it meant two—which did not seem important enough to worry about. Hull agreed that "it made little difference either way" and suggested that the American delegates at Dumbarton Oaks be permitted to settle the question as they saw fit. When Roosevelt gave his assent to this idea, Stettinius asked for his advice on the veto problem. "Although," according to the under secretary, "this had been raised previously with the President on several occasions this time he seemed confused on the issue and both Mr. Hull and I had to explain the matter in some detail before it was clear to him." Even then, FDR had no guidance to offer. Hull pointed out, though, that the Russians could expect to be voted down "practically unanimously" on this question at the full United Nations conference and that "in their own self-interest" they should see that point now and accept the Anglo-American position to avoid embarrassment in the future. Later, when the State Department officials were driving to the secretary's apartment, Hull advised his under secretary to stress this point strongly in his talks with Gromyko—an approach that could not, under the circumstances, have made the Soviet chairman any more yielding.[36]

Both sides got down to cases when the Joint Steering Committee met at ten o'clock on 7 September—the meeting scheduled for 6 September having been postponed until Cadogan received additional instructions from London. Although Eden authorized the British chairman to yield on the majority vote issue, Cadogan failed to do so on this occasion, perhaps because he did not feel that the time had come to play what he regarded as his highest card. The Americans also refused to come all the way around to the Soviet position. Instead, they proposed the replacement of all fractions with a statement that substantive votes in the Security Council would require seven votes to pass. Although this kept them in conformity with Stettinius's faulty mathematics, it failed to attract any support from either the British or the Russians.[37]

Nor, despite some trading of concessions on minor issues, was any progress made on the veto question. Cadogan's new instructions confirmed what he already knew: the Foreign Office would not budge on the issue of a party to a dispute voting in the council, which it regarded as "a matter of fundamental principle. If we yield ground here," the Foreign Office continued, "we shall undermine the moral authority of the new organization from the start." The others remained equally obdurate, with the Soviets maintaining their position, as Stettinius put it, "without discussion." The only new development was Cadogan's acceptance of the American idea of voluntary abstention as a possible solution to the problem, provided that the country abstaining be required to accept and comply with the decision of the other members. This only brought the British and American positions into full concordance, however; it left the Russians and their Western allies as far apart as ever.[38]

Gromyko proved more willing to talk openly at lunch with Stettinius and Cadogan. In a tone that Stettinius described as "discouraged," the Russian chairman discussed his perception of the lack of progress being made at the conference. "I am 99% sure," he said, "I could clean up everything except the voting procedure and this is a serious matter with us." The other chairmen, sensing that Gromyko was on the verge of giving up on their efforts, stressed that a final document that left the veto question unsettled would probably never be approved by the rest of the world, let alone their own governments. The possibility of putting the issue off for later was, to use Cadogan's term, an "illusion"; if the delegates did so, the British chairman went on, "one simply wouldn't get a World Organization." In addition, Cadogan warned that if the section on voting procedure had to be omitted from the Dumbarton Oaks proposals, Eden would probably insist on issuing a footnote explaining the British position to the rest of the world, which could only damage the reputation of the Soviet Union. Stettinius added that the United States might have to release a similar statement, especially to satisfy the governments of Latin America. Gromyko, visibly disturbed by these developments, changed his mind and expressed a desire to stay at Dumbarton Oaks until the problem could be solved. He remained, however, as wooden as before on the nature of the best solution.[39]

Having failed thus far to move Gromyko, the British and Americans decided to try two new strategies. The first was Cadogan's idea and came from his lack of confidence in Gromyko's intellectual abilities. "From some of the things he said," Cadogan wrote in his diary, "it became clear that he didn't understand the point himself, so [he] can't have put the arguments properly to Moscow." The British chairman thus proposed to the Foreign Office that it have Sir Archibald Clark Kerr, their ambassador in the Soviet Union, present the British position directly to Molotov. He also told Stettinius that, in his view, Gromyko "probably has not presented the facts to Moscow accurately" and suggested that the American ambassador, W. Averell Harriman, should support Clark Kerr's arguments. Stettinius agreed, even though he was then working out the details for a new tactic of his own.[40]

What Stettinius had in mind was bringing out what he called his "biggest and last remaining gun"—President Roosevelt. At a critical moment earlier in the veto debate Secretary Hull had prevailed upon Gromyko to change his mind without success; now Stettinius thought that the time had come to see if Roosevelt might not have better luck. He discussed the matter with the president on 7 September, emphasizing that the success of the entire conference seemed to hinge on this one issue. The problem, he said, was that the Soviets were "being stubborn" and would not yield on other remaining points until the voting procedure question was settled. "Why not call in Gromyko?" was FDR's response. He could fit him into his schedule, he said, after the press conference slated for the next morning. Stettinius, who did not want to face another unproductive meeting of the Joint Steering Committee, asked for an earlier time, preferably before 10 A.M. The president replied that he was busy that night but, if Gromyko "would not be offended," he would be glad to receive him in his bedroom at 9:30 in the morning.[41]

Stettinius telephoned Gromyko immediately and said that the president had expressed a desire to talk with him on the voting issue, "which he felt was of over-riding importance" to the success of their efforts at Dumbarton Oaks. He then asked the Russian chairman if he would be willing to call upon Roosevelt, taking care, as Hull had advised, "not to put it on the basis of the President sending for him." Far from insulted by this request, Gromyko replied that he would be delighted to discuss the matter with Roosevelt and agreed to meet Stettinius at the main entrance to the White House the following morning.[42]

Roosevelt appeared cheerful when Stettinius ushered Gromyko into his bedroom at 9:30 A.M. In an attempt to create a warm atmosphere before getting down to business, the president spoke briefly of his hopes for another meeting with Stalin and of the progress of the war in Europe. He said that both the Soviets in the East and the Anglo-Americans in the West had succeeded too well lately and had overrun their respective lines of supply, creating "a period of pause for consolidation" on both fronts—a remark that must have had special meaning for a Soviet ambassador concerned about the effect of the Warsaw uprising on American opinion. Roosevelt also remarked on a telegram he had received from General Patrick J. Hurley, his personal representative in China, who reported that Molotov was not interested in the Chinese Communists—and that they were not really Communists anyway but, as Roosevelt put it, "agrarians." Most likely, Roosevelt brought this matter up to reassure Gromyko that he did not regard China as a stumbling block to postwar cooperation between the United States and the Soviet Union.[43]

When he finally got around to the subject of Dumbarton Oaks, FDR said that he understood the voting question to be the "only one fundamental point" that remained open. Gromyko, who still hoped to trade away his government's positions on lesser matters, replied that he thought there were other issues— but backed down when pressed on the point by Stettinius. The president then made a concession of his own, announcing to the Russian ambassador that the United States would accept a simple majority on council votes "if it would help him at home." After Gromyko smiled his approval, Roosevelt turned to what Stettinius called "the major issue." Traditionally in America, the president said, husbands and wives having trouble are never permitted to vote on their own case, although they are always afforded an opportunity to testify—to state their case. It should be the same, he thought, within the family of nations. He then told what Stettinius described as a "beautiful story" tracing the American notion of fair play back to the days of the founding fathers, and stressed the difficulty that any sort of break with this concept, such as that contained in the Soviet proposal, would cause him in the Senate.[44]

Gromyko, according to Stettinius, "did not seem at all depressed" by the president's remarks. He asked a few questions but was primarily concerned with finding out how he might best present the American position, which really mixed two principles in a confusing way, to his superiors in Moscow. Stettinius took this opportunity to ask the Russian chairman if it would be helpful for the Americans to send a message on the question directly to Marshal Stalin. This idea had been proposed by Harry Hopkins, who thought that it was the best way to break the logjam at Dumbarton Oaks. Following Hopkins's advice, Stettinius had already asked Charles E. Bohlen, the chief of the State

Department's Division of Eastern European Affairs and an adviser to the American group, to prepare a draft of a cable on the subject. When Gromyko said that he would leave the matter of a direct message up to the Americans' judgment, Stettinius produced this draft and handed it to Roosevelt, who suggested a number of changes—including a reference to the husband and wife simile that he had employed earlier in the meeting.[45]

The resulting message, which went out later in the day, presented the American position clearly. After mentioning his bedroom meeting with Gromyko, Roosevelt said that traditionally in the United States parties to a dispute have never voted on their own case and that American public opinion would "neither understand nor support" a plan for world organization that violated this principle. Other nations, he thought, would take a similar view, leaving him entirely convinced that smaller states would find it hard to accept an organization in which the Great Powers attempted to "set themselves up above the law" by voting on their own disputes in the council. Finally, he said, he would have "real trouble" with the Senate. Thus, the president hoped, Stalin would find it possible to instruct his delegation to accept the Anglo-American position on voting and permit the conversations at Dumbarton Oaks to be concluded speedily and with "outstanding success."[46]

Before adjourning his talk with Gromyko, Roosevelt embarrassed Stettinius by bringing up the question of arrangements for the Chinese phase of the Dumbarton Oaks Conference. Mentioning the Chinese conversations, in which the Soviets were not supposed to be involved, was a diplomatic faux pas that made both of the delegation chairmen uneasy. Stettinius could not let the issue pass, however, without pressing Gromyko for a quick conclusion to the Russian phase of the conference, suggesting that talks with the Chinese might begin in three or four days. Gromyko did not object but was made palpably nervous by this turn of events; he feared, with good reason, that Stettinius intended to use the idea of interim talks with the Chinese to put added pressure on the Soviet group to concede. Roosevelt ended the meeting on an upbeat note by saying that he wanted, by the time he returned from his upcoming conference with Churchill at Quebec, both a signed document and a report on the "great success" that had been achieved at Dumbarton Oaks. "This is an order to you," he concluded.[47]

With both Stettinius and Gromyko occupied at the White House, the Joint Steering Committee meeting scheduled for 8 September had to be canceled. Cadogan said he did not mind the inconvenience, however, because he knew it meant that the Russian was being grilled by the president on the voting issue. When Gromyko finally showed up at Dumbarton Oaks at 11 A.M., he asked the other two chairmen for a meeting "for the express purpose of eliminating as many brackets as possible." If this request raised any hopes for Stettinius and Cadogan, it could not have been for long. Gromyko did offer some minor concessions but remained unwavering on the two questions relating to voting in the council. Stettinius, trying to break the deadlock on these issues, reiterated Roosevelt's statement that the United States would agree to the Soviet plan for making decisions by a simple majority—then qualified it by adding "if it should prove necessary in order to reach agreement on the joint recommendations as a whole." Gromyko apparently expected the British to yield on this question as well. But Cadogan refused, proclaiming that he would do so only if the Russians gave in on the issue of voting by parties to a dispute. As the British chairman saw it, this quid pro quo had become the only possible solution; the Soviets would have to ask themselves the question—"Do you want a world organization or do you not?"—and act accordingly.[48]

What Cadogan referred to as acting accordingly would have to be done in Moscow, of course, and the delegates' nerves began to fray as they waited for Gromyko to receive additional instructions from home. Even trying to avoid the issue and concentrate on other topics failed to help very much; Cadogan, increasingly irritated by the slow progress in the Joint Steering Committee, came by 9 September to view the Russians as "slow and sticky and rather stupid." Gromyko's tension found expression in a Stalinesque telephone call to Stettinius at midnight on 10 September. The Soviet ambassador phoned to remind the American chairman that the Chinese talks could not begin until the current conversations were completed. Stettinius, mystified by a call for this purpose at such an hour, agreed that this was correct and asked if anything had turned up to give the Russians concern. "No, nothing had happened," Gromyko replied. After a pause, the Soviet chairman said that he expected some delay in hearing from Moscow but that it would be unfair to place all the blame for this on the Soviets because the Americans themselves had made so many changes in the draft proposals. Stettinius, not wanting to add to Gromyko's pressures, remarked that he would put off a meeting of the Joint Steering Committee until the Russians had something to report. "Or you have something to report," Gromyko responded. On the American side, Hull expressed the tension growing at Dumbarton Oaks. He told Stettinius on 12 September that "planning for Europe without Stalin present was something which ought to be seriously considered"—a remark that betrayed an expanding theme in American thinking about the postwar world. Clearly, the conference was building toward a climax.[49]

The climax came on 13 September. In that morning's meeting of the Joint

Steering Committee, Gromyko announced that he had received his long-awaited instructions from home—and that the Soviet position on voting in the council remained unchanged. Stettinius asked if this represented his government's final word on the subject, and Gromyko answered that "this was the case," that the Soviet position was "final and unalterable." There could be, he went on, no backing away from the principle of unanimity, which the Soviet Union had always, from the beginning of negotiations on a postwar organization, considered to be a matter of the "very greatest importance." Stettinius responded that the United States felt just as strongly about its view of the matter, about the principles of fairness and equity. He could not see, as Gromyko had already learned from the president, how the American public, the world public, the United States Senate, or the smaller nations of the world could ever accept a proposal that permitted a party to a dispute to vote on its own case, particularly if that party was a Great Power with a veto in the council. Describing the Soviet chairman's announcement as a "great blow," Stettinius said that it might very easily mean that no general conference to create a world organization could ever be held. Certainly, he argued, many small nations would refuse to participate in the sort of organization that it would produce. Cadogan, also disappointed by Gromyko's revelation, added that he did not think that any of the British dominions would join the kind of organization that the Soviets envisioned.[50]

The developing impasse put everyone in what Cadogan described as a blue mood. Even Stettinius lost his usual sense of buoyancy. He could not, he said, see at that moment how any purpose might be served by issuing any document from Dumbarton Oaks—their failure to agree on this one issue had rendered all of their other efforts meaningless. Cadogan also wondered what they should do next. He had nothing to suggest, he said, except that they should all give thought to the matter. Stettinius agreed, pointing out that they must give especially careful consideration to the public effect of the Soviet position. Both Parliament and the American Congress would want an explanation of the issues involved, he thought, and he did not see how they could avoid making each of the Big Three's views on this subject known to the public. Cadogan remarked that no matter how the situation might be construed "it is bound to be most awkward." Releasing no statement would indicate to the world that the Dumbarton Oaks talks had failed, whereas saying anything at all was bound to be embarrassing. He really did not know, he said, what would be the best thing to do under the circumstances.[51]

Gromyko, who had been accepting this criticism in silence, could only retreat behind the well-worn principle of unanimity. Where that was concerned, he said, there was "no possibility of any kind of change." Nor did he agree that other nations would have difficulty accepting the Soviet view. Great Power unanimity had been the understood basis for all postwar plans, the Russian chairman argued, because everyone recognized that only the large countries had the military resources required to maintain peace and security— and thus were entitled to a special position in the postwar organization. Small powers would accept this, he thought, because their main desire was to live in the kind of peaceful world that only an international body dominated by the Great Powers could provide. This situation, he argued, had "been taken for granted by everyone" until now.[52]

Cadogan and Stettinius did not take issue with Gromyko's major premise. It was true, they thought, that everyone understood and accepted the idea of a special status being afforded to the Great Powers who must bear the lion's share of the responsibility for maintaining peace. But the situation would become very different when a permanent member of the council was involved in a dispute; then, Stettinius argued, the world would expect that all countries be treated the same. Consider, the American chairman continued, what would happen in a hypothetical incident where the United States took military action against Mexico. Under the terms of the Soviet proposal, the result would be an "impossible situation" in which the United States could prevent the council from even considering the matter. Gromyko—probably relieved by Stettinius's choice of examples—replied that it seemed narrow-minded to assume that the Great Powers, which were taking on the heavy burden of world peace, would necessarily get involved in disputes. Instead, they should be expected to cooperate with other nations in the future—just as they have been doing during the present war. Cadogan replied that this might be true but that other nations were likely to think otherwise. Part of the problem here was that the Soviets' perception of the postwar world was heavily colored by the experiences of the war emergency itself, when lesser allies had accepted the dominance of the major powers as the price of victory, while the Anglo-Americans expected that the smaller nations would soon reassert their traditional desire for independence. Certainly the British had been hearing this view from the dominions. Unrealistic as it may seem, the Soviet view was based upon both their needs and their perception of power. The Russians believed that the Great Powers could, through their actions and decisions, determine whether future international relations would be shaped by prewar or wartime principles, and they preferred the latter because they recognized that they were the only foundation on which their continued hegemony over Eastern Europe could be built.[53]

Realizing that his substantive arguments were getting him nowhere, Gromyko switched tactics. It should not be necessary, he said, to point out that the Soviets had already made a number of concessions—if that word could be used in connection with the current conversations where all three nations were working toward common agreement. Nor had these concessions always related to small matters. On several important questions, Gromyko claimed, the Soviet Union had given in because it appreciated the great significance of reaching agreement in these talks. Unmoved, the British and American delegations responded that all three groups had made concessions of importance; neither side should expect the other to yield anything more on that score.[54]

Stettinius wanted to get back to the issue at hand. Did the Soviets really think, he inquired, that other nations would accept their proposal? Sobolev responded that he had "no doubt of this." Gromyko agreed, provided that the Great Powers presented the proposition unanimously—what he regarded as the key to the success of whatever they came up with at Dumbarton Oaks. The Russian chairman also thought that Stettinius was making too much of the veto matter because other countries were less interested in details about voting procedure in the council than they were about the overall effectiveness of the new world organization. Smaller nations understood that the Great Powers had not failed them so far—they were winning the war, after all—and would be willing to continue to extend their confidence to them in the future. Sobolev remarked that the real threat to their success lay in the Anglo-American proposal, which was reversing the existing situation of unanimity among the Great Powers and undermining their authority throughout the world. If the proposed peacekeeping organization failed to materialize, he concluded, it would be for this reason. Stettinius replied that they might have to accept such a result, that the American position on voting would, like that of the Soviets, remain unalterable "regardless of future events."[55]

Pasvolsky expressed his growing discouragement by remarking that the time had come to consider whether it was still feasible to construct the type of organization that the conference had been working toward. If the Big Three could not agree on a method of voting for the settlement of disputes, he thought, perhaps it would be necessary to leave the idea of enforcement out of plans for the organization altogether. Dunn added that the only reasonable course of action might be to change the form of the proposed charter to an agreement whereby the Great Powers would simply consult one another in the event of a crisis; as things stood now, he went on, it could not be expected that the other nations would agree to the use of military force. Jebb agreed with this analysis. There seemed, he said, to be no choice but to remove enforcement provisions from the charter if any sort of an agreement was to be reached. The British delegate also pointed out that this would not be easy to accomplish; the conferees would have to create a document that was very different from the present draft—hardly the work of a few days. He was not sure, he said, whether the effort would prove to be worth the trouble. Cadogan remarked that "he did not believe the world would think much of such a document."[56]

This exchange had a sobering effect on the committee members, who recognized that what they were now considering was the creation of an organization as ineffectual as the League of Nations—a body whose failures they had all grown used to deprecating. Dunn was the first to crack, asking for the time to make what he called "a rather full statement." They must not, he said, lose sight of the fact that they had been cooperating fully up to this point, or that their very presence at Dumbarton Oaks was a mark of their shared desire to continue their cooperation into the postwar period. This kind of cooperation was proving hard, he thought, because it was new. Still, he did not see why, as long as they continued to work together, they should not be able to draw up a document on which they could all eventually agree. The resulting charter might be quite different from what they had all envisioned initially and might not provide for the particular kind of machinery featured in their present drafts. But this would not mean that they had failed—not if they all continued to cooperate and refused to permit disagreement to creep into their relations after the war. Cadogan applauded Dunn's remarks. So did Stettinius, who said that whatever happened in the next few days, the three groups must leave Dumbarton Oaks in agreement with one another. What hope could there be, he asked, for peace and security in the future if the three nations did not remain shoulder-to-shoulder after the war, just as they had during it? It is a matter, he said, on which "the very future of civilization depends."[57]

Characteristically, Stettinius focused on the public relations dimension of the problem. He said that there must be "no whisper" that any serious disagreements have arisen among the conferees at Dumbarton Oaks. Cadogan added that there existed a terrible danger of speculation by the press and others if their difficulties in reaching an agreement should be permitted to leak out. Gromyko gave his assurance that there would be no disclosure by anyone in the Soviet group. The Americans, more aware than Gromyko of the difficulties involved in maintaining official secrecy in an open society, pointed out that the conferees would now have to act quickly to come up with something that they could all agree on before reporters got wind of their troubles. They thought that this might be possible, however, considering the fact that the final product now seemed likely to be much shorter than any of their current drafts.[58]

Stettinius said that he had what might be an easier solution. What did the others think, he asked, of leaving the question of voting in the council for the full United Nations conference to decide? Sobolev objected that it "would not be possible to do that," and was seconded by Jebb. Considering his earlier remarks to Gromyko about what would happen in such a situation, it is difficult to imagine that Stettinius intended this as a serious proposal. In fact, the American chairman was probably trying to embarrass the Russians—an intention that he soon betrayed by inquiring why they were afraid of leaving the matter for later. Did Gromyko think that his proposal would have such a negative effect on the rest of the world? As if this were not a sufficiently sour note on which to end the meeting, Cadogan announced that he would have to consult his government before he could consent to the drafting of a new type of document. Thus the session ended with the three groups able to agree on nothing except the need to maintain secrecy about their disagreement.[59]

This meeting of the Joint Steering Committee proved to be the turning point in the conference at Dumbarton Oaks. Before 13 September all participants seemed to think that full agreement was possible; afterward, they vacillated between trying to create a patched up document and despairing of their efforts to reach any sort of an agreement at all. Failure now seemed entirely too possible, if not imminent. Webster tried not to think about it; "I have hardly dared write," he recorded in his diary, "in these days of crisis." Stettinius was also in the doldrums, describing this period as the "low point" of the conference. "It looks as if an impasse has been reached," he wrote on 14 September, "and we cannot tell whether we will be able to work it out to a successful conclusion or whether the conference will blow up." The American chairman took what comfort he could from conversations with such old hands at diplomacy as Joseph Grew and Edwin C. Wilson, who told him that there never had been a conference that did not appear to be "completely broken down at one stage or another." If this lent perspective to Stettinius's problem, it did not give him any better idea how to solve it. The Dumbarton Oaks Conference, on which everyone's hopes for a peaceful postwar world had been based, now seemed on the verge of failure.[60]

9 *Conflict and Compromise*

If the conference at Dumbarton Oaks was to have any chance of producing a plan for a postwar world organization, some solution had to be found to the impasse that had developed over the key issue of the Great Power veto in the Security Council. It was obvious that neither side was simply going to accept the other's position—each had indicated by 13 September that it regarded the stakes as much too high for that. There remained only the possibility of compromise, of finding some formula capable of satisfying both the Soviets and the Anglo-Americans that their respective principles and interests would be protected in the postwar organization they were struggling to create. No one could have supposed that this would be easy; indeed, some of the delegates had already come to doubt whether it was even possible. And as if things weren't bad enough in Georgetown, the conflicting aspirations of the Big Three were being underscored daily by the news from Poland, where the Warsaw uprising provided the delegates and their governments with a preview of the coming dispute over Eastern Europe—a dispute that was already causing some on both sides to question the wisdom as well as the likelihood of their continued cooperation. Clearly, the meeting at Dumbarton Oaks, like East-West relations in general, had come to a crossroads. They could have conflict or compromise—or, as would turn out to be the case, they could have both.

The search for a solution to the veto problem began almost immediately, with both the British and American groups gathering to discuss their options as soon as the Joint Steering Committee adjourned at noon on 13 September. The British meeting, which reflected the unhappy mood that had settled over Cadogan's delegates, produced no results of any consequence. Someone half-heartedly proposed referring the voting question to a conference of foreign ministers, but the group dismissed this as impossible. Another suggested solution would have created the organization first and authorized it to work out the details of voting in the council later. Even Webster finally rejected this idea—and he had proposed it. "It was a hateful time," Webster concluded. Cadogan was only a little more optimistic in outlining the options for the Foreign Office. There were, as far as he could see, four possible alternatives, although none really seemed very promising. One was to produce what he called a "watered-down document" that would omit any reference to a Security Council. This idea he called a "bad solution" because it would create world-wide disappointment and make the conference a failure. A second alternative would include plans for a council but leave out the principle of unanimity with the understanding that the Great Powers would always take action on that basis. Cadogan doubted whether the Soviets would feel safe enough to approve such an undocumented arrangement. Third, Cadogan thought that the charter might call upon a permanent member involved in a dispute to forgo the use of its veto voluntarily. He did not believe that in practice the Soviet Union would ever take such a recommendation, however, so there would be no real point in making it. And fourth, the British leader proposed that the Great Powers might be required to give up the use of their veto during the first stages of the procedure for settling disputes in which they were involved. Thus the organization could still investigate, urge suitable solutions, and formulate recommendations, which meant that the permanent members would not be "entirely above the law." Only this last alternative appealed to Cadogan at all, but he was not sure that anyone at the conference would be willing to accept it.[1]

The American group had somewhat better luck, with several delegates offering new compromise proposals that held out at least some hope of success. One solution would have permitted a Great Power to vote when involved in a dispute but required an extraordinary majority—say, the votes of nine out of eleven members—before any sort of action could be taken. Another solution would have referred all decisions involving members of the council to a select committee drawn from the General Assembly. And a third, suggested by Breckinridge Long, would have placed all such cases in the hands of the full assembly, where a three-quarters majority including all parties to the dispute would be required for any decision. Pasvolsky proposed a different kind of solution—one based on the type of issue involved. This formula, which Pasvolsky had first suggested to the American group during its preconference meeting on 17 August and which was similar to Cadogan's preferred alternative, called for leaving the veto intact only where enforcement decisions were concerned; all other kinds of cases would require the Great Power involved to abstain from voting. The Americans failed to adopt any of these proposals, deciding only to include all of them in a memorandum for Hull and Stettinius.[2]

The veto was also the main topic of an emergency meeting of the Formulation Group, convened at Stettinius's request later that afternoon. After several hours of discussion, the delegates worked out what the American chairman described as "an informal compromise solution" to the problem. This new formula maintained the veto on votes concerning enforcement action but not on the peaceful settlement of disputes—exactly what Pasvolsky had suggested to the American group a few hours before. The representatives of all three powers found this idea acceptable in principle, and Cadogan advocated it so strongly that the official British history of diplomacy during the Second World War erroneously credited him with its invention. Still, despite the fact that Sobolev showed "some signs of being interested" in the compromise proposal, the Anglo-Americans doubted if the Kremlin would ever accept it.[3]

They would, in fact, have trouble enough with their own superiors. A hopeful Stettinius explained the new formula to Hull, who described it as "a substantial concession to the Soviet point of view and the absolute minimum of what we could accept." The secretary of state added that the proposal looked good to him and that his "curbstone opinion" was favorable—but that he could not approve it in any final way until after he had discussed it with the president. Cadogan found himself in much the same position with Eden. The two chairmen thus agreed to put the matter before Churchill and Roosevelt, who were then together in Quebec for conversations on military strategy. Cadogan was delegated to present the proposal when he journeyed to Canada for consultations with the prime minister and Eden on 14 September—much to the annoyance of Hull and Stettinius, who had been left out of the president's party on the grounds that the talks were to be entirely military. As it turned out, the British chairman had a bad time of it at Quebec. When Cadogan finally steered the conversation around to Dumbarton Oaks during lunch on 15 September, both the president and the prime minister "rambled hopelessly." He repeatedly "tried to pin them down to the point, but they always wandered away." "It's quite impossible to do business this way," the British chairman fumed. The results of the meeting also proved discouraging: neither Churchill nor FDR was willing to support the compromise proposal. As Hull described the situation in his memoirs, "the President and the Prime Minister were so busy with their discussions at Quebec that they simply did not have the time to give the question the serious consideration it deserved." Stettinius, worried that the president did not understand the issues involved, requested a meeting with Roosevelt at Hyde Park. When FDR refused, saying that he was tired, was expecting Churchill for a visit, and would not change his mind on the proposal anyway, the conferees were back where they had been on 13 September.[4]

When Cadogan reported the bad news to Gromyko, the Russian chairman said that Stalin had reached a similar conclusion. Worse yet, the marshal's reply to President Roosevelt's telegram on the veto question had been received in the White House Map Room and, as Harry Hopkins put it, said "'No' with a loud bang." Voting in the council, Stalin argued, must reflect the principles of coordination and unanimity among the Big Four on all questions, "including those which directly relate to one of these nations." He thought that the initial American proposal, which called for a special procedure regarding voting in case of a dispute that involved one or more permanent members of the council, had been correct—"otherwise will be brought to naught the agreement achieved at the Tehran Conference." Stalin also hinted at his motives for demanding an absolute veto. What unanimity presupposed, he said, was "that among these powers there is no room for mutual suspicions," whose development the Soviet Union could not ignore, in light of "the presence of certain absurd prejudices" that "often hinder an actually objective attitude toward the USSR." Under such circumstances, the Russian leader reasoned, the Soviet Union could not take the risk of surrendering its right to a veto.[5]

Stalin's telegram suggested the way in which outside political questions—including mutual suspicions—were now intruding at Dumbarton Oaks. On both sides, the veto dispute reflected the mistrust growing between the Anglo-Americans and the Russians—mistrust that would ultimately develop into the cold war. Day-to-day differences among the Allies, which were perhaps made inevitable by their imminent victory in the struggle that had drawn them together, were dangerously exacerbated during the summer of 1944 by an expanding awareness of their conflicting political systems and security needs. By the time the conference opened at Dumbarton Oaks, the leaders of the American group were already coming to view the Russians as less of a policeman and more of a threat to peace, a change of opinion that grew during the conference and had a telling effect on their hardening attitude toward the veto question. In fact, their behavior regarding that issue is difficult to explain except in terms of their more general attitude toward the Soviet Union. In less than a month's time, the American group had moved from almost unanimous support of the USSR's position regarding the Great Power veto to a vigorous rejection of that view. It seemed, moreover, that the harder the Soviets pressed for the retention of their right to vote on all questions, the more certain Stettinius and Hull became that it must be denied to them, a reaction that suggested their growing suspicions about the Kremlin's postwar objectives. The State Department's top officers were probably attributing their own motives to the British when they decided that Cadogan's refusal to compromise on the veto was "based perhaps on a desire to be certain the Soviets do not obtain a position whereby they could control all of Europe" after the war; the Americans were confident, at any rate, that "more than Dumbarton Oaks was probably involved" here for all of the participants. They knew, of course, that this was becoming increasingly true for themselves.[6]

It was also true for the British. Churchill's bad opinion of Soviet intentions is well known, and Eden proved equally determined to avoid anything that might add to the USSR's postwar advantages on the continent of Europe. For some members of the British War Cabinet, the veto issue became an early test of will regarding the postwar distribution of power—what Clement Attlee and Lord Cranborne referred to as a "show-down" with the Russians in their telegram to Churchill rejecting the compromise formula of 13 September. If there remained a residue of wartime good will for the Soviet Union among some members of the British group at Dumbarton Oaks—Webster, for instance—it was evaporating as rapidly among them as it was among the Americans.[7]

The reason for this change of sentiment could be found in Eastern Europe—on whose shoals the Grand Alliance would soon be wrecked. Most pressing at the time was the problem of Poland, over whose borders and government the Allies seemed destined to disagree. The Dumbarton Oaks Conference opened in the midst of the tragic Warsaw uprising, which saw the Polish Home Army annihilated by German forces while the advancing Red Army paused at the approaches to the city. Although Stalin's motives in this affair remain an uncertain blend of his willingness to sacrifice non-Communist Poles, caution caused by overstretched lines of supply, and confusion at a surprisingly strong German counteroffensive, his failure to support the insurrection shocked Western observers as an example of what Churchill termed "strange and sinister behavior." Ambassador Halifax, anxious to make sure that the Americans did not miss the point, called Stettinius at home on 28 August—a Sunday—to say that he was "very disturbed about the Polish situation." Throughout the conference, the uneven battle in Warsaw raged on, taking its toll not only in Polish patriots but in the relations between the Russians and Anglo-Americans as well. Each day, news from Dumbarton Oaks was required to share headline space with the latest tales of horror from Warsaw—a juxtaposition that had to have some effect on the negotiators.[8]

It was not supposed to be that way. Stettinius told reporters during a press conference on 10 August that the Polish situation would not be discussed at Dumbarton Oaks because "that was a current situation whereas the Dumbarton Oaks conference was for . . . the future." What they intended to do here, the American chairman went on, was to create an international organization "to deal with such conflicts in the future rather than the present." But events in Warsaw forced the negotiators to leave their ivory tower and to consider the immediate consequences of their lofty formulas—just as the Polish uprising inevitably entered into relations between the Allies. By the end of August, Churchill and Roosevelt were pressuring Stalin for permission to use Soviet air bases to land planes engaged in dropping supplies to the beleaguered Poles.

Stalin's stubborn refusal added to tension over the insurrection and its meaning, as well as enhancing the Westerners' growing sense of how difficult it was
to do business with the Soviets. After many strained cables, Moscow finally
granted the desired landing rights on 9 September, followed by a movement of
Red Army contingents into position for entering the city along the Vistula. But
this was a case of too little too late. Despite their forward movement, the
Soviets did not come to the relief of the Polish Home Army, and reports from
Warsaw grew more depressing during the second half of September—just as
the conference at Dumbarton Oaks was stumbling toward its deadlocked
conclusion. For the Americans in particular, the parallel between the tragic
denouement in Warsaw and their hardening attitude toward granting the
Soviets an unlimited veto could not have been simply coincidental.[9]

The clearest evidence of this fact came in the State Department's efforts to
understand why the Kremlin was clinging so tenaciously to an absolute veto.
These assessments always returned to the same point: the Soviets intended to
dominate Eastern Europe after the war and did not want to risk any interference from the new United Nations Organization. Thus, at the time of the
climax of the veto crisis on 16 September, Stettinius, Pasvolsky, Hackworth,
and Hayden Raynor agreed that the Soviets might be stalling the Dumbarton
Oaks talks intentionally because they did not want to see the matter settled—
and a peacekeeping body created—until after the war in Europe had ended
with their armies firmly in control of the East. Ambassador Harriman reached a
similar conclusion when queried by the State Department about the Soviets'
motives for refusing to compromise. He did not believe, he cabled, that Stalin
had finally decided to reverse his policy of cooperation with the West, because
the Russian leader still desired "above all else to take a leading role in international affairs"—something that he could not do on his own. Still, cooperating
with Stalin presented something of a problem for Western diplomats, "in part
because words have a different connotation to the Soviets than they have to us."
This would constitute, he thought, a real difficulty in Eastern Europe and
particularly in Poland, where the term "friendly government" would mean for
Stalin "a hand picked government which will insure Soviet domination." Harriman could not even say for sure, he went on, that Molotov understood Western
objections about the Polish situation. With this in mind, the ambassador
thought that the Soviets had a good reason for being stubborn about the veto.
They had never, even early in the war, been very willing to consult with their
allies about events in Eastern Europe. Since then, Harriman pointed out, their
victories over the Germans had strengthened their bargaining position with the
West, and they were now putting into effect their policies for the upcoming

peace. They would operate unilaterally if necessary; they did not, Harriman believed, feel the need "to foster our cooperation" any longer where Eastern Europe was concerned. "It might well be," he concluded, "that the change in developments has brought to the surface the underlying attitudes" of noncooperation that Stalin had harbored all along. But whether that was true or not, it now seemed clear that the Soviets regarded control over Eastern Europe as more important than the creation of a postwar organization, especially one in which they might not have full veto powers.[10]

This assessment was not very far off the mark. Stalin viewed a Soviet-led Communist hegemony in Eastern Europe as his most important postwar objective and was willing, if necessary, to sacrifice his friendly relations with the West in order to achieve it. But as late as 1944, he hoped that such a result would not prove necessary—that his control over what he regarded as the Soviet Union's sphere of influence would be accepted, and perhaps ratified, by his wartime allies. This possibility was what Stalin saw in Roosevelt's idea of a postwar organization dominated by the Four Policemen: it would, by assigning the USSR to peacekeeping responsibility for Eastern Europe, insure his power over that vital area, while granting the Soviet Union an important role in global relations and guaranteeing its permanent status as a Great Power as well. If structured properly, a peacekeeping body could harmonize with all of the Soviet leader's foreign policy objectives; no wonder, then, that he proved so willing to turn away from unilateralism and to embrace the principle of postwar planning at Tehran.[11]

The situation looked quite different, however, by the time of Dumbarton Oaks. Then the United States plan was no longer the Rooseveltian equivalent of the *Dreikaiserbund* that Stalin had approved; it now exhibited a concern for the rights of smaller powers that could only alarm the Soviet dictator. Litvinov had tried to warn Harriman about the effect of this change on the eve of the conference's opening when he said that "the day of the small nation was over," that the Great Powers would now have to be the dominating factor in world affairs. Worse, the Americans had turned away from regionalism, the principle by which the Kremlin expected to be given authority over its nearest neighbors, in favor of a universalistic approach that might open the way for the West to meddle in the Soviet sphere. This change in approach raised the possibility, at least, of an Anglo-American conspiracy to use the world body against the USSR in Eastern Europe—something that Stalin had been conditioned to believe both by experience and by ideology. If such a thing should happen it would force the Soviet leader to choose between his need to control the nations on his borders and his desire to play a major role in international affairs through cooperation with the West. It would not, as we have seen, be a difficult choice.[12]

The veto dispute proved to be the last straw for Stalin. The idea of the Four Policemen depended upon unanimity, a fact that the State Department's original acceptance of an unqualified Great Power veto attested to. But at Dumbarton Oaks, the Anglo-Americans had united in opposition to this principle and were pursuing an approach that would open the door for all of the U.N.'s policing machinery, even enforcement action, to be used against the Soviet Union. The Russians were, according to Jebb, genuinely shocked by the Western view on the veto. As a Marxist-Leninist, Stalin saw only too clearly the isolation that awaited his nation in an organization whose members were almost unanimously capitalist. As a Russian, he expected his Western allies to take advantage of their overwhelming number of votes within the peacekeeping body and turn its authority against him. The Anglo-Americans had nothing to fear from abandoning unanimity because they could always count on each other, Stalin thought, not to mention the French and the Chinese, to come to their defense in the council. But the Soviet leader saw an absolute veto as his only defense—and he clung to it tenaciously. It would be better, as Stalin saw it, to have no world organization at all than to have one that might endanger the security of the Soviet Union by providing a vehicle for Western intervention in Eastern Europe. To approve an organization in which the Great Powers would not have an unlimited veto was worse than utopian; it was positively foolhardy.[13]

In this context, the Anglo-American reaction to the Warsaw uprising must have affected Stalin's perception of Dumbarton Oaks. The cables that he received from Churchill and Roosevelt demonstrated both a worrisome interest in Eastern European affairs and a willingness to become involved militarily there, at least to the extent of dropping supplies to the beleaguered Poles by air. This meddling aroused Stalin's awareness of the coming storm over Poland, made him question the utility of continued cooperation with the West, and enhanced his misgivings about participating in a world organization where he would not have an absolute veto. As Molotov told Clark Kerr, the Westerners' behavior was "contrary to the spirit of Allied cooperation." Why did the British government not warn the Soviets of plans for the uprising in advance? he asked. Was this not a repetition of what had happened in April 1943 when the Polish government was permitted to make its "slanderous" accusations about the executions at Katyn? Now, according to Molotov, the Anglo-Americans themselves seemed determined to make the Soviet Union appear responsible for the "Warsaw adventure," which the Poles had brought on themselves. Thus, much as it did for the British and Americans, the Polish imbroglio highlighted for Stalin the practical implications of the veto controversy and added to his determination to see it settled only on his own terms.[14]

This did not mean, however, that Stalin was about to give up on the idea of a postwar organization. In some ways, the conference at Dumbarton Oaks was proving the value of cooperation. It had enhanced Soviet prestige and illuminated its global responsibilities. It had, through Roosevelt's plan for international trusteeships, sowed discord among the capitalist Western nations. And it had raised the possibility of distributing worldwide military bases among the Great Powers, some of which would surely fall into the hands of the Soviet Union. There remained, clearly, much for Stalin to gain by staying with his plan for participation in an international organization. Giving up, on the other hand, could only make things worse. As Arkady Sobolev told the interpreter Berezhkov at a crucial moment at Dumbarton Oaks, "nothing good could come from a sharpening of the conflict" developing between East and West. But, as Stalin was painfully aware, the conflict was already being sharpened by events in Eastern Europe, over which the Soviet leader had no intention of yielding. Litvinov tried to explain this to Harriman by saying that "it was unreasonable to consider that the interests of 30 million Poles should be given equal weight with those of 180 million Russians. Where the interests of the Russians conflicted with those of the Poles, the Poles would have to give way." For Stalin, all of this meant maintaining his policy of keeping two arrows in his quiver: he would continue to pursue negotiations for the potentially useful postwar organization but would revert to unilateralism if the talks took a direction that threatened the Soviet Union's vital security interests in Eastern Europe. He nearly reached for the latter arrow over the veto dispute at Dumbarton Oaks.[15]

The possibility of this result soon became apparent in the talks themselves. In a conversation with Stettinius on 18 September, Gromyko, who according to Sobolev had never liked the Formulation Group's two-level plan, ruled out the idea of finding any compromise formula on the veto. The position of his government, the Russian chairman said, was now "final and would not be changed regardless of whether the conversations were prolonged a week or a year." The Soviet Union, he emphasized, "would never consider joining an organization in which a major power involved in a dispute did not vote." There could be no doubt that this was the Soviet Union's last word on the subject; if the British and Americans did not relent on the veto issue there would be no postwar organization—at least none that included the USSR among its members. Stalin's policy of cooperation with the West was on the verge of breaking down.[16]

As members of the American group began to realize the seriousness of the situation, Stettinius faced a rebellion within his own delegation. Several of the State Department planners had never felt completely comfortable with the idea of restricting the Great Power veto, a fact that Hackworth had pointed out on 4 September—before the veto controversy had reached crisis proportions. Their doubts were enhanced by the impasse that developed on 13 September, when it became apparent that the price of rejecting the unqualified veto might be the absence of Soviet participation in the postwar organization. Breckinridge Long, who thought that this price was too high and feared that the secretary of state might not be getting the whole story concerning the issue, called on Hull personally to tell him that the American group was itself far from unanimous about limiting the Great Power veto. He also told Stettinius that he was worried "about the trend of things" at Dumbarton Oaks, where the Russians were now insisting on the original American position—which he thought the American group had been wrong to reject in the first place. Stettinius replied that there was no reason for Long to "get in a lather," that the negotiators were looking for a compromise solution to the problem.[17]

The excitable Long did not give up, however. The assistant secretary of state argued, during an all-day meeting of the American group on 18 September, that the United States should preserve the Soviet Union's postwar cooperation by accepting its view of the veto question. The American delegation had, in Long's opinion, grown far too intransigent about a position that had really only solidified during the conversations themselves—and then essentially in support of the British. As Long saw it, any deviation from Great Power unanimity was unrealistic for two reasons. First, an organization that attempted to act without the support of a Great Power—or, worse, against one—was bound to fail, perhaps causing the kind of world conflagration that it was supposed to prevent. And second, the United States Senate would never agree to American participation in such an organization, ensnaring President Roosevelt in the same sort of difficulty that had stymied the previous efforts of Woodrow Wilson. The best way to avoid both of these fatal pitfalls, Long argued, was for the American group to return to its original position on the veto.[18]

Long found powerful supporters among the military advisers at Dumbarton Oaks. The uniformed delegates, who had always feared the wartime consequences of an outright break with the Soviets, thought that the time had come for the United States to yield on the veto question. General Embick stressed the importance that the Joint Chiefs of Staff placed on Soviet entrance into the war against Japan; without the Red Army, he thought, an invasion of the home islands might well result in double the number of American casualties. The

Soviet Union's support was so vital, according to Admiral Hepburn, that anything that "may give her an excuse for limiting her assistance should be avoided." The officers also questioned the value of a postwar organization that did not include the Soviet Union; such a body would almost certainly prove to be, in Hepburn's word, "useless." The same could be said, of course, about an organization missing the United States—but not Great Britain, which the generals and admirals predicted would be less important in the postwar world and would have to go along with whatever the Soviets and the Americans decided between them. This meant that the British view on the veto, unlike that of the Soviets, could probably be rejected without sacrificing the United Nations' chances for success. In any event, the military advisers argued, "the realistic fact" was that the veto in the council did not "go to the heart of the question" of power and was therefore merely academic. Practically speaking, they thought, a Great Power had a veto over the actions of the council whether it was formally acknowledged or not—the alternative being the disruption of the international organization and probably a new world war. No Great Power could realistically be expected to place the interests of the peacekeeping body above its own, which meant that it would accede or not in the decisions of the council depending upon whether and how its vital interests were affected. It would be preferable, the officers argued, to have the great nations exercise this power legally, through the veto, rather than by rendering the council impotent through their refusal to obey its lawful wishes. The Russian proposal for unanimity, Hepburn concluded, "merely makes this evident." Sooner or later this fact of life would have to be absorbed by the smaller states; the only question was whether it would be now or later when it might possibly be too late.[19]

Long and the military advisers developed a three-part proposal designed to break the impasse at Dumbarton Oaks. First, they suggested a renewed effort to persuade Roosevelt, Churchill, and Stalin to accept the compromise formula of 13 September. If this failed, they went on, the United States should propose another alternative plan whereby parties to a dispute not represented on the Security Council would be invited to take part in its deliberations and vote on their own cases. Such a procedure would leave the Great Power veto intact but would also, Long maintained, restore a measure of equity to the decision-making process by permitting all parties to a dispute to vote. And finally, if this too was rejected by the others, the American group should return to its original position and support the Soviet call for unqualified unanimity among the permanent members of the council.[20]

Several members of the American delegation took issue with all of these ideas. Pasvolsky disagreed with Long's recollection of the American group's preconference debates, contending that the United States's position on the Great Power veto had not changed as abruptly as the assistant secretary of state thought. This continuity was particularly true, Pasvolsky argued, concerning the views of Hull and Roosevelt, who had never entirely accepted the idea of an unqualified veto—and who had rejected it outright as soon as the issues involved became clear. Bowman agreed with Pasvolsky's interpretation and added that he did not remember there ever having been a question of permitting Great Powers to vote on enforcement decisions when they were involved in the dispute. In fact, both Long and Pasvolsky were partly correct. The confusion arose from poor communication within the American delegation—which had originally caused the group to think that it was reflecting the opinions of the president and secretary of state when it voted in August to support the unlimited Great Power veto. If Pasvolsky knew better, he had not said so at the time.[21]

Cohen and Bowman also disputed the idea that failing to yield to the Russians might endanger Soviet participation in the war against Japan. They said that although it was far from clear what effect the conversations at Dumbarton Oaks might have on Stalin's wartime decisions, they suspected that he would enter the war in the Far East or not depending upon his perception of the national interests of the Soviet Union—not out of friendship for the United States. They also warned against focusing too narrowly on the need for Soviet participation in the U.N., especially if this resulted in an agreement on the veto that alienated the British dominions, the Latin American republics, and other nations, some of which might then refuse to join the new organization. A United Nations, they thought, that included the Soviet Union but no one else might be worse than the other way around.[22]

A similar view was expressed by State Department Latin American adviser John Moors Cabot. Cabot argued that the Latin American countries would never accept an unqualified veto, which they would look upon as an attempt to make them rubber stamp a system whereby the Great Powers could "rule or ruin as they see fit." The nations of Latin America, Cabot contended, had two main postwar security interests—protection against each other and protection against a possible resurgence of Yankee imperialism. From their perspective, an organization that included the Russian proposal for an absolute veto would be unnecessary to do the former and incapable of doing the latter. It would be, therefore, worse than useless. Cabot also thought that some members of the American delegation were trying too hard to please the Soviets and forgetting about the important place of the Western Hemisphere in United States security.

He asked the military representatives if they really thought that maintaining an "uneasy understanding" with the Soviet Union was worth endangering hemispheric solidarity and good will, goals that the Roosevelt administration had pursued with great care. Finally, Cabot disagreed with the notion that it was not feasible to bring sanctions against a Great Power. Preventing aggression by the major nations, he argued, would ultimately have to be the test of the new world body because small powers were in no position to endanger world peace. And even if action against a powerful nation should result in war, as Long predicted, it would always be better in the future, as it would have been in the past, to take on an offending Great Power singly than to await the creation of an "aggressor cartel."[23]

Hull and Stettinius saw little merit in the ideas presented by Long and the uniformed delegates. They did not believe that the consequences of rejecting the Soviet position could be so dire as the military advisers predicted and, acting on the advice of Harry Hopkins, asked Admiral Willson to find out if General Marshall shared the concern expressed by the uniformed members of the American group. When Marshall, the most respected of all American military leaders during the Second World War, replied in a noncommittal fashion, Hull and Stettinius decided to continue the course they had already established and risk a falling out with the Soviet Union. Not that they thought such a result was very likely. Stettinius, whose own nerves had been tested by the controversy, remarked that he felt the American group had gotten "a little bit hysterical" over the veto issue. "I think," the American chairman went on, "the Admirals and Generals and some of our political advisors have lost their grip and are not thinking straight about this thing at all."[24]

Hull announced his final decision when he met with the American group "to canvass the whole situation" on 19 September. The secretary of state emphasized his belief that the veto controversy would not permanently affect the Kremlin's commitment to international cooperation. "The Soviet Union," he thought, "might get off the lines but if this happens she would have to come back into line in time because she would discover that any course other than cooperation was against her own interests." With the group's decision made, the Americans quickly closed ranks. At a meeting on the following evening, Long and the military representatives "backed down completely, several members of that group pleading a misunderstanding of the basic issues involved, including the Russian position." Although there is no record of what convinced them, it seems likely that the erstwhile dissenters were now viewing the veto question with the same kind of mistrust of the Soviets that had previously caused them to doubt their ally's intentions to enter the war against Japan.

They had, at any rate, now moved into line with the developing attitudes that would turn most State Department officers into cold warriors within the next few months.[25]

The British, meanwhile, were having a different sort of disagreement. The rejection of the compromise formula had completely deflated Cadogan, who now regarded any further attempts to reach agreement at Dumbarton Oaks as tantamount to chasing a will-o'-the-wisp. According to Webster, the British chairman had grown convinced that a postwar organization was impossible and was finally inclined to give up on his efforts to create one. Ambassador Halifax, similarly discouraged, wanted to adopt a plan first suggested by Walter Lippmann—never a supporter of the Wilsonian vision of world order—that the Great Powers should confine themselves in the postwar period to enforcing the peace against the defeated Axis states. Webster and Jebb disagreed with the pessimistic outlook of their superiors. They thought that there remained hope, that patient diplomacy might break the voting impasse—if not at Dumbarton Oaks, then later.[26]

The key question in the British debate—what to do next?—became the final problem of the Soviet phase of the conference. Stettinius, speaking to a meeting of the Joint Steering Committee on 17 September, said that he saw three possibilities. First, the Russians, British, and Americans could simply terminate the conversations with a statement that they had found it impossible to arrive at an agreement. This, he thought, was unthinkable because "civilization as we know it and the entire future of the world" depended upon the Great Powers' ultimate success at creating a world peacekeeping organization. Second, they could publish the document as agreed to and leave the question of voting in the council up to a general conference of the United Nations. Stettinius did not think, however, that this approach would be acceptable to the Soviet Union—indeed, he knew that it would not. And third, the delegates could finish as much of the proposal as possible at Dumbarton Oaks, with each group reporting the results to its own government for further study. They could then reconvene at a later date to resolve whatever differences remained between them. This, Stettinius concluded, was the procedure preferred by the United States.[27]

Cadogan and Gromyko agreed with Stettinius's reasoning. The British chairman, who had apparently regained some of his composure, said that he was certain neither Churchill nor Eden would like the first idea of merely breaking up the discussions—which would anyway give the false impression that they had accomplished nothing at Dumbarton Oaks. Cadogan also thought that his government would object to the second alternative because it would be unwise to enter a general conference without prior agreement among the Great Powers. Gromyko, who seemed less disturbed than his British and American counterparts by the events of the past few days, remarked that they should be careful not to issue a statement implying failure to reach an agreement. Stressing that this was only his personal view, the Russian chairman said that they would do better to emphasize their achievements by saying that they had arrived at agreement on many important questions but that consideration of some issues had not yet been completed. Gromyko also said he thought that the Soviet government would object to holding a general meeting before the voting question was resolved.[28]

Stettinius then presented a specific proposal, which he and Hull had decided on before that day's meeting of the Joint Steering Committee. It called for closing down the talks with the Russians as soon as possible, holding conversations with the British and Chinese immediately thereafter, and issuing press releases that would indicate the progress made at Dumbarton Oaks while explaining that there were "certain open points" that would have to be studied in more detail. The plan also provided for a second set of Great Power conversations, to be held no later than 15 November at a place not yet determined, although Stettinius expressed a preference for a city in the American Midwest. Gromyko and Cadogan raised no objections to this procedure, "seemed to receive it favorably" according to Stettinius, and agreed to wire home for instructions about putting it into effect.[29]

With all hope of complete success abandoned, the atmosphere at Dumbarton Oaks grew increasingly depressed. The conference had become, to use Robert Frost's phrase, "a diminishing thing," and the delegates did not know what to do with it. Some, like Webster, engaged in postmortem examinations of the corpse. The British historian thought that there were several reasons for the present jam, including insufficient preparations, too much publicity, and excessively detailed proposals. As he told members of the American group, whom he described as "down" on 18 September, the conference had tried to go too far too fast, attempting to settle in three weeks a problem that had gone unsolved over centuries of human history. The Americans "gloomily acquiesced" in this analysis but had no suggestions about what to do next.[30]

A few of the Americans searched for ways to make things difficult for the Soviets, who increasingly looked to them like the villains of the story. Pasvolsky, for instance, amused himself by planning to make a statement for the record in the Joint Steering Committee that the Russians were responsible for most of the disagreements at Dumbarton Oaks—the implication being that the conference's failure was primarily their fault. Stettinius, who apparently refused to give up on the possibility of convincing Gromyko to change his mind on the veto, kept busy presenting new arguments to the Soviet chairman—even after it was clear that the Kremlin's decision was final. On 18 September, for example, he warned Gromyko that the voting controversy, which could not possibly be kept secret, would result in "considerable anti-Soviet discussion in the American press." Gromyko, unmoved, replied that if there had to be a break among the Great Powers on this issue, they might just as well have it now rather than at some later conference. Hull, who was perhaps considering a little Soviet baiting of his own, suggested that Stettinius try to get the Soviet chairman's comments in writing.[31]

Stettinius also considered other, more positive ways to break the deadlock at Dumbarton Oaks. He discussed with Hull the possibility of asking Roosevelt to send another message to Stalin, which neither really thought would do much good. He also met with Gromyko and sounded him out informally on whether he thought there was a chance that a meeting of foreign ministers or chiefs of state might solve the problem. The Russian chairman responded, according to Stettinius, "rather negatively" but with a clear conviction that something had to be done. "You can't have an international organization without us," Gromyko said. "We can't have one without you. And there has to be unanimity between us and the other powerful states. The moment . . . this breaks down there is war." As each of the American chairman's efforts fell short of the mark, Stettinius grew more—the word is Cadogan's—"fussed" at the possibility of failure. "He should have thought of this before!" Cadogan concluded.[32]

As this last remark indicated, Cadogan was also feeling the effects of waiting for what could only be bad news. Always acerbic, the British chairman's comments in his diary became increasingly shrill after the rejection of the compromise voting proposal. On 18 September, for instance, he attended an embassy party and found it insufferable. "A million people in a small, hot room," he wrote, "and a noise in which one couldn't hear oneself scream." It was, he concluded, "a foretaste of Hell." Much of Cadogan's anxiety came from his desire to return to England, which only added to his impatience over the lack of progress being made at Dumbarton Oaks. He reacted on 19 September to Gromyko's unwillingness either to end the Russian phase of the conference or begin the Chinese talks by describing the situation as hopeless and complaining that he "might be here for 10 weeks." Desperate to get away, the British chairman cabled London to say that he was wasting his time in America and to request permission to come home, leaving Jebb in charge under Halifax. When he was still in Washington a few days later, he pronounced his personal benediction on the conference. "I wish people knew when they had, or should have had, enough of a bad thing," he wrote.[33]

In fact, everyone had had enough of Dumbarton Oaks. All that remained was to find a way to end the conference as gracefully as possible while preserving at least the illusion of continued agreement among the Great Powers. To this end, the delegates put finishing touches on the document containing their plan—an exercise that, according to the dejected Cadogan, did not "matter now" anyway. Maintaining appearances also meant avoiding altogether the impossible issue of voting in the Security Council, so that when the peripheral question of voluntary abstention came up in the Joint Steering Committee on 19 September, the British said emphatically that the entire voting problem was taboo for now and that it "should be settled as a whole rather than in parts." The next day, the three chairmen agreed to delete all substantive points concerning voting in the council and to replace them with a statement that the question was still under consideration by their governments.[34]

The Joint Steering Committee did not meet for a week following this decision. The ostensible cause of this hiatus was that the British and Russians were awaiting instructions from home, but it also reflected the delegates' despair about reaching a final agreement at Dumbarton Oaks. When the Joint Steering Committee finally reconvened on 27 September following Gromyko's receipt of new instructions from Moscow, it was only for the purpose of wrapping up the conference. No one made any attempt to deal constructively with the voting issue; indeed, Gromyko added to the deadlock by remarking that his government's agreement to a general conference of the United Nations in the future was contingent upon prior British and American acceptance of the Soviet position on the veto. The delegates did manage to agree on an interim communiqué, which described the conversations as useful and said that they had led to a large measure of agreement on the shape of a postwar peacekeeping organization. They also agreed in principle on the form of a somewhat longer communiqué to be issued at the completion of the Chinese talks, a date set tentatively for 9 October. This statement, which was designed to present the Dumbarton Oaks proposals to the world and to announce future conversations on the same subject, ran into difficulty from the British, who refused to name 15 November as the date of renewed talks, and from the Soviets, who objected to a final paragraph expressing that the Great Powers intended to cooperate "with all other Governments" engaged in defeating the Axis states to enforce the terms of surrender.[35]

As the Russian phase of the conference edged toward completion, Stettinius regained some of his usual optimism. He refused to look upon the Dumbarton Oaks talks as a failure, even if they had not achieved a finished product in accordance with the State Department's designs. "Personally, I am not discouraged," he wrote in his diary on 19 September. "While it looks as if we will not have a 100 percent victory, I think it will be at least 75 percent"—and there was no use asking what could be done with three-quarters of a world organization. Hull and Roosevelt shared this view of the situation. The secretary of state, who would leave the State Department on 2 October—his seventy-third birthday— never to return, thought that the Dumbarton Oaks Conference had accomplished more than might reasonably have been expected of it; the differences that had surfaced there meant only that the new world organization would have to wait a while longer to be born. As for the president, it does not appear that he ever thought of the conversations as developing anything more than a preliminary working paper to facilitate further study and negotiations. Drafting a finished plan would have made no sense anyway, he told Stettinius, because Churchill—and perhaps Stalin as well—had not even begun to consider some of the key issues involved.[36]

Roosevelt's remark about Churchill turned out to be prophetic. By the end of September, as the talks with the Soviet Union were concluding, the prime minister was reversing his opinion on the Great Power veto—by all accounts the most important issue of the conference. The first indication of this came on 25 September, when Churchill forwarded to Washington a telegram from Jan Christian Smuts, prime minister of the Union of South Africa. Smuts, whose advice Churchill respected and was likely to weigh heavily, said that he had initially viewed the Soviet attitude on the veto as absurd but that he was now having second thoughts. The Kremlin's attitude, Smuts wrote, was based on its concern for the Soviet Union's "honour and standing . . . amongst her Allies"; on whether, that is, "she is trusted and treated as an equal or is still an outlaw and Pariah" among nations. This made the current disagreement more than a mere difference of opinion. "It touches Russian *amour propre* and produces an inferiority complex and might poison European relations with far-reaching results." In addition, Smuts thought, the Soviets were inevitably growing conscious of their newly won power, an awareness that was attested to by their unwillingness to compromise on the veto issue. This realization might make them more grasping and dangerous, calling into question the nature of their future relations with Germany and Japan "and even France, not to mention lesser countries." There was, moreover, no way to avoid the reality of Soviet power. If a world organization was formed without the Russians, the South African reasoned, they would become the "power centre of another group" and "we shall be heading for World War 3." But if no such organization was formed by the victorious nations, they would all "stand stultified before history." "The dilemma," Smuts concluded, "is a very grave one and the position into which we may be drifting should be avoided at all costs."[37]

Under the circumstances, Smuts argued, the smaller nations must be persuaded to make concessions to the Soviet view and not insist on a theoretical
equality with the Great Powers. Standing on principle now might mean that no
world body could be created—a result that would prove ultimately most
devastating for the lesser states themselves. Thus, the United States and Great
Britain should use their influence "in favour of common sense and safety-first
rather than status for the smaller countries" by supporting the Soviet position.
In addition, Smuts thought, there was much to be said for the principle of
unanimity among the Great Powers, at least for the uncertain years of the
immediate postwar period. The most important thing now was to build mutual
trust and confidence among the major victors; certainly "at the present stage a
clash should be avoided at all costs." In the short run, unanimity could do little
harm, the South African prime minister reasoned, and it might even provide a
brake on the rising ambitions of the Soviet leaders. Thus, Smuts advised, the
whole situation should be reconsidered in light of its far-reaching implications
and a modus vivendi found that could prevent "a catastrophe of the first
magnitude."[38]

Smuts's defection had a decided effect on Churchill. In a personal minute
dated 20 September, the British prime minister had expressed his agreement
with Smuts's views and ordered them circulated within the War Cabinet. On 3
October, as the Chinese phase of the conference was getting under way, he
cabled Roosevelt that he was now "pretty clear that the only hope is that the
three great powers are agreed." To soften the blow, Churchill said that it was
"with regret" that he had "come to this conclusion contrary to my first
thought." In addition to the arguments presented by Smuts, the British prime
minister had reasons of his own for reversing his stand on an unqualified Great
Power veto. He was, as he informed Stalin during their meeting in Moscow later
in the month, beginning to worry about how limits on the veto might affect
British colonial interests in such places as Hong Kong. Whom, he wondered,
could Great Britain count on for support if the Security Council voted to settle
a dispute over retention of its colony there? Surely not China or the equally
anticolonial United States. Or France, which especially if led by a revanchist
Charles de Gaulle, might be too jealous of British grandeur to help. That would
leave the Soviet Union—hardly the sort of reed that Churchill wanted to lean
on to save the empire. Thus, despite the Foreign Office's continued lobbying
for its original view, British self-interest joined Soviet self-interest in rejecting
what had become the American position on the veto.[39]

Roosevelt responded with a calmness that belied the importance he placed
on the issue. His reply, cabled to Churchill on 4 October, finessed the problem

by calling for "compromise by all the parties concerned," which FDR thought "ought to tide things over for a few years until the child learns to toddle." The president also asked the prime minister not to discuss the veto issue with "Uncle Joe" in Moscow, apparently out of concern that Churchill would concede the game before the American leader had a chance to play his cards. "That is a matter," Roosevelt wrote, "which the three of us can I am sure work out together." Not satisfied with this, Roosevelt took the advice of Harry Hopkins and sent a cable to Stalin informing him that Churchill had no authority to speak on the president's behalf, that Ambassador Harriman would take part in the discussions only as an observer, and that there were no world problems—political or military—in which the United States did not have an interest. One historian has argued that this message, with its clear implication of the American stake in Eastern Europe, might best be used to date the beginning of the cold war. It was also, not coincidentally, the last word on the subject of the veto question during the conference at Dumbarton Oaks.[40]

10 Bring on the Chinese

No one expected the Chinese phase of the Dumbarton Oaks Conference to amount to much. Because making any major changes in the draft proposals would jeopardize the fragile agreement just completed between the Anglo-Americans and the Soviets—something that neither of the Western allies wanted to risk—the Chinese talks were relegated in advance to a status that was little more than ceremonial, or, as the Foreign Office put it, "informative." This role was, to be sure, in keeping with Roosevelt's original purpose for including China in conversations with the Great Powers, which had been primarily to enhance Chiang Kai-shek's position as a peacekeeper in Asia. But benign as this objective may have been, it could not have encouraged the delegates at Dumbarton Oaks to take any Chinese suggestions very seriously; the Asians were there, after all, to be blessed, not to reform the church. By October 1944, moreover, even this reason for including the Chinese was being called into question by Chiang's own behavior. Not only had the Chinese leader failed to prosecute the war against Japan with anything like the vigor expected of a Great Power, but he had also engaged his top American adviser, General Joseph Stilwell, in a bitter quarrel that would shortly lead to the American's recall. Under the circumstances, neither the British nor the Americans were in any mood to debate the Chinese about points in a proposal that could not really be amended anyway.[1]

The Chinese promised to be more cooperative at Dumbarton Oaks than they were in Chungking. When their official delegation visited the State Department on 30 August, its chairman, Columbia educated V. K. Wellington Koo, said that he had "no disposition to quibble over any details"; the "most important thing," he concluded, "was to agree to *something*." Still, their second-rate status at the conference must have rankled the Chinese. First they had to wait in the wings while the Big Three took over center stage, a development that the Chinese ambassador in Washington, Wei Tao-ming, told the press he was "not too happy about"—especially because it was caused by the "technicality" of Soviet neutrality in their war against Japan. Then the Russian talks dragged on for weeks longer than anyone had anticipated, embarrassing the Chinese by highlighting their relative unimportance at the conference. By the time that the second round of conversations actually got under way, almost a month after Koo's remarks at the State Department, the proud Chinese chairman may have regretted his promise to cooperate fully with the British and Americans.[2]

For their part, the Americans attempted to shelter the sensibilities of the Chinese—at least insofar as formalities were concerned. Stettinius apologized profusely to Koo for keeping the Chinese waiting and assured him that the delay had been "caused by conditions beyond our control." He also followed protocol to the letter in planning for the opening of the Chinese talks. Thus, all the pomp and circumstance of the first session with the Russians was repeated in the music room on 29 September for the benefit of the Chinese—complete with reporters and newsreel photographers. Secretary of State Hull made one of his last public appearances to welcome the new delegates. Cadogan, who had been persuaded by Stettinius to stay in Washington for the end of the Soviet talks, represented the British and gave what he laconically referred to as "my usual little speech." Koo, able to take the floor at last, delivered what Breckinridge Long described as a "felicitous address characteristic of his understanding and use of the English language." If window dressing was what the Chinese talks were all about, they were off to an appropriate start.[3]

The hosts proved less accommodating about plans for conducting the talks themselves. Although Stettinius agreed, at Koo's request, to give the Chinese a chance to study the draft document by adjourning the conference for the weekend following the opening session, he made it clear that the conversations would have to be completed in time for the scheduled release of the joint communiqué on 9 October. He even tried during the first meeting of the Joint Steering Committee to set that as the official date for concluding the second phase of the conference. But the Chinese chairman, who had been cooling his heels for six weeks while the Russian talks languished, refused to agree in advance to be rushed by those who had just kept him waiting. A similar difference of opinion threatened to develop over the procedure for dealing with any suggestions that the Chinese might make for changes in the proposals. As early as 23 September, the American group had considered a plan whereby Chinese amendments would not be included in the Dumbarton Oaks document itself but placed in a separate paper for presentation to the general United Nations conference, thus putting the ideas of the Chinese delegation on a very different footing from those presented by the representatives of the other Great Powers. Such a procedure, Stettinius explained on 2 October, was the only way to insure that the Dumbarton Oaks document, which had already been adopted before the Russians went home, could be published as scheduled one week later. Koo, who recognized a fait accompli when he heard one, gave this plan his tentative approval while reserving his government's right to offer changes in the proposals in the future, perhaps in the form of a supplementary paper. Ultimately, the Chinese would honor their American sponsors' request in this matter—and surrender whatever chance they had to play a meaningful role at Dumbarton Oaks.[4]

In fact, the need for haste was only one of Stettinius's motives for putting a cap on the influence of the Chinese. Equally important was his lack of confidence in the Asians' understanding of what was required in a postwar international organization. Back on 12 July, the American chairman had met to discuss the future world body with H. H. Kung, Chiang Kai-shek's vice premier and minister of finance, and Liu Chieh, the Chinese chargé d'affaires in the United States, and decided that China's views on the subject were "extremely idealistic." A study of the Chinese proposals undertaken by Joseph Grew, Harley Notter, and Joseph Ballantine of the State Department's Office of Far Eastern Affairs produced a similar assessment. As the Americans saw it, the Chinese plans placed too much emphasis on social and economic concerns and too little on security—exactly the criticism of the American tentative proposals that the Soviets had made a few weeks before. In addition, according to Notter, the Chinese put excessive faith in the rule of international law, which they thought should be employed to resolve all nonviolent disputes, and in the ability of the world organization to bring about changes in the internal affairs of its member states. If not kept under tight control, such idealistic views could lead to the kind of long and complicated debates for which the British and Americans, tired from their six weeks of bickering with the Soviets, no longer had any patience.[5]

Still, discussion of important issues could not be completely stifled. Some deference had to be paid to the right of the Chinese to have opinions—even if they were not going to be taken very seriously. With this in mind, Stettinius called a meeting of the Joint Steering Committee on the afternoon of 2 October to brief the Chinese delegates on the questions left unsettled at the end of the Russian talks. The most important of these, of course, was the problem of voting in the Security Council, which Stettinius told the Chinese had been primarily responsible for the delay in concluding the Soviet phase of the conference. After summarizing the various positions on the two main voting issues of the Great Power veto and the size of the majority, the American chairman asked the Chinese for their questions and advice. Victor Hoo, the vice minister for foreign affairs in Chiang's government, asked for a clarification about the principle of unanimity—the basis for the Soviet Union's insistence on an unlimited veto. Would it be destroyed, he wondered, if one of the Great

Powers abstained from voting in the council? Pasvolsky replied that voluntary abstention had been considered as one of the possible solutions to the veto dispute but had presented so many problems that it was eventually dropped. His own view, however, was that abstention by a permanent member might serve as a "recognized exception" to the principle of unanimity. A difficulty here, Hoo thought, could come from requiring the abstaining member to provide military forces if their use was voted by the council—perhaps, to state a ridiculous case, even against themselves. Jebb and Pasvolsky agreed that this was a problem, the American adding that it might be solved by including reservations about voluntary abstention in the proposed agreements for the provision of forces by the Great Powers. In general, however, the abstaining member would have to be bound by the decisions of the council, Pasvolsky thought. What, Hoo inquired, would then be the point of abstention? Pasvolsky responded that there might be a case in which a nation would have no particular objection to some proposed action but would not want to be on record as favoring it. Jebb, who had replaced Cadogan as the main spokesman of his group for the Chinese phase of the conversations, said that the British shared Hoo's objection and were now opposed to the inclusion of a provision for voluntary abstention. Certainly it was not the answer to the veto squabble.[6]

Wellington Koo wondered about another aspect of the veto problem. When the Russians spoke of the necessity of permitting a party to a dispute to vote, he asked, did they mean only the permanent members of the Security Council? Yes, Stettinius answered. Jebb agreed and added that this was one of Great Britain's main objections to the Soviet position because "it meant that there would be one rule for the great powers and another for the small powers." Pasvolsky said that the arrangement could be extended to the smaller states as well, but that it would make little difference whether a nonpermanent member of the council, which would not have the right of veto, voted in its own case or not. Except, Hoo noted, if the nonpermanent member's vote was needed to make a majority. Nobody mentioned that it might matter a great deal to the nation involved—all the more so, perhaps, because a small state would be more vulnerable than a large one to any action voted by the council.[7]

Hoo was also unclear about the status of states that might be invited to attend meetings of the council when matters affecting their interests were under consideration. Would they be permitted to vote? The Anglo-Americans said no, that had never been intended. Anyway, Jebb added, their voting would be precluded by the rule that parties to a dispute should not do so. Hoo regarded this rationale as insufficient. Not all decisions of the council would involve actual disputes, he remarked, and not all nations whose interests were affected would be parties to whatever dispute was under debate. Nevertheless, the Westerners replied, there had been no thought that nonmembers would be permitted to vote in the council. Still not satisfied, Hoo observed that this was a change from the procedure followed by the League of Nations—a remark that revealed the much higher esteem in which that organization was held by the Chinese than by the other Great Powers. As the British and Americans were discovering, debating these questions with the Chinese presented problems that were almost the opposite of those raised by debating them with the Soviets.[8]

Koo asked about the various formulas that had been considered as solutions to the veto dispute. Stettinius and James Dunn said that several ideas had been developed by the Joint Formulation Group but that these had not been brought up for consideration by the three chairmen. Pasvolsky remarked that one avenue the planners had explored was the possibility of separating the Security Council's functions into two categories—one requiring unanimity and the other denying parties to a dispute the right to vote. The best method for doing this, he went on, drew a distinction between peaceful settlement, which would call for the exclusion of parties to a dispute, and the use of force, which would require the unanimous approval of the Great Powers—the compromise formula rejected by Roosevelt, Churchill, and Stalin in mid-September. This approach would, of course, eventually provide the basis for the voting plan approved at Yalta and adopted at San Francisco, but at this time it was, according to Pasvolsky, "not a considered formula but the result of exploratory discussions." That this undervalued the extent to which the plan had been considered at the conference was revealed by Jebb, who said that the proposal "had not found favor in any high quarter"—to which it would hardly have been referred without serious discussion first at Dumbarton Oaks. Koo, apparently noticing this contradiction, asked whether this plan could be called "the main compromise formula" to emerge from the Soviet talks. Jebb and Stettinius said no, this would be going too far; it was even doubtful, the American chairman claimed, whether either Roosevelt or Hull could remember the proposal's terms. It is difficult to say why the Anglo-Americans were going to such lengths to understate the importance of the compromise voting formula. Perhaps they believed it had been firmly rejected and did not want to see it adopted now by the Chinese. Or, more likely, they may have wanted to avoid appearing weak by advocating any compromise at all.[9]

The Chinese also inquired whether other compromise formulas had been considered. Dunn and Jebb said that several others had been discussed by the Formulation Group but that none had contained much merit. One, mentioned by Pasvolsky, would have authorized the Security Council to request that a party to a dispute decline to vote. On consideration, however, the planners had decided that such an approach was not feasible—he did not say why—and had returned to the principle of automatically excluding a party from voting in its own case. Jebb and Webster brought up another possible formula, which would have required the unanimity of the entire council except for the permanent member that was involved in a dispute. But this, too, had been rejected by the Formulation Group, according to the British delegates. Koo thought that the Westerners had painted a terribly bleak picture, one that did not make their chances for creating a successful world body look very bright. The question of voting in the council must be resolved, he said, because the Chinese considered it to be the "root of the whole question of an organization." He promised to give the matter more thought.[10]

Having exhausted the voting issue, Koo asked what other points were still under consideration, as the note at the end of the draft document had put it. This question provoked a bit of a controversy between the British and Americans, who maintained different views about what in fact constituted the conference's unfinished business. Stettinius and Pasvolsky listed the issues of territorial trusteeship, the liquidation of the League of Nations, the statute of an international court of justice, and initial membership in the new organization as the main points that remained open. Pasvolsky added that although the question of trusteeship, which involved creating a successor to the league's mandate system, had not been discussed at Dumbarton Oaks, it was an important subject and might be handled in the near future through an exchange of papers among the Great Powers. The Americans' willingness to raise the trusteeship issue with the anticolonial Chinese clearly troubled Jebb—so much so that he invoked the name of Sir Alexander Cadogan to say that the departed chairman did not include that question on his list of points that were still under consideration. He also warned the Foreign Office that the issue had come up again, still colored by American "misunderstanding and ill-informed criticism" of British colonial purposes. "The Americans misrepresent us," he concluded, "we rightly resent this, and so it goes on." Back at Dumbarton Oaks, Jebb argued that trusteeship had not even been considered during the Russian talks, so it could not properly be regarded as remaining under consideration now. It was simply a matter of definition. Because the same was also true of the question of liquidating the League of Nations, Jebb went on, the British interpreted the statement at the end of the proposals to include only the issues of the statute of the court and of initial membership. Pasvolsky, who liked to get in the last word, said that the note could fairly be interpreted either way.[11]

The tactful Koo did not press the issue, changing the subject to inquire about the question of initial membership in the new organization. Did it mean, he asked, which countries would be invited to the general conference of the United Nations? Jebb said yes and added that "there had not been entire agreement" on this matter. The problem, Pasvolsky elaborated, did not concern the present United Nations—those states actually involved in fighting the war against the Axis powers. Everyone agreed that they should be invited to attend. But, Pasvolsky continued, the Russians had objected to adding the Associated Nations to the initial list, preferring instead to restrict charter membership to those states that had been in the Grand Alliance during the war. Turkey, Stettinius added, was an example of a debatable nation. Koo wondered how the problem might be settled, adding that he did not see any likely compromise. The Americans replied that it would have to be resolved at the diplomatic level, but that they thought a solution would grow easier to find as the war neared its conclusion.[12]

The Westerners were not, of course, telling the Chinese quite the whole story. They had left out the most politically delicate part—the Soviet Union's insistence on membership in the new world body for all sixteen of its constituent republics, or the X-matter, as the security-conscious Americans called it. It was probably, in fact, the need for security that explained this obvious omission, which demonstrated just how little the Anglo-Americans trusted the Chinese. Roosevelt proved more trusting, however. To Stettinius's horror, the president mentioned the still-secret Soviet proposal to the Chinese delegates when they visited the White House on 3 October—probably because he wanted to add to his ammunition against it by asking the Chinese how many provinces there were in their country. He had, it will be recalled, committed a similar gaffe in a meeting with the Brazilian ambassador a few weeks earlier. Stettinius attempted to undo the damage in a session of the Joint Steering Committee the next day, when he reviewed the whole controversy for the Chinese and implored them not to make the Russian demand public. After pointing out that "in all probability it will never be possible to agree to the Soviet proposal," the American chairman said that the real danger lay in prematurely publicizing the controversy. He thought that "the whole civilized world would by shocked by such a proposal," which might, if it became public knowledge, lead to attacks on the Soviet Union in the United States and elsewhere and endanger all of their hopes for the creation of a postwar organization. After Halifax added that he agreed with Stettinius, that the matter must "remain locked in the minds" of those who already knew about it, Koo promised that no word of the Soviet proposal would escape from the Chinese delegation.[13]

Also concerning the question of membership, Koo said that the Chinese were glad to see France singled out for eventual inclusion as a permanent member of the council. This may have surprised the Americans, who had previously noted that any mention of membership for France had been omitted from the Chinese plan. In any event, Koo now wondered what was meant by the phrase "in due course" as it referred to French admittance to the security agency. Stettinius replied that it meant "as soon as the French people are able to elect a government which is plainly one of their own choosing"—a classic statement of the rather invidious way in which the Americans viewed this problem. Perhaps sensing that there was too much starch in the under secretary's tone, Dunn said that no specific formula had been worked out, and Pasvolsky added that this matter, too, would probably have to be resolved diplomatically. Webster pointed out that it was not even clear whether the decision would be made before the new organization was actually in operation; the only certain thing was that the other four permanent members would have to agree before France came in.[14]

The Chinese also made several criticisms of the draft document and suggested additions that they thought would strengthen it. In general, these reflected the greater emphasis that the Chinese placed on moral principles and international law as the foundations of world peace—what Stettinius had referred to when he called their ideas "extremely idealistic." But they also demonstrated China's desire to create an organization with teeth in it. Predictably, some of the Chinese suggestions took the British and Americans back over familiar ground, trying their patience with the idea of conducting a second round of similar talks so soon after completing the first—as well as with the newcomers to the conference themselves. This inevitably limited the effectiveness of any arguments presented by the Chinese, a result that Koo seemed to understand only too well. Thus, from the beginning of the conversations, the Chinese chairman refused to press very hard for his own ideas and usually retreated as soon as his Western counterparts began to raise objections. If this spared Koo the pain of experiencing Anglo-American impatience, it also meant that his government's ideas received only a very brief hearing at Dumbarton Oaks.[15]

During the first plenary session on 2 October, Koo pointed out what he regarded as the main weakness in the draft charter—its lack of a detailed statement of principles to guide the new organization. What principles were included in the document seemed, to the Chinese chairman, to be far too general to do much good; certainly they were considerably less specific than those presented in the more "idealistic" Chinese plan. Pasvolsky explained, however, that the new organization's principles had been left intentionally vague because to try to do otherwise would have involved the planners in no end of difficulty. It would be better, they decided, to let the details evolve over time. Koo seemed satisfied with this response but, somewhat uncharacteristically, raised the matter again in that afternoon's meeting of the Joint Steering Committee, remarking that he thought a more specific statement of principles was needed "for the general guidance of the Assembly and the council in the settlement of disputes." Pasvolsky suggested the compromise of including some of the Chinese ideas as a preamble to the eventual United Nations charter, and the Chinese chairman, apparently satisfied with this proposal, did not return to this issue at Dumbarton Oaks.[16]

Koo also expressed apprehension about one of the principles that was included in the draft document, which required that all members refrain from the use of force "in any manner inconsistent with the purposes of the Organization." What, the Chinese chairman asked, would prevent member states from employing force whenever they chose to do so and claiming that its use was not inconsistent with the world body's purposes? The Anglo-Americans explained that, except for self-defense, no unilateral use of force was permitted without the approval of the Security Council. Koo, who might have pointed out that this definition appeared nowhere in the document, "seemed satisfied," according to Stettinius. Victor Hoo saw just the opposite problem in this principle and asked for explicit assurance that the organization would not regard the use of force in self-defense as violating its purposes. After receiving such assurance, the Chinese let the matter drop.[17]

The Chinese could see that this discursive approach was getting them nowhere. If they were to make any impression at all on the Dumbarton Oaks proposals—even in a separate document—they would have to come up with more specific ideas. By the morning of 3 October, Koo was prepared to do so. In that day's plenary session, which was the second of three held during the brief Chinese phase of the conference, he listed seven points that he thought would strengthen the new organization and insure its wide support among the smaller nations of the world. Three of these had to do with various aspects of international law—a subject that the Chinese thought had been given short shrift in the Russian talks. First, Koo suggested that some reference be made to a body of law or specific principles of justice as criteria for the settlement of disputes between nations. This would, according to the Chinese leader, expedite enforcement, reinforce confidence in the new organization, and give assurance to smaller states that the world body was not intended to become merely an instrument of power politics. The Chinese did not, at this point, have any specific laws or principles to propose, Koo said, but thought that international law should be progressively codified and become the basis for decisions by the world organization as the two developed together over time.[18]

Fostering that kind of joint development was the idea behind the second of Koo's proposals. This was the codification of international law by the General Assembly, which would eventually provide the world organization with a kind of legislative function. The Chinese chairman also reminded the British and Americans that his government's plan had included an international law codification commission to study problems and propose conventions to ratify new laws in the future. The Americans saw serious difficulties with this proposal. It had, for one thing, been rejected by the Soviet Union when the United States had suggested it at Dumbarton Oaks, and no one in the American group wanted to bring the issue up with the Russians again. In addition, as Green Hackworth pointed out, codification of international law had never worked very well when attempted in the past by either the League of Nations or various inter-American conferences. And finally, codification—like legislation—always involved compromises and the acceptance of the lowest common denominator; much better, the American group now thought, to develop law through the world court and other judicial processes, where principles, not politics, would prevail.[19]

Third, Koo proposed that the world court be granted compulsory jurisdiction over peaceful disputes. This provision should be, he thought, in the charter of the new United Nations Organization, not just in the statute of the court itself. What the Chinese idea meant, as the British and Americans interpreted it, was that all decisions of the court would be subject to enforcement by the Security Council—a proposition that put far more authority in the hands of the judicial body than the other Great Powers were willing to grant. It would also tie the court and the peacekeeping organization too tightly together and would run afoul of the Russians by practically eliminating the Great Power veto where justiciable disputes were concerned. Thus, the Anglo-Americans argued that any statement defining the jurisdiction of the court should await that body's establishment and should be placed in its statute rather than in the charter of the new international organization.[20]

Koo's fourth point called for a provision that would guarantee international respect for the political independence and territorial integrity of member states. Such a statement naturally meant more to the Chinese, who had only secured abolition of the unequal treaties and regained respect for their own independence during the Second World War, than it did to the other Great Powers. But, by suggesting what Long called "Article X phraseology," this proposal raised the Anglo-Americans' fears of recreating what they saw as one of the major shortcomings of the League of Nations—its inability to provide for peaceful change among its members. To prevent this from happening again, the American group thought that any provision involving guarantees would have to be coupled with a more specific definition of peaceful change; otherwise, the United Nations would repeat the mistake of the league by becoming strictly the protector of the status quo. Most of the Americans, however, regarded any specific definition as difficult, if not impossible, to achieve. Jebb agreed with this assessment, adding that it would be a great mistake to put anything in the organization's charter that might become an impediment to peaceful change. Koo, who defended his proposal in a meeting of the Formulation Group on 4 October, replied that his government had introduced these provisions to safeguard states against aggression, not to perpetuate the status quo. But, Hackworth said, aggression was already outlawed by one of the principles of the new body, which required members to refrain from the threat or use of force. Moreover, Pasvolsky added, respect for political independence and territorial integrity were also covered by the principle that established the sovereign equality of all peace-loving states. Thus, according to the British and Americans, Koo's proposal was unnecessary as well as dangerous.[21]

Fifth, Koo called for a definition of aggression. Such a provision would, according to the Chinese chairman, facilitate swift action by the Security Council, inspire confidence in the world organization, restrain potential aggressors, and make it possible for world opinion to recognize an aggressor immediately. The definition would not have to be comprehensive, Koo said, but should at least provide examples or illustrations of what the creators of the international body meant by the term. The British and Americans had, of course, been over this issue at length with the Soviets. They explained to Koo that they thought it impossible to arrive at a satisfactory, all-inclusive definition of aggression—or, for that matter, of threats to or breaches of the peace. The methods of aggressors would inevitably change with time, they argued, and even a list of examples would run the risk of being perceived as an exclusive definition that might limit the council's actions in the future. Thus it would be safer to leave the question of what constituted aggression for the Security Council to decide on a case-by-case basis.[22]

Sixth, the Chinese still supported the idea of an international air force, a plan for the creation of which had been included in their tentative proposals. Such a force, Koo thought, if placed directly under the control of the Security Council, would make it possible to punish aggressors quickly while serving as a potent symbol of the Security Council's authority. As during the Russian phase of the conference, this question was referred to a special military group, which met later in the afternoon of 3 October. At this meeting, the American representatives—Generals Strong and Fairchild and Admiral Train—went over the debate they had had on the subject with the Soviets and explained why they thought the present provision concerning military forces would be flexible enough to provide air power when necessary. The Chinese said, however, that they had something much stronger in mind, including perhaps the abolition of all national air forces. A plan of this sort, which would certainly have facilitated enforcement by the new world organization, seemed hopelessly impractical to the Anglo-Americans, who had already gone as far along this road as they thought they could. The other Great Powers, as the Chinese were coming to realize, intended to rely more on their own strength than on that of the world body to protect their postwar interests and security.[23]

Koo's last proposal called for provisions to enhance the new organization's role in fostering cultural cooperation as a means of preventing conflict. The Chinese preconference plans had provided for the creation of an international cultural relations office, which would prepare propaganda designed to promote worldwide understanding and friendship, encourage international peace movements, alleviate possible causes of ill-feeling among nations, and effect various kinds of cultural exchanges. The principle here was the dubious one that, in international relations, familiarity breeds respect. Although, as the British and Americans pointed out, this sort of thing was already generally provided for in the draft document, Koo thought that a more explicit supplementary statement would be useful. In this one case, the other delegates saw no good reason to object.[24]

During the first meeting of the Formulation Group on 3 October, the Chinese agreed to reduce their suggested changes from seven to three. The three remaining proposals, about which the British and Americans had raised the fewest objections, included the adjustment of international disputes according to principles of justice and law, the development and revision of international law by the General Assembly, and the promotion of cultural cooperation by the new organization. Consideration of the other four points was postponed indefinitely. The next morning, at a meeting of the steering committee, the British and American chairmen accepted these suggestions, which Jebb described as "quite harmless," as official proposals emanating from the Chinese phase of the conference—a decision that they regarded as more important for saving Chinese face than for any improvement it might produce in the draft document.[25]

The next question was how these suggestions ought to be handled. Koo hoped to publish them along with the Dumbarton Oaks document on 9

October—thus insuring the additional proposals (and the talks that produced them) a status equal to those endorsed by the Russians. Stettinius and Halifax doubted the wisdom of this idea, however, because it would merely accentuate the difference between the draft charter, approved by all four powers, and the supplementary proposals, approved by only three. It would be better, they argued, to wait to publish the Chinese-British-American suggestions until after they had been accepted by the Soviet Union as well. In addition, the Westerners feared that any attempt to add the new proposals to the upcoming communiqué would jeopardize Stalin's willingness to proceed with publication as scheduled on 9 October. Reluctantly, the Chinese chairman agreed to the postponement with the understanding that the new proposals would be discussed with the Russians before the meeting of the general United Nations conference. Pasvolsky then raised another issue that promised to be equally complicating. This referred to the list of additional suggestions, which he thought should be broadened to include the two other unresolved questions of territorial trusteeship and liquidation of the League of Nations. Stettinius argued that the British would never accept these additions, however, and the proposal was dropped. The important thing, as the American chairman saw it, was to conclude the Chinese talks without provoking any new disputes.[26]

Stettinius must, therefore, have been apprehensive when Koo asked for a special meeting of the steering committee to present his government's ideas on the voting question. There were, according to the Chinese chairman, several questions of principle that deserved additional consideration—a statement that could not have done much to ease his American counterpart's concern. As it turned out, however, Stettinius need not have worried; Koo had no desire to do anything more than contribute to a general understanding of the voting issue by presenting his own opinions, most of which accorded with those of the British and Americans. He thought, for example, that a decision must be made on the best way to distinguish between procedural and substantive questions, especially if one would require a simple majority and the other a two-thirds vote of the council. The new organization should benefit from the experience of the League of Nations, Koo said, where the failure to define the difference between the two had sometimes produced paralyzing disagreements. This experience suggested that it would be a good idea to enumerate the questions covered by each category. But because he recognized that a complete list would be impossible to devise, the Chinese chairman favored a compromise that would offer a definition but leave the final distinction up to the council when necessary.[27]

Most of Koo's presentation dealt with the three related questions of the principle of unanimity, abstention from voting, and the size of the majority required for action by the council. On the first topic, the Chinese chairman agreed with the British and American view that unanimity was worthwhile and ought to be maintained except where one of the permanent members of the council was involved in a dispute. His government did not see, he said, how a party to a dispute could ever be permitted to vote in its own case, especially if it had the power to veto any decisions. Koo did not suggest any new compromise solutions to the problem—perhaps because the possibility of ever finding one had been presented so discouragingly by the Anglo-Americans.[28]

Koo's views on abstention prompted more debate, especially as they related to the question of how to determine the size of a majority vote when one or more members abstained. It had to be determined, the Chinese chairman said, whether abstention was to be permitted and, if so, what its effect should be both on the enforcement responsibility of the member that declined to vote and on the number of votes required to make up a majority. First Koo, perhaps playing the devil's advocate, wondered whether the other groups would object to prohibiting abstention altogether on the grounds that it caused too many problems—especially where the Great Power veto was concerned—and that members of the council should always be willing to show their "true colors" by voting, as Stettinius put it. Jebb and Pasvolsky said no, they would not necessarily object. Stettinius agreed, stressing that a nation sitting on the council should recognize its obligation to act as a trustee for other states and vote. Webster raised the strongest objections. He did not believe, he said, that there existed any precedent for denying members of an organization the right to abstain, or that it would be possible to make a state vote if it did not wish to do so. Koo added that trying to require everyone to vote might have the undesirable effect of causing a member that did not want its position recorded to absent itself from the council, thus further reducing the force and authority of the meeting at which a vote for action was taken. Failing to provide for abstention could, in this way, prove dangerously divisive for the new organization.[29]

But, Koo wondered, if abstention were to be permitted, how should the council's votes be counted? Should the abstaining state's vote be included with the affirmative or the negative? This question would be especially important, Koo pointed out, if action by the Security Council required approval by a majority of its entire membership and not just of those present and voting. And what if the abstaining member was a Great Power? In such cases, according to the Chinese chairman, some way would have to be found to prevent the abstaining nation (or nations) from invalidating the decision of the council. Webster thought that this could not be done, that an abstaining member's vote would have to be regarded as a negative one. The only alternative, he reasoned, was to count it with the affirmative—that is, if a positive decision required a majority of all eleven members. Jebb agreed that in effect an abstention would have to amount to a negative vote. Pasvolsky argued, however, that it might be possible to stipulate the opposite; such a provision, he thought, would not only solve the problem at hand but might discourage abstention as well.[30]

Halifax offered another suggestion—determining a majority only among those members who were present and voting. Otherwise, he argued, abstention by several states could block action by the council even if no member was on record as opposed to it. As a worst case, the British ambassador raised the possibility of a vote in which all five Great Powers favored action—thus preserving the principle of unanimity—but were stymied by the abstention of all of the smaller states. Pasvolsky said that this should not concern them, however, because an action agreed upon by the permanent members that could not command the support of at least one of the other nations on the council would have to be regarded as undesirable anyway. Still, the American had to admit that Halifax's idea presented a possible way out of their dilemma. Hoo, sensitive as always to the special problems of smaller nations, pointed out that some of the reasons for abstention might be eliminated by providing for a secret ballot in the council; then nonpermanent members, which might feel more vulnerable than their stronger counterparts, would not have to fear reprisals. This might even make it practicable to prohibit abstention, Hoo thought. Jebb disagreed that this was an issue because no small nation would ever have to be fearful of acquiescing in a decision approved by all of the Great Powers, but Stettinius thought that Hoo's proposal was very interesting and contained considerable merit.[31]

Hoo also reasoned that some of the problems of abstention could be solved by eliminating the concept of a majority and requiring a fixed number of affirmative votes before the council could take action. Pasvolsky agreed—not surprisingly, since he had made a similar proposal in the Russian phase of the conference—and suggested seven as the number to be required. Jebb said that he was inclined to agree as well, provided that the question was not complicated by permitting abstention. Dunn, who saw for the first time that this might be possible, remarked that Hoo's formula constituted an improvement over previous thinking on the subject. Beyond anybody's expectations, the Chinese were contributing valuable ideas to the planning for a postwar organization.[32]

On 7 October, the last day of the conference at Dumbarton Oaks, the Formulation Group met to discuss the problem of transition from the League of Nations to the new world peacekeeping organization. The greatest difficulty here was the difference in membership of the two world bodies. Of the forty-five members of the league, only twenty-nine (including France) were among the United and Associated Nations; thus sixteen states would be left out. Although four of these countries were enemy states, and Soviet-occupied Estonia, Latvia, and Lithuania constituted a "special case," there remained the possibility that the others might object to the league's dissolution, especially if it were not conducted in what Webster called "a decent and orderly fashion." In addition, fifteen of the new organization's proposed members, including of course the United States, did not belong to the league. These differences in membership, the Formulation Group recognized, would render impossible a simple passage of power from the old world body to the new; the transition would have to be handled issue by issue and in a way that, as Koo put it, "would leave no loopholes for claims or recriminations." The planners discussed several of the more complicated issues, including adoption of the league's responsibilities for minorities and mandates, disposition of its assets and liabilities, and transference of treaties that assigned powers and duties to the league, but could draw no definite conclusions. They thus approved Jebb's suggestion that all three delegations—and the Soviet Union, if it so desired—should prepare research papers on the subject of the league for exchange and for the development of a joint proposal before the meeting of the full United Nations conference.[33]

The Dumbarton Oaks Conference ended on an upbeat note, with the heads of the three delegations praising themselves and each other in a final plenary session on 7 October. In fact, the Chinese conversations, unlike those with the Soviets that had preceded them, had accomplished more and raised fewer difficulties than anticipated. In mid-September, radio commentator Wilfred Fleisher had reported that the Chinese were "about to ruffle the smooth waters of the Dumbarton Oaks Conference" by making a plea for racial equality in the new United Nations Organization. Of course this never happened—nor did anything else that embarrassed the British and Americans, although Cadogan had been worried enough to ask the Foreign Office for instructions. On the other hand, the Chinese made what Hull described as "cogent observations" about the draft proposal, brought up a number of issues that would be raised again by smaller nations at the San Francisco conference, and illuminated important lacunae in the preliminary plan. Stettinius and Halifax were undoubtedly sincere when they closed the conference by thanking the Chinese for their cooperation; if only, they must have thought, they had been so lucky in their dealings with the Soviets.[34]

Conclusion:
Quod Severis Metes

The Dumbarton Oaks plan was released as scheduled at noon on 9 October 1944. The accompanying communiqué, which had been the source of so much difficulty in the waning days of the Soviet phase of the conference, revealed little of the turmoil that had prevented the delegates from completing their proposals. It said only that the attached plan indicated a framework of basic agreement among the Big Four, to be followed by more complete proposals to serve as a basis of discussion at a full United Nations conference in the future. The plan itself also expressed more confidence than most of the departing delegates felt. With the exception of voting in the Security Council and a few other unnamed questions said to be "still under consideration," the proposals claimed to present a complete draft charter for the new United Nations Organization. The impression it all gave was that the conference at Dumbarton Oaks had finally accomplished what a war-weary world was hoping for—a plan for permanent peace.[1]

But had it? The answer, of course, is no. Regardless of how the questions that were listed as "still under consideration" might be answered by the Great Powers, the new world body would not have the force or the authority to maintain the kind of international security that had been its original goal. Gone from the plan were the strongest proposals for enforcing the peace—the undiluted Four Policemen backed by an international air force—as well as the idea of requiring mandatory settlement of justiciable disputes by the world court. Worse, what security apparatus remained in the proposals had been hamstrung by the perhaps inevitable inclusion of provisions to protect the national sovereignty of member states and to remove domestic concerns from the new organization's jurisdiction. If, as Lord Cranborne, Churchill's secretary of state for the dominions, claimed in defending the plan in a House of Lords debate, the new United Nations would have a "really serviceable set of teeth," they would not be so sharp as earlier proposals would have made them.[2]

This dulling may have been predictable. Shortly after the conference opened, on 24 August, columnist Edgar Ansel Mowrer had written, in an article "Woodrow Wilson at Dumbarton Oaks," that despite their grander ambitions, the statesmen of 1944 would turn inevitably to a universal security system "not very different from the first League of Nations." The American and British plans had, in fact, been moving steadily in that direction with each successive draft—partly in response to complaints from smaller states and partly out of their own desire to create an organization that would be something more than the police force of the Big Four. And although a revitalized league carried less appeal for the Soviet Union, even Gromyko saw good reasons to go that way at Dumbarton Oaks. The United Nations would, as a result, be a combination of both the Four Policemen and the League of Nations ideas. Considering the state of world politics at the time, it could hardly have been otherwise.[3]

At the heart of the new organization's political difficulties lay the expansive postwar ambitions of the Great Powers themselves. In the years of study that preceded the meetings at Dumbarton Oaks, some English and American planners had seemed to envision a world body whose deliberations would ultimately replace power politics as the final arbiter of international relations. Such thinking, which would later be depicted as naive and idealistic, did not seem so utopian at the time—primarily because the terrors of the world war made other, more nationalistic, concerns pale into selfish insignificance. But all of this was changing by August 1944, when the winding down of the war was causing the Great Powers to become increasingly aware of their own postwar objectives, so that traditional nationalism was replacing the prevention of the next war as the dominant force in postwar policy-making. What this meant was that the Big Three saw the defense of their own security, the protection of their own interests, and the enjoyment of the fruits of their victory in the world war as more important than the creation of an international organization to maintain future world peace. These goals were not necessarily mutually exclusive— indeed, to some extent the Great Powers had always seen their paramount role in the new world body as both a mark and a means of their postwar dominance. And the United States, in particular, would later come to identify preservation of world peace with the protection of its own national security. But if, as became apparent at Dumbarton Oaks, the sharing of power inherent in any world organization threatened to interfere with the achievement of their national ambitions, the Great Powers would sacrifice at least the substance if not the idea of the security body and depend upon their own resources to defend their interests. Although this tendency may have been most pronounced among the Soviets, it could be seen in the behavior of the British and Americans at Dumbarton Oaks as well, as all three of the Great Powers found themselves, in the words of Matthew Arnold, "wandering between two worlds, one dead, the other powerless to be born."

The task of the Dumbarton Oaks Conference was also made more complicated by the developing conflict among the Great Powers themselves. To whatever extent the political and ideological differences dividing the Big Three had been forgotten during the war, they were remembered at Dumbarton Oaks. One of Cadogan's first acts after arriving in Washington, in fact, was to warn Stettinius that the Soviets intended to make serious mischief in Eastern Europe—a view that was not, of course, unheard of within the American State Department. It was in this context, highlighted daily by news of the tragic uprising in Warsaw, that the Anglo-Americans perceived the veto controversy with the Soviet Union. As they saw it, the Soviets intended to use the new organization as an instrument to legitimize their postwar hegemony over their smaller neighbors; that, they thought, was why Stalin clung so tenaciously to the unlimited Great Power veto. They employed similar reasoning to explain Russian interest in requiring weaker states to furnish bases to the peacekeeping body. Nor did the Soviets trust the intentions of their Western allies. In addition to fearing that the point of the veto dispute was to clear the way for their erstwhile friends to employ the world organization against them, the Russians thought that the Americans, especially, meant to use the United Nations, saturated as it would inevitably be with their capitalist friends and clients, to cement their control over the entire world. This, in their view, was why the State Department had shifted its emphasis from a regional to a universal organization—an interpretation that could only have been strengthened by the telegram that Roosevelt sent to Stalin in October linking continued talks about the postwar body to American interest in Eastern Europe. And even the British had to balance their concern over the Soviet menace with their suspicion that the United States intended to employ the new world organization to make the sun finally set on their empire. Not only did such concerns make a mockery of the contemporary idea of Great Power unity, but they made each of the Big Three doubt the possibility of their long-term cooperation as well. The most surprising thing, perhaps, is that they bothered to go through with the creation of a new world body at all.[4]

They had a number of good reasons for doing so. The Dumbarton Oaks Conference had been too heavily publicized to be permitted to fail without damaging the authority of the Great Powers and demoralizing the public throughout the world. As Jebb pointed out, the conference might better have been held with less fanfare in "some rather less spectacular place"; then the possibility of failure would not have been so difficult for the participants to accept. And, of course, the leading delegates had their own reputations to worry about. More important than appearances, though, was the continued hope that a peacekeeping body might work—that it might even lead, through daily contact and compromises, to an improvement in the already deteriorating relations among the Great Powers. Besides, what was the alternative? "The practical choice at this time," Joseph Grew said during an NBC broadcast on the prospective United Nations, "is clearly between an organization of the type proposed at Dumbarton Oaks and international anarchy." The planners had to avoid, added Assistant Secretary of State Archibald MacLeish, both the errors of the cynics, who thought that there must always be war, and those of the perfectionists, who would accept nothing less than an ideal world order. A world organization, as Stettinius argued, was really the only hope for preventing a Third World War—thus it had to be tried "for the sake of everything we hold dear and for our as yet unborn generations." Even Stalin, who might fairly be regarded as one of the cynics, expressed similar sentiments in his speech on 6 November commemorating the anniversary of the Bolshevik revolution. The same conclusion also resulted from a concern for realpolitik. This came up in the United States when Hull and Pasvolsky discussed the possibility of scrapping plans for a new world organization. "But if you cut loose," Hull said, "then you have nothing but regional organizations" to maintain security. "That is it," Pasvolsky replied. "If we ask for the privilege, everybody else will." Even the Japanese, he reminded the former secretary of state, had described their plans for the conquest of Asia as a new Monroe Doctrine. "If we start dividing the world into regions," Pasvolsky concluded, "it will push them [the Soviets] into a combine." The result would be rival power blocs—and probably war. The Great Powers, then, would simply have to find some way to reconcile their differences about plans for the new world organization; no other choice seemed thinkable.[5]

The same problems that had plagued the conference at Dumbarton Oaks continued to hinder efforts to find answers for the questions that were blandly described as still under consideration in the final communiqué. This was particularly true where the Great Power veto was concerned. Churchill's complete defection to the Russian position on the voting issue while in Moscow did not mean that the conflict between East and West had been put to rest. The developing disagreement over Eastern Europe, temporarily relegated to the back burner by the spheres-of-influence approach adopted by Stalin and Churchill in October, still threatened to bring Allied relations to the boiling point in the future. If anything, in fact, American awareness of the "percentages" deal made the State Department more committed than ever to the need for a voting formula that would check both Soviet and British ambitions. Stalin, too, could only have grown more convinced of the need to preserve his veto during the autumn of 1944 as the United States expressed increasing interest in the political reconstruction of Eastern Europe—an area that the marshal regarded as his nation's vital security zone. Thus, the lack of trust among the Great Powers that had surfaced at Dumbarton Oaks threatened to make the successful completion of their plans for a postwar organization extremely difficult, if not impossible, to achieve.[6]

The State Department's growing suspicion of the Soviets could be seen even in its postconference efforts to devise a workable voting plan. In a meeting on 4 November, the planners agreed that something like the compromise formula developed at Dumbarton Oaks was the best that they could hope to get. They thus drafted a plan whereby procedural questions, including the pacific settlement of disputes, could be decided by any seven votes—a compromise between a simple and a two-thirds majority of the eleven-member council—while decisions on all other matters, including enforcement action, would also require the concurrence of all five permanent members. Thus the veto would remain in effect where it seemed most important—the use of military and other sanctions to enforce the council's decisions. But now Leo Pasvolsky, who had developed the compromise formula in the first place, had a new concern; a Great Power should not, he thought, be permitted to veto council decisions about whether a regional security organization was consistent with the purposes of the parent United Nations or whether a dispute should be referred by the council to a regional body for peaceful settlement. These matters, Pasvolsky argued, should be added to the list of procedural questions for which the agreement of the Great Powers was not required; otherwise the Soviets, and perhaps the British, might use regional organizations to subvert the goals of the new international body and to control their own parts of the globe. Harley Notter pointed out that such a provision would also limit the control of the United States over the inter-American system, but the rest of the group agreed with Pasvolsky that this risk was necessary to check Soviet activity in the Balkans. When the other two Great Powers objected to this change in the formula, however, the Americans agreed in January 1945 to the retention of the veto in votes determining the legitimacy of peacekeeping by a regional organization—at least in part to protect their own freedom of action in the Western Hemisphere. As it often had before, the United States was vacillating between structuring the new United Nations to further its own postwar ambitions and using it to prevent the British and Russians from furthering theirs.[7]

Other, more cynical, Americans were beginning to wonder if the entire idea of a world organization had not been a mistake. The influential columnist Walter Lippmann told Alger Hiss over lunch on 20 October that he viewed the

Security Council as really just a continuation of the Grand Alliance in disguise. This sort of thing might be useful, he thought, for enforcing peace terms on Germany and Japan, but it was dangerous to suppose that it might also be able to police the world. The State Department's George F. Kennan, still two years away from his rise to influence as the architect of the containment doctrine, took an even stronger position. In January 1945, he wrote to Assistant to the Secretary of State—and later Ambassador to the Soviet Union—Charles E. Bohlen that there was no basis in reality for what he called the new League of Nations. "We are badly enmeshed in our own unsound slogans," he argued, and have confused the Russians—who anyway fear a trick—by permitting them to think that we have been proposing "a cleverly disguised statute for the collaboration of the strong in the brow-beating of the weak." This would, Kennan thought, accentuate rather than ameliorate the problems of the post-war world by doing no good in Eastern Europe while ultimately disappointing the heightened hopes of the Soviet Union. The solution, according to the State Department's second highest official in Moscow, was to "bury" the Dumbarton Oaks agreements, taking the out offered by the Soviets over the veto dispute. The United States should not stake the future of Europe, Kennan concluded, on the flawed assumption of a community of aims with the Russians—an idea that was only wishful thinking anyway; instead, it should renounce all coop-eration with the USSR and draw a line between the two systems in Eastern Europe. Although this extreme view of the situation would eventually become enshrined in American policy-making, it found little favor in the State Depart-ment of 1945. Still, it expressed something of the mistrust toward the Soviet Union that was growing within official circles in the United States.[8]

Stalin's continuing suspicions were also evident in the negotiations following Dumbarton Oaks. He responded to the American compromise voting formula on 27 December by saying he would still have to insist on maintaining unanim-ity among the Great Powers in the council. There must be, the Soviet leader argued, "full agreement of powers which are permanent members of the coun-cil bearing upon themselves the main responsibility for maintenance of peace and security"; any other approach could, he thought, have fatal consequences for the success of the new world organization. Ambassador Harriman, who had presented the compromise plan to Stalin, attempted to explain the marshal's reaction in a telegram to the State Department on the following day. Harriman emphasized that even as a Great Power the Soviet Union remained "suspicious of the underlying attitude" that most of the world's nations had taken since 1917 toward its goals and aspirations. It thus expected to be misunderstood and dealt with unfairly by other members of the Security Council, especially where its intentions to dominate its neighbors in Eastern Europe were concerned. "The court, they believe, is stacked against them," the ambassador wrote, and nothing less than an absolute veto could make them feel secure in what they regarded as a willfully hostile world. The Soviets, he concluded, had made up their minds on the question of voting in the council and only a firm and definite stand on the part of the British and Americans would have any chance of persuading them to change their position.[9]

Such a stand was exactly what the State Department now had in mind. In passing Harriman's message on to Roosevelt a few days later, Stettinius emphasized the need to get tough with the Soviets—an approach that the secretary hoped the president would take in his upcoming summit meeting with Stalin and Churchill at Yalta. To have any hope of succeeding, this plan would require that Roosevelt line up the support of the British prime minister, who had rejected the compromise formula at Quebec in September and had actually gone over to Stalin's point of view following the completion of the Dumbarton Oaks Conference. Unless the unpredictable Churchill could be persuaded to change his mind again, it seemed likely that Roosevelt would go to Yalta as the odd man out among the Big Three and that the American president, far from being in a position to get tough with Stalin, would be lucky to reach a compromise voting formula that State Department planners could accept.[10]

Meanwhile, Churchill's defection was generating a major debate within the British government. When, in September, the prime minister had first expressed his changing sentiments, Whitehall had apparently given way without putting up much of a struggle. Almost immediately, the Foreign Office had taken the view that accepting the Soviet position was a lesser evil than failing to establish a postwar organization altogether—exactly the opposite of the approach then being taken by its delegates at Dumbarton Oaks. On a more positive note, the Foreign Office now thought that "the Russian thesis would seem to safeguard some of the interests which we possess outstandingly as an Imperial power with far flung and sometimes disputed possessions," such as the Falkland Islands. An unlimited veto might therefore serve British purposes as well as Soviet ones, a consideration that certainly recommended it to the empire-minded Churchill. A new British position on the key issue of the conference thus seemed all but an accomplished fact.[11]

But then the British group returned from Dumbarton Oaks, intent on defending its actions there against the prime minister's latest interference. Jebb, Webster, and Cadogan all weighed into the controversy during mid-October, attacking both Churchill and those members of the War Cabinet, such as Sir Stafford Cripps, who had so quickly adopted the prime minister's views. As

Webster informed Eden on 23 October, the British delegates were certain that any organization created through the acceptance of a Soviet-style veto would only be a sham, incapable of fulfilling the goals that the Foreign Office had set for it through years of planning. The British government should not, Webster argued, be in such a hurry to abandon its principles on so important a question, especially in light of the use to which the Soviets might be expected to put an unrestricted veto in Eastern Europe. The united front presented by the returning British group steadied a wavering Eden but had little effect on Churchill, who was finding it increasingly difficult to believe that any of the Great Powers could accept less than the Soviet position.[12]

The Foreign Office responded by renewing its search for a compromise voting formula. By the end of November, Cadogan was ready to give Eden some alternative approaches to the problem, although he still contended that the former British attitude was entirely correct. Cadogan's preferred compromise solution was the same one the American State Department was working on at the time: a Great Power involved in a dispute could not veto recommendations for pacific settlement, only for enforcement action. Although this approach seemed promising as a means of safeguarding everyone's interests, Cadogan doubted whether the Soviets would be willing to accept it. Thus planners in the Foreign Office had also devised two entirely new ways of dealing with the veto problem. One would have denied a Great Power the right to vote on its own case but given it the option of settling the dispute through a method that was different from the one the Security Council usually followed. Under this special procedure, the council would serve only as a conciliator, taking no votes and imposing no sanctions. A second new approach would have permitted a Great Power to deny the council the authority to deal with any dispute in which it was involved. Cadogan thought it possible that the Soviets might stick to their guns and reject all of these proposals, in which case he argued that the British should refuse to proceed with the drawing up of plans for an international organization and look elsewhere for ways to insure their postwar security.[13]

A more immediate problem, however, was Churchill's unwillingness to compromise with his own government's planners. The prime minister responded to Cadogan's proposals by informing Eden that "I must warn you that as far as I can see the Foreign Office view differs fundamentally from mine"; he remained, he said, "in entire agreement with the Russians." Then, to the Foreign Office's obvious relief, both the Soviets and the Americans showed signs of coming around to the compromise formula rejected at Quebec and Moscow. By the end of December, planners in each of the Great Powers had accepted it as the only practicable solution to the veto problem; all that remained was for the national leaders to strike a final bargain at Yalta.[14]

Churchill gave way with surprising ease. As 1944 came to a close, he had promised Eden that if the Soviets agreed to a compromise he would not press his views. A month later, his growing concern over events in Eastern Europe had made him only too happy to reestablish a united front with the Americans, especially now that his fears for the empire had been allayed by the American plan's assurance that Great Britain could always veto any proposal calling for action by the council. He thus embraced the compromise voting formula at Yalta and took the lead in trying to explain it to Stalin, who admitted that he had not yet studied the proposal. "Uncle Joe" did not prove to be as difficult to persuade as the Anglo-Americans had feared. Once he was convinced that the formula really meant what it said—that the Soviet Union could indeed veto any council action—Stalin indicated his approval of the plan, which Molotov accepted formally on the following day. Immediately thereafter, the X-matter was also resolved, with the British and Americans accepting White Russia and the Ukraine as initial members of the new world organization and the Soviets dropping their request for membership for the other fourteen constituent republics. Churchill and Stalin also agreed to Roosevelt's suggestion that the British and Americans could each have two additional seats in the General Assembly if they so desired.[15]

These issues resurfaced at the San Francisco conference in the Spring of 1945. By 30 April, the end of the first week of proceedings there, the question of initial membership in the United Nations Organization, which everyone thought had been answered at Yalta, was once again straining Soviet-American relations almost to the breaking point. The problem was not that the United States had changed its mind about extra votes for the Soviet Union. Despite considerable public criticism of the three-vote agreement, Roosevelt and Truman had stuck by the American promise to support the inclusion of the Ukraine and White Russia, while declining the option to take two extra seats for themselves. At San Francisco, however, the issue was made more complicated by the presence of some forty-six nations, many of which had ideas of their own on the question of the new world body's initial membership. The delegations from the Latin American states, in particular, which made up almost half of the United Nations, refused to vote for the inclusion of the Soviet republics unless Argentina, a nation that had only entered the war in March 1945, was also added to the list of charter members. The United States had no difficulty with this demand—Stettinius had, it will be recalled, tried to provide for Argentina at Dumbarton Oaks—but the Soviets were outraged. Molotov found the connection of the two issues incomprehensible, especially in light of an American refusal to grant admittance to the Lublin Poles, and argued forcefully against offering immediate membership to the "fascist" government of Argentina. The Russians were easily out-voted in the large plenary session at San Francisco, however, and Argentina was admitted—along with the Soviet republics—by a tally of thirty-two to four, with ten abstentions.[16]

This outcome held some troubling implications for the Soviet foreign minister. First it appeared that the United States had used its Latin American clients, which it claimed a surprising inability to control, as a cat's paw to place conditions on a promise already made—and on which, Molotov must have feared, it was looking for an excuse to renege. Then it marshaled the votes of those same states to win an overwhelming victory in the plenary session, where the Americans seemed to have only too much control. Thus Molotov saw that the United States could have it both ways at San Francisco—it could employ the supposed independence of the smaller states to force new issues on the Soviets, then insure their favorable resolution simply by calling for a vote. As Stalin had always suspected would happen, the Soviets now found themselves feeling increasingly isolated and vulnerable, truly the black sheep in the family of nations.[17]

Such feelings had a decided impact on the issue of the Great Power veto, which was also resurrected at San Francisco. By May 1945, many Americans feared that an unlimited veto was too high a price to pay for Soviet cooperation in a world peacekeeping organization. Acting Secretary of State Grew—Stettinius, who had replaced Hull as secretary, was leading the American delegation in San Francisco—wrote in a private memorandum on 19 May that the Great Power veto would leave the U.N. "powerless to act against the one certain future enemy, Soviet Russia," making "its power to prevent a future world war . . . but a pipe dream." At the same time, events in San Francisco were causing the Soviets to move in the opposite direction—to take a firmer grip on the veto, which they saw increasingly as their one life preserver in a shark-infested capitalist sea. Thus the Yalta compromise on the issue, always a bit unsteady, was carrying an additional weight of suspicion on both sides; the slightest push from either direction might cause the whole arrangement to topple over.[18]

Once again the shove came from the smaller nations. Led by the delegation from Australia, they sought clarification about what they regarded as ambiguities in the Yalta formula, which permitted the Great Powers to veto enforcement action but not procedural questions. Into which category, they wondered, would fall a proposal to take up a dispute for discussion in the Security Council? The Americans were certain that such a proposal was procedural and could not be vetoed; the Soviets were just as certain that it was the opposite. Both claimed the Yalta agreements as their authority—and argued that the other side was trying to reinterpret the voting formula to suit its own purposes. Stettinius thought the matter was serious enough to take up with Truman, who responded that the United States would stand firm on its view of the Yalta compromise. When, a few days later, the Soviet delegation received the same sort of instructions from Stalin, the San Francisco conference had reached what Senator Vandenberg called its "zero hour." Once again it seemed possible that the veto issue, which had been the source of so much trouble at Dumbarton Oaks, might wreck everyone's plans for a postwar international organization.[19]

To break this deadlock, Truman attempted the strategy that FDR had employed when faced with the same problem at Dumbarton Oaks—a direct appeal to Stalin. At Stettinius's urging, the president instructed Harry Hopkins, who was in Moscow trying to negotiate a settlement to the Polish impasse, to present the case for the American interpretation of the Yalta formula directly to the Soviet leader. Hopkins did so on 6 June, during his last meeting with Stalin. The real issues involved here, according to the American, were freedom of discussion in the new world body and the right of any member to bring any dispute before the Security Council, principles that the United States thought had been safeguarded at Yalta. Molotov, who had recently returned to Moscow from San Francisco, replied that the Soviet position was based on the distinction between peaceful disputes and enforcement that had made the Yalta compromise possible; thus anything pertaining to enforcement, including its discussion in the council, required the concurrence of all the permanent members. Stalin apparently had not heard the question explained in this way before. He took Molotov aside and, after remarking that he thought it was "an insignificant matter," agreed to accept the American position. In so doing, he also revealed his concern about what was happening at San Francisco. The small nations, he told Hopkins, were attempting there "to exploit and even to create differences between the great powers" for their own ends. Worse, "certain statesmen" seemed far too interested in getting hold of the votes of the smaller states—what Stalin described as "a dangerous and slippery path" for the Great Powers to follow.[20]

Gromyko expressed a similar concern in San Francisco a few days later. The subject this time was the General Assembly, a branch of the new world body that the Soviets were finding it increasingly difficult to trust in light of small-nation behavior at the organizing conference. In particular, the Russians objected to a clause in the charter that gave the assembly the right to discuss any matter "within the sphere of International relations," language that Gromyko thought needed to be qualified in some way to exclude interference in the domestic affairs of member states. When the United States resisted, the head of the Soviet delegation informed Stettinius that he had received firm instructions from Moscow not to sign the charter unless it was changed in accordance with the Russian view. "We all had a nervous night," Senator Vandenberg wrote in his diary. "There was a chance that the Soviets would kick everything over at the last minute." Finally, as the conference was coming to a close, the Soviet Union accepted a compromise that granted the assembly the right to discuss all matters "within the scope of the Charter," thus excluding debate over domestic concerns while permitting discussion on a broad range of issues.[21]

All of these successful compromises, which made a United Nations Organization possible, could not revitalize the Dumbarton Oaks proposals. They still lacked the kind of teeth required to maintain permanent peace and bore only a superficial resemblance to the stronger if more visionary schemes of the wartime planners, whose original ideas for world order seemed about as meaningful in the new world of 1945 as would a dictionary for a language that nobody spoke. The vocabulary of peace, so often employed during the war, had been replaced by the language of national security—and it was almost impossible to make a coherent translation of one into the other. This change had begun at the time of the conference at Dumbarton Oaks, when the idea of a forceful United Nations had run afoul of the Great Powers' growing concern over their own interests and security, both of which pointed in the direction of expanded unilateralism on the part of each of the Big Three. Over the next few years of East-West conflict culminating in cold war, the American desire for collective security would lead to the creation of a very different kind of international organization in the North Atlantic Treaty Organization. With NATO, as opposed to the United Nations, the conflicting security needs of the United States and the Soviet Union would no longer have to be a problem—the Americans could promote their own interests while denying the legitimacy of the Russians'. The Warsaw Pact would, of course, serve the same purpose for the Soviets. Thus the contradictions posed by the need for cooperation between two such different systems were resolved by institutionalizing the conflicts between them, precisely the opposite of what the wartime vision of a continuing United Nations Organization had been supposed to achieve. This vision, and the kind of U.N. it might have led to, were among the first casualties of the cold war.

Shortly after the close of the Dumbarton Oaks Conference, Clare Booth Luce, then a Republican representative from Connecticut, had compared the United Nations proposal to the Holy Alliance of Czar Alexander I. Both seemed, she wrote, a "curiously Russian [she might also have said American] blend of shrewdness and mysticism, generosity and ambition." Perhaps that was too much to ask of any one organization; perhaps it was inevitable, as happened at Dumbarton Oaks, that the contradictory elements would cancel each other out, that, as Jebb put it, the delegates had aimed too high for "this wicked world." Still, the fact remains that the Great Powers, which may have begun by trying to do too much, ended by doing too little. They created an organization that would fail to fulfill Tennyson's happy dream of a parliament of man, a federation of the world, primarily because they feared the effect that such a strong body might have on their own national objectives for the postwar era. The result would be a permanent state of cold war between them, provoked by the kind of differences that only their continuing cooperation in a peacekeeping body might have given them a chance to resolve. Thus the inscription above the entry at Dumbarton Oaks turned out to be prophetic— the Great Powers would reap as they had sown.[22]

Appendix: Members of the Four Groups at Dumbarton Oaks

United States

Edward R. Stettinius, Jr., under secretary of state; Isaiah Bowman, president of Johns Hopkins University and special adviser to the secretary of state on post-war problems; Benjamin V. Cohen, legal counsel, Office of War Mobilization; James C. Dunn, director, Office of European Affairs, State Department; Henry P. Fletcher, special adviser to the secretary of state; Joseph C. Grew, director, Office of Far Eastern Affairs, State Department; Green H. Hackworth, legal adviser, State Department; Stanley K. Hornbeck, special assistant to the secretary of state; Breckinridge Long, assistant secretary of state for congressional relations; Leo Pasvolsky, special assistant to the secretary of state and executive director, Committee on Post-war Programs; Edwin C. Wilson, director, Office of Special Political Affairs, State Department; Lieutenant General Stanley D. Embick, Joint Strategic Survey Committee of Joint Chiefs of Staff; Major General Muir S. Fairchild, Joint Strategic Survey Committee of Joint Chiefs of Staff; Admiral Arthur Hepburn, chairman, general board of the U.S. Navy; Vice Admiral Russell Willson, Joint Strategic Survey Committee of Joint Chiefs of Staff; and Rear Admiral Harold Train, Joint Post-war Committee of the Joint Chiefs of Staff.

American advisers and principal officials of the Secretariat included: Charles Bohlen, chief, Division of Eastern European Affairs, State Department; John M. Cabot, chief, Division of Caribbean and Central American Affairs, State Department; O. Benjamin Gerig, assistant chief, Division of International Security and Organization, State Department; Alger Hiss, assistant to director, Office of Special Political Affairs, State Department; Michael McDermott, special assistant to secretary of state; Harley Notter, chief, Division of International Security and Organization, State Department; Hayden Raynor, special assistant to Edward Stettinius; Easton Rothwell, assistant chief, Division of International

Security and Organization, State Department; and Charles Yost, executive secretary to Policy Committee, State Department.

Soviet Union

Andrei Gromyko, ambassador in Washington; Arkady Sobolev, minister-counselor of Soviet embassy in London; Semen Zarapkin, head, American section, Foreign Ministry; Major General Nikolai Slavin, Soviet general staff, liaison officer with Allied Military Missions in Moscow; Rear Admiral Konstantin Rodionov, chief, Administrative Division, Navy Ministry; Professor Sergei A. Golunsky, Soviet Foreign Ministry; Professor Sergei B. Krylov, professor of International Law, Moscow University; Grigori Dolbin, Protocol Section, Foreign Ministry; Mikhail Yunin, secretary; and Valentin M. Berezhkov, counselor, Foreign Ministry.

Great Britain

Sir Alexander Cadogan, permanent under secretary of state for foreign affairs; Gladwyn Jebb, counselor, Foreign Office; Sir William Malkin, legal adviser, Foreign Office; A. H. Poynton, Colonial Office; Admiral Sir Percy Noble, Military Mission in Washington; Lieutenant General Gordon Macready, Military Mission in Washington; Air Marshal Sir William Welch, Military Mission in Washington; Colonel Capel Dunn, military assistant to the secretary of War Cabinet; Peter Loxley, private secretary to Sir Alexander Cadogan; Paul Falla, Economic and Reconstruction Department, Foreign Office; and Professor Charles K. Webster, professor of International History, London School of Economics, and researcher for Foreign Office.

China

V. K. Wellington Koo, ambassador in London; Victor Chi-tsai Hoo, vice minister of foreign affairs; Wei Tao-ming, ambassador in Washington; General Shang Chen, chief, Military Mission in Washington; Major General P. T. Mow, director of the Washington office of the Commission on Aeronautical Affairs; Rear Admiral Liu Ten-fu, naval attaché of the Chinese embassy in Washington; Major General Chu Shih-ming, military attaché of the Chinese embassy in Washington; Pu Hsueh-Feng, counselor of the Supreme Defense Council; Chang Chung-fu, director, Department of American Affairs, Ministry of Foreign Affairs; T. L. Soong, delegate, United Nations Monetary and Financial Conference; Liu Chieh, minister-counselor, Chinese embassy in Washington; and Kan Lee, commercial counselor, Chinese embassy in Washington.

Notes

Chapter 1

1. Rosenman, *Public Papers and Addresses of Franklin D. Roosevelt*, 6:406–11; and Department of State, *Peace and War*, pp. 484–85.

2. Roosevelt's speech is quoted in Notter, *Postwar Foreign Policy Preparation*, p. 18. For Wilson's campaign during World War I, see also Hilderbrand, *Power and the People*, pp. 136–41.

3. The *Washington Post*, 13 November 1939; and Commission to Study the Organization of Peace, Preliminary Report, November 1940, quoted in Divine, *Second Chance*, p. 33. See also Notter, *Postwar Foreign Policy Preparation*, p. 19; and Divine, *Second Chance*, pp. 29–34.

4. See Gelfand, *The Inquiry*; and Notter, *Postwar Foreign Policy Preparation*, p. 19.

5. Pasvolsky's memoranda are quoted in Notter, *Postwar Foreign Policy Preparation*, pp. 20, 453–54. See also Russell, *United Nations Charter*, p. 17; Department of State, *Bulletin* 2:19; Hull, *Memoirs*, 2:1626–27; Kolko, *The Politics of War*, pp. 243–44, 348–50; and Campbell, *Masquerade Peace*, p. 4.

6. Department of State, *Bulletin* 2:19; and Hull, *Memoirs*, 2:1627. See also Russell, *United Nations Charter*, p. 17. Members of the advisory committee were Pasvolsky; Under Secretary Welles; R. Walton Moore, counselor; George S. Messersmith, assistant secretary; Adolph A. Berle, Jr., assistant secretary; Green H. Hackworth, legal adviser; Herbert Feis, economic adviser; Henry F. Grady, assistant secretary; Stanley K. Hornbeck, political adviser; Jay Pierrepont Moffat, chief, Division of Political Affairs; Hugh Wilson, special assistant to the secretary; James C. Dunn, political adviser; Breckinridge Long, assistant secretary; Norman H. Davis, former head delegate to the disarmament conferences in London and Geneva; and George Rublee, director of the Intergovernmental Committee on Political Refugees.

7. Department of State, *Bulletin* 2:153; see also Hull, *Memoirs*, 2:1628.

8. Hugh R. Wilson, memorandum arising from conversations in Mr. Welles's office, 19 and 26 April and 1 May 1940, printed in Notter, *Postwar Foreign Policy Preparation*, pp. 458–60. See also Russell, *United Nations Charter*, p. 21.

9. Wilson, memorandum arising from conversations.

10. See Hull, *Memoirs*, 2:1629–30; and Notter, *Postwar Foreign Policy Preparation*, p. 28.

11. Roosevelt, Annual Message to Congress, 6 January 1941, 77th Cong., 1st sess., pp. 44–47, H. Doc. 1; and Department of State, Departmental Order 917-A, 3 February 1941, printed in Notter, *Postwar Foreign Policy Preparation*, pp. 517–18.

12. Department of State, *Bulletin* 4:575–76 and 6:75–76.

13. Pasvolsky, memorandum to Under Secretary Welles, 11 April 1941, printed in Notter, *Postwar Foreign Policy Preparation*, p. 462; and Hull, *Memoirs*, 2:1631–32.

14. Pasvolsky to Hull, "Proposal for the Organization of Work for the Formulation of Postwar Foreign Policies," 12 September 1941, printed in Notter, *Postwar Foreign Policy Preparation*, pp. 464–67.

15. Hull, *Memoirs*, 2:1631; and Hull to Roosevelt, 22 December 1941, printed in Notter, *Postwar Foreign Policy Preparation*, pp. 63–65.

16. Department of State, *Bulletin* 5:125. Initial members of the advisory committee were Secretary Hull; Under Secretary Welles; Norman H. Davis; Ambassador Myron C. Taylor; Dean Acheson, assistant secretary; Hamilton Fish Armstrong, editor, *Foreign Affairs*; Adolph A. Berle, Jr.; Isaiah Bowman, president, Johns Hopkins University; Benjamin V. Cohen, general counsel, National Power Policy Committee; Herbert Feis; Green H. Hackworth; Harry C. Hawkins, chief, Department of State Division of Commercial Policy; Anne O'Hare McCormick, editorial staff, the *New York Times*; Breckinridge Long; John Van A. MacMurray, special assistant to the secretary; and Leo Pasvolsky.

17. Welles, *Where Are We Heading?*, p. 15. See also Churchill, *The Second World War*, 3:437; and *Foreign Relations of the United States, 1941* (hereafter *FRUS*), 1:364–67.

18. Notter, *Postwar Foreign Policy Preparation*, p. 79; and record of conversation between Welles and Roosevelt, 12 February 1942, in Harley Notter File, Records of the Department of State (hereafter Notter File, RDS).

19. Notter, *Postwar Foreign Policy Preparation*, p. 93; see also Welles, *Where Are We Heading?*, pp. 20–21.

20. Chart of postwar problems, in Notter, *Postwar Foreign Policy Preparation*, pp. 85–86; and record of meeting of Subcommittee on Political Problems, 21 February 1942, Notter File, RDS.

21. Notter, *Postwar Foreign Policy Preparation*, pp. 88–89; and minutes, Advisory Committee on Postwar Foreign Policy, 4 April 1942, Notter File, RDS.

22. Roosevelt, Memorandum to Myron C. Taylor, 1 September 1941, Secretary's File, Franklin D. Roosevelt Papers; and Hull, *Memoirs*, 2:1120. See also Russell, *United Nations Charter*, p. 43.

23. Department of State, *Bulletin* 7:781–83; and the *New York Times*, 20 June 1942. See also Department of State, *Bulletin* 6:531–34; and Notter, *Postwar Foreign Policy Preparation*, pp. 101–3.

24. Wallace's speech upon accepting the annual award of *The Churchman*, 8 June 1942, reported in the *New York Times*, 9 June 1942; and "Notes," 1–3 July 1942, Notter File, RDS.

25. Henry R. Luce, "The American Century," *Life*, 17 February 1941, 61–65; and Welles's speech, 17 June 1942, quoted in the *New York Times*, 18 June 1942. Welles's final point had been developed in an earlier policy memorandum that stated: "Two basic points must be made about this security mechanism: first, it cannot be created artificially by a stroke of the pen when hostilities cease but, whatever its ultimate form, must grow more or less naturally out of security mechanisms created during the war; second, its ultimate form will be largely conditioned by the character of the international political organization which arises after the war." Charles W. Yost, "Objectives and Priorities in an International Security Program," (S-Undistributed 17), 3 April 1942, Notter File, RDS.

26. Hull's speech, 23 July 1942, printed in the *New York Times*, 24 July 1942. Hull

had been thinking of the "isolationists" in an earlier meeting of the advisory committee when he alluded to "sinister influences" that would attempt to prevent an effective postwar settlement. Minutes, Advisory Committee on Postwar Foreign Policy, 2 May 1942, Notter File, RDS.

27. Stassen's speech, 22 June 1942, quoted in the *New York Times*, 23 June 1942.

28. "Notes," 14–26 September, Notter File, RDS. See also Notter, *Postwar Foreign Policy Preparation*, pp. 108–12.

29. Churchill is quoted in Notter, *Postwar Foreign Policy Preparation*, p. 112; the other quotation is from Yost, "Objectives and Priorities," Notter File, RDS. See also Hull, *Memoirs*, 2:1640–41, for a discussion of Churchill's ideas presented to Roosevelt in the message "Morning Thoughts: Note on Postwar Security"; and Brief no. 1, British Delegation to Washington Conference, U5617/180/70, FO 371.

30. Notter, *Postwar Foreign Policy Preparation*, p. 126; and minutes, Organizational Meeting of the Advisory Committee on Postwar Foreign Policy, 12 February 1942, Notter File, RDS.

31. Notter, *Postwar Foreign Policy Preparation*, p. 126; and "French Proposals for an International Force," (S-Undistributed 27), 27 October 1942, Notter File, RDS.

32. "Critique of the *Ad Hoc* Type of International Force" (S-Undistributed 26), 25 November 1942, Notter File, RDS.

33. Notter, *Postwar Foreign Policy Preparation*, pp. 128–29.

34. Hull to members of the advisory committee, 12 July 1943, quoted in Notter, *Postwar Foreign Policy Preparation*, p. 164; *New Republic*, 16 August 1943, 211; and "Declaration of Four Nations on General Security" in *FRUS, 1943*, 1:755–56. See also Notter, *Postwar Foreign Policy Preparation*, pp. 162–64.

35. Hull, *Memoirs*, 2:1637. See also Israel, *War Diary of Breckinridge Long*, pp. 281, 322–25, and 327–28; Dallek, *Franklin D. Roosevelt and American Foreign Policy*, p. 421; and "Draft Constitution of International Organization," printed in Notter, *Postwar Foreign Policy Preparation*, 472–83.

36. Hull, *Memoirs*, 2:1644–45. See also Divine, *Second Chance*, pp. 104–5, 172–82.

37. The Charter of the United Nations, 14 August 1943, and Commentaries, 7 September 1943, Notter File, RDS; see also Notter, *Postwar Foreign Policy Preparation*, pp. 175–76.

38. The Charter of the United Nations, 14 August 1943, Notter File, RDS.

39. Commentaries, 7 September 1943, Notter File, RDS.

40. The *New York Times*, 12 March 1943; and Acheson, *Present at the Creation*, p. 88. See also Campbell and Herring, *Diaries of Edward R. Stettinius*, pp. xxi–xxv.

41. *Congressional Record*, 78th Cong., 1st sess., 21 September 1943, H. Con. Res. 25, p. 7729; *Congressional Record*, 78th Cong., 1st sess., 16 March 1943, S. Res. 114, p. 2030; and the *New York Times*, 6 November 1943. See also Campbell and Herring, *Diaries of Edward R. Stettinius*, pp. 9–13; Israel, *War Diary of Breckinridge Long*, pp. 329–30; and *Congressional Record*, 78th Cong., 1st sess., 5 November 1943, S. Res. 192, p. 9222.

42. Sherwood, *Roosevelt and Hopkins*, p. 757. See also Acheson, *Present at the Creation*, p. 47; and Edward R. Stettinius, Jr., calendar notes, 6 October and 27 November 1943, Stettinius Papers.

43. A chart of the reorganized State Department, as well as a detailed description of

Stettinius's plan, is in Department of State, *Bulletin* 10:43–67. See also Notter, *Postwar Foreign Policy Preparation*, pp. 215–17; and Hull, *Memoirs*, 2:1650.

Chapter 2

1. "Declaration of Four Nations on General Security," 1 November 1943, in *FRUS, 1943*, 1:756. See also Divine, *Second Chance*, p. 184; and Notter, *Postwar Foreign Policy Preparation*, pp. 169–71, 246–47.
2. "Plan for the Establishment of an International Organization for the Maintenance of International Peace and Security," 23 December 1943, in *FRUS, 1944*, 1:615. See also minutes of Informal Political Agenda Group, meeting 1 (9 December 1943) and meeting 2 (16 December 1943), Notter File, RDS; Barton, "The Dumbarton Oaks Conference," pp. 74–75; and Notter, *Postwar Foreign Policy Preparation*, pp. 250–51.
3. "Tentative Views of the Subcommittee on International Organization," 12 March 1943, Notter File, RDS; and "Plan for the Establishment," in *FRUS, 1944*, 1:617. See also minutes of Informal Political Agenda Group, meeting 6 (21 December 1943) and meeting 8 (22 December 1943), Notter File, RDS; Russell, *United Nations Charter*, p. 246; Barton, "The Dumbarton Oaks Conference," p. 76; and minutes of meeting between Roosevelt and Stalin, 29 November 1943, in *FRUS, 1943, Cairo and Tehran*, pp. 530–32, 622.
4. "Tentative Views of the Subcommittee on International Organization," 12 March 1943, Notter File, RDS; "Draft Constitution of International Organization," July 1943, and The Charter of the United Nations, 14 August 1943, in Notter, *Postwar Foreign Policy Preparation*, pp. 472–83, 526–32; minutes of Informal Political Agenda Group, meeting 2 (16 December 1943), Notter File, RDS; Russell, *United Nations Charter*, p. 242; and Barton, "The Dumbarton Oaks Conference," p. 78.
5. Minutes of Informal Political Agenda Group, meeting 2 (16 December 1943), Notter File, RDS; Russell, *United Nations Charter*, pp. 247–48; and Barton, "The Dumbarton Oaks Conference," pp. 78–79.
6. Minutes of Informal Political Agenda Group, meeting 5 (17 December 1943) and meeting 7 (21 December 1943), Notter File, RDS.
7. "Plan for the Establishment," 23 December 1943, in *FRUS, 1944*, 1:617–18. See also Russell, *United Nations Charter*, p. 249; and Barton, "The Dumbarton Oaks Conference," pp. 80–81.
8. "Plan for the Establishment," 23 December 1943, in *FRUS, 1944*, 1:618–19. See also minutes of Informal Political Agenda Group, meeting 8 (22 December 1943), Notter File, RDS.
9. Memorandum, Secretary of State Hull to President Roosevelt, 19 December 1943, Pasvolsky Papers. See also Hull, *Memoirs*, 2:1649.
10. "Notes on Meeting of Secretary Hull with President Roosevelt at the White House on February 3, 1944," presumably written by Pasvolsky, Pasvolsky Papers; and "Memory Notes, Talks with FDR," 8 February 1944, apparently written by Notter as relayed

through Pasvolsky, Notter File, RDS. See also Notter, *Postwar Foreign Policy Preparation*, p. 256.

11. "Notes on Meeting, February 3, 1944," Pasvolsky Papers; and "Memory Notes," 8 February 1944, Notter File, RDS.

12. "Notes on Meeting, February 3, 1944," Pasvolsky Papers; "Memory Notes," 8 February 1944, Notter File, RDS; minutes of meeting between Roosevelt and Stalin, 29 November 1943, in *FRUS, 1943, Cairo and Tehran*, pp. 531–32; and Sherwood, *Roosevelt and Hopkins*, p. 717.

13. "Notes on Meeting, February 3, 1944," Pasvolsky Papers; and Welles, *Where Are We Heading?*, pp. 31–32, 49–50.

14. "Notes on Meeting, February 3, 1944," Pasvolsky Papers; minutes of meeting between Roosevelt and Stalin, 28 November 1943, in *FRUS, 1943, Cairo and Tehran*, pp. 484–85; and Hull, *Memoirs*, 2:1597.

15. Hull, *Memoirs*, 2:1650; and the acting secretary of state (Stettinius) to the ambassador in the Soviet Union (Harriman), 10 February 1944, in *FRUS, 1944*, 1:622–23. See also memorandum, James C. Dunn to Stanley Hornbeck, 9 February 1944, Notter File, RDS.

16. Eden, *Memoirs*, p. 43. See also Notter, *Postwar Foreign Policy Preparation*, p. 247; Woodward, *British Foreign Policy*, pp. 433–35; Brief no. 1, U5617/180/70, FO 371; and "The Four-Power Plan" (Jebb), 20 October 1942, U742/742/70, FO 371.

17. Woodward, *British Foreign Policy*, pp. 435–36; Brief no. 1, U5617/180/70, FO 371; "The Four-Power Plan" (Cripps), 19 November 1942, W.P.(42)532, CAB 66, vol. 31; and minutes of British War Cabinet, 23 November 1942, War Cab. 157, CAB 65, vol. 28.

18. Personal minute, prime minister to Eden, 18 October 1942, 100/7, PREM 4; and Eden to Prime Minister, 19 October 1942, 100/7, PREM 4. See also Eden to Halifax, 15 October 1942, A4.410.4.15, Halifax Papers.

19. Personal minute, prime minister to Eden, 21 October 1942, 100/7, PREM 4.

20. Churchill, *The Second World War*, 4:803–5.

21. Foreign Office, "Aide-Mémoire: Suggested Principles Which Would Govern the Conclusion of Hostilities with the European Members of the Axis," 16 July 1943, in *FRUS, 1943, Washington and Quebec*, p. 702; and Eden to Churchill, 27 March 1943, FO 800/404. See also Eden, *Memoirs*, p. 438; Churchill, *The Second World War*, 4:802–3; Churchill to Eden, 30 March 1943, FO 800/404; and McNeill, *America, Britain and Russia*, pp. 320–21, 354.

22. Diary of Charles K. Webster, 15 June 1943, printed in Reynolds and Hughes, *The Historian as Diplomat*, p. 20; and McNeill, *America, Britain and Russia*, p. 321. See also Brief no. 1, U5617/180/70, FO 371; and Woodward, *British Foreign Policy*, pp. 434–35.

23. "The Four-Power Plan" (Eden), 8 November 1942, W.P.(42)516, CAB 66, vol. 30. See also minutes of British War Cabinet, 23 November 1942, War Cab. 157, CAB 65, vol. 28.

24. "The United Nations Plan," 16 January 1943, W.P.(43)31, CAB 66, vol 33.

25. Brief no. 1, U5617/180/70, FO 371. See also Eden to Churchill, 27 March 1943, FO 800/404; Report by Gladwyn Jebb, W.P.(43)217-Annex, CAB 66, vol. 37; and War Cab. 53(43) Conclusions-Confidential Annex, 13 April 1943, CAB 65, vol. 38.

26. Brief no. 1, U5617/180/70, FO 371. See also W.P.(43)217, CAB 66, vol. 37; and War Cab. 86(43) Conclusions, 16 June 1943, CAB 65, vol. 34.

27. "United Nations Plan for Organizing Peace," 7 July 1943, W.P.(43)300, CAB 66, vol. 38.

28. McNeill, *America, Britain and Russia*, pp. 322–23; and Hull, *Memoirs*, 2:1298–99, 1649.

29. Webster, "The Making of the Charter of the United Nations," p. 23. See also Woodward, *British Foreign Policy*, p. 445.

30. McNeill, *America, Britain and Russia*, pp. 323–26.

31. Stalin, *Great Patriotic War*, p. 59; and minutes of Roosevelt-Stalin meeting, 29 November 1943, in *FRUS, 1943, Cairo and Tehran*, p. 532. See also McNeill, *America, Britain and Russia*, p. 357; and Feis, *Churchill, Roosevelt, Stalin*, p. 270; and Brief no. 1, U5617/180/70, FO 371.

32. Minutes of Roosevelt-Stalin meeting, 29 November 1943, in *FRUS, 1943, Cairo and Tehran*, p. 531. See also McNeill, *America, Britain and Russia*, p. 356; Mastny, *Russia's Road to the Cold War*, p. 218; and minutes of Roosevelt-Stalin meeting, 1 December 1943, in *FRUS, 1943, Cairo and Tehran*, p. 596.

33. Mastny, *Russia's Road to the Cold War*, p. 218; and Ulam, *The Rivals*, p. 16.

34. Ulam, *The Rivals*, p. 18.

35. Memorandum by Mr. Leo Pasvolsky, special assistant to the secretary of state, 15 March 1944, in *FRUS, 1944*, 1:629; and text of a telegram from the British ambassador at Moscow to the Foreign Office, 5 April 1944, in *FRUS, 1944*, 1:635. See also British summary of topics, 15 February 1944, and American topical outline, 17 February 1944, in *FRUS, 1944*, 1:624–26; and FO minute by Jebb, 15 June 1944, U5697/180/70, FO 371.

36. Memorandum of conversation by the secretary of state with Ambassador Molotov, 29 March 1944, in *FRUS, 1944*, 1:634. See also the secretary of state to the ambassador in the Soviet Union, 9 February 1944, in *FRUS, 1944*, 4:824–26; memorandum prepared in the Division of European Affairs, "Current Problems in Relations with the Soviet Union," 24 March 1944, in *FRUS, 1944*, 4:839–42; Feis, *Churchill, Roosevelt, Stalin*, pp. 283–302; and memo, "Probable Post-War Tendencies in Soviet Foreign Policy," 29 April 1944, 21/5, PREM 4.

37. Hull, *Memoirs*, 2:1653. See also "Possible Plan for a General International Organization," 29 April 1944, printed in Notter, *Postwar Foreign Policy Preparation*, pp. 582–91.

38. FO minute, 10 January 1944, U180/180/70, FO 371; and Richard Law, "Explanatory Note," 19 April 1944, quoted in Woodward, *British Foreign Policy*, p. 452. See also "Tentative Proposals by the United Kingdom for a General International Organization," 3 July 1944, W.P.(44)370, CAB 66, vol. 52; and Woodward, *British Foreign Policy*, pp. 451–52.

39. Record of meeting at the Foreign Office, 3 April 1944, U2585/180/70, FO 371. See also Memorandum A, W.P.(44)370, CAB 66, vol. 52; and Woodward, *British Foreign Policy*, pp. 452–53.

40. Memorandum A, W.P.(44)370, CAB 66, vol. 52. See also record of meeting at the Foreign Office, 14 April 1944, U3388/180/70, FO 371; draft record of meeting of A. P. W. Committee, 22 April 1944, U3532/180/70, FO 371; and Woodward, *British Foreign Policy*, pp. 452–53.

41. Memorandum B, W.P.(44)370, CAB 66, vol. 52; and record of meeting held at the Foreign Office, 11 April 1944, U3131/180/70, FO 371.

42. Memorandum C, W.P.(44)370, CAB 66, vol. 52; and FO minute by Cadogan, 26 March 1944, U2295/180/70, FO 371. See also record of meeting at Foreign Office, 30 March 1944, U2543/180/70, FO 371.

43. Memorandum D, W.P.(44)370, CAB 66, vol. 52; and record of meeting on the colonies and the Washington talks at Foreign Office, 27 July 1944, U6731/180/70, FO 371.

44. Memorandum E, W.P.(44)370, CAB 66, vol. 52; see also Eden, *Memoirs*, p. 514.

45. Note by prime minister, "The Postwar World Settlement," 8 May 1944, U4194/180/70, FO 371. See also Eden to prime minister, "Outline Scheme for the Establishment of a Permanent World Organization," 3 May 1944, U3872/180/70, FO 371; and FO minute by Webster, 29 April 1944, U4036/180/70, FO 371.

46. FO memorandum by Webster, 9 May 1944, U4035/180/70, FO 371; and FO paper on Western Europe, June 1944, U5407/180/70, FO 371. The emphasis is Eden's. See also FO minute by Jebb, 1 May 1944, U4378/180/70, FO 371.

47. Record of Prime Ministers' meeting (44)12, 11 May 1944, 30/7, PREM 4; and Eden to Duff Cooper, 25 July 1944, U6594/180/70, FO 371. See also FO minute, "Western Europe," 9 May 1944, U4105/180/70, FO 371.

48. FO minute, "British Policy Towards Europe," 12 May 1944, U4366/180/70, FO 371. See also FO minute, "Britain and Western Europe," 11 April 1944, U4199/180/70, FO 371; and note by prime minister, "The Postwar World Settlement," 8 May 1944, U4194/180/70, FO 371.

49. Jebb to R. I. Campbell, 19 May 1944, U5624/180/70, FO 371; and FO minute by Cadogan, 15 May 1944, U4367/180/70, FO 371. See also FO minute by Jebb, 11 May 1944 and FO minute by Eden, 13 May 1944, ibid.

50. FO minute by Jebb, 29 May 1944, U5050/180/70, FO 371; and Jebb to R. I. Campbell, 19 May 1944, U5624/180/70, FO 371. See also FO minute by Cadogan, 15 May 1944, U4367/180/70, FO 371.

51. Prime minister's personal minute, 21 May 1944, U4635/180/70, FO 371; and FO minute by Jebb, 29 May 1944, U5050/180/70, FO 371.

52. FO minute by Jebb, 24 June 1944, U5877/180/70, FO 371; FO minute by Cadogan, 24 June 1944, ibid.; FO minute by Jebb, 8 July 1944, U6441/180/70, FO 371; and "Tentative Proposals by the United Kingdom," 22 July 1944, in *FRUS, 1944*, 1:672.

53. Campbell and Herring, *Diaries of Edward R. Stettinius*, pp. 52–54. See also Stettinius to Harriman, 7 March 1944, in *FRUS, 1944*, 4:947; report to the secretary of state by Under Secretary Stettinius on his mission to London, 7–29 April 1944, in *FRUS, 1944*, 3:3; memorandum by Stettinius on conversations with Churchill in London, Notter File, RDS; memorandum of conversation by Bowman with Churchill, 15 April 1944, Stettinius Papers; and account by Dr. Bowman of his private talk with the prime minister, 15 April 1944, U3316/180/70, FO 371.

54. Campbell and Herring, *Diaries of Edward R. Stettinius*, p. 55. See also report by Stettinius on mission to London, in *FRUS, 1944*, 3:15–17; FO minute by Cadogan, 19 April 1944, U3409/180/70, FO 371; memorandum of conversation by Bowman with Jebb, Cadogan, Charles Webster, 19 April 1944, Stettinius Papers; Stettinius diary,

London mission, 15, 16, and 19 April 1944, Stettinius Papers; and Howard Bucknell, Jr., to Hull, 18 May 1944, in *FRUS, 1944*, 1:636–37.

55. Campbell and Herring, *Diaries of Edward R. Stettinius*, pp. 60, 63. See also Stettinius diary, London mission 11, 16, and 24 April 1944, Stettinius Papers; Hull to Stettinius, 17, 18, and 20 April 1944, 740.0011/Stettinius Mission, RDS; FO minute by Cadogan, 14 April 1944, U4024/180/70, FO 371; and FO minute, 25 April 1944, U3847/180/70, FO 371.

56. J. G. Ward to Michael Wright, 2 May 1944, U3409/180/70, FO 371; interview with Dr. Bowman in Sir Alexander Cadogan's room, 19 April 1944, U3409/180/70, FO 371; and record of conversation, Bowman and Jebb at Foreign Office, 12 April 1944, U6284/180/70, FO 371.

57. See Hull to Tom Connally, 17 April 1944, Hull Papers; Notter, *Postwar Foreign Policy Preparation*, pp. 259–63; Hull, *Memoirs*, 2:1657–59; and Divine, *Second Chance*, pp. 195–96.

58. See Notter, *Postwar Foreign Policy Preparation*, pp. 264–65; Divine, *Second Chance*, pp. 197–98; Hull, *Memoirs*, 2:1659, 1662; and Vandenberg, *Private Papers*, pp. 104–7.

59. Department of State, *Bulletin* 10:510. See also Vandenberg to Hull, 3 May 1944, Hull Papers; Vandenberg, *Private Papers*, pp. 99, 102–4; Israel, *War Diary of Breckinridge Long*, pp. 348–50; Hull, *Memoirs*, 2:1660–61, 1667–69; and Vandenberg to John Foster Dulles, 2 June 1944, Dulles Papers.

60. Memorandum of conversation by the secretary of state, 30 May 1944, in *FRUS, 1944*, 1:637–38; and Washington to Foreign Office, 31 May 1944, U4928/180/70, FO 371.

61. See Hull, *Memoirs*, 2:1586–87; Dallek, *Roosevelt and American Foreign Policy*, pp. 389, 428–29; Eden, *Memoirs*, p. 437; and Schaller, *The U.S. Crusade in China*, pp. 90–91.

62. Churchill, *The Second World War*, 4:133; and Churchill to Eden, 21 October 1942, ibid., pp. 561–62. See also account by Dr. Bowman of talk with prime minister, 15 April 1944, U3316/180/70, FO 371; Dilks, *Diaries of Sir Alexander Cadogan*, p. 488; and Woodward, *British Foreign Policy*, p. 420.

63. Campbell and Herring, *Diaries of Edward R. Stettinius*, p. 53; and memorandum by Stanley K. Hornbeck, 28 October 1943, Notter File, RDS. See also account by Dr. Bowman, 15 April 1944, U3316/180/70, FO 371.

64. Memorandum by Harry Hopkins, 22 March 1943, Hopkins Papers. See also Eden's report of trip to Washington, 28 March 1943, FO 800/404; and Eden, *Memoirs*, p. 437.

65. Churchill to Roosevelt, 26 October 1943, in *FRUS, 1943, Cairo and Tehran*, p. 41; account by Dr. Bowman, 15 April 1944, U3316/180/70, FO 371; and the British Foreign Office to the British embassy in the United States, 4 June 1944, in *FRUS, 1944*, 1:640–41. See also FO minute by Jebb, 2 June 1944, U4928/180/70, FO 371; Woodward, *British Foreign Policy*, p. 420; and Thorne, *Allies of a Kind*, pp. 305–7.

66. Minutes of Roosevelt-Stalin meeting, 29 November 1943, in *FRUS, 1943, Cairo and Tehran*, pp. 530–31. See also minutes of Roosevelt-Stalin meeting, 1 December 1943, ibid., p. 596; McNeill, *America, Britain and Russia*, p. 356; Ulam, *The Rivals*, p. 38; and Moscow to Ottawa, 15 March 1944, U4778/180/70, FO 371.

67. Stalin to Roosevelt, 12 November 1943, in *FRUS, 1943, Cairo and Tehran*, pp. 82–83. See also Soviet chargé d'affaires to the acting secretary of state, 2 October 1943, in *FRUS, 1943*, 1:537–38; Stalin to Roosevelt, 6 October 1943, ibid., 548; "Summary of Proceedings of the Third Session of the Tripartite Conference," 21 October 1943, ibid., 593–94; memorandum of conversation by the secretary of state, 21 October 1943, ibid., 602–3; Roosevelt to Chiang Kai-shek, 30 October 1943, in *FRUS, 1943, Cairo and Tehran*, pp. 55–56; and Feis, *The China Tangle*, pp. 99–101.

68. Aide-mémoire, the Soviet embassy to the Department of State, 9 July 1944, in *FRUS, 1944*, 1:645; and the British Foreign Office to the British embassy in the United States, 4 June 1944, ibid., 640–41. See also Notter, *Postwar Foreign Policy Preparation*, p. 278; memorandum of conversation by Stettinius with Ambassador Halifax, 6 June 1944, Stettinius Papers; FO minute by Jebb, 2 June 1944, U4928/180/70, FO 371; and Foreign Office to Washington, 12 June 1944, U5466/180/70, FO 371.

69. Feis, *Churchill, Roosevelt, Stalin*, p. 253; Schaller, *U.S. Crusade in China*, pp. 179–80; Clubb, *China and Russia*, pp. 326–30, 334–45; Schwartz, *Tsars, Mandarins, and Commissars*, pp. 137–38; Ulam, *The Rivals*, pp. 90–92; and Djilas, *Conversations with Stalin*, p. 182.

70. Memorandum of conversation by the secretary of state, 10 July 1944, in *FRUS, 1944*, 1:646; and Hull to Harriman, 14 July 1944, ibid., 651–52. See also aide-mémoire, the Soviet embassy to the Department of State, 20 July 1944, ibid., 669–70; Foreign Office to Washington, 16 July 1944, U6366/180/70, FO 371; Hull to Harriman, 7 July 1944, in *FRUS, 1944*, 1:644; and Notter, *Postwar Foreign Policy Preparation*, pp. 167–82.

71. Aide-mémoire, the Department of State to the Soviet embassy, 12 July 1944, in *FRUS, 1944*, 1:650–51. See also Foreign Office to Washington, 18 July 1944, U6439/180/70, FO 371; Notter, *Postwar Foreign Policy Preparation*, pp. 281–82; and Mastny, *Russia's Road to the Cold War*, pp. 167–82.

72. Soviet embassy to the Department of State, 9 July 1944, in *FRUS, 1944*, 1:645; and aide-mémoire, the Department of State to the Soviet embassy, 12 July 1944, ibid., 650–51. See also aide-mémoire, the British embassy to the Department of State, 15 March 1944, ibid., 633; Foreign Office to Washington, 18 July 1944, U6439/180/70, FO 371; and Harriman to Hull, 8 July 1944, 500.cc/7-844, RDS.

73. Department of State, *Bulletin* 10:84; aide-mémoire, the Soviet embassy to the Department of State, 20 July 1944, in *FRUS, 1944*, 1:669–70; and Harriman to Hull, 4 August 1944, ibid., 704. See also Halifax to Foreign Office, 27 July 1944, U6599/180/70, FO 371; Notter, *Postwar Foreign Policy Preparation*, pp. 282–84; and Jebb to Campbell, 19 May 1944, U5624/180/70, FO 371.

74. Rudolph E. Schoenfield, chargé d'affaires at the U.S. embassy near the Netherlands government-in-exile, London, to Hull, 1 June 1944, in *FRUS, 1944*, 1:639.

75. Department of State, *Bulletin* 10:509. See also Notter, *Postwar Foreign Policy Preparation*, pp. 266–67.

76. Department of State, *Bulletin* 10:552–53. See also Israel, *War Diary of Breckinridge Long*, pp. 355–56; and "History of the President's Statement of 15 June 1944, on International Organization," 19 June 1944, Pasvolsky Papers.

77. Department of State, *Bulletin* 10:152–53.

78. *Nation*, 24 June 1944, 722; *Time*, 26 June 1944, 18; and FO minute by Jebb, 21 June 1944, U5639/180/70, FO 371. The emphasis is Jebb's. See also *Chicago Daily Tribune*, 19 June 1944; Ely Culbertson to Roosevelt, 16 June 1944, Official File 5557, Roosevelt Papers; Divine, *Second Chance*, pp. 206–8; and Barton, "The Dumbarton Oaks Conference," pp. 113–14.

Chapter 3

1. See Campbell, *Masquerade Peace*, p. 26; and Green, "The Dumbarton Oaks Conversations," in Green Papers.
2. British Foreign Office to the British embassy in the United States, 4 June 1944, in *FRUS, 1944*, 1:640. See also Washington to Foreign Office, 5 June 1944, U5095/180/70, FO 371; Israel, *War Diary of Breckinridge Long*, p. 355; Warren Kelchner, Division of International Conferences, to Stettinius, 25 June 1944, Notter File, RDS; Foreign Office to Washington, 8 June 1944, U5095/180/70, FO 371; memorandum of conversation, Stettinius calling Pasvolsky, 7 July 1944, Stettinius Papers; and Jebb to R. I. Campbell, 19 May 1944, U5624/180/70, FO 371.
3. British Foreign Office to the British embassy in the United States, 4 June 1944, *FRUS, 1944*, 1:640; and Soviet delegation at Dumbarton Oaks, 11 August 1944, 500.cc/8-1144, RDS. See also Clark Kerr to Molotov, 21 July 1944, U6652/180/70, FO 371; Soviet embassy in Washington to Department of State, 9 July 1944, *FRUS, 1944*, 1:645; memorandum of conversation by the secretary of state, 12 June 1944, ibid., 641–42; memorandum of telephone conversation by Stettinius with Hull, 7 June 1944, Stettinius calendar notes, Stettinius Papers; Washington to Foreign Office, 8 June 1944, U5241/180/70, FO 371; and Notter, *Postwar Foreign Policy Preparation*, pp. 284–85.
4. Stettinius diary, 12 and 19 April 1944, Stettinius Papers; and Dilks, *Diaries of Sir Alexander Cadogan*, pp. 617–18. See also J. G. Ward to Michael Wright, 2 May 1944, U3409/180/70, FO 371; and memorandum of conversation by Stettinius with Gromyko, 6 June 1944, 500.cc/6-644, RDS.
5. Dilks, *Diaries of Sir Alexander Cadogan*, p. 654; memorandum of conversation, Stettinius with Hull, 8 June and 12 August 1944, Stettinius Papers; Cadogan to Foreign Office, 17 August 1944, U6916/180/70, FO 371; and Stettinius diary, 20 August 1944, Stettinius Papers. See also FO minute by Jebb, 20 July 1944, U6538/180/70, FO 371; Dilks, *Diaries of Sir Alexander Cadogan*, pp. 654–55; and Stettinius calendar notes, 20 August 1944, Stettinius Papers.
6. Stettinius diary, 20 August 1944, Stettinius Papers; Stettinius calendar notes, 21 August 1944, Stettinius Papers; *New York Herald Tribune*, 21 August 1944; and Dilks, *Diaries of Sir Alexander Cadogan*, p. 655.
7. Dilks, *Diaries of Sir Alexander Cadogan*, p. 656; and Stettinius diary, 21 August 1944, Stettinius Papers. See also Green, "The Dumbarton Oaks Conversations," Department of State, *Bulletin* 11:459; memorandum, Stettinius to Roosevelt, 21 August 1944, *FRUS, 1944*, 1:713–14; memorandum from Division of International Conferences, 12

August 1944, Notter File, RDS; and Notter, *Postwar Foreign Policy Preparation*, p. 301.

8. Memorandum, Stettinius to Roosevelt, 21 August 1944, *FRUS, 1944*, 1:714. See also Stettinius diary, 21 August 1944, Stettinius Papers; Notter, *Postwar Foreign Policy Preparation*, pp. 305–6; and Barton, "The Dumbarton Oaks Conference," pp. 221–22. For a complete list of delegates to the conference, see Appendix.

9. Memorandum, Stettinius to Roosevelt, 21 August 1944, *FRUS, 1944*, 1:714–15; Stettinius diary, 21 August 1944, Stettinius Papers; and "Proposals Regarding Informal Record of the Conversations," 21 August 1944, Notter File, RDS.

10. Stettinius diary, 21 August 1944, Stettinius Papers; Reynolds and Hughes, *Historian as Diplomat*, p. 44; and Dilks, *Diaries of Sir Alexander Cadogan*, pp. 656–57. See also Stettinius calendar notes, 21 August 1944, Stettinius Papers, and *FRUS, 1944*, 1:714, n. 94.

11. Webster, "The Making of the Charter of the United Nations," 25; and Dilks, *Diaries of Sir Alexander Cadogan*, p. 656. See also Stettinius diary, 21 August 1944, Stettinius Papers.

12. Notter, *Postwar Foreign Policy Preparation*, p. 306.

13. Memorandum, Stettinius to Hull, 22 August 1944, *FRUS, 1944*, 1:716. See also Notter, *Postwar Foreign Policy Preparation*, pp. 292, 306–7; and memorandum, Hull to Roosevelt, 11 July 1944, Notter File, RDS.

14. Notter, *Postwar Foreign Policy Preparation*, pp. 306–8; and memorandum, Stettinius to Roosevelt, 28 August 1944, *FRUS, 1944*, 1:738.

15. Notter, *Postwar Foreign Policy Preparation*, pp. 308–9; and memorandum, Stettinius to Roosevelt, 28 August 1944, *FRUS, 1944*, 1:738.

16. Notter, *Postwar Foreign Policy Preparation*, pp. 310–11; memorandum, Stettinius to Hull, 24 August 1944, *FRUS, 1944*, 1:730, n. 13; and note by General Ismay, July 1944, U6805/180/70, FO 371.

17. Notter, *Postwar Foreign Policy Preparation*, pp. 311–12; and Foreign Office to Washington, 18 July 1944, U6471/180/70, FO 371. See also Stettinius diary, 22 August 1944, Stettinius Papers.

18. Stettinius diary, 22 August 1944, Stettinius Papers; bills for the catering services are also included.

19. The *New York Times*, 23 August 1944.

20. Mowrer, "Woodrow Wilson at Dumbarton Oaks," 24 August 1944, in Sweetser Papers; and the *New York Times*, 23 August 1944.

21. Webster's diary, 21 August 1944, quoted in Reynolds and Hughes, *Historian as Diplomat*, p. 44. See also meeting of Steering Committee, 19 August 1944, Notter File, RDS; Green, "The Dumbarton Oaks Conversations," Department of State, *Bulletin* 11:459; and the *New York Times*, 23 August 1944.

22. Stettinius diary, 23 August 1944, Stettinius Papers; the *New York Times*, 23 August 1944; and Dilks, *Diaries of Sir Alexander Cadogan*, p. 657. See also the *New York Herald Tribune*, 24 August 1944.

23. Statement by the Committee of the State Department Correspondents Association, 24 August 1944, Notter File, RDS. See also Stettinius diary, 24 August 1944, Stettinius Papers.

24. Dilks, *Diaries of Sir Alexander Cadogan*, p. 657; and statement by the heads of the

American, British, and Soviet groups, 24 August 1944, Notter File, RDS. See also Stettinius diary, 24 August 1944, Stettinius Papers; and Barton, "The Dumbarton Oaks Conference," pp. 246–47.

25. Dilks, *Diaries of Sir Alexander Cadogan*, p. 659. See also Stettinius diary, 24 and 29 August 1944, Stettinius Papers; statement by the heads of the American, British, and Soviet delegations, 29 August 1944, in Department of State, *Bulletin* 11:233; statement by the under secretary of state, 29 August 1944, ibid., 233–34; and the *New York Times*, 30 August 1944.

26. The *Detroit Free Press*, 31 August 1944. See also the *New York Times*, 30 August 1944; and Campbell, *Masquerade Peace*, p. 30.

27. Stettinius calendar notes, 5 September 1944, Stettinius Papers. See also Department of State, press and radio news conference transcript, 5 September 1944, RDS.

28. Stettinius calendar notes, 1 September 1944, Stettinius Papers. See also Russell, *United Nations Charter*, p. 412; and Campbell, *Masquerade Peace*, pp. 30–31.

29. Memorandum of conversation, Stettinius calling Michael Wright, 6 July 1944, Stettinius Papers; Dilks, *Diaries of Sir Alexander Cadogan*, p. 657; the *New York Times*, 24 August 1944; and International Security Organization memoranda for Pasvolsky, 30 September, 5, 10 and 11 October 1944, Notter File, RDS.

30. Feis, *Churchill, Roosevelt, Stalin*, p. 309; and Berezhkov, "Dumbarton Okse," part 1, pp. 179–80.

31. Gerald L. K. Smith to Hull, 20 August 1944, Long Papers.

32. Memorandum of telephone conversation, Long and Mrs. Gerald L. K. Smith, 22 August 1944, Long Papers; and memorandum of telephone conversation, Mrs. Smith and Long's secretary, Mrs. Winifred A. Kunz, 23 August 1944, Long Papers. See also Barton, "Dumbarton Oaks Conference," p. 263.

33. Stettinius diary, 25 August 1944, Stettinius Papers.

34. Smith to Hull, 23 August 1944, Long Papers.

35. Nicholas, *Washington Despatches*, pp. 407–8.

36. Memorandum of conversation, Alger Hiss and Dorothy Detzer, 30 November 1944, Hiss File, RDS. See also Stettinius to Leo Pasvolsky, 30 November 1944, Pasvolsky File, RDS.

37. See Stettinius diary, 25 and 28 August 1944, Stettinius Papers; Berezhkov, "Dumbarton Okse," part 1, pp. 180–82; and Barton, "The Dumbarton Oaks Conference," pp. 266–68.

38. *Time*, 4 September 1944, 23. See also the *New York Times*, 28 August 1944; and Dilks, *Diaries of Sir Alexander Cadogan*, p. 659.

39. Dilks, *Diaries of Sir Alexander Cadogan*, pp. 662–63. See also Stettinius diary, 10 September 1944, Stettinius Papers; and "Plans for the Tour," Stettinius Papers.

40. See Berezhkov, "Dumbarton Okse," part 2, pp. 176–177; and Barton, "The Dumbarton Oaks Conference," pp. 386–87.

41. *Time*, 4 September 1944, 23; and Dilks, *Diaries of Sir Alexander Cadogan*, p. 663.

Chapter 4

1. Notter, *Postwar Foreign Policy Preparation*, p. 301. See also Cadogan to Foreign Office, 17 August 1944, U6916/180/70, FO 371.

2. Stettinius to Hull, "Progress Report on Dumbarton Oaks Conversations," 23 August 1944, *FRUS, 1944*, 1:717; radio commentary by Upton Close, 3 September 1944, synopsis in Stettinius Papers; and "Proposals for the Establishment of a General International Organization," *FRUS, 1944*, 1:890. See also Stettinius diary, 23 August 1944, Stettinius Papers; memorandum on an international security organization, *FRUS, 1944*, 1:708; Cadogan to Foreign Office, 12 September 1944, U7353/180/70, FO 371; and Stettinius to Hull, "Progress Report on Dumbarton Oaks Conversations," 22 August 1944, *FRUS, 1944*, 1:716.

3. Memorandum on an international security organization by the Soviet Union, 12 August 1944, *FRUS, 1944*, 1:708; Stettinius to Hull, "Progress Report on Dumbarton Oaks Conversations," 23 August 1944, *FRUS, 1944*, 1:717; and Dilks, *Diaries of Sir Alexander Cadogan*, p. 657. See also Notter, *Postwar Foreign Policy Preparation*, pp. 308–9.

4. Stettinius calendar notes, 21 August 1944, Stettinius Papers; Stettinius diary, 24 August 1944, Stettinius Papers; and memorandum of conversation, Stettinius calling Hull, 24 August 1944, Stettinius Papers.

5. Informal minutes of meeting of the Joint Steering Committee, 25 August 1944, RDS; FO minute on Memorandum A, 29 March 1944, U2585/180/70, FO 371; and Webster, "The Making of the Charter of the United Nations," p. 29.

6. Stettinius diary, 25 August 1944, Stettinius Papers; and informal minutes of meeting of the Joint Steering Committee, 25 August 1944, RDS. See also Malinin, "Regarding International Security Organization" enclosed in Moscow to Washington, 25 July 1944, RG-84, RDS; and Moscow to Ottawa, 15 March 1944, U4778/180/70, FO 371.

7. Informal minutes of meeting of the Joint Steering Committee, 25 August 1944, RDS. See also "United States Tentative Proposals for a General International Organization," 18 July 1944, *FRUS, 1944*, 1:664.

8. Informal minutes of meeting of the Joint Steering Committee, 25 August 1944, RDS; Russell, *United Nations Charter*, pp. 304–6; and Webster, "The Making of the Charter of the United Nations," p. 29.

9. Stettinius to Hull, "Progress Report on Dumbarton Oaks Conversations," 25 August 1944, *FRUS, 1944*, 1:733. See also informal minutes of meeting of the Joint Steering Committee, 25 August 1944, RDS.

10. Stalin is quoted in Taubman, *Stalin's American Policy*, p. 49; and Stettinius to Hull, "Progress Report on Dumbarton Oaks Conversations," 25 August 1944, *FRUS, 1944*, 1:733.

11. Stettinius to Hull, "Progress Report on Dumbarton Oaks Conversations," 29 August 1944, *FRUS, 1944*, 1:747; Stettinius diary, 29 August 1944, Stettinius Papers; and Jebb to Nigel Ronald, 15 September 1944, U7503/180/70, FO 371.

12. Stettinius to Hull, "Progress Report on Dumbarton Oaks Conversations," 6 September 1944, *FRUS, 1944*, 1:772, 783. See also informal minutes of meeting of the Joint

274   Notes to Pages 91–96

Steering Committee, 7 September 1944, RDS; and Stettinius diary, 7 and 8 September 1944, Stettinius Papers.

13. Stettinius diary, 11 September 1944, Stettinius Papers; and informal minutes of meeting of the Joint Steering Committee, 12 September 1944, RDS.

14. Stettinius diary, 11 and 12 September 1944, Stettinius Papers; and informal minutes of meeting of the Joint Steering Committee, 12 September 1944, RDS.

15. Annex to Stettinius to Hull, "Progress Report on Dumbarton Oaks Conversations," 9 September 1944, FRUS, 1944, 1:791. See also Stettinius diary, 9 September 1944, Stettinius Papers; informal minutes of meeting of the Joint Steering Committee, 9 September 1944, RDS; and Stettinius to Hull, "Progress Report on Dumbarton Oaks Conversations," 9 September 1944, FRUS, 1944, 1:789.

16. Informal minutes of meeting of the Joint Steering Committee, 9 September 1944, RDS; and Foreign Office to Cadogan, 15 September 1944, U7424/180/70, FO 371. See also Stettinius diary, 9 September 1944, Stettinius Papers; and Cadogan to Foreign Office, 18 September 1944, U7424/180/70, FO 371.

17. Stettinius to Hull, "Progress Report on Dumbarton Oaks Conversations," 19 and 20 September 1944, FRUS, 1944, 1:825, 829–30; Stettinius diary, 20 September 1944, Stettinius Papers; Moscow to Ottawa, 15 March 1944, U4778/180/70, FO 371; and informal minutes of meeting of Joint Steering Committee, 20 September 1944, RDS.

18. "Proposals for the Establishment of a General International Organization," FRUS, 1944, 1:898; and Stettinius diary, 27 September 1944, Stettinius Papers. See also informal minutes of meeting of Joint Steering Committee, 17 and 20 September 1944, RDS; Russell, United Nations Charter, pp. 423–24; Stettinius to Hull, "Progress Report on Dumbarton Oaks Conversations," 27 September 1944, FRUS, 1944, 1:838–39; and Hiss to Stettinius, 23 September 1944, Hiss File, RDS.

19. Stettinius to Hull, "Progress Report on Dumbarton Oaks Conversations," 13 September 1944, FRUS, 1944, 1:797; minutes of meeting of American group, 13 September 1944, RDS.

20. Stettinius to Hull, "Progress Report on Dumbarton Oaks Conversations," 23 August 1944, FRUS, 1944, 1:717; and Cadogan to Foreign Office, 12 September 1944, U7353/180/70, FO 371.

21. Memorandum on an international security organization by the Soviet Union, 12 August 1944, FRUS, 1944, 1:708; and "United States Tentative Proposals for a General Security Organization," FRUS, 1944, 1:653. See also Russell, United Nations Charter, pp. 360–61; and Stettinius to Hull, "Progress Report on Dumbarton Oaks Conversations," 23 August 1944, FRUS, 1944, 1:717.

22. "Tentative Proposal by the United Kingdom for a General International Organization," 22 July 1944, FRUS, 1944, 1:673; Stettinius to Hull, "Progress Report on Dumbarton Oaks Conversations," 23 August 1944, FRUS, 1944, 1:717; FO minute by J. G. Ward, 4 September 1944, U7196/180/70, FO 371; and Russell, United Nations Charter, pp. 361–62.

23. Shatrov, translation of article in War and the Working Class, no. 14 (January 1944), Sweetser Papers; Taubman, Stalin's American Policy, pp. 88–89; and McNeill, America, Britain and Russia, p. 506.

24. Stettinius diary, 28 August 1944, Stettinius Papers; and Hull, Memoirs, 2:1679.

See also W.P.(44)443, 12 August 1944, CAB 66, vol. 53; Stettinius to Hull, "Progress Report on Dumbarton Oaks Conversations," 28 August 1944, *FRUS, 1944*, 1:738; informal minutes of meeting of the Joint Steering Committee, 28 August 1944, ibid., 742–43; and Stettinius, memorandum, 29 August 1944, ibid., 751–52.

25. Kolko, *The Politics of War*, p. 273; Notter, *Postwar Foreign Policy Preparation*, p. 318, n. 19; Russell, *United Nations Charter*, pp. 361–62; and Rothstein, *Soviet Foreign Policy*, 2:49–50.

26. Hull, *Memoirs*, 2:1679. See also Stettinius calendar notes, 11 February 1944, Stettinius Papers; Notter, *Postwar Foreign Policy Preparation*, p. 318, n. 19; Russell, *United Nations Charter*, pp. 360–61; and *FRUS, 1944*, 4:811–13, 820–23, 944–45.

27. Stettinius diary, 28 August 1944, Stettinius Papers. See also Reynolds and Hughes, *Historian as Diplomat*, p. 45.

28. FO minute by J. G. Ward, 4 September 1944, U7196/180/70, FO 371; and Foreign Office to Cadogan, 6 September 1944, ibid.

29. Stettinius memorandum, 29 August 1944, *FRUS, 1944*, 1:753. See also Stettinius diary, 28–29 August 1944, Stettinius Papers; Hull, *Memoirs*, 2:1680; and Notter, *Postwar Foreign Policy Preparation*, p. 318.

30. Stettinius diary, 29 August 1944, Stettinius Papers; and Hull, *Memoirs*, 2:1680. See also Stettinius, memorandum, 29 August 1944, *FRUS, 1944*, 1:751–53.

31. Roosevelt to Stalin, 31 August 1944, *FRUS, 1944*, 1:760; Stalin to Roosevelt, 7 September 1944, *FRUS, 1944*, 1:782–83; and Moscow to Ottawa, 15 March 1944, U4778/180/70, FO 371.

32. Stettinius diary, 14 September 1944, Stettinius Papers; and Shatrov, article in *War and the Working Class*, Sweetser Papers. See also Edgar Snow, record of interview with Maxim Litvinov, 6 October 1944, Roosevelt Papers; Mastny, *Russia's Road to the Cold War*; pp. 219–22; and memorandum of conversation, Pasvolsky and Arkady Sobolev, 28 September 1944, Pasvolsky Papers. The Americans and British agreed at Yalta to support a Soviet request at the general United Nations conference for the inclusion of the Ukraine and Byelorussia in the world organization.

33. Stettinius to Hull, "Progress Report on the Dumbarton Oaks Conversations," 7 September 1944, *FRUS, 1944*, 1:777. See also Stettinius diary, 29 August 1944, Stettinius Papers; Cadogan to Foreign Office, 12 September 1944, U7353/180/70, FO 371; and informal minutes of meeting of the Joint Steering Committee, 31 August 1944, RDS.

34. Stettinius to Hull, "Progress Report on the Dumbarton Oaks Conversations," 7 September 1944, *FRUS, 1944*, 1:777. See also Stettinius diary, 29 August 1944, Stettinius Papers; and informal minutes of meeting of the Joint Steering Committee, 31 August 1944, RDS.

35. Stettinius to Hull, "Progress Report on the Dumbarton Oaks Conversations," 13 September 1944, *FRUS, 1944*, 1:796; and Proposals for the Establishment of a General International Organization, ibid., 891. See also minutes of meeting of American group, 13 September 1944, Pasvolsky Papers; informal minutes of meeting of Joint Steering Committee, 13 September 1944, RDS; Notter, *Postwar Foreign Policy Preparation*, p. 396; and Russell, *United Nations Charter*, p. 435.

36. Memorandum on an international security organization by the Soviet Union, 12

August 1944, *FRUS, 1944*, 1:717–18; Stettinius diary, 24 August 1944, Stettinius Papers; Cadogan to Foreign Office, 23 August 1944, U7010/180/70, FO 371; Russell, *United Nations Charter*, pp. 362–63, 397–98; and minutes of American group meeting, 16 August 1944, Hull Papers.

37. "Tentative Proposals by the United Kingdom for a General International Organization," 22 July 1944, *FRUS, 1944*, 1:673; and Stettinius to Hull, "Progress Report on Dumbarton Oaks Conversations," 25 August 1944, ibid., 733. See also Stettinius to Hull, "Progress Report on Dumbarton Oaks Conversations," 23 and 28 August 1944, ibid., 717, 737; informal minutes of meeting of the Joint Steering Committee, 25 August 1944, RDS; and Stettinius diary, 28 August 1944, Stettinius Papers.

38. Stettinius diary, 6 September 1944, Stettinius Papers. See also Stettinius to Hull, "Progress Report on Dumbarton Oaks Conversations," 6 September 1944, *FRUS, 1944*, 1:777, 783; and Stettinius diary, 7 and 8 September 1944, Stettinius Papers.

39. "Proposals for the Establishment of a General International Organization," *FRUS, 1944*, 1:892. See also Russell, *United Nations Charter*, pp. 438–39.

40. Great Britain, *Commentary on Dumbarton Oaks Proposals for the Establishment of a General International Organization*, Notter File, RDS. See also Russell, *United Nations Charter*, pp. 438–39.

41. Great Britain, *Commentary on Dumbarton Oaks Proposals*, Notter File, RDS. See also Stettinius to Hull, "Progress Report on Dumbarton Oaks Conversations," 24 and 31 August 1944, *FRUS, 1944*, 1:729, 755; and Russell, *United Nations Charter*, pp. 426–27.

42. Stettinius to Hull, "Progress Report on Dumbarton Oaks Conversations," 7 September 1944, *FRUS, 1944*, 1:777. See also Stettinius to Hull, "Progress Report on Dumbarton Oaks Conversations," 20 September 1944, ibid., 830; Stettinius to Roosevelt, "Progress Report on Dumbarton Oaks Conversations," 27 September 1944, ibid., 838; Formulation Group draft, 9 September 1944, RDS; and "Proposals for the Establishment of a General International Organization," *FRUS, 1944*, 1:900.

43. Russell, *United Nations Charter*, p. 427.

44. Stettinius to Hull, "Progress Report on Dumbarton Oaks Conversations," 5 September 1944, *FRUS, 1944*, 1:767; and Foreign Office to Cadogan, 13 September 1944, U7353/180/70, FO 371. See also memorandum of conversation, Stettinius calling Leahy, 7 July 1944, Stettinius Papers; Stettinius to Hull, "Progress Report on Dumbarton Oaks Conversations," 29 August 1944, *FRUS, 1944*, 1:746; and preliminary report of Nomenclature Group, 4 September 1944, Fletcher Papers. Other nations later suggested alternate names. Chile proposed "World Community of Nations," and Mexico recommended "Permanent Union of Nations." See U.N. charter draft revision, 9 April 1945, Pasvolsky Papers.

45. Stettinius to Hull, 9 September 1944, *FRUS, 1944*, 1:790. See also "Draft Design for Charter of General International Organization," 10 April 1944, Sweetser Papers; and Stettinius to Hull, 9 and 12 September 1944, *FRUS, 1944*, 1:789–90, 795.

46. Stettinius diary, 21 August 1944, Stettinius Papers.

47. Ibid., 24 and 28 August 1944.

48. FO minute by Jebb, 7 April 1944, U3661/180/70, FO 371. See also memorandum of conversation, Pasvolsky and Arkady Sobolev, 28 September 1944, Stettinius Papers; Stettinius diary, 24 and 28 August 1944, Stettinius Papers; and Nicolson, *The War Years*, p. 409.

Chapter 5

1. "Tentative Proposals by the United Kingdom," 22 July 1944, *FRUS, 1944*, 1:673. See also Stettinius to Hull, "Progress Report on Dumbarton Oaks Conversations," 23 August 1944, *FRUS, 1944*, 1:717; Webster, "The Making of the Charter of the United Nations," p. 30; Ottawa to Dominions Office, 2 August 1944, U6760/180/70, FO 371; Russell, *United Nations Charter*, pp. 197–99, 290–94; and "Tentative Proposals of the United Kingdom," 22 July 1944, *FRUS, 1944*, 1:673–74.

2. Stettinius to Hull, "Progress Report on Dumbarton Oaks Conversations," 23 and 31 August 1944, *FRUS, 1944*, 1:717, 755; and record of meeting at Foreign Office, 3 April 1944, U2585/180/70, FO 371. See also "United States Tentative Proposals," 18 July 1944, *FRUS, 1944*, 1:655; "Tentative Views," 12 March 1943, Notter File, RDS; memorandum on an international security organization by the Soviet Union, 12 August 1944, *FRUS, 1944*, 1:708; and Stettinius to Hull, "Progress Report on Dumbarton Oaks Conversations," 24 August 1944, ibid., 729.

3. Informal minutes of meeting of Joint Steering Committee, 31 August 1944, RDS; Stettinius to Hull, "Progress Report on Dumbarton Oaks Conversations," 31 August 1944, *FRUS, 1944*, 1:755; and "Proposals for the Establishment of a General International Organization," ibid., 892.

4. Stettinius to Hull, "Progress Report on Dumbarton Oaks Conversations," 5, 8, 14, and 19 September 1944, *FRUS, 1944*, 1:768, 784, 807, 825; Stettinius diary, 8 September 1944, Stettinius Papers; and FO to Cadogan, 15 September 1944, U7424/180/70, FO 371.

5. "Proposals for the Establishment of a General International Organization," *FRUS, 1944*, 1:892. See also Stettinius to Hull, "Progress Report on Dumbarton Oaks Conversations," 31 August 1944, ibid., 755; "United States Tentative Proposals," 18 July 1944, ibid., 656; and Russell, *United Nations Charter*, pp. 365, 377–78.

6. Informal minutes of meeting of Joint Steering Committee, 9 September 1944, RDS. See also Stettinius to Hull, "Progress Report on Dumbarton Oaks Conversations," 31 August 1944, *FRUS, 1944*, 1:755; and note for the secretary of state, 7 September 1944, U7235/180/70, FO 371. The Canadians wanted "secondary" powers like themselves to have more authority than the "smaller" states. See memorandum of conversation, Lester B. Pearson, Canadian chargé d'affaires in Washington and John Hickerson, 31 August 1944, Stettinius Papers; and Ottawa to Dominions Office, 2 August 1944, U6760/180/70, FO 371.

7. Informal minutes of meeting of Joint Steering Committee, 9 September 1944, RDS. See also Russell, *United Nations Charter*, pp. 364–65.

8. Note for the secretary of state, 7 September 1944, U7235/180/70, FO 371. See also informal minutes of meeting of Joint Steering Committee, 9 September 1944, RDS.

9. "Proposals for the Establishment of a General International Organization," *FRUS, 1944*, 1:892. See also Stettinius to Hull, "Progress Report on Dumbarton Oaks Conversations," 19 and 20 September, ibid., 825, 829; and informal minutes of meeting of Joint Steering Committee, 19 September 1944, RDS.

10. Russell, *United Nations Charter*, pp. 366–67.

11. "Proposals for the Establishment of a General International Organization," *FRUS,*

1944, 1:893. See also Benjamin Gerig and Charles W. Yost, memorandum by the assistant chief of the Division of International Security and Organization, and the executive secretary of the Policy Committee, 20 November 1944, RDS; Stettinius to Hull, "Progress Report on the Dumbarton Oaks Conversations," 14 September 1944, *FRUS, 1944*, 1:807; and Russell, *United Nations Charter*, pp. 366–67.

12. "Proposals for the Establishment of a General International Organization," *FRUS, 1944*, 1:893; and Gerig and Yost, memorandum, 20 November 1944, RDS.

13. Russell, *United Nations Charter*, p. 366. See also Stettinius to Hull, "Progress Report on Dumbarton Oaks Conversations," 14 September 1944, *FRUS, 1944*, 1:807; and "Proposals for the Establishment of a General International Organization," ibid., 891.

14. Record of discussion between Dr. Bowman and Sir William Malkin, 22 April 1944, U3835/180/70, FO 371. See also draft statute of the Permanent Court of International Justice with the revisions proposed, 15 August 1944, RDS.

15. Stettinius diary, 24 August 1944, Stettinius Papers; minutes of meeting of American group, 17 August 1944, RDS; Notter, *Postwar Foreign Policy Preparation*, pp. 267–68; and Russell, *United Nations Charter*, pp. 382–86.

16. Stettinius to Hull, "Progress Report on Dumbarton Oaks Conversations," 22 August 1944, *FRUS, 1944*, 1:716; informal record of Legal Subcommittee, 24 August 1944, Hackworth Papers; and Russell, *United Nations Charter*, p. 866.

17. Draft statute of the Permanent Court of International Justice with the revisions proposed, 15 August 1944, RDS. See also informal record of Legal Subcommittee, 24 August 1944, Hackworth Papers; and FO minute, 13 July 1944, U6197/180/70, FO 371. The United States delegation agreed to create a new court, in part because it was not firmly wedded to the idea of continuing the Permanent Court and in part because an entirely new tribunal would be easier to sell to the Senate. See Philip C. Jessup, "The International Court of Justice of the United Nations—With Text of Statute," *Foreign Policy Reports* 21 (August 15, 1945): 160–61.

18. Informal record of Legal Subcommittee, 24 August 1944, Hackworth Papers; and Russell, *United Nations Charter*, pp. 382–83.

19. Russell, *United Nations Charter*, p. 383. See also informal record of Legal Subcommittee, 31 August 1944, Hackworth Papers.

20. Informal record of Legal Subcommittee, 31 August 1944, Hackworth Papers; and "Proposals for the Establishment of a General International Organization," *FRUS, 1944*, 1:895.

21. Stettinius to Hull, "Progress Report on Dumbarton Oaks Conversations," 1 September 1944, *FRUS, 1944*, 1:761. See also record of meeting at Foreign Office, 11 April 1944, U3137/180/70, FO 371; and informal record of Legal Subcommittee, 31 August 1944, Hackworth Papers.

22. FO minute by Jebb, 3 May 1944, U4098/180/70, FO 371. See also Green H. Hackworth, "The International Court of Justice," Department of State, *Bulletin* 13:216; and Russell, *United Nations Charter*, pp. 892–93.

23. Sergei B. Krylov, *Materials for the History of the United Nations*, quoted in Russell, *United Nations Charter*, p. 888, n. 49. See also Lawrence Preuss, "The International Court and the Problem of Compulsory Jurisdiction," Department of State, *Bulletin* 13:471–72; and informal record of meeting of the Legal Subcommittee, 24 and 31

August 1944, Hackworth Papers.

24. Stettinius to Hull, "Progress Report on Dumbarton Oaks Conversations," 6 September 1944, *FRUS, 1944*, 1:771; informal record of meeting of Legal Subcommittee, 6 September 1944, Hackworth Papers; "Proposals for the Establishment of a General International Organization," *FRUS, 1944*, 1:895; and Webster, "The Making of the Charter of the United Nations," p. 30.

25. Webster, "The Making of the Charter of the United Nations," p. 26; and Jebb to R. I. Campbell, 19 May 1944, U5624/180/70, FO 371.

Chapter 6

1. See Luard, *History of the United Nations*, 1:6–8; and Moscow to Ottawa, 15 March 1944, U4778/180/70, FO 371.

2. Account by Dr. Bowman, 15 April 1944, U3316/180/70, FO 371. See also informal minutes of the Joint Steering Committee, 28 August 1944, RDS; and memorandum of conversation, Michael Wright and Dunn, 14 August 1944, Pasvolsky File, RDS. There is no evidence to confirm the contention of Herbert Feis that there was disagreement at Dumbarton Oaks over a permanent council seat for China. The British and Soviets had, of course, objected previously to promoting China to Great Power status with permanent council membership, but they did not voice this opinion during the discussions at Dumbarton Oaks. See Feis, *Churchill, Roosevelt, Stalin*, p. 431. Feis may have based this view on the fear of Charles K. Webster that Soviet unwillingness to sign a joint communiqué with the Chinese reflected a desire to remove them from the ranks of the Great Powers. See Reynolds and Hughes, eds., *Historian as Diplomat*, p. 47.

3. Stettinius diary, 24 August 1944, Stettinius Papers; informal minutes of the Joint Steering Committee, 28 August 1944, RDS; discussion with Dr. Isaiah Bowman, 14 April 1944, U3445/180/70, FO 371; and "Proposal for the Establishment of a General International Organization," *FRUS, 1944*, 1:893. See also Stettinius diary, 28 August and 1 September 1944, Stettinius Papers; memorandum, meeting between Stettinius, Pasvolsky, Dunn, Cadogan, Malkin, and Jebb, 17 August 1944, Pasvolsky File, RDS; memorandum, meeting between Hull, Dunn, Hackworth, and Pasvolsky, 19 August 1944, ibid.; and FO minute, 31 August 1944, U7098/180/70, FO 371.

4. Memorandum, meeting between Hull, Dunn, Hackworth, and Pasvolsky, 19 August 1944, Pasvolsky File, RDS; meeting of American group, 31 August 1944, RDS; Stettinius to Roosevelt, "Brazil's Place on Council," 31 August 1944, President's Secretary File: Dumbarton Oaks, Roosevelt Papers; Russell, *United Nations Charter*, p. 400; and Hull, *Memoirs*, 2:1678. The current Brazilian government proved less sensitive, however, and asked only for an elected seat on the council. See Rio de Janeiro to Washington, 19 October 1944, *FRUS, 1944*, 1:932–33.

5. Stettinius diary, 24 August 1944, Stettinius Papers.

6. Informal minutes of the Joint Steering Committee, 28 August 1944, RDS; Hull, *Memoirs*, 2:1678; and FO minute, 31 August 1944, U7098/180/70, FO 371.

7. Stettinius diary, 28 August 1944, Stettinius Papers.

8. Meeting of American group, 31 August 1944, RDS; Stettinius to Roosevelt, "Brazil's Place on Council," 31 August 1944, Roosevelt Papers; Barton, "The Dumbarton Oaks Conference," pp. 305–6; and K. Davis, "FDR as a Biographer's Problem," p. 3. One country whose sentiments the State Department failed to consider was Canada, which was adamantly opposed to granting a permanent council seat to Brazil. See Canada to Dominions Office, 4 September 1944, U7235/180/70, FO 371.

9. Meeting of American group, 31 August 1944, RDS.

10. Stettinius to Roosevelt, "Brazil's Place on Council," 31 August 1944, Roosevelt Papers.

11. Stettinius diary, 31 August 1944, Stettinius Papers; Sherwood, *Roosevelt and Hopkins*, p. 718; *FRUS, 1943, Cairo and Tehran*, pp. 530–33; meeting between Hull and Roosevelt, 3 February 1944, *FRUS, 1944*, 1:620–21; and Barton, "The Dumbarton Oaks Conference," pp. 312–13. See also memorandum by the Joint Chiefs of Staff to the secretary of state, enclosed in General George C. Marshall to the secretary of state, 3 August 1944, 500.cc/8-344, RDS.

12. Stettinius diary, 31 August and 2 September 1944, Stettinius Papers; and Stettinius to Hull, "Progress Report on Dumbarton Oaks Conversations," 3 September 1944, *FRUS, 1944*, 1:764–65.

13. Stettinius calendar notes, 15 June 1944, Stettinius Papers. See also "Tentative Proposals by the United Kingdom," 22 July 1944, *FRUS, 1944*, 1:674; interview with Dr. Bowman, 19 April 1944, U3409/180/70, FO 371; minutes of Joint Steering Committee, 28 August 1944, RDS; FO minute, 28 June 1944, U6441/180/70, FO 371; and "Tentative Views," 12 March 1943, Notter File, RDS.

14. Stettinius to Hull, "Progress Report on Dumbarton Oaks Conversations," 24 August 1944, *FRUS, 1944*, 1:729; minutes of Joint Steering Committee, 28 August 1944, RDS; and "Proposals for the Establishment of a General International Organization," *FRUS, 1944*, 1:893.

15. Russell, *United Nations Charter*, p. 445; and "Proposals for the Establishment of a General International Organization," *FRUS, 1944*, 1:894. See also Stettinius to Hull, "Progress Report on Dumbarton Oaks Conversations," 30 August 1944, *FRUS, 1944*, 1:754; Gerig and Yost, memorandum, 20 November 1944, RDS; and Reynolds and Hughes, *Historian as Diplomat*, p. 46.

16. Memorandum on an international security organization by the Soviet Union, 12 August 1944, *FRUS, 1944*, 1:709; "Possible Plan for a General International Organization," 29 April 1944, in Notter, *Postwar Foreign Policy Preparation*, p. 507; and "United States Tentative Proposals," 18 July 1944, *FRUS, 1944*, 1:659. See also Moscow to Ottawa, 15 March 1944, U4778/180/70, FO 371; and Russell, *United Nations Charter*, p. 458.

17. Meeting of American group, 17 August 1944, RDS; meeting between Hull, Dunn, Hackworth, and Pasvolsky, 19 August 1944, Pasvolsky File, RDS.

18. Meeting of the American group, 17 August 1944, RDS; and meeting between Hull, Dunn, Hackworth, and Pasvolsky, 19 August 1944, Pasvolsky File, RDS.

19. Stettinius diary, 24 August 1944, Stettinius Papers. See also Stettinius calendar notes, supplementary notes on conversation with the president, 24 August 1944, ibid.

20. Berezhkov, "Dumbarton Okse," part 1, p. 173; Stettinius diary, 22 August 1944, Stettinius Papers; Stettinius to Hull, "Progress Report on Dumbarton Oaks Conversa-

tions," 22 August 1944, *FRUS, 1944*, 1:716; and "Tentative Proposals by the United Kingdom," 22 July 1944, ibid., 677–79.

21. "Tentative Proposals by the United Kingdom," 22 July 1944, *FRUS, 1944*, 1:678–79.

22. Stettinius to Hull, "Progress Report on Dumbarton Oaks Conversations," 24 August 1944, ibid., 728.

23. Ibid.; and Russell, *United Nations Charter*, pp. 457–59.

24. "Proposals for the Establishment of a General International Organization," *FRUS, 1944*, 1; 895. See also Stettinius to Hull, "Progress Report on Dumbarton Oaks Conversations," 1 September 1944, ibid., 761; Gerig and Yost, memorandum, 20 November 1944, RDS; and Russell, *United Nations Charter*, p. 459.

25. Hull, *Memoirs*, 2:1690, 1692; and the *New York Times*, 17 August 1944. See also Dulles, *War or Peace*, pp. 123–25; Department of State, *Bulletin* 11:206; and Divine, *Second Chance*, pp. 216–17.

26. Notter, *Postwar Foreign Policy Preparation*, p. 321. See also Hull, *Memoirs*, 2:1693–94.

27. Hull, *Memoirs*, 2:1694. See also Notter, *Postwar Foreign Policy Preparation*, pp. 221–22; and Russell, *United Nations Charter*, pp. 459–60.

28. Stettinius to Hull, "Progress Report on Dumbarton Oaks Conversations," 14 September 1944, *FRUS, 1944*, 1:808. See also Foreign Office to Cadogan, 15 September 1944, U7424/180/70, FO 371; and Stettinius to Hull, "Progress Report on Dumbarton Oaks Conversations," 20 and 27 September 1944, *FRUS, 1944*, 1:829, 838–39.

29. "Proposals for the Establishment of a General International Organization," *FRUS, 1944*, 1:895–96; and Stettinius to Hull, "Progress Report on Dumbarton Oaks Conversations," 19 September 1944, ibid., 825.

30. "Proposals for the Establishment of a General International Organization," *FRUS, 1944*, 1:896. See also Russell, *United Nations Charter*, pp. 457–62; Gerig and Yost, memorandum, 20 November 1944, RDS; Stettinius to Hull, "Progress Report on Dumbarton Oaks Conversations," 3 September 1944, *FRUS, 1944*, 1:765; and Barton, "Dumbarton Oaks Conference," p. 326.

31. "Proposals for the Establishment of a General International Organization," *FRUS, 1944*, 1:896. See also N. Malinin, "Regarding International Security Organization," *Zvezda*, no. 4 (1944), RDS; and Moscow to Ottawa, 15 March 1944, U4778/180/70, FO 371.

32. Memorandum on an international security organization by the Soviet Union, 22 August 1944, *FRUS, 1944*, 1:708–10. See also Stettinius to Hull, "Progress Report on Dumbarton Oaks Conversations," 22 August 1944, ibid., 715–16; and Brief no. 1, U5617/180/70, FO 371.

33. Stettinius to Hull, "Progress Report on Dumbarton Oaks Conversations," 22 August 1944, *FRUS, 1944*, 1:716; and Russell, *United Nations Charter*, p. 465.

34. Gerig and Yost, memorandum, 20 November 1944, RDS; Cadogan to Foreign Office, 12 September 1944, U7353/180/70, FO 371; and "Proposals for the Establishment of a General International Organization," *FRUS, 1944*, 1:896.

35. Gerig and Yost, memorandum, 20 November 1944, RDS.

36. Memorandum on an international security organization by the Soviet Union, 12 August 1944, *FRUS, 1944*, 1:710; J. F. de Barros Pimentel, "The Use of Force in the

Structure of Peace," 500.cc/7-2244, RDS; and "United States Tentative Proposals," 18 July 1944, *FRUS, 1944*, 1:661.

37. Meeting of Joint Steering Committee, 4 September 1944, RDS. See also meeting of Joint Steering Committee, 7 September 1944, ibid.; and "Proposals for the Establishment of a General International Organization," *FRUS, 1944*, 1:896.

38. S-Undistributed 26, "Critique of the *Ad Hoc* Type of International Force," 25 November 1942, Notter File, RDS; B. Stein, "From the History of the Preparation of the League of Nations Statutes," *Historical Journal*, nos. 2–3 (1944), in Moscow Dispatch no. 425, 500.cc/50, RDS; and Dorsey Gasseway Fischer, second secretary of embassy in London, to Hull, 11 May 1944, 500.cc/45, RDS.

39. "Critique of the *Ad Hoc* Type of International Force," 25 November 1942, Notter File, RDS; and translation of *Zvezda* article, in Moscow to Washington, 25 July 1944, 500.cc/7-2544, RDS.

40. NBC Broadcast, "Building the Peace," 3 March 1945, Sweetser Papers. See also Maurice Léon to Hull, 14 April 1944, 500.cc/74, RDS; and remarks by Norman H. Davis in Political Subcommittee, 1 May 1943, Notter File, RDS.

41. "Tentative Proposals by the United Kingdom for a General International Organization," *FRUS, 1944*, 1:686. See also report by War Cabinet Post-Hostilities Planning Subcommittee, 24 April 1944, U3630/180/70, FO 371; and FO minute, 11 May 1944, U3991/180/70, FO 371. One such "quarter" was Canada, which thought an international police force a good idea. See note by Canadian Working Committee on Post-Hostilities Problems, 6 March 1944, U5014/180/70, FO 371.

42. Wallace is quoted in Divine, *Second Chance*, p. 80. See also Wallace to Roosevelt, 5 February 1943, Wallace Papers.

43. S-Undistributed 47, "An International Air Force," undated, Notter File, RDS.

44. Ibid. See also Divine, *Second Chance*, p. 83.

45. See Sherry, *Preparing for the Next War*, pp. 22, 43, 166–68; and P. Smith, *The Air Force Plans for Peace*, pp. 39–53.

46. *Documents on Polish-Soviet Relations*, 2:338–39. See also translation of *Zvezda* article, in Moscow to Washington, 25 July, 1944, 500.cc/7-2544, RDS; and memorandum on an international security organization by the Soviet Union, 12 August 1944, *FRUS, 1944*, 1:711.

47. "Tentative Proposals by the United Kingdom for a General International Organization," *FRUS, 1944*, 1:686; and General Ismay to prime minister, 1 September 1944, U7320/180/70, FO 371.

48. Informal record of the first meeting of the Security Subcommittee, 23 August 1944, Hackworth Papers; and Dilks, *Diaries of Sir Alexander Cadogan*, p. 657. See also Stettinius to Hull, "Progress Report on Dumbarton Oaks Conversations," 24 August 1944, *FRUS, 1944*, 1:730.

49. Memorandum of conversation, Stettinius calling John J. McCloy, 29 July 1944, Stettinius Papers; and memorandum of conversation, Stettinius calling Dunn, 29 July 1944, ibid. See also Stettinius to Hull, "Progress Report on Dumbarton Oaks Conversations," 24 August 1944, *FRUS, 1944*, 1:730; and the diary of Henry L. Stimson, 31 July 1944, Stimson Papers.

50. P. Smith, *The Air Force Plans for Peace*, pp. 39–53.

51. Memorandum on meeting of Security Subcommittee, 23 August 1944, Notter File, RDS.

52. Summary of proceedings of the Military Subcommittee, Notter File, RDS; and informal record of the first meeting of the group of military representatives, 24 August 1944, Hull Papers. See also meeting of American group, 25 August 1944, RDS.

53. Informal record of the first meeting of the group of military representatives, 24 August 1944, Hull Papers. See also summary of proceedings of the Military Subcommittee, Notter File, RDS; and report by War Cabinet Post-Hostilities Planning Subcommittee, 24 April 1944, U3630/180/70, FO 371.

54. Summary of proceedings of the Military Subcommittee, Notter File, RDS. See also memorandum on meeting of Security Subcommittee, 23 August 1944, ibid.; and Stettinius diary, 24 August 1944, Stettinius Papers.

55. S-Undistributed 47, "An International Air Force," Notter File, RDS; and FO minute by Cadogan, 15 May 1944, U3991/180/70 FO 371.

56. S-Undistributed 47, "An International Air Force," Notter File, RDS.

57. Stettinius to Hull, "Progress Report on Dumbarton Oaks Conversations," 30 August 1944, FRUS, 1944, 1:753–54; FO minute by Cadogan, 11 May 1944, U3991/180/70, FO 371; and Stettinius diary, 30 August 1944, Stettinius Papers. See also informal record of second meeting of military group, 30 August 1944, Hull Papers.

58. Dilks, Diaries of Sir Alexander Cadogan, p. 659; Russell, United Nations Charter, p. 469; and Hull, Memoirs, 2:1696.

59. Vandenberg to Hull, 29 August 1944, Long Papers. See also Hull, Memoirs, 2:1696–97; and Campbell, Masquerade Peace, pp. 44–45.

60. Memorandum by Frederick G. Ribble, 20 April 1944, Pasvolsky Papers. See also Campbell, Masquerade Peace, pp. 43–45; and Hull, Memoirs, 2:1696–97.

61. Long to Hull, 12 September 1944, Hull Papers; and the Constitution of the United States, article 1, section 8, clause 10. See also Long diary, 30 August 1944, Long Papers; Long to Hull, 11 September 1944, Hull Papers; Hull, Memoirs, 2:1696–99; and "Use of Armed Force in the Maintenance of Peace and Security," in Hackworth to Hull, 31 August 1944, Hull Papers. Hackworth later suggested publishing the appendix to win public support for American involvement in the proposed peacekeeping organization. Others feared, however, that to do so might alienate Latin American nations, against whom most of the interventions Hackworth listed had been directed. See Long to Hackworth, 31 October 1944, Hiss File, RDS.

62. Dilks, Diaries of Sir Alexander Cadogan, p. 659; and Cadogan to Foreign Office, 1 September 1944, U7123/180/70, FO 371.

63. Dilks, Diaries of Sir Alexander Cadogan, p. 660; prime minister's minute, 29 August 1944, and Eden to Cadogan, 4 September, U7261/180/70, FO 371.

64. Dilks, Diaries of Sir Alexander Cadogan, p. 660.

65. Ibid.; Cadogan to Foreign Office, 5 September 1944, U7248/180/70, FO 371; and Stettinius diary, 5 September 1944, Stettinius Papers.

66. Dilks, Diaries of Sir Alexander Cadogan, pp. 660–61; General Ismay to prime minister, 1 September 1944, U7320/180/70, FO 371; and Chiefs of Staff to Joint Staff Mission, 4 September 1944, U7240/180/70, FO 371. See also minutes of meeting of Chiefs of Staff, 1 September 1944, U7197/180/70, FO 371; memo by War Cabinet Post-Hostilities Planning Staff, 4 September 1944, U7240/180/70, FO 371; and Sir Stafford Cripps to Eden, 3 September 1944, U7402/180/70, FO 371.

67. Stettinius diary, 5 September 1944, Stettinius Papers.

68. Roosevelt to Eichelberger, 11 January 1944, Roosevelt Papers; Stettinius calendar

notes, 6 September 1944, Stettinius Papers; and Stettinius diary, 29 August and 6 September 1944, *FRUS, 1944*, 1:749 and 772–73.

69. Stettinius diary, 6 September 1944, *FRUS, 1944*, 1:773.

70. Stettinius diary, 6 September 1944, Stettinius Papers.

71. Dilks, *Diaries of Sir Alexander Cadogan*, p. 661. The emphasis is Cadogan's. See also Cadogan to Foreign Office, 7 September 1944, U7326/180/70, FO 371; Stettinius to Hull, "Progress Report on Dumbarton Oaks Conversations," 7 September 1944, *FRUS, 1944*, 1:778; and minutes of meeting of Joint Steering Committee, 7 September 1944, RDS.

72. Stettinius diary, 8 September 1944, Stettinius Papers.

73. Stettinius to Hull, "Progress Report on Dumbarton Oaks Conversations," 12 September 1944, *FRUS, 1944*, 1:795; minutes of meeting of Joint Steering Committee, 12 September 1944, RDS; and informal record of the first meeting of the Security Subcommittee, 23 August 1944, Hackworth Papers.

74. Formulation Group's draft proposal of 9 September 1944, RDS. See also Stettinius to Hull, "Progress Report on the Dumbarton Oaks Conversations," 20 September 1944, *FRUS, 1944*, 1:829–30.

75. "Proposals for the Establishment of a General International Organization," *FRUS, 1944*, 1:896–97. See also informal record of second meeting of military group, 30 August 1944, Hull Papers; and Gerig and Yost, memorandum, 20 November 1944, RDS.

76. "Tentative Proposals of the United Kingdom for a General International Organization," 22 July 1944, *FRUS, 1944*, 1:686–87. See also Russell, *United Nations Charter*, p. 472.

77. Stettinius to Hull, "Progress Report on Dumbarton Oaks Conversations," 25 September 1944, *FRUS, 1944*, 1:734. See also informal minutes of meeting of Joint Steering Committee, 25 September 1944, RDS; Russell, *United Nations Charter*, pp. 261–62; and "United States Tentative Proposals," 18 July 1944, *FRUS, 1944*, 1:662.

78. "Proposals for the Establishment of a General International Organization," *FRUS, 1944*, 1:897. See also memorandum on an international security organization by the Soviet Union, 12 August 1944, ibid., 710; informal record of second meeting of military group, 30 August 1944, Hull Papers; Gerig and Yost, memorandum, 20 November 1944, RDS; and Russell, *United Nations Charter*, p. 262.

Chapter 7

1. "United States Tentative Proposals," 18 July 1944, *FRUS, 1944*, 1:663; and War Cab. 88(44) Conclusion, 7 July 1944, CAB 65, vol. 43.

2. "Tentative Proposals by the United Kingdom for a General International Organization," 22 July 1944, *FRUS, 1944*, 1:686; notes by General Ismay, July 1944, U6805/180/70, FO 371; Russell, *United Nations Charter*, pp. 476–77; and Gerig and Yost, memorandum, 20 November 1944, RDS.

3. Memorandum on an international security organization by the Soviet Union, 12 August 1944, *FRUS, 1944*, 1:709.

4. S-124, "Method of Achieving a System for the Regulation of Arms and Armed Forces," 6 June 1944, Notter File, RDS.

5. Reynolds and Hughes, *Historian as Diplomat*, p. 467. See also Foreign Office to Cadogan, 15 September 1944, U7424/180/70, FO 371; and Stettinius to Hull, "Progress Report on Dumbarton Oaks Conversations," 5 September, 1944, *FRUS, 1944*, 1:768.

6. Stettinius to Hull, "Progress Report on Dumbarton Oaks Conversations," 5 September 1944, *FRUS, 1944*, 1:768; "United States Tentative Proposals," 18 July 1944, ibid. 663; and Chiefs of Staff to Joint Staff Mission, 7 September 1944, U4392/180/70, FO 371.

7. Memorandum, "Commentaries at Dumbarton Oaks: Regulation of Armaments," 13 February 1946, Notter File, RDS; and Gerig and Yost, memorandum, 20 November 1944, RDS.

8. Memorandum, "Commentaries at Dumbarton Oaks: Regulation of Armaments," 13 February 1946, Notter File, RDS. See also Foreign Office to Cadogan, 15 September 1944, U7424/180/70, FO 371; Gerig and Yost, memorandum, 20 November 1944, RDS; Stettinius to Hull, "Progress Report on Dumbarton Oaks Conversations," 14 and 19 September 1944, *FRUS, 1944*, 1:807 and 825; Formulation Group draft, 6 September 1944, Chapter 9, "Regulation of Armaments," RDS; and Russell, *United Nations Charter*, p. 477.

9. "United States Tentative Proposals," 18 July 1944, *FRUS, 1944*, 1:653; and Russell, *United Nations Charter*, pp. 398–99.

10. "United States Tentative Proposals," 18 July 1944, *FRUS, 1944*, 1:653. See also American group meeting, 16 August 1944, Hull Papers; and Russell, *United Nations Charter*, pp. 398–99.

11. International Security Organization 43, "Role of Local and Regional Agencies in the Maintenance of Security and Peace," 17 August 1944, RDS. See also memorandum, "Principal Objective Which We Hope to Attain in the Forthcoming Conversations at Dumbarton Oaks," 12 August 1944, Stettinius Papers.

12. Reynolds and Hughes, *Historian as Diplomat*, p. 35. See also record of meeting with dominion prime ministers, 27 April 1944, U4098/180/70, FO 371; "Tentative Proposals by the United Kingdom," 22 July 1944, *FRUS, 1944*, 1:672–73; and W.P.(44)370, 3 July 1944, CAB 66, vol. 52.

13. "Tentative Proposals by the United Kingdom," 22 July 1944, *FRUS, 1944*, 1:672–73. See also Eden to prime minister, 3 May 1944, U3872/180/70, FO 371.

14. Stettinius to Hull, "Progress Report on Dumbarton Oaks Conversations," 25 August 1944, *FRUS, 1944*, 1:733; minutes of meeting of Joint Steering Committee, 7 September 1944, RDS; Stettinius diary, 8 September 1944, Stettinius Papers; Russell, *United Nations Charter*, pp. 472–73.

15. *War and the Working Class*, no. 24 (15 December 1944), quoted in Harriman to Stettinius, 21 December 1944, Stettinius Papers. See also transcript of telephone conversation, Hull and Pasvolsky, 10 May 1945, Pasvolsky Papers.

16. "United States Tentative Proposals," 18 July 1944, *FRUS, 1944*, 1:661. See also Notter, *Postwar Foreign Policy Preparation*, pp. 274–75; War Cab. 88(44) Conclusion, 7 July 1944, CAB 65, vol. 43; and meeting of Joint Steering Committee, 9 September 1944, RDS.

17. "Proposals for the Establishment of a General International Organization," *FRUS,*

1944, 1:900. See also Russell, *United Nations Charter*, p. 474.

18. Stettinius diary, 12 September 1944, Stettinius Papers; Hull, *Memoirs*, 2:1697–98; and Russell, *United Nations Charter*, p. 475.

19. Meeting of American group, 13 September 1944, RDS.

20. Stettinius to Hull, "Progress Report on Dumbarton Oaks Conversations," 13 September 1944, *FRUS, 1944*, 1:797; meeting of Joint Steering Committee, 13 September 1944, RDS; FO minute by Cadogan, 14 July 1944, U6306/180/70, FO 371; and Gerig and Yost, memorandum, 20 November 1944, RDS.

21. "Proposals for the Establishment of a General International Organization," *FRUS, 1944*, 1:900. See also Gerig and Yost, memorandum, 20 November 1944, RDS; War Cab. 88(44) Conclusion, 7 July 1944, CAB 65, vol. 43; and minutes of meeting of Joint Steering Committee, 19 September 1944, RDS.

22. "Proposals for the Establishment of a General International Organization," *FRUS, 1944*, 1:898. See also International Security Organization 43, "Role of Local and Regional Agencies in the Maintenance of Security and Peace," 17 August 1944, RDS; Gerig and Yost, memorandum, 20 November 1944, RDS; and minutes of meeting of Joint Steering Committee, 19 September 1944, RDS.

23. Memorandum of conversation by Bowman with Cadogan and Webster, 24 April 1944, Stettinius Papers; record of conversation by Bowman with Jebb, 12 April 1944, U6284/180/70, FO 371; "United States Tentative Proposals," 18 July 1944, *FRUS, 1944*, 1:665–67; and Louis, *Imperialism at Bay*, pp. 378–91.

24. Memorandum of conversation by Bowman with Law, 11 April 1944, Stettinius Papers; memorandum of conversation by Bowman with Churchill, 15 April 1944, ibid.; memorandum of conversation by Bowman with Oliver Stanley, colonial secretary, ibid.; FO minute by Cadogan, 21 July 1944, U6284/180/70, FO 371; and Woodward, *British Foreign Policy*, p. 440, n. 2.

25. Record of meeting on the colonies at the Washington talks, 27 July 1944, U6731/180/70, FO 371. See also FO minute by Cadogan, 21 July 1944, U6284/180/70, FO 371.

26. Louis, *Imperialism at Bay*, p. 382. See also Sir George Gator to Cadogan, 28 July 1944, U6683/180/70, FO 371; and FO minute by Cadogan, 21 July 1944, U6284/180/70, FO 371.

27. FO minute by Cadogan, 21 July 1944, U6284/180/70, FO 371; and FO minute by Jebb, 24 July 1944, U6519/180/70, FO 371. See also Sir George Gator to Cadogan, 28 July 1944, U6683/180/70, FO 371.

28. FO minute, note for secretary of state on W.P.(44)406, by Jebb, U6772/180/70, FO 371. See also memo by Poynton, 26 July 1944, CO 968/156/pt. 1; minutes of meeting by Poynton, 27 July 1944, CO 968/156/pt. 1; and Poynton to Jebb, with draft paper, 7 July 1944, U6284/180/70, FO 371.

29. Reynolds and Hughes, *Historian as Diplomat*, pp. 38–39; and FO minute by Cadogan, 26 July 1944, U6519/180/70, FO 371. See also Russell, *United Nations Charter*, pp. 342–43.

30. Knox is quoted in Gilchrist, "The Japanese Islands," 642–43.

31. Grew to Hull, 11 July 1944, Hull Papers.

32. Russell, *United Nations Charter*, pp. 346–47. See also comments on trusteeship proposals as of 17 July 1944, group 1, Working Book B, RDS; and Hull, *Memoirs*, 2:1466.

33. Millis, *The Forrestal Diaries*, p. 8; memorandum of conversation, Forrestal calling Stettinius, 7 July 1944, Stettinius Papers; and Notter, *Postwar Foreign Policy Preparation*, p. 387. See also Stettinius diary, 29 July 1944, Stettinius Papers; and memorandum for secretary, 1 August 1944, ibid.

34. Meeting of American group, 18 July 1944, Stettinius Papers; and Notter, *Postwar Foreign Policy Preparation*, pp. 295–96.

35. Memorandum by the Joint Chiefs of Staff to the secretary of state, 3 August 1944, *FRUS, 1944*, 1:701, 703; and Hull, *Memoirs*, 2:1466. For a view similar to Marshall's, see Admiral William D. Leahy to Hull, 16 May 1944, *FRUS, 1945, Malta and Yalta*, pp. 106–8.

36. Halifax to Eden, 15 September 1944, CO 968/160/14814/11. See also meeting of American Steering Committee, 31 July 1944, RDS; Cadogan to Foreign Office, 10 September 1944, U7387/180/70, FO 371; Notter, *Postwar Foreign Policy Preparation*, pp. 295–96; and Louis, *Imperialism at Bay*, p. 390.

37. Taubman, *Stalin's American Policy*, pp. 73–98; Stettinius diary, 22 August 1944, Stettinius Papers; minutes of meeting of Joint Steering Committee, 25 August 1944, RDS.

38. Memorandum of conversation, Pasvolsky and Sobolev, 28 September 1944, *FRUS, 1944*, 1:847. See also U.S. draft of a declaration by the United Nations on national independence, 9 March 1943, *FRUS, 1943*, 1:747–49; and Hull, *Memoirs*, 2:1236.

39. Memorandum of conversation, Pasvolsky and Sobolev, 28 September 1944, *FRUS, 1944*, 1:848.

40. Stettinius to Hull, "Progress Report on Dumbarton Oaks Conversations," 31 August and 1 September 1944, *FRUS, 1944*, 1:756, 762; *FRUS, 1943, Cairo and Tehran*, p. 532; "United States Tentative Proposals," 18 July 1944, *FRUS, 1944*, 1:662; "Tentative Proposals by the United Kingdom," 22 July 1944, ibid., 687; Chiefs of Staff memorandum, "United Nations Bases," April 1944, U3177/180/70, FO 371; and record of meeting at Foreign Office, 12 April 1944, ibid.

41. Stettinius to Hull, "Progress Report on the Dumbarton Oaks Conversations," 5 September 1944, *FRUS, 1944*, 1:767–68; and Joint Staff Mission to Chiefs of Staff, 2 September 1944, U7371/180/70, FO 371. See also meeting of Joint Steering Committee, 4 September 1944, RDS.

42. Stettinius, "Flash Items for the President," 6 September 1944, Stettinius Papers. See also Stettinius diary, 5 September 1944, Stettinius Papers; and Hull to embassy, Rio de Janeiro, 23 June 1944, Hiss File, RDS.

43. Stettinius, "Flash Items for the President," 6 September 1944, Stettinius Papers. See also Stettinius to Hull, "Progress Report on Dumbarton Oaks Conversations," 4 September 1944, *FRUS, 1944*, 1:765; and Stettinius diary, 5 September 1944, Stettinius Papers.

44. Harriman to Harry Hopkins, 10 September 1944, *FRUS, 1944*, 4:989. For correspondence on American and British attempts to win Soviet cooperation in aiding the Warsaw underground, see *FRUS, 1944*, 3:1372–98.

45. Report of Subcommittee on Soviet Proposal for Bases, 5 September 1944, Fletcher Papers. See also Hull to Winant, 8 September 1944, Stettinius Papers.

46. Stettinius diary, 5 September 1944, Stettinius Papers.

47. Proposals of the American group concerning the Formulation Group draft, 6

September 1944, Fletcher Papers.

48. Stettinius diary, 6 September 1944, Stettinius Papers.

49. Foreign Office to Cadogan, 23 September 1944, U7438/180/70, FO 371; Hull to Winant, 8 September 1944, Stettinius Papers; and Stettinius to Hull, "Progress Report on the Dumbarton Oaks Conversations," 8 September 1944, *FRUS, 1944*, 1:784. See also Gerig and Yost, memorandum, 20 November 1944, RDS; Stettinius diary, 8 September 1944, Stettinius Papers; Joint Staff Mission to Chiefs of Staff, 2 September 1944, U7371/180/70, FO 371; and Stettinius to Hull, "Progress Report on the Dumbarton Oaks Conversations," 12 and 20 September 1944, *FRUS, 1944*, 1:795, 829.

50. "United States Tentative Proposals," 18 July 1944, *FRUS, 1944*, 1:661.

51. Stettinius to Hull, "Progress Report on Dumbarton Oaks Conversations," 4 September 1944, *FRUS, 1944*, 1:766. See also Gerig and Yost, memorandum, 20 November 1944, RDS.

52. Stettinius to Hull, "Progress Report on Dumbarton Oaks Conversations," 4 September 1944, *FRUS, 1944*, 1:766; and Gerig and Yost, memorandum, 20 November 1944, RDS.

53. "Proposals for the Establishment of a General International Organization," *FRUS, 1944*, 1:898.

Chapter 8

1. See Russell, *United Nations Charter*, pp. 445–50.

2. Informal minutes of the Joint Steering Committee, 13 September 1944, *FRUS, 1944*, 1:798–804.

3. Minutes of group meeting number 8, 10 August 1944, Hull Papers; memorandum by the Joint Chiefs of Staff to the secretary of state, 3 August 1944, *FRUS, 1944*, 1:702–3; and S-131 Preliminary, "International Enforcement Measures," 18 July 1944, Notter File, RDS.

4. Minutes of group meeting number 8, 10 August 1944, Hull Papers.

5. Ibid.

6. Ibid.

7. Memorandum, "How the Interests of the United States are Safeguarded," 4 May 1944, Pasvolsky Papers.

8. "United States Tentative Proposals," 18 July 1944, *FRUS, 1944*, 1:658. See also minutes of group meetings number 8 and 10, 10 and 16 August 1944, Hull Papers.

9. Minutes of group meeting number 6, 7 August 1944, Pasvolsky Papers; and minutes of group meeting number 8, 10 August 1944, Hull Papers.

10. Minutes of group meeting number 8, 10 August 1944, Hull Papers; and Cadogan to Foreign Office, 17 August 1944, U6916/180/70, FO 371.

11. Minutes of group meeting number 8, 10 August 1944, Hull Papers; and minutes of group meeting number 10, 16 August 1944, RDS.

12. Minutes of group meeting number 9, 15 August 1944, RDS; minutes of group meeting number 10, 16 August 1944, Hull Papers; minutes of group meeting number

11, 17 August 1944, RDS; and Barton, "The Dumbarton Oaks Conference," pp. 199–201.

13. Minutes of group meeting number 11, 17 August 1944, RDS; meeting of groups 1 and 2, 17 August 1944, RDS; and International Security Organization 79, "A Minute on Views as to Alternative Procedures of Voting in the Executive Council When a Party to a Dispute Is a Member with Continuing Tenure," 19 August 1944, RDS.

14. Cadogan to Foreign Office, 17 August 1944, U6916/180/70, FO 371. See also meeting between Hull, Dunn, Hackworth, and Pasvolsky, 19 August 1944, Pasvolsky File, RDS; International Security Organization 79, "A Minute," 19 August 1944, RDS; conversation between Dunn, Pasvolsky, Jebb, and Webster, 16 August 1944, Pasvolsky File, RDS; the *New York Times*, 20 August 1944; Barton, "The Dumbarton Oaks Conference," p. 206; and Reynolds and Hughes, *Historian as Diplomat*, p. 43.

15. Russell, *United Nations Charter*, p. 446, n. 10; and meeting between Hull, Dunn, Hackworth, and Pasvolsky, 10 August 1944, RDS. See also Russell, *United Nations Charter*, pp. 407–8; Barton, "The Dumbarton Oaks Conference," pp. 203–6; Hull, *Memoirs*, 2:1677–78; and Stettinius diary, 24 August 1944, *FRUS, 1944*, 1:731.

16. Hull, *Memoirs*, 2:1678. See also Stettinius to Hull, "Progress Report on Dumbarton Oaks Conversations," 24 August 1944, *FRUS, 1944*, 1:729; and Russell, *United Nations Charter*, p. 446, n. 10.

17. Meeting between Hull, Dunn, Hackworth, and Pasvolsky, 19 August 1944, RDS; Stettinius diary, 24 August 1944, *FRUS, 1944*, 1:731; memorandum for the president, 23 August 1944, RDS; and Russell, *United Nations Charter*, pp. 407–8, 446.

18. Woodward, *British Foreign Policy*, p. 456. See also Dilks, *Diaries of Sir Alexander Cadogan*, pp. 654–55; FO minute by Cadogan, July 1944, U6441/180/70, FO 371; memorandum on an international security organization by the Soviet Union, 12 August 1944, *FRUS, 1944*, 1:706–11; meeting between Cadogan, Malkin, Jebb, Stettinius, Pasvolsky, and Dunn, 17 August 1944, Pasvolsky File, RDS; and Reynolds and Hughes, *Historian as Diplomat*, pp. 42–43.

19. Stettinius to Hull, "Progress Report on Dumbarton Oaks Conversations," 24 August 1944, *FRUS, 1944*, 1:729; informal minutes of meeting 2 of the General Organization Committee, 24 August 1944, RDS; Reynolds and Hughes, *Historian as Diplomat*, p. 48; and Dilks, *Diaries of Sir Alexander Cadogan*, pp. 657–58.

20. Informal minutes of meeting 2 of General Organization Committee, 24 August 1944, RDS; FO minute by Cadogan, July 1944, U6441/180/70, FO 371; and Stettinius to Hull, "Progress Report on Dumbarton Oaks Conversations," 24 August 1944, *FRUS, 1944*, 1:729.

21. Stettinius diary, 25 August 1944, Stettinius Papers. See also meeting between Cadogan, Malkin, Jebb, Stettinius, Pasvolsky, and Dunn, 17 August 1944, Pasvolsky File, RDS; Stettinius to Hull, "Progress Report on Dumbarton Oaks Conversations," 24 August 1944, *FRUS, 1944*, 1:729; and Stettinius diary, 25 August 1944, Stettinius Papers.

22. Stettinius to Hull, "Progress Report on Dumbarton Oaks Conversations," 25 August 1944, *FRUS, 1944*, 1:733; and Cadogan to Foreign Office, 28 August 1944, U7098/180/60, FO 371. See also Dilks, *Diaries of Sir Alexander Cadogan*, p. 658; and Stettinius diary, 25 August 1944, Stettinius Papers.

23. Informal minutes of meeting of the Joint Steering Committee, 28 August 1944, RDS. See also Woodward, *British Foreign Policy*, p. 457.

24. Informal minutes of meeting of the Joint Steering Committee, 28 August 1944, RDS.

25. Ibid.

26. Ibid.

27. Ibid.

28. Ibid.

29. Stettinius diary, 29 August 1944, Stettinius Papers.

30. Ibid.

31. Memorandum to Hull, "Certain Views Expressed Recently by Members of American Group," 29 August 1944, RDS; and Stettinius diary, 29 August 1944, Stettinius Papers.

32. Stettinius to Hull, "Progress Report on Dumbarton Oaks Conversations," 4 September 1944, *FRUS, 1944*, 1:766–67; Cadogan to Foreign Office, 4 September 1944, U7204/180/70, FO 371; and Dilks, *Diaries of Sir Alexander Cadogan*, p. 659.

33. Dilks, *Diaries of Sir Alexander Cadogan*, pp. 659–63; and Stettinius diary, 29 August 1944, Stettinius Papers. See also Cadogan to Foreign Office, 4 September 1944, U7204/180/70, FO 371; and Stettinius diary, 4 September 1944, Stettinius Papers.

34. Dilks, *Diaries of Sir Alexander Cadogan*, p. 660; and Stettinius diary, 5 September 1944, Stettinius Papers.

35. Stettinius diary, 5 September 1944, Stettinius Papers.

36. Ibid., 6 September 1944.

37. Stettinius to Hull, "Progress Report on Dumbarton Oaks Conversations," 7 September 1944, *FRUS, 1944*, 1:777; Foreign Office to Cadogan, 6 September 1944, U7223/180/70, FO 371; minutes of meeting of Joint Steering Committee, 7 September 1944, RDS; and Dilks, *Diaries of Sir Alexander Cadogan*, p. 661.

38. Stettinius to Hull, "Progress Report on Dumbarton Oaks Conversations," 7 September 1944, *FRUS, 1944*, 1:777; and Foreign Office to Cadogan, 6 September 1944, U7223/180/70, FO 371. See also minutes of meeting of Joint Steering Committee, 7 September 1944, RDS; and Dilks, *Diaries of Sir Alexander Cadogan*, p. 661.

39. Stettinius diary, 7 September 1944, Stettinius Papers; and Dilks, *Diaries of Sir Alexander Cadogan*, p. 661. See also Cadogan to Foreign Office, 7 September 1944, U7274/180/70, FO 371.

40. Dilks, *Diaries of Sir Alexander Cadogan*, p. 661; and Stettinius diary, 6 September 1944, Stettinius Papers. See also Woodward, *British Foreign Policy*, p. 457; Cadogan to Foreign Office, 7 September 1944, U7274/180/70, FO 371; and Hull to Harriman, 11 September 1944, 500.cc/9-1144, RDS. Harriman advised against raising the issue with Molotov because of FDR's telegram to Stalin.

41. Stettinius diary, 7 September 1944, Stettinius Papers; and memorandum of conversation by the secretary of state, 31 August 1944, RDS.

42. Stettinius diary, 7 September 1944, Stettinius Papers.

43. Stettinius diary, 8 September 1944, Stettinius Papers. See also Stettinius, *Roosevelt and the Russians*, p. 22.

44. Stettinius diary, 8 September 1944, Stettinius Papers.

45. Ibid. See also Stettinius diary, 7 September 1944, Stettinius Papers; and draft cable by Charles E. Bohlen, 8 September 1944, RDS.

46. Roosevelt to Harriman, 8 September 1944, Roosevelt Papers.

47. Stettinius diary, 8 September 1944, Stettinius Papers.

48. Dilks, *Diaries of Sir Alexander Cadogan*, p. 662; Cadogan to Foreign Office, 8 September 1944, U7281/180/70, FO 371; and Stettinius diary, 8 September 1944, Stettinius Papers.

49. Dilks, *Diaries of Sir Alexander Cadogan*, p. 662; and Stettinius diary, 11 and 12 September 1944, Stettinius Papers. See also meeting of American group, 11 September 1944, RDS.

50. Minutes of meeting of Joint Steering Committee, 13 September 1944, RDS; and Woodward, *British Foreign Policy*, p. 457. See also Dilks, *Diaries of Sir Alexander Cadogan*, p. 664; and Cadogan to Foreign Office, 13 September 1944, U7374/180/70, FO 371.

51. Dilks, *Diaries of Sir Alexander Cadogan*, p. 664; and minutes of meeting of Joint Steering Committee, 13 September 1944, RDS. See also Stettinius diary, 13 September 1944, Stettinius Papers.

52. Minutes of meeting of Joint Steering Committee, 13 September 1944, RDS.

53. Ibid. See also Mastny, *Russia's Road to the Cold War*, pp. 218–24.

54. Minutes of meeting of Joint Steering Committee, 13 September 1944, RDS.

55. Ibid.

56. Ibid.; and Cadogan to Foreign Office, 13 September 1944, U7374/180/70, FO 371.

57. Minutes of meeting of Joint Steering Committee, 13 September 1944, RDS.

58. Ibid.

59. Ibid.

60. Reynolds and Hughes, *Historian as Diplomat*, p. 48; and Stettinius diary, 14 September 1944, Stettinius Papers.

Chapter 9

1. Reynolds and Hughes, *Historian as Diplomat*, p. 48; and Cadogan to Foreign Office, 13 September 1944, U7374/180/70, FO 371.

2. Meeting of American group, 13 September 1944, RDS; Israel, *War Diary of Breckinridge Long*, pp. 379–80; and minutes of meeting of American group, 17 August 1944, RDS.

3. Stettinius diary, 13 September 1944, Stettinius Papers; and Dilks, *Diaries of Sir Alexander Cadogan*, p. 664. See also Reynolds and Hughes, *Historian as Diplomat*, p. 48; "Compromise Proposal Drafted by the Formulation Group," 13 September 1944, *FRUS, 1944*, 1:805–6; and Woodward, *British Foreign Policy*, p. 458.

4. Hull, *Memoirs*, 2:1701–2; Stettinius diary, 14 September 1944, Stettinius Papers; and Dilks, *Diaries of Sir Alexander Cadogan*, pp. 665–66. See also Stettinius to Roosevelt,

15 September 1944 and Roosevelt to Stettinius, 15 September 1944, *FRUS, 1944*, 1:812–14; and prime minister to Cadogan, 13 September 1944, 75/2/part 1, PREM 4. Hull's concern with being left behind was well founded. Secretary of the Treasury Morgenthau, who had been disputing with Hull over several foreign policy issues, was invited to attend the conference at Quebec, during which Churchill and Roosevelt approved the so-called Morgenthau Plan for the political and economic dismemberment of Germany. "In Christ's name," Hull exclaimed to Stettinius, "what has happened to the man?" See Dilks, *Diaries of Sir Alexander Cadogan*, p. 666; and Woodward, *British Foreign Policy*, pp. 47–72.

5. Stettinius diary, 14 September 1944, Stettinius Papers; and Stalin to Roosevelt, 14 September 1944, *FRUS, 1944*, 1:806–7. See also Dilks, *Diaries of Sir Alexander Cadogan*, p. 666; and Stettinius to Roosevelt, "Progress Report on Dumbarton Oaks Conversations," 17 September 1944, *FRUS, 1944*, 1:816–18.

6. Memorandum of meeting between Stettinius, Pasvolsky, Hackworth, and Hayden Raynor, 16 September 1944, Stettinius Papers. See also Reynolds and Hughes, *Historian as Diplomat*, p. 43; and Hull, *Memoirs*, 2:1703.

7. Deputy prime minister to foreign secretary, 15 September 1944, U7374/180/70, FO 371. See also Woodward, *British Foreign Policy*, p. 458; and Reynolds and Hughes, *Historian as Diplomat*, p. 43.

8. Churchill is quoted in Mastny, *Russia's Road to the Cold War*, p. 186; Halifax is quoted in Stettinius diary, 28 August 1944, Stettinius Papers. See also Ciechanowski, *The Warsaw Rising of 1944*; and Werth, *Russia at War*, p. 876.

9. Stettinius, memorandum of press conference, 10 August 1944, Hackworth Papers. See also Moscow to Foreign Office, 9 September 1944, FO 800/412; Ciechanowski, *The Warsaw Rising of 1944*; Roosevelt to Churchill, 26 August and 15 September 1944, and Churchill to Roosevelt, 25 and 29 August and 4 and 5 September 1944, in Loewenheim, Langley, and Jonas, *Roosevelt and Churchill*, pp. 566–73; and Mastny, *Russia's Road to the Cold War*, pp. 188–89.

10. Meeting between Stettinius, Pasvolsky, Hackworth, and Hayden Raynor, 16 September 1944, Stettinius Papers; and Harriman to Hull, 20 September 1944, 500.cc/9-2044, RDS. See also Bohlen to Hull, 8 September 1944, Hull Papers; and Harriman to Hull, 19 September 1944, 500.cc/9-1944, RDS.

11. Taubman, *Stalin's American Policy*, pp. 68–69.

12. Harriman to Hull, 23 August 1944, 500.cc/8-2344, RDS. See also Mastny, *Russia's Road to the Cold War*, pp. 220–21.

13. Jebb to Nigel Ronald, 15 September 1944, U7503/180/70, FO 371. See also Taubman, *Stalin's American Policy*, pp. 88–89; Harriman to Stettinius, 28 December 1944, 500.cc/12-2844, RDS; and Moscow to Foreign Office, 15 September 1944, FO 800/412.

14. Moscow to Foreign Office, 9 September 1944, FO 800/412. See also Mastny, *Russia's Road to the Cold War*, p. 221.

15. Berezhkov, *Gody diplomaticheskoi sluzhby* [The years of diplomatic service], pp. 290–91; and Harriman to Hull, 19 September 1944, 500.cc/9-1944, RDS. See also Taubman, *Stalin's American Policy*, pp. 89–90; and Mastny, *Russia's Road to the Cold War*, p. 221.

16. Stettinius to Hull, "Progress Report on Dumbarton Oaks Conversations," 18 September 1944, *FRUS, 1944*, 1:821. See also memorandum of conversation, Pasvolsky with Sobolev, 28 September 1944, RDS.

17. Stettinius diary, 15 September 1944, Stettinius Papers. See also "Proposals of American Group for Changes in the Formulation Group's Draft," 4 September 1944, Fletcher Papers; and Israel, *War Diary of Breckinridge Long*, pp. 379–80.

18. Meeting of American group, 18 September 1944, RDS; note, "Consequences of Disagreement," undated, Long Papers; Stettinius diary, 18 September 1944, Stettinius Papers; and Long diary, 19 September 1944, Long Papers.

19. Meeting of American group, 18 September 1944, RDS; Stettinius diary, 18 and 20 September 1944, Stettinius Papers; aide-mémoire, Hepburn to Stettinius, undated, Stettinius Papers; memorandum, unsigned, to Stettinius, 18 September 1944, Hull Papers.

20. Meeting of American group, 18 September 1944, RDS; and memorandum, unsigned, to Stettinius, 18 September 1944, Hull Papers.

21. Meeting of American group, 18 September 1944, RDS; and Stettinius diary, 18 September 1944, Stettinius Papers.

22. Memorandum for the secretary of state, "Dumbarton Oaks Situation," RDS. Although this memorandum was unsigned, the names of Bowman, Grew, Edwin Wilson, Hornbeck, and Cohen were penciled in the margin.

23. Memorandum, Cabot to Stettinius, 19 September 1944, Stettinius Papers.

24. Stettinius diary, 19 September 1944, Stettinius Papers.

25. Hull, *Memoirs*, 2:1703–4; and memorandum for Stettinius, 21 September 1944, Stettinius Papers. See also Stettinius diary, 20 September 1944, Stettinius Papers; and Kennan, *Memoirs*, pp. 220–23.

26. Dilks, *Diaries of Sir Alexander Cadogan*, pp. 666–67; and Reynolds and Hughes, *Historian as Diplomat*, pp. 48–49.

27. Minutes of Joint Steering Committee, 17 September 1944, RDS. See also Stettinius diary, 17 September 1944, Stettinius Papers.

28. Minutes of Joint Steering Committee, 17 September 1944, RDS. See also Dilks, *Diaries of Sir Alexander Cadogan*, p. 666.

29. "U.S. Proposal of Possible Procedure," 17 September 1944, RDS; and Stettinius to Roosevelt, "Progress Report on Dumbarton Oaks Conversations," 17 September 1944, *FRUS, 1944*, 1:816. See also Cadogan to Foreign Office, 15 September 1944, U7388/180/70, FO 371.

30. Reynolds and Hughes, *Historian as Diplomat*, pp. 48–49. See also Jebb to Nigel Ronald, 15 September 1944, U7503/180/70, FO 371.

31. Hiss to Pasvolsky, 22 September 1944, Pasvolsky Papers; and Stettinius diary, 18 September 1944, Stettinius Papers.

32. Stettinius diary, 18 September 1944, Stettinius Papers; and Dilks, *Diaries of Sir Alexander Cadogan*, p. 667.

33. Dilks, *Diaries of Sir Alexander Cadogan*, pp. 667–68.

34. Ibid., p. 667; and Stettinius to Hull, "Progress Report on Dumbarton Oaks Conversations," 19 September 1944, *FRUS, 1944*, 1:824–25. See also minutes of meeting of Joint Steering Committee, 20 September 1944, RDS.

35. Stettinius to Roosevelt, "Progress Report on Dumbarton Oaks Conversations," 27 September 1944, *FRUS, 1944*, 1:838–41. See also Harriman to the secretary of state, 7 October 1944, 500.cc/10-744, RDS.

36. Stettinius diary, 19 and 21 September 1944, Stettinius Papers. See also Hull, *Memoirs*, 2:1703–4; and "Notes of the Secretary's Remarks to the American Group in His Office," 19 September 1944, RDS. See also memorandum for Mrs. Roosevelt, 21 September 1944, Office File 5557, Roosevelt Papers.

37. Churchill to Roosevelt, 25 September 1944, 500.cc/9-3044.

38. Ibid.

39. Churchill to Roosevelt, 3 October 1944, *FRUS, 1944*, 4:1002. See also prime minister's personal minute, 20 September 1944, U7593/180/70, FO 371; Woodward, *British Foreign Policy*, pp. 459–62; Russell, *United Nations Charter*, pp. 519–20; FO minute by N. Butler, 25 September 1944, U7469/180/70, FO 371; and Resis, "The Churchill-Stalin Secret 'Percentages' Agreement," pp. 372–73.

40. Roosevelt to Churchill, 4 October 1944, *FRUS, 1945, Malta and Yalta*, p. 7. See also Sherwood, *Roosevelt and Hopkins*, pp. 832–34; Roosevelt to Harriman, 4 October 1944, *FRUS, 1945, Malta and Yalta*, pp. 6–7; and Resis, "The Churchill-Stalin Secret 'Percentages' Agreement," p. 386.

Chapter 10

1. Foreign Office to Cadogan, September 1944, U7416/180/70, FO 371. See also Feis, *The China Tangle*, pp. 145–207; and Stettinius diary, 21 June and 13 September 1944, Stettinius Papers.

2. Long diary, 30 August 1944, Long Papers (the emphasis is Long's); and report on radio commentary by Royal Arch Gunnison, 26 August 1944, Stettinius Papers. See also Long diary, 27 September 1944, Long Papers.

3. Stettinius diary, 27 September 1944, Stettinius Papers; Dilks, *Diaries of Sir Alexander Cadogan*, p. 669; and Long diary, 29 September, 1944, Long Papers.

4. Stettinius diary, 13 and 27 September 1944, Stettinius Papers; Stettinius to Hull, "Progress Report on Dumbarton Oaks Conversations," 29 September and 2 October 1944, *FRUS, 1944*, 1:850–51, 861; Hull, *Memoirs*, 2:1707; Halifax to Foreign Office, 3 October 1944, U7651/180/70, FO 371; meeting of Joint Steering Committee, 27 September 1944, RDS; and Jebb to Foreign Office, 5 October 1944, U7659/180/70, FO 371.

5. Stettinius diary, 12 July 1944, Stettinius Papers. See also Harley Notter, "Points for the Special Private Conversations," 4 September 1944, RDS; and "Tentative Chinese Proposals for a General International Organization," 23 August 1944, *FRUS, 1944*, 1:718–28.

6. Informal minutes of meeting of the Joint Steering Committee, 2 October 1944, RDS.

7. Ibid.

8. Ibid.; and "Tentative Chinese Proposals for International Organization," 23 August 1944, *FRUS, 1944,* 1:718–28.

9. Informal minutes of meeting of the Joint Steering Committee, 2 October 1944, RDS.

10. Ibid.

11. "Proposals for the Establishment of a General International Organization," 9 October 1944, *FRUS, 1944,* 1:900; Jebb to Foreign Office, 8 October 1944, U7714/ 180/70, FO 371; and informal minutes of meeting of the Joint Steering Committee, 2 October 1944, RDS.

12. Informal minutes of meeting of the Joint Steering Committee, 2 October 1944, RDS.

13. Ibid.; and extracts of meeting of the Joint Steering Committee, 4 October 1944, *FRUS, 1944,* 1:868–69.

14. Informal minutes of meeting of the Joint Steering Committee, 2 October 1944, RDS. See also "Document Prepared for Special Conversations with the Chinese," 8 September 1944, Notter File, RDS.

15. Stettinius to Hull, "Progress Report on Dumbarton Oaks Conversations," 2 and 3 October 1944, *FRUS, 1944,* 1:861–64; and informal minutes of meeting of the Joint Steering Committee, 3 October 1944, RDS.

16. Stettinius to Hull, "Progress Report on Dumbarton Oaks Conversations," 2 October 1944, *FRUS, 1944,* 1:862. See also informal minutes of meeting of the Joint Steering Committee, 2 October 1944, RDS.

17. Stettinius to Hull, "Progress Report on Dumbarton Oaks Conversations," 2 October 1944, *FRUS, 1944,* 1:862.

18. Stettinius to Hull, "Progress Report on Dumbarton Oaks Conversations," 3 October 1944, *FRUS, 1944,* 1:863–64; and Jebb to Foreign Office, 3 October 1944, U7643/ 180/70, FO 371.

19. Stettinius to Hull, "Progress Report on Dumbarton Oaks Conversations," 3 October 1944, *FRUS, 1944,* 1:863–64; "Tentative Chinese Proposals for a General International Organization," 23 August 1944, *FRUS, 1944,* 1:722; and meeting of American group, 3 October 1944, RDS.

20. Stettinius to Hull, "Progress Report on Dumbarton Oaks Conversations," 3 and 4 October 1944, *FRUS, 1944,* 1:864–66; and "Document Prepared for Special Conversations with the Chinese," 8 September 1944, Notter File, RDS.

21. "Note on Proposals for the Establishment of a General International Organization," 27 September 1944, Long Papers. See also Stettinius to Hull, "Progress Report on Dumbarton Oaks Conversations," 3 October 1944, *FRUS, 1944,* 1:864; meeting of Joint Formulation Group, 3 October 1944, RDS; meeting of American group, 3 October 1944, RDS; and record of meeting at Foreign Office, 3 April 1944, U7585/180/70, FO 371.

22. Stettinius to Hull, "Progress Report on Dumbarton Oaks Conversations," 3 October 1944, *FRUS, 1944,* 1:864; meeting of American group, 3 October 1944, RDS; and meeting of Joint Formulation Group, 3 October 1944, RDS.

23. "Tentative Chinese Proposals for a General International Organization," 23 August 1944, *FRUS, 1944,* 1:726; Stettinius to Hull, "Progress Report on Dumbarton Oaks Conversations," 3 October 1944, *FRUS, 1944,* 1:864–65; informal record of meeting of

military representatives, 3 October 1944, Long Papers; and Notter, *Postwar Foreign Policy Preparation*, p. 332.

24. Stettinius to Hull, "Progress Report on Dumbarton Oaks Conversations," 3 October 1944, *FRUS, 1944*, 1:865; "Tentative Chinese Proposals for a General International Organization," 23 August 1944, *FRUS, 1944*, 1:723; and meeting of Joint Formulation Group, 3 October 1944, RDS.

25. Jebb to Foreign Office, 4 October 1944, U7659/180/70, FO 371. See also meeting of Joint Formulation Group, 3 and 4 October 1944, RDS; and Stettinius to Hull, "Progress Report on Dumbarton Oaks Conversations," 4 October 1944, *FRUS, 1944*, 1:866–67.

26. Stettinius to Hull, "Progress Report on Dumbarton Oaks Conversations," 3 October 1944, *FRUS, 1944*, 1:865; meeting of Joint Steering Committee, 4 October 1944, RDS; Jebb to Foreign Office, 5 October 1944, U7659/180/70, FO 371; and meeting of American group, 3 October 1944, RDS.

27. Minutes of meeting of Joint Steering Committee, 5 October 1944, RDS.

28. Ibid.

29. Ibid.

30. Ibid.

31. Ibid

32. Ibid.

33. Stettinius to Hull, "Progress Report on Dumbarton Oaks Conversations," 7 October 1944, *FRUS, 1944*, 1:883; FO minute, 13 July 1944, U6197/180/70, FO 371; and meeting of Joint Formulation Group, 7 October 1944, RDS.

34. Radio commentary by Wilfred Fleisher, 9 September 1944, Stettinius Papers; and Hull, *Memoirs*, 2:1707. See also Cadogan to Foreign Office, 29 September 1944, U7584/180/70, FO 371; meeting of Joint Formulation Group, 6 October 1944, RDS; and "Remarks by the Secretary of State at the Closing Session," Department of State, *Bulletin* 11:374–75.

Conclusion

1. Press release issued by the Department of State, 9 October 1944, *FRUS, 1944*, 1:889–90; and "Proposals for the Establishment of a General Organization," *FRUS, 1944*, 1:900.

2. "The Dumbarton Oaks Tentative Proposals" (British), 18 October 1944, Sweetser Papers.

3. Mowrer, "Woodrow Wilson at Dumbarton Oaks," 24 August 1944, Sweetser Papers.

4. See analysis of article in *War and the Working Class*, in Harriman to Stettinius, 12 March 1945, Notter File, RDS; and Jebb to Nigel Ronald, 15 September 1944, U7503/180/70, FO 371.

5. Memorandum on NBC broadcast, Sweetser Papers; transcript of telephone conver-

sation, Hull and Pasvolsky, 19 May 1945, Pasvolsky Papers; Jebb to Nigel Ronald, 15 September 1944, U7503/180/70, FO 371; and Stettinius, quoted in Divine, *Second Chance*, p. 247. See also Stalin, *Great Patriotic War*, pp. 137–42.

6. See Resis, "The Churchill-Stalin Secret 'Percentages' Agreement."

7. Meeting of State Department planners to discuss voting procedure in Security Council, 4 November 1944, RDS; Stettinius to Harriman, 5 December 1944, *FRUS, 1945, Malta and Yalta*, pp. 58–60; Harriman to Stettinius, 19 December 1944, ibid., pp. 60–61; memorandum of conversation, Pasvolsky and Gromyko, 11 January 1945, ibid., pp. 68–73; acting counselor of British embassy in Washington (Michael Wright) to Pasvolsky, 14 January 1945, ibid., p. 77; and Pasvolsky to Wright, 17 January 1945, *FRUS, 1945*, 1:22–23.

8. Memorandum of conversation, Hiss and Walter Lippmann, 20 October 1944, Hiss File, RDS; and Kennan to Bohlen, 26 January 1945, Bohlen Papers.

9. Stalin to Roosevelt, 27 December 1944, Roosevelt Papers; and Harriman to Stettinius, 28 December 1944, 500.cc/12-2844, RDS.

10. Stettinius to Roosevelt, 2 January 1945, 500.cc/1-245, RDS.

11. FO minute by J. G. Ward, 22 September 1944, U7469/180/70, FO 371; and FO minute by N. Butler, 25 September 1944, ibid. See also FO minute by J. G. Ward, 20 September 1944, U7593/180/70, FO 371; and draft memo, "World Organization and Voting Rights of the Great Powers," 12 October 1944, U7664/180/70, FO 371.

12. FO minute by Webster, 23 October 1944, U7919/180/70, FO 371. See also FO minute by Jebb, 13 October 1944, U7737/180/70, FO 371; Cadogan to Cripps, 30 October 1944, 30/10, PREM 4; FO minute by Cadogan, 31 October 1944, U7919/180/70, FO 371; and prime minister's personal minute, 6 October 1944, 30/10, PREM 4.

13. Memorandum on world organization by Cadogan, 22 November 1944, 30/10, PREM 4.

14. Prime minister's personal minute, 6 December 1944, 30/10, PREM 4. See also Roosevelt to Churchill, 5 December 1944; minute by Eden, 12 and 29 December 1944; and note by Jebb, 5 December 1944, all ibid.

15. "Protocol of Proceedings of the Crimean Conference," 11 February 1945, *FRUS, 1945, Malta and Yalta*, p. 976; Woodward, *British Foreign Policy*, pp. 491–92; prime minister's personal minute, 30 December 1944, 30/10, PREM 4; W.P.(45)12, 5 January 1945, ibid.; W.P.(45)4 Conclusions, 11 January 1945, ibid.; and Clemens, *Yalta*, pp. 218–26.

16. Russell, *United Nations Charter*, p. 638. See also Vandenberg, *Private Papers*, pp. 179–82; and Divine, *Second Chance*, pp. 290–91.

17. McNeill, *America, Britain and Russia*, pp. 594–96; and Russell, *United Nations Charter*, p. 639.

18. Grew, *Turbulent Era*, 2:1446. See also Divine, *Second Chance*, pp. 293–94.

19. Vandenberg, *Private Papers*, pp. 201–6. See also Truman, *Memoirs*, 1:285–86; Russell, *United Nations Charter*, pp. 716–19; and McNeill, *America, Britain and Russia*, pp. 600–601.

20. Sherwood, *Roosevelt and Hopkins*, p. 911. See also Stettinius, *Roosevelt and the Russians*, pp. 319–21; and Truman, *Memoirs*, 1:287.

21. Vandenberg, *Private Papers*, p. 214. See also Russell, *United Nations Charter*, pp. 770–75; and Divine, *Second Chance*, pp. 296–97.

22. Clare Booth Luce, "Waging Peace," in *New York Herald Tribune*, 22 October 1944, copy in Hiss File, RDS; and Jebb to Nigel Ronald, 15 September 1944, U7503/180/70, FO 371.

Bibliography

Manuscript Collections

United Kingdom

Cambridge, England
  Churchill College Library, Cambridge University
    First Earl of Halifax Papers
London, England
  Public Record Office, Kew Branch
    Records of the Cabinet
      CAB 65
      CAB 66
    Records of the Colonial Office
      CO 968
    Records of the Foreign Office
      FO 371
      FO 414
      FO 800
      FO 954
      Papers of Alexander Cadogan
      Papers of Anthony Eden
    Records of the Prime Minister
      PREM 3
      PREM 4

United States

Charlottesville, Virginia
  Alderman Library, The University of Virginia
    Edward R. Stettinius, Jr., Papers
Hyde Park, New York
  Franklin D. Roosevelt Library
    Harry Hopkins Papers
    Franklin D. Roosevelt Papers
    Henry A. Wallace Papers
New Haven, Connecticut
  Yale University Library
    Henry L. Stimson Papers

Princeton, New Jersey
  Seeley G. Mudd Library, Princeton University
    John Foster Dulles Papers
    James Forrestal Papers
Washington, D.C.
  Library of Congress
    Charles E. Bohlen Papers
    Henry P. Fletcher Papers
    James Frederick Green Papers
    Green H. Hackworth Papers
    Cordell Hull Papers
    Breckinridge Long Papers
    Leo Pasvolsky Papers
    Arthur Sweetser Papers
  National Archives
  General Records of the Department of State
    Alger Hiss File
    Harley Notter File
    Leo Pasvolsky File

Published Documents

Documents on Polish-Soviet Relations, 1939–1945. 2 vols. London: Heinemann, 1961.
Union of Soviet Socialist Republics, Ministry of Foreign Affairs. *Correspondence between the Chairman of the Council of Ministers of the U.S.S.R. and the Presidents of the U.S.A. and the Prime Ministers of Great Britain during the Great Patriotic War of 1941–1945.* 2 vols. Moscow: 1957.
United Kingdom. *Parliamentary Debates*, Commons, 5th series, vol. 391.
United Nations. Information Organization. *Documents of the United Nations Conference on International Organization.* 22 vols. Vol. 3, *Dumbarton Oaks Proposals: Comments and Proposed Amendments.* New York: 1945.
U.S. Congress. *Congressional Record.* 78th Cong., 1st and 2d sess. 1943–44.
U.S. Department of State. *Bulletin.* Vols. 7–12.
———. *Foreign Relations of the United States, 1943, China.* Washington, D.C., 1957.
———. *Foreign Relations of the United States: Conference of Washington and Quebec, 1943.* Washington, D.C., 1970.
———. *Foreign Relations of the United States: Conferences of Cairo and Tehran, 1943.* Washington, D.C., 1961.
———. *Foreign Relations of the United States, 1944.* Vol. 1, *General.* Washington, D.C., 1966.
———. *Foreign Relations of the United States, 1944.* Vol. 3, *British Commonwealth and Europe.* Washington, D.C., 1965.
———. *Foreign Relations of the United States, 1944.* Vol. 4, *Europe.* Washington, D.C., 1966.

_____. *Foreign Relations of the United States, 1944*. Vol. 5, *Near East, South Asia, Africa, Far East*. Washington, D.C., 1965.

_____. *Foreign Relations of the United States, 1944*. Vol. 6, *China*. Washington, D.C., 1967.

_____. *Foreign Relations of the United States: Conference at Quebec, 1944*. Washington, D.C., 1972.

_____. *Foreign Relations of the United States, 1945*. Vol. 1, *General: The United Nations*. Washington, D.C., 1967.

_____. *Foreign Relations of the United States: Conferences of Malta and Yalta, 1945*. Washington, D.C., 1955.

_____. *Peace and War: United States Foreign Policy, 1931–1941*. Washington, D.C., 1944.

Newspapers and Magazines

Chicago Daily Tribune
Detroit Free Press
Life
Nation
New Republic
New York Herald Tribune
New York Times
Time
Washington Post

Published Sources

Acheson, Dean. *Present at the Creation: My Years in the State Department*. New York: W. W. Norton, 1969.

Berezhkov, Valentin M. *Gody diplomaticheskoi sluzhby*. Moscow: Mezhdunarodnye otnosheniia, 1972.

_____. "O Konferntsii v Dumbarton Okse v 1944 godu." *Novaya i noveyshaya istoria*. Part 1, Jan.–Feb., 1970, 166–82. Part 2, Mar.–Apr., 1970, 173–93.

Blum, John Morton. *From the Morgenthau Diaries*. 3 vols. Vol. 3, *Years of War, 1941–1945*. Boston: Houghton Mifflin, 1967.

Bohlen, Charles E. *Witness to History*. New York: W. W. Norton, 1973.

Churchill, Winston S. *The Second World War*. 6 vols. Vol. 3, *The Grand Alliance*. Vol. 4, *The Hinge of Fate*. Vol. 5, *Closing the Ring*. Vol. 6, *Triumph and Tragedy*. Boston: Houghton Mifflin, 1948–1953.

Colville, John. *The Fringes of Power: Downing Street Diaries, 1939–1945*. London: Hodder and Stoughton, 1985.

De Gaulle, Charles. *The Complete War Memoirs of Charles de Gaulle.* New York: Simon and Schuster, 1964.

Dilks, David, ed. *The Diaries of Sir Alexander Cadogan, 1938–1945.* New York: G. P. Putnam's Sons, 1972.

Djilas, Milovan. *Conversations with Stalin.* New York: Harcourt, Brace and World, 1962.

Dulles, John Foster. *War or Peace.* New York: Macmillan, 1950.

Eden, Anthony. *The Memoirs of Anthony Eden: The Reckoning.* Boston: Houghton Mifflin, 1965.

Green, James Frederick. "The Dumbarton Oaks Conversations." U.S. Department of State *Bulletin* 11 (1944): 459–65.

Grew, Joseph C. *Turbulent Era: A Diplomatic Record of Forty Years, 1904–1945.* Edited by Walter Johnson. 2 vols. Boston: Houghton Mifflin, 1952.

Harriman, W. Averell. *America and Russia in a Changing World: A Half Century of Personal Observation.* Garden City, N.Y.: Doubleday, 1971.

Harriman, W. Averell, and Abel, Elie. *Special Envoy to Churchill and Stalin.* New York: Random House, 1975.

Hull, Cordell. *The Memoirs of Cordell Hull.* 2 vols. New York: Macmillan, 1948.

Israel, Fred L., ed. *The War Diary of Breckinridge Long, 1939–1944.* Lincoln: University of Nebraska Press, 1966.

Jessup, Philip C. "The International Court of Justice of the United Nations—With Text of Statute." *Foreign Policy Reports* 21 (August 15, 1945): 150–84.

Kennan, George F. *Memoirs (1925–1950).* 2 vols. Boston: Little, Brown, 1967.

Khrushchev, Nikita S. *Khrushchev Remembers.* Boston: Little, Brown, 1970.

Kimball, Warren F., ed. *Churchill and Roosevelt: The Complete Correspondence.* 3 vols. Vol. 1, *Alliance Emerging, October 1933–November 1942.* Vol. 2, *Alliance Forged, November 1942–February 1944.* Vol. 3, *Alliance Declining, February 1944–April 1945.* Princeton: Princeton University Press, 1984.

Krylov, S. D. *Materialy k istorii Organizatsii Ob'yedinennykh Natsiy.* Moscow: Idz. Akad. Nauk. S.S.S.R., 1949.

Leahy, William D. *I Was There.* New York: McGraw-Hill, 1950.

Lippmann, Walter. *United States War Aims.* Boston: Little, Brown, 1944.

Loewenheim, Francis L.; Langley, Harold D.; and Jonas, Manfred, eds. *Roosevelt and Churchill: Their Secret Wartime Correspondence.* London: Barrie and Jenkins, 1975.

Luce, Henry R. "The American Century." *Life,* 17 February 1941, 61–65.

Malinin, N. "K voprosu o sozdanii mezhdunarodnoi organizatsii bezopasnosti." *Voina: rabochii klass.* 15 December 1944, 4–8.

Millis, Walter, ed. *The Forrestal Diaries.* New York: Viking, 1951.

Moran, Lord. *Churchill: Taken from the Diaries of Lord Moran—The Struggle for Survival, 1940–1965.* Boston: Houghton Mifflin, 1966.

Nicholas, Herbert G., ed. *Washington Despatches, 1941–1945.* Chicago: University of Chicago Press, 1981.

Nicolson, Harold. *Diaries and Letters of Harold Nicolson.* 2 vols. Vol. 2, *The War Years, 1939–1945.* New York: Atheneum, 1967.

Notter, Harley. *Postwar Foreign Policy Preparation, 1939–1945.* Washington, D.C.: U.S. Department of State, 1950.

Pasvolsky, Leo. "Dumbarton Oaks Proposals," U.S. Department of State *Bulletin* 11 (1944): 702–6.

————. *Russia in the Far East.* New York: Macmillan, 1922.

Perkins, Frances. *The Roosevelt I Knew.* New York: Viking, 1947.

Reynolds, P. A., and Hughes, E. J., eds. *The Historian as Diplomat: Charles K. Webster and the United Nations, 1939–1946.* London: Martin Robertson, 1976.

Rosenman, Samuel I., ed. *Public Papers and Addresses of Franklin D. Roosevelt.* 13 vols. Vol. 6, *The Constitution Prevails, 1937.* Vol. 13, *1944–1945.* New York: Harper and Bros., 1941, 1950.

Stalin, Josef V. *War Speeches, Orders of the Day, and Answers to Foreign Press Correspondents during the Great Patriotic War.* London: Hutchinson, 1946.

Stettinius, Edward R., Jr. *Roosevelt and the Russians: The Yalta Conference.* Garden City, N.Y.: Doubleday, 1949.

Stimson, Henry L., and Bundy, McGeorge. *On Active Service in Peace and War.* New York: Harper and Bros., 1948.

Truman, Harry S. *Memoirs.* 2 vols. Vol. 1, *Year of Decisions.* Garden City, N.Y.: Doubleday, 1955.

Vandenberg, Arthur H., Jr., ed. *The Private Papers of Senator Vandenberg.* Boston: Houghton Mifflin, 1952.

Webster, Charles K. "The Making of the Charter of the United Nations." *History* 32 (March 1947): 16–38.

Welles, Sumner. *Seven Decisions that Shaped History.* New York: Harper and Bros., 1944.

————. *The Time for Decision.* New York: Harper and Bros., 1944.

————. *Where Are We Heading?* New York: Harper and Bros., 1946.

Willkie, Wendell. *One World.* New York: Simon and Schuster, 1943.

Books and Articles

Ambrosius, Lloyd E. "Wilson, the Republicans, and French Security after World War I." *Journal of American History* 49 (1972): 341–52.

Anderson, Terry H. *The United States, Great Britain, and the Cold War, 1944–47.* Columbia: University of Missouri Press, 1981.

Barnard, Ellsworth. *Wendell Willkie—Fighter for Freedom.* Marquette: Northern Michigan University Press, 1966.

Bialer, Seweryn, ed. *Stalin and His Generals.* New York: Pegasus, 1969.

Bishop, Jim. *FDR's Last Year.* New York: Morrow, 1974.

Bourquin, Maurice. *Vers Une Novelle Société des Nations.* Neuchâtel: Editions de la Baconnière, 1945.

Burns, James MacGregor. *Roosevelt: The Lion and the Fox.* New York: Harcourt, Brace and World, 1956.

————. *Roosevelt: The Soldier of Freedom.* New York: Harcourt Brace Jovanovich, 1970.

Campbell, Thomas M. *Masquerade Peace: America's UN Policy, 1944–1945.* Tallahassee: Florida State University Press, 1973.

———. "Nationalism in America's UN Policy, 1944–1945." *International Organization* 27 (1973): 25–44.

Campbell, Thomas M., and Herring, George C., eds. *The Diaries of Edward R. Stettinius, Jr., 1943–1946*. New York: Franklin Watts, 1975.

Chandler, Harriette L. "The Transition to Cold Warrior: The Evolution of W. Averell Harriman's Assessment of the U.S.S.R.'s Polish Policy." *East European Quarterly* 10 (1976): 229–45.

Ciechanowski, Jan. *Defeat in Victory*. Garden City, N.Y.: Doubleday, 1947.

———. *The Warsaw Rising of 1944*. Cambridge: Cambridge University Press, 1974.

Claude, Inis L. *Swords into Plowshares: The Problems and Progress of International Organization*. New York: Random House, 1959.

Clemens, Diane Shaver. *Yalta*. New York: Oxford University Press, 1970.

Clubb, O. Edmund. *China and Russia: The Great Game*. New York: Columbia University Press, 1971.

Connell-Smith, Gordon. *The Inter-American System*. London: Oxford University Press, 1966.

Considine, Bob. "Stettinius—Dynamo in the State Department." *Readers Digest* 46 (March 1945): 11–14.

Dallek, Robert. *Franklin D. Roosevelt and American Foreign Policy, 1932–1945*. New York: Oxford University Press, 1979.

Dallin, Alexander. *The Soviet Union and the United Nations*. New York: Praeger, 1962.

Davis, Forrest. "What Really Happened at Tehran?" *Saturday Evening Post*, part 1, 13 May 1944; part 2, 20 May 1944.

Davis, Kenneth S. "FDR as a Biographer's Problem." *The Key Reporter* 50:1 (Autumn 1984): 1–3.

Davis, Lynn E. *The Cold War Begins: Soviet-American Conflict over Eastern Europe*. Princeton: Princeton University Press, 1974.

Davis, Vincent. *Postwar Defense Policy and the U.S. Navy, 1943–1946*. Chapel Hill: University of North Carolina Press, 1966.

Deane, John R. *The Strange Alliance*. New York: Viking, 1947.

Deutscher, Isaac. *Stalin: A Political Biography*. London: Oxford University Press, 1967.

Divine, Robert A. *Second Chance: The Triumph of Internationalism in America during World War II*. New York: Atheneum, 1967.

Duggan, Laurence. *The Americas: The Search for Hemispheric Security*. New York: Henry Holt, 1949.

Evatt, Herbert Vere. *The United Nations*. Cambridge: Harvard University Press, 1948.

Feis, Herbert. *The China Tangle: The American Effort in China from Pearl Harbor to the Marshall Mission*. Princeton: Princeton University Press, 1953.

———. *Churchill, Roosevelt, Stalin: The War They Waged and the Peace They Sought*. Princeton: Princeton University Press, 1957.

Gaddis, John L. *The United States and the Origins of the Cold War*. New York: Columbia University Press, 1972.

Gardner, Lloyd C. *Architects of Illusion: Men and Ideas in American Foreign Policy, 1941–1949*. Chicago: Quadrangle, 1970.

Gelfand, Lawrence E. *The Inquiry: American Preparations for Peace, 1917–1919*. New Haven: Yale University Press, 1963.

Gietz, Axel. *Die neue Alte Welt: Roosevelt, Churchill und die europäische Nachkriegsord-nung.* Munich: William Fink, 1986.

Gilchrist, Huntington. "The Japanese Islands: Annexation or Trusteeship?" *Foreign Affairs* 22 (July 1944): 635–43.

Graebner, Norman A., ed. *An Uncertain Tradition: American Secretaries of State in the Twentieth Century.* New York: McGraw-Hill, 1961.

Gray, Richard B., ed. *International Security Systems: Concepts and Models of World Order.* Itasca, Ill.: F. E. Peacock, 1969.

Guggenheim, Paul. *L'Organisation de la Société Internationale.* Neuchâtel: Editions de la Baconnière, 1944.

Harbutt, Frazier J. *The Iron Curtain: Churchill, America, and the Origins of the Cold War.* New York: Oxford University Press, 1986.

Hess, Gary R. "Franklin Roosevelt and Indochina." *Journal of American History* 49 (1972): 353–68.

Hilderbrand, Robert C. *Power and the People: Executive Management of Public Opinion in Foreign Affairs, 1897–1921.* Chapel Hill: University of North Carolina Press, 1981.

Holborn, Louise W., ed. *War and Peace Aims of the United Nations.* 2 vols. Boston: World Peace Foundation, 1943–48.

Hurstfield, Julian G. *America and the French Nation, 1939–1945.* Chapel Hill: University of North Carolina Press, 1986.

King, Frank P. "British Policy and the Warsaw Uprising." *Journal of European Studies* 4 (1974): 1–18.

Kolko, Gabriel. *The Politics of War: The World and United States Foreign Policy, 1943–1945.* New York: Random House, 1968.

Ledermann, Laszlo. *Les Precurseurs de L'Organisation Internationale.* Neuchâtel: Editions de la Baconnière, 1945.

Leffler, Melvyn P. "The American Conception of National Security and the Beginnings of the Cold War, 1945–48." *The American Historical Review* 89(2) (April 1984): 346–81.

Louis, Wm. Roger. *Imperialism at Bay: The United States and the Decolonization of the British Empire, 1941–1945.* New York: Oxford University Press, 1978.

Luard, Evan. *A History of the United Nations.* 2 vols. Vol. 1, *The Years of Western Domination, 1945–1955.* New York: St. Martin's Press, 1982.

McNeill, William H. *America, Britain and Russia: Their Cooperation and Conflict, 1941–1946.* London: Oxford University Press, 1953.

Marks, Frederick W. *Wind Over Sand: The Diplomacy of Franklin Roosevelt.* Athens: University of Georgia Press, 1988.

Mastny, Vojtech. *Russia's Road to the Cold War: Diplomacy, Warfare, and the Politics of Communism, 1941–1945.* New York: Columbia University Press, 1979.

Matloff, Maurice. *Strategic Planning for Coalition Warfare, 1943–1944.* Washington, D.C.: Historical Division, Department of the Army, 1959.

Pogue, Forrest C. *George C. Marshall.* 4 vols. Vol. 3, *Organizer of Victory, 1943–1945.* New York: Viking, 1973.

Polonsky, Anthony, ed. *The Great Powers and the Policy Question, 1941–1945.* London: London School of Economics and Political Science, 1976.

Poole, Walter S. "From Conciliation to Containment: The Joint Chiefs of Staff and the

Coming of the Cold War." *Military Affairs* 42 (1978): 12–16.

Pratt, Julius W. *The American Secretaries of State and Their Diplomacy*. Vols. 12 and 13, *Cordell Hull, 1933–1944*. Edited by Robert H. Ferrell and Samuel F. Bemis. New York: Cooper Square Publishers, 1964.

Range, Willard. *Franklin D. Roosevelt's World Order*. Athens: University of Georgia Press, 1959.

Resis, Albert. "The Churchill-Stalin Secret 'Percentages' Agreement on the Balkans, Moscow, October, 1944." *The American Historical Review* 83(2) (April 1978): 368–87.

Riggs, Robert E. "Overselling the UN Charter—Fact and Myth." *International Organization* 14 (1960): 277–90.

Robins, Dorothy B. *Experiment in Democracy: The Story of U.S. Citizen Organizations in Forging the Charter of the United Nations*. New York: The Parkside Press, 1971.

Rossinger, Lawrence. *China's Wartime Politics*. Princeton: Princeton University Press, 1945.

Rothstein, Andrew. *Soviet Foreign Policy during the Patriotic War*. 2 vols. London: Hutchinson, 1944–46.

Rozek, Edward J. *Allied Wartime Diplomacy, A Pattern in Poland*. New York: John Wiley and Sons, 1958.

Russell, Ruth B., with Muther, Jeanette E. *A History of the United Nations Charter: The Role of the United States, 1940–1945*. Washington, D.C.: The Brookings Institution, 1958.

Sainsbury, Keith. *The Turning Point: Roosevelt, Stalin, Churchill, and Chiang Kai-Shek, 1943: The Moscow, Cairo, and Tehran Conferences*. Oxford: Oxford University Press, 1985.

Schaller, Michael. *The U.S. Crusade in China, 1938–1945*. New York: Columbia University Press, 1979.

Schwartz, Harry. *Tsars, Mandarins, and Commissars: A History of Chinese-Russian Relations*. London: Victor Gollancz, 1964.

Sherry, Michael S. *Preparing for the Next War: American Plans for Postwar Defense, 1941–45*. New Haven: Yale University Press, 1977.

Sherwood, Robert E. *Roosevelt and Hopkins, An Intimate History*. New York: Harper and Bros., 1948.

Smith, Gaddis. *American Diplomacy during the Second World War, 1941–1945*. New York: John Wiley and Sons, 1965.

Smith, Perry McCoy. *The Air Force Plans for Peace, 1943–1945*. Baltimore: Johns Hopkins University Press, 1970.

Snell, John L. *Illusion and Neutrality: The Diplomacy of Global War*. Boston: Houghton Mifflin, 1963.

Stoler, Mark. "From Continentalism to Globalism: General Stanley D. Embick, the Joint Strategic Survey Committee, and the Military View of American National Policy during the Second World War." *Diplomatic History* 6 (1982): 303–21.

Stuart, Graham. *The Department of State*. New York: Macmillan, 1949.

Summers, Robert E., ed. *Dumbarton Oaks*. The Reference Shelf, vol. 18, no. 1. New York: H. H. Wilson, 1945.

Takayuki, Ito. "The Genesis of the Cold War: Confrontation over Poland, 1941–1944."

In *The Origins of the Cold War in Asia*, edited by Yonosunke Nagai and Akira Iriye. Tokyo: University of Tokyo Press, 1977.

Tang Tsou. *America's Failure in China*. Chicago: University of Chicago Press, 1963.

Taubman, William. *Stalin's American Policy: From Entente to Detente to Cold War*. New York: W. W. Norton, 1982.

Thorne, Christopher. *Allies of a Kind: The United States, Britain, and the War against Japan, 1941–1945*. New York: Oxford University Press, 1978.

Ulam, Adam B. *Expansion and Coexistence: The History of Soviet Foreign Policy, 1917–1967*. New York: Frederick A. Praeger, 1968.

————. *The Rivals: America and Russia since World War II*. New York: Viking, 1971.

————. *Stalin: The Man and His Era*. New York: Viking, 1973.

Varg, Paul. *The Closing of the Door: Sino-American Relations, 1936–1946*. East Lansing: Michigan State University Press, 1973.

Walker, Richard L. *The American Secretaries of State and Their Diplomacy*, Vol. 14, *Edward R. Stettinius, Jr*. Edited by Robert H. Ferrell and Samuel F. Bemis. New York: Cooper Square Publishers, 1965.

Walters, F. P. *A History of the League of Nations*. London: Oxford University Press, 1952.

Werth, Alexander. *Russia at War*. New York: Dutton, 1964.

Westerfield, H. Bradford. *Foreign Policy and Party Politics: Pearl Harbor to Korea*. New Haven: Yale University Press, 1955.

Wheeler-Bennett, John W., and Nicholls, Anthony. *The Semblance of Peace*. New York: Macmillan, 1972.

Wilson, Theodore A. *The First Summit: Roosevelt and Churchill at Placentia Bay, 1941*. Boston: Houghton Mifflin, 1969.

Woodward, Sir Llewellyn. *British Foreign Policy in the Second World War*. London: Her Majesty's Stationery Office, 1982.

Yergin, Daniel. *Shattered Peace: The Origins of the Cold War and the National Security State*. Boston: Houghton Mifflin, 1978.

Dissertations

Barton, Keith M. "The Dumbarton Oaks Conference." Ph.D. dissertation, Florida State University, 1974.

Campbell, Thomas M. "Edward R. Stettinius and the Founding of the United Nations." Ph.D. dissertation, University of Virginia, 1964.

Schwark, Stephen J. "The State Department Plans for Peace, 1941–1945." Ph.D. dissertation, Harvard University, 1985.

Index

Taylor, Myron C., 15, 30, 262 (n. 16)
Tehran Conference, 31, 36, 37, 40, 45,
    60, 61, 72, 177, 183, 195, 212, 215
Tennyson, Alfred Lord, 257
Thompson, Sir Llewellyn, 191
Thorne, Christopher, 60
Train, Admiral Harold, 90, 175, 240
Treaties, 134–35, 244
Treaty of Versailles (1919), 58, 165
Truman, Harry S., 175, 253, 255
Trusteeship, 15–16, 37, 47, 51, 56–57,
    69, 170–81, 217, 234, 241
Turkey, 235

Union of Soviet Socialist Republics
    (USSR). *See* Soviet Union
United Nations Authority, 15
United Nations conference (San Fran-
    cisco), 81, 100, 112, 115, 117, 119,
    120, 233, 253–56
United Nations Organization, 1; based
    on mistakes in League of Nations, 2,
    26, 33, 49–50; planning for, 3, 4, 7–8;
    Roosevelt's early views on, 5–6; first
    plans in State Department for, 9; basis
    in Atlantic Charter, 13; plans of Sub-
    committee on Political Problems for,
    14–15; and transition to postwar pe-
    riod, 15, 167–70; various plans in
    United States, 17–18, 19; membership
    in, 19, 34, 92, 94–101, 234, 235–36;
    and world government, 20, 26, 36, 49,
    51, 65; and peacekeeping force, 21–
    23, 50, 140–43, 156; and bases, 23,
    45, 143, 145, 159, 170–81, 217, 247;
    discussed at Moscow Foreign Minis-
    ters' Conference, 24; Security Council,
    25, 31–32, 33–34, 35, 38, 40, 43, 46,
    47, 49, 55–56, 90, 92–93, 106, 108,
    109, 111, 115, 122–58, 159–208,
    209–12, 214, 218–28, 231–34, 241–
    43, 245, 248–49, 254–55, 277 (n. 6);
    and disarmament, 26, 159–163, 186;
    planning for in U.S. Congress, 27–28;
    relationship to League of Nations, 30,
    234, 243–44; expulsion of members,

34; location of, 36, 105–7; nomencla-
    ture of, 36, 74, 105–6, 276 (n. 44);
    general assembly, 36–37, 43, 47, 49,
    55–56, 65, 87, 93, 106, 108–15, 157,
    160, 162, 163, 170, 188, 210, 237–
    38, 240, 253, 255–56; and colonies,
    36–37, 47, 51, 56–57, 69, 92, 170–
    81, 247; early plans for in Foreign Of-
    fice, 37–38, 39–44; Soviet planning
    for, 44–47; International Court of Jus-
    tice, 47, 49, 65, 93, 108, 113, 115–20,
    135–36, 234, 238, 245, 278 (n. 17);
    auxiliary organizations in, 47, 51, 63,
    65, 86–93, 94, 240; and justice, 50,
    237–38, 240; timing of creation, 51;
    and international air force, 73, 142–
    56, 239–40, 245; basic principles of,
    85–86; and aggression, 86, 137–38,
    239; Economic and Social Council,
    86–93, 103, 109, 113; and human
    rights, 91–92, 135; secretariat, 93,
    106; and discrimination, 93, 185; ba-
    sic shape of, 93–94, 236; and "associ-
    ated powers," 95; and Soviet request
    for sixteen votes, 95, 235, 253, 275
    (n. 32); and termination of member-
    ship, 101–3; amendments to charter,
    103–5; and domestic questions, 135–
    36, 185, 195, 231, 245, 256; and use
    of force, 136–37, 140, 156, 237; and
    sanctions, 138–39, 186; military staff
    committee, 156–58, 160, 165; and re-
    gional security organizations, 159,
    163–70, 215, 249; trusteeship council,
    170–81, 217, 234; and economic re-
    lief, 181–82; and peaceful change,
    238–39; and cultural cooperation, 240
United Nations Relief and Rehabilitation
    Administration, 100
United States, 1, 16, 19, 21, 49; as key to
    postwar organization, 2; plans for
    postwar organization, 4, 6, 7–36; entry
    into World War II, 5; relationship to
    postwar peacekeeping, 36; in British
    plans, 38–39, 41–42, 43, 51–53, 60,
    79; on France as Great Power, 40; in